Form-Oriented Analysis

T0181670

Dirk Draheim · Gerald Weber

Form-Oriented Analysis

A New Methodology to Model Form-Based Applications

With 83 Figures

 Springer

Dirk Draheim
Institute of Computer Science
Freie Universität Berlin
Takustr. 9
14195 Berlin, Germany
draheim@acm.org

Gerald Weber
Department of Computer Science
The University of Auckland
Private Bag 92019
Auckland 1020, New Zealand
g.weber@cs.auckland.ac.nz

http://www.formcharts.org/

ACM Computing Classification (1998): D.2.1, D.2.2

ISBN 978-3-642-05822-6   e-ISBN 978-3-540-26893-2

Springer is a part of Springer Science+Business Media

springeronline.com

© Springer-Verlag Berlin Heidelberg 2010
Printed in Germany

Cover design: KünkelLopka, Heidelberg

Printed on acid-free paper   45/3142/YL - 5 4 3 2 1 0

Preface

This book presents a special purpose modeling technique for the analysis and design of an important system class, namely form-based enterprise systems. Recent discussions on modeling languages emphasize that there is a strong demand for such domain-specific modeling languages. The class of form-based enterprise systems includes, for example, web shops as well as ERP and B2B solutions and can be said to be paradigmatic for enterprise computing. This book was motivated by the widespread interest in this type of business application from professionals as well as from scientists. The book adapts well-established basic modeling techniques in a novel way in order to achieve a modeling framework optimized for the indicated application domain.

Besides its practical parts the book details theoretical achievements, which lead to real improvements in the application domain of the book. It explains how to model a form-based enterprise system during the analysis and specification phase, and how these models translate into good design. Typical form-based applications have common properties that can be molded into specialized diagram types for such applications. Such a diagram type is the formchart, the central artifact that is described in the book. The formchart is a good example of customized diagrams according to the most recent proposed profiling techniques.

If form-based enterprise systems are modeled with typical general purpose modeling approaches without such customizations, there are a number of obstacles the modeler will face. For example, if one employs use case modeling together with interaction diagrams, the analyst will be confronted with three problems. First of all, the method has to be adapted to the form-based application, since no specific guidance for this special application type is part of the general method. Secondly, the model will become complex for even small-sized problems, since every diagram has to repeat common properties of this very specific application class. Hence the model tends to become highly redundant, and the important distinguishing information is diluted. Furthermore, a third problematic aspect is that current analysis methods are traditionally rather oriented towards event-driven and complex GUI-based applications but not towards form-based applications. Hence the customization demand for form-based applications is particularly high.

Conversely, there are certain benefits the reader of the book can reap by employing the new customized artifacts presented in this book. The reader can obtain faster results and more significant models, because the common properties of enterprise systems are already incorporated in the semantics of the modeling method. The new artifact types presented in this book incorporate the results of studying form-based systems in general, knowledge that a software engineer can hardly obtain in the limited setting of a running project. Our method provides a separation of concerns by splitting the general semantic structure of such applications from the specific information about business logic in the concrete single project. The foundation of the new techniques is fully elaborated in the book for the working developer confronted with everyday problems in professional IT projects. In the same way, the scientist interested in performing novel research on enterprise systems can use this formal reference.

The book is divided into four parts. The first part is a detailed discussion of the new modeling method for form-based systems from a practitioner's viewpoint and explains how the proposed techniques can actually be employed in a project. The second part is about tool support and exemplifies how the concepts introduced in the first part can be exploited by several different implementing technologies. The third part provides the semantic foundation of the different kinds of diagrams and tools introduced in the first and second parts. The fourth part serves as a summary and provides a discussion of related work.

After the introduction the book starts with an in-depth motivation for the new techniques. It is shown that the considered system class encompasses a wide range of important enterprise systems from mainframe/terminal systems through ubiquitous COTS software to modern web applications. The explanations in the book are deliberately based on a realistic running example in order to make a difference. Throughout the book the concepts are exemplified with an online bookshop. This example is not an arbitrary choice of the authors – the important TPC-W benchmark, for example, also uses a standardized online bookshop as a representative example of typical business functionality. The form-oriented information system model is introduced. Different kinds of diagrams for these models, i.e., screen diagrams, page diagrams, form storyboards, and formcharts are introduced for the user interface state part of these models. All of these, and the further model components, i.e., dialogue constraints and the layered data models, are introduced immediately with unambiguous semantics and are used in modeling the running example. Then, techniques for decomposition and refinement are discussed. A parsimonious data modeling language is elaborated. A message approach to the modeling of data interchange is outlined. The book is not primarily about software engineering processes; however, it provides a discussion on how the proposed artifacts can be exploited in an entire software engineering life cycle. The interplay of some proposed best practices that are centered around descriptiveness, artifact orientation, feature orientation, and reuse are discussed. For each concept we show how it can be used to add sustainable value to the respective software engineering activities.

The second part discusses issues of architecture, design, and implementing technology. From this discussion concepts and concrete prototypical technologies for forward engineering, reverse engineering, and the implementation of web presentation layers are derived.

The third part of the book presents the semantic foundation of form-oriented analysis. First, several alternatives for tool support are discussed and given a conceptual basis using an integrated source code model. Then, precise semantics for the form-oriented diagram types are given. For this purpose, a new, lightweight, semantics framework approach is introduced as an alternative to current multi-level metamodeling techniques. Along the lines of the framework approach precise semantics of formcharts, layered data modeling, and the dialogue constraint language are given. This is followed by a discussion of the semantic of the proposed parsimonious data modeling approach. A formal type system for the interplay of server actions and pages of submit/response style systems is provided.

The fourth part provides a focused description of the widely accepted modeling approaches in use. The discussion shows the differences between these approaches and the new method, but it also shows how our method is integrated with standard modeling techniques. For each related method we discuss how it could be applied to enterprise systems and how form-oriented analysis provides a more convenient solution. Therefore this chapter provides a different view on the benefits of form-oriented analysis to the reader. Finally, a summary of the main contributions is provided.

The reader should have some experience with object-oriented programming languages. First-hand experience with visual modeling languages and the graphical tools for them is helpful. Basic knowledge of SQL is also desired for some advanced excursions, but this can be postponed until needed. Related approaches are comprehensively introduced, so that even a reader who is new to these other approaches can follow the arguments.

The book targets professionals, i.e., working software engineers and decision makers, researchers in computer science, and upper-level graduate students who are interested in enterprise systems. Care must be taken, because professionals, researchers, and students typically have different objectives, different dispositions, and different opinions with respect to software engineering topics. This is due to the fact that goals and driving forces are different in industry and academia. Consequently, readers may have different attitudes towards the several parts of the book; see the figure below for a guess. In the figure, supposed main interests are shaded gray, whereas minor interests are left blank.

Professionals actually working on enterprise software will gain a deepened understanding of form-based systems from the abstract system viewpoint pro-

Part I Modeling Form-Based Systems	Part II Tool Support	Part III Semantics	Part IV Conclusion
Presentation of Form-Oriented Analysis	Practical Justification	Precise Reference Manual	Summary

Professional

Presentation of Form-Oriented Analysis	Preliminary Semantics	Entry Point for Further Investigations	Discussion of Related Work

Scientist

Presentation of Form-Oriented Analysis	Learning Aid		Summary

Student

vided by form-oriented analysis. Many developers already use ad hoc techniques tailored to form-based systems like naive page diagrams or click dummies. These ad hoc techniques arise naturally when developing form-based systems but lack an elaborated conceptual basis. The book allows these developers to strengthen these techniques in practice. Readers can employ the approach directly in projects, because every concept introduced comes with precise semantics and the mutual dependencies between the concepts are elaborated, too. The prototypical forward and reverse engineering tools are suitable for convincing the professional about the potential practical impact of the form-oriented approach. The third part of the book is less important for the professional. If a semantical clarification is needed, this part can serve as a precise reference manual. The professional can use the fourth part as a detailed summary.

Researchers might be especially interested in the third part of the book as an entry point for further investigations. Upper-level graduate students will benefit from the presentation of state-of-the-art knowledge about the development, architecture, and design of enterprise systems in the organizing framework of form-oriented analysis. The second part of the book will help students to grasp more easily the concepts of form-oriented analysis.

Since enterprise applications are a particularly important class of software, almost every IT professional, computer scientist, or computer science student may have some interest in gaining at least an overview of the fundamentals of enterprise computing. The book is written with the different objectives of professionals, researchers, and students in mind. In industry productivity eventually targets return on investment. Product quality and product quantity are limited by productivity. Productivity is limited by the availability of resources. Knowledge acquisition is needed to improve productivity. Academic activity spans two areas that have to be integrated: research and education. While academic research has a subtle target, i.e., the construction of knowledge, higher

education has the tangible responsibility to produce well-prepared professionals. Academic research is driven by the pressure to get contributions published
in the scientific peer community. Higher education is driven by the demands
of the yet uneducated. Altogether these differences result in the following: one
and the same concept can be perceived totally differently by individuals in
industry and in academia. We encourage all who try to keep an open mind
and hope that this book provides valuable information or inspiration.

  We are indebted to Martin Große-Rhode for his encouragement and advice.
We want to thank our editor Ralf Gerstner for his support and guidance. We
would also like to thank the reviewers who made many helpful comments.

Berlin, August 2004   *Dirk Draheim*
Auckland, August 2004   *Gerald Weber*

Contents

Part I Modeling Form-Based Systems

1	**Introduction**	3
	1.1 Enterprise Systems	4
	1.2 Modeling Enterprise Systems	5
	1.3 High-Level Transactional Programming	6
	1.4 A Parsimonious Relational Notation	6
	1.5 A Descriptive Approach to the Software Development Process	7
2	**The Form-Based System Paradigm**	9
	2.1 The Submit/Response Style Interface	10
	2.2 A Message-Based Model of Data Interchange	20
3	**Exploring the Online Bookshop**	23
	3.1 The Dialogue Model	24
	3.2 The Persistent Data Model	30
	3.3 An Exemplary Submit/Response Style System	32
4	**Form Storyboarding**	35
	4.1 Page Diagrams	36
	4.2 Form Storyboards	41
5	**Formcharts and Dialogue Specification**	49
	5.1 Form-Oriented Information System Models	49
	5.2 The Dialogue Model	55
	5.3 The Layered Data Model	59
	5.4 Dialogue Specification	66
	5.5 The Bookstore Formchart and Data Model	74

6   Model Decomposition and Refinement 97
   6.1   Model Union 97
   6.2   Formchart Decomposition 98
   6.3   Formchart Hierarchies 100
   6.4   A Feature-Driven Approach 102
   6.5   State Sets and State Specialization 104
   6.6   Decomposition of Page Diagrams and Form Storyboards ... 107
   6.7   Model Refinement 107

7   Data Modeling 109
   7.1   The Parsimonious Data Modeling Language 111
   7.2   The Data Access Language DAL 114
   7.3   The Transaction Data Access Language TDAL 121
   7.4   Constraints 125
   7.5   Style Formats 141

8   Message-Based Modeling of Data Interchange 147
   8.1   Connectivity of Enterprise Systems 147
   8.2   The Message-Based System Viewpoint 150
   8.3   Data Interchange Model 152
   8.4   Data Interchange Specification 156
   8.5   The Relation to Data Flow Diagrams 160
   8.6   The Interplay of Formcharts and Data Interchange Diagrams . 162
   8.7   Topic Bundles 164

9   A Descriptive Approach 165
   9.1   Descriptiveness, Prescriptiveness, and the Software Process ... 168
   9.2   Metaphor A Posteriori 170
   9.3   On Desktop Metaphors 172
   9.4   On Real-World Modeling 173
   9.5   Visual Modeling De-emphasized 175
   9.6   Artifact Orientation 176
   9.7   The High-Level Programming Viewpoint 177
   9.8   Advanced Systems Modeling Approaches 180

Part II Tool Support

10   Forward Engineering and Reverse Engineering 187
   10.1   Forward Engineering 188
   10.2   Reverse Engineering 193
   10.3   Source-Code-Opaque Reverse Engineering 196

11 **Typed Server Pages** 199
    11.1 Type-Safe Interplay of Forms and Scripts 200
    11.2 Functional Decomposition of Server Pages 214
    11.3 Higher-Order Server Pages 221
    11.4 A Comparison of Web Technologies 224

Part III Semantics

12 **The Integrated Source Code Paradigm** 229
    12.1 Towards Structured Collaborative Work 229
    12.2 Structured Artifacts 232
    12.3 The Syntax Model Approach 233
    12.4 A Closer Look at Languages 235
    12.5 The Integrated Source Code Paradigm 237
    12.6 A Flexible Generic Textual Format for Data 241
    12.7 Generative Programming 244

13 **State History Diagrams** 249
    13.1 State History Diagrams and Class Diagrams 249
    13.2 Discussion of Formchart Semantics 258
    13.3 Semantics of Dialogue Constraints 260
    13.4 Path Expressions 267

14 **Semantics of the Data Model** 271
    14.1 Semantics of the Temporal Model 271
    14.2 Alternative Fundamental Models 274
    14.3 Discussion 279

15 **Semantics of Web Signatures** 283
    15.1 Formal Semantics of Web Signature Recovery 283
    15.2 Coding Guidelines for Typed Server Pages 287
    15.3 Formal Definition of the NSP Type System 299

Part IV Conclusion

16 **A Comparison of Modeling Methods** 325
    16.1 User Interface Modeling 325
    16.2 Web Site Modeling 326
    16.3 Data Modeling 328
    16.4 Model-Oriented Specification Languages 329
    16.5 Structured Analysis 331
    16.6 Object-Oriented Analysis and Design 335
    16.7 Model-Driven Architecture 338

17 Summary 343
   17.1 Contributions to Modeling Form-Based Systems 343
   17.2 Contributions to Modeling in General 347

References 351

Index 367

List of Figures

2.1 Example pages of the online bookshop 10
2.2 Ultra-thin client based submit/response style systems 12
2.3 SAP R/3 system architecture 12
2.4 Example formchart for a system login capability............. 17

3.1 Welcome screen of the online bookshop.................... 24
3.2 Login screen of the online bookshop 25
3.3 Registration screen of the online bookshop.................. 26
3.4 Category screen of the online bookshop 27
3.5 Book page of the online bookshop 27
3.6 Shopping cart of the online bookshop 28
3.7 Order information page of the online bookshop.............. 30
3.8 Search result page of the online bookshop 31
3.9 Data model of the online bookshop 32

4.1 Page diagram 37
4.2 Screen diagram 39
4.3 List of options for a single conceptual option 40
4.4 Form storyboard 42
4.5 Page images 44
4.6 Form storyboard annotated with interaction information 45
4.7 Message storyboard.................................... 47

5.1 The information system model of form-oriented analysis 50
5.2 A first formchart example 56
5.3 Two alternative formcharts for the same model.............. 57
5.4 Formchart naming conventions 57
5.5 Opaque references in the information model 61
5.6 Formchart notational elements 67
5.7 Three-valued logic in OCL............................... 68
5.8 Meaning of path expressions in the formchart 72

5.9 Complete formchart for the bookstore example 75
5.10 Login, registration and logout feature of the online bookshop .. 76
5.11 Conditional server/page transitions 79
5.12 Refinement of a server input constraint...................... 80
5.13 Browsing feature of the online bookshop..................... 85
5.14 Shopping cart feature of the online bookshop 88
5.15 Buying feature of the online bookshop 90
5.16 Reuse of the login and registration subdialogues 91
5.17 Managing user data in the online bookshop 92
5.18 Search feature of the online bookshop 93
5.19 Graphical representation of a client output constraint 96

6.1 Named partitioning of a formchart........................... 99
6.2 Hierarchical formchart decomposition 100
6.3 Structured analysis: leveled data flow diagram 101
6.4 A flat formchart.. 101
6.5 Additional features of the bookstore 103
6.6 Modeling with state set notation 104
6.7 Using state set notation for the bookstore features............ 105
6.8 Modeling enabling conditions based on state specialization..... 106

7.1 The PD model of the bookshop 112
7.2 A submodel of the bookshop 116
7.3 A relation of arity 3 128
7.4 A partial order in the data model 129
7.5 A composition constraint 132

8.1 Example datatype interchange diagram 153
8.2 Model subsystem in a DTIM............................... 154
8.3 Edges between actions within the same model................ 155
8.4 Example DTIMs of the login dialogue....................... 160
8.5 A DTIM and an equivalent DFD 161

10.1 The Angie language related tool suite 187
10.2 Grammar of the language Angie............................ 190
10.3 Bookstore login capability 192
10.4 Revangie: example screen classifications 198

11.1 CPDS and CPTS.. 201
11.2 Model 2 architecture...................................... 216
11.3 Model 2 architecture versus NSP functional decomposition 218
11.4 Example interaction diagram 221
11.5 Higher-order server pages design example................... 224

12.1 PD core syntax model 234
12.2 Multiplicity syntax model 234

12.3 A cutout message storyboard 243

13.1 Frameworks for state history diagrams and formcharts 252
13.2 A formchart is derived from the semantic framework 255
13.3 The object net over a formchart is a path 256
13.4 A login subdialogue as UML state machine 259
13.5 Semantics of path expressions in DCL......................266
13.6 Example of path expressions 268
13.7 UML tree definition 269

15.1 Example form message type 293
15.2 Example cyclic form message type 296
15.3 Example complex form message type........................297
15.4 List definitions 308

16.1 The Seeheim model of user interfaces 326
16.2 Data flow diagram..333
16.3 Use case diagram...337

Part I

Modeling Form-Based Systems

1

Introduction

What is the business logic of an enterprise system? How do I specify it in such a way that I know how to transform it into a running system, by skill and by automated tool support? This book gives a self-contained introduction to the modeling and development of business logic for enterprise systems.

Enterprise systems are a distinct and highly complex class of systems. They are characterized by their importance for enterprises themselves, making them mission critical, by their extreme multi-user capability, by their tolerance of heavy loads, and by their tight integration with the business processes, which makes every enterprise system installation unique. In short, they are one of the most fascinating yet most demanding disciplines in software engineering. This book is in the first instance intended to be a conceptual introduction to and comprehensive overview of enterprise systems modeling.

Enterprise applications can be singled out within the domain of database applications in general through a number of typical characteristics, which are usually not discriminating if seen in isolation, but which together characterize enterprise applications. An example of a database application very different from enterprise applications is a typical genome database. Enterprise applications store amongst other things data describing events in time. The enterprise system is critical for ensuring data consistency and allowing action consistent with those data in particular. An enterprise system installation controls a certain defined part of an organization. Installing and using the system a second time in parallel for the same business processes leads to serious problems. The correct assignment of the installation to a part of an organization is itself a basic element of this consistency effort, otherwise outdated data is used. This does not mean that multiple installations with correct information about their domain cannot cooperate. It just means that enterprise system installations are in a certain sense territorial. This can be pinned down to the data they manage.

This book explains enterprise systems in the novel form-oriented framework, which is easy to learn and practically applicable yet theoretically powerful. It introduces the form-based system specification as the key notion for the conceptual definition of business logic. It explains state-of-the-art modeling languages and their usage for specifying business logic and for the subsequent building of enterprise systems. The techniques presented here are applicable to enterprise systems of all sizes.

1.1 Enterprise Systems

Enterprise systems are a type of system where so-called business rules are automated. The term business rule refers to a high-level data manipulation rule, which is executable manually or mechanically. But business rules can contain straightforward computations, which we expect today to be executed by a system, or which we even require to be done, not only for convenience, but also for security and data integrity, like the tax on a purchase computed by a cash desk.

There is an intricate relationship between business rules and enterprise systems. Enterprise systems have a distinctive look and feel, because they are mainly systems for managing business rules. On the other hand, if you have a business rule, it is at least conceivable that it will be executed or supported by an enterprise system. Take as an example your mortgage. If you ask your banker about it, the banker should and probably will draw up a financing plan in which you can see what you have to pay each month and what you still owe afterwards. The banker will get this perhaps from the intranet web portal of the bank created by a part of the bank's enterprise application.

In this book we will encounter a uniform viewpoint on business rules, the form-based metaphor. We will learn a general method for describing business rules as functionalities, or *features* of a form-based system. The motivation is not in any way the assumption that business rules must be executed with form-based systems. It is rather the goal to have a common notation, which allows comparisons of different business rules in a common language. If we therefore model a business rule like the mortgage computer above as a part of a form-based system, it is based solely on the assumption that it is *possible* to model the system in such a way, but not on the belief that it is necessary to do so.

One interesting advantage of this uniform modeling approach for form-based systems is, indeed, that by subsuming business applications under this model we single out a well-defined category of system properties in the following, slightly tricky sense. By viewing every business rule as performed with a form-based application, we abstract from the properties of the application, which make no difference in this type of interface. For example, whether a system is used from a touch screen on dedicated terminals, or as a web application over the Internet, might not make a difference with respect to the description of the form-based interface. These differences nevertheless can and should be recognized, but they somehow belong to a different kind of property. The key advantage is to gain a useful classification of different types of system requirements. We therefore introduce the term *business logic requirement* in order to refer to such requirements, which we can express as requirements of the system within our form-based metaphor. In other words, the subsumption of applications under the form-based metaphor is our operative method to separate the business logic requirements from the whole requirement mix. Business logic requirements form the part of an organization's business rules that are to be mechanically executed by the enterprise system.

A full requirements description of a system will consist of the business logic requirements gained in this way as well as all more general requirements. In this book we focus solely on the domain of business logic requirements. This does not reduce the importance of the other requirements in any way. Making the modeling and implementation of business logic requirements more efficient is an encouragement that more care should be taken for these other requirements as well.

1.2 Modeling Enterprise Systems

In this book a semantically precise notion of form-based systems is explained, and called the notion of *submit/response style applications*. This gives us an exactly defined concept of form-based systems.

This notion of submit/response style systems is therefore the framework in which we can model business rules, and it can be seen as a novel concept of a *virtual business machine*, i.e., a machine, which is directly able to execute business logic, regardless of whether it includes human interaction or not. We can now forge the important notion with which we want to refer to business logic requirements in their form as executable programs of this virtual machine. We call the program of this virtual machine the *business logic* of the application.

These considerations lead to another key concept in our considerations, namely *executable specification*. If our business logic can be conceived as the program of a virtual business machine, then our specification method is nothing less than a high-level programming language. In fact, some decades ago, the concept of such languages for data-centric applications appeared so natural that the terminology "fourth generation languages" was coined for these types of languages. This term "fourth generation language" can now be said to be tied to the even more specialized look and feel of such a language, like ABAP-4 in the SAP system. Like this example, fourth generation languages are typically tightly integrated into single-vendor platforms. The modeling method presented here can nevertheless be seen as an integration of practical experiences from fourth generation languages into a state-of-the-art modeling style. In principle it is therefore conceivable that a future business platform running as a virtual machine on common platforms can interpret business logic directly.

1.3 High-Level Transactional Programming

A central topic in this book is the distinction between high-level programming and specification. High-level programming is a programming paradigm, which is on the abstraction level of specifications. Yet a high-level programming paradigm must be effectively translatable in efficient code on standard platforms.

The vision of high-level programming is certainly not restricted to the idea of a fully automated translation. This idealized concept of the translation of the functional specification into a running system on a current platform is neither state-of-the art, nor the most desirable concept. The high-level programming vision rather exploits the broad range of programming notions. Consider higher programming languages, which indeed started as a kind of abstract notation, but which were often not translated automatically, but manually. The task of the programming language was to encode knowledge about good program design.

The most intuitive use of a high-level program is perhaps as an input for a generator. The generator translates the system description into a target code, i.e., it can be compared to a compiler approach. However, the translation process is more transparent, in that the target code can be customized. The difference between a high-level programming paradigm and a general specification paradigm is that the former allows only those specifications that are known to be translatable into code. This is not a contradiction of the previous statement that the translation can also be transformed manually. However, one must be aware of that the code generated from the high-level program may not be a complete implementation: it may well be that there are still system parts that have to be developed manually on the target platform. One could also say that there are also tasks of tuning, which have to be done manually, since the problem is not to generate *some* code that fulfills the specification and is executable, but to generate efficient code.

1.4 A Parsimonious Relational Notation

Throughout the book we use class diagrams for data modeling. We start our examples with some currently discussed modeling approaches, e.g., UML and OCL. From the problems encountered there we will advance to a new, simple data modeling notion, the PD models. It has not just a simple format, but also a precisely defined meaning, its *semantics*. This notation is especially good for training and educational purposes, being an excellent primer for the sometimes more abstruse and feature-laden notations used in industry. It is particularly designed as a preparation of the diverse modeling landscape in industry and research. In industry projects as well as in scholarly discussions one might encounter a whole range of different data modeling notations, like ER diagrams and UML diagrams, but also database schemes, which all turn out to be related approaches to data modeling. The PD model notation in this book is an introduction to the commonalities of all these notations. The PD notation provides a good preparation for the very important skill nowadays to be able to quickly grasp new notations.

You will be well prepared if you keep your mind open, and if you are trained to identify the common concept behind these notations.

Industry notations, like UML, have the property that they must possess deliberately ambiguous semantics, in order to capture a number of differing notions under the umbrella of a unified notation – hence the name. In contrast, the notion used in this book has a fixed format as well as semantics. Of course you are encouraged to use the PD modeling notation presented here in your projects. Hopefully you will experience the advantages of a lightweight yet feature-rich approach that is tailored for today's enterprise applications.

1.5 A Descriptive Approach to the Software Development Process

Form-oriented analysis proposes artifacts for modeling. These artifacts are accompanied by recommendations on when and how to produce these artifacts. However, these recommendations must not be misunderstood as prescriptions – form-oriented analysis is a descriptive approach to software development. This means, first and foremost, that it should not be used to restrict the working software developer in any way. For example, we propose a couple of artifacts for the visualization of our form-oriented information system models, i.e., screen diagrams, page diagrams, form storyboards, formcharts, which differ with respect to granularity, comprehensibility, and preciseness.

Coarse grain modeling is motivated by certain demands of the requirements elicitation process, e.g., the need for lightweight communication with the domain expert, or a desired jump start to modeling. Then, for the sake of a convenient presentation the different kinds of artifacts are presented in this book in the manner of a strict stage-wise process, as if we were proceeding in a project from informal to more and more formal documents. However, this should not convey the impression that the proposed artifacts can only be exploited in a defined proceedings.

The arguments of form-oriented analysis aim at empowering the developer, they aim at improving the modeling of enterprise systems under the overall umbrella of *artifact orientation*. Ideally, form-oriented analysis provides the conceptual underpinning for some personal best working practices that the developer has already discovered by him- or herself, though in an ad hoc manner, or that he or she has learned from a colleague – typically from a senior developer.

In a wider sense, the descriptive approach has several properties, which are not mutually exclusive:

- Orthogonality with respect to process models.
- Focus on conceptual insight.
- Free approach.
- Holistic approach.

Software development methods can have a product model aspect and a process model aspect. Different software development methods can put different foci on these aspects. Actually, we argue that a concrete software development method can be advantageous with respect to product modeling even without reference to any process model. As we have already mentioned, form-oriented analysis techniques and tools are *orthogonal* to process model aspects, too.

Form-oriented analysis focuses on *conceptual insight*. It tries to foster a precise understanding of the certain widespread class of enterprise applications. This does by no means imply that we do not propose concrete formats, concrete tools, and concrete activities. It just means that concrete formats, concrete tools, and concrete activities are subject to concrete elaboration and must not be overemphasized, i.e., they must not be considered more important than the understanding of the system semantics.

The form-oriented analysis approach does not strictly follow any other dominating paradigm. This does not mean that it is completely decoupled from proven techniques and concepts defined so far in the software development community. On the contrary, we believe that form-oriented concepts can be also used in scenarios where other techniques are already successfully established. It just means that form-oriented analysis is *free* from the dictates of other paradigms and metaphors.

Similarly, form-oriented analysis is not restricted to a certain modeling level or process stage, say, requirements specification, analysis or design. As a *holistic* approach form-oriented analysis is open for equal discussions of all kinds of problems the working software engineer is faced with. The only restriction of form-oriented analysis is a self-restriction: it does not aim at being a general purpose approach, but utilizes assumptions about the systems that it is designed for.

2

The Form-Based System Paradigm

Enterprise systems encompass online transaction processing systems, enterprise resource planning systems, electronic data interchange, and e-commerce. This means the system class of interest can contain a small web shop as well as a huge system like the SABRE flight reservation system, which connected 59,000 travel agents in the year 2002 [155].

In this chapter we give an outline of our model for enterprise applications. An enterprise system can be seen as an installed and running enterprise application. The basic type of enterprise system we call a *unit system*: that is, a system which we consider as a single unit for our purposes. From the user's perspective a unit system is a black box. It is characterized by the interfaces through which it is accessed. Each unit system is a single unit of abstraction, it is a single *abstract data object*. The interface of a unit system which is directly accessible for us is the *human–computer interface* for interaction with the user. A unit system can also have an interface to other unit systems, and we will call this a *service interface* . Of the two kinds of interfaces of a unit system the human–computer interface is the more tangible one, therefore we begin our outline of the system modeling approach with this type of interface. In our method, the human–computer interface for communication with one unit system is session based, and we call it the *submit/response* style interface. One can conceive of another kind of interface which is sessionless and resembles a mail client with its mailbox. We will discuss such an interface designed for communication with multiple unit systems later in the book. But here we concentrate on the session-based interface type. It captures the key concepts behind several widespread interface types for enterprise applications, e.g., web interfaces. In one sentence one can say that the submit/response style interface models the human–computer interaction as an alternating exchange of messages between the user and the computer. But before we try to understand submit/response style systems in this way we look at them solely from the perspective of the user.

2.1 The Submit/Response Style Interface

We introduce the class of submit/response style interfaces by using a familiar application as an example, namely an online bookshop as can be found frequently in a similar form on the Web. Chapter 3 is devoted solely to an informal description of this example bookstore.

We have designed the following considerations in such a way that the reader can participate in the development of the ideas about the interface types. This is intended to be neither a historic line of development nor a necessary argument; it is just considered to be helpful, instructive, and easy to follow.

Submit/response style interfaces show at each point in time a page to the user, the *current page*. Two such pages, which are taken from our example bookstore, are shown in Fig. 2.1, i.e., a page showing the contents of the user's shopping cart and a page for gathering personal data.

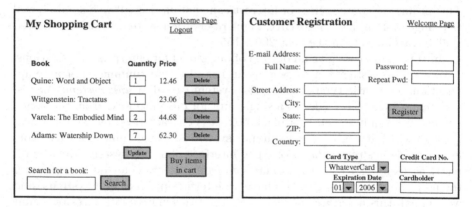

Fig. 2.1. Example pages of the online bookshop

A submit/response style interface allows the user to perform two kinds of interactions with the interface: we call them *page edits* and *page change*. Page changes are singular interactions which change the page, i.e., the current page is replaced by a new page. Page edits are interactions with the current page, namely the filling out of a form or resetting a form. Forms are the only editable parts of the page, and are made of input elements. These input elements can be quite sophisticated by themselves. A very sophisticated form element is a text field that allows the input of formatted text, as can be found in some interface technologies.

There is a hierarchy in these two kinds of interaction. Take the search option as an example. First you enter keywords by page interaction. Then you press the search button and the system shows the page with the search results by performing a page change. The page edit is always a preparation for the page change in this style. We call this the *two-staged interaction* paradigm of submit/response systems.

During the heyday of GUI-based client/server programming such interfaces were often considered as bare metal legacy technology. The advent of the web browser as a new thin client has shown many reasons why submit/response style interfaces are here to stay. On the one hand there are proven system architectures for submit/response style systems. Classical mainframe architectures like CICS are still in use and being constantly improved. Some ubiquitous commercial off-the-shelf (COTS) products are successful because they have a mature system architecture. They provide working solutions for enterprise applications, and they take into account the substantial non-functional requirements of enterprise applications. New vendor-neutral and platform-independent enterprise computing approaches like J2EE are emerging, targeting the same driving forces such as the classical approaches.

But submit/response style systems do not just have proven software architectures. Surprisingly, submit/response style interfaces can have cognitive advantages, too. This means that submit/response style interaction can foster usability in many cases, simply because it is often the natural solution with respect to an automated enterprise functionality.

2.1.1 Proven System Architecture for Submit/Response Style Systems

Enterprise applications are data-centric and transaction-based. The submit/response style interface is not tied to any specific technology. On the contrary, the same characteristics can be found in many technologies, e.g., HTML-based clients and mainframe terminals. Even the screens of a GUI-based COTS system follow the submit/response style interface metaphor.

An important class of systems with submit/response style interfaces are systems with ultra-thin clients, encompassing terminals and HTML browsers, see Fig. 2.2. Ultra-thin clients are used for creating an interface tier that does not contain business logic in itself. Ultra-thin clients cache the user interaction on one page in the client layer. The page sequence control logic – or workflow controller – is also not hosted by the client layer but rather by the server layer. Ultra-thin clients fit neatly into the transactional system architecture, be it one of the classical proposals [23, 130] or a more recent proposal [181]. Transactional system architectures successfully target many problems: system load, performance maintainability, scalability, security, and others.

The interaction with a system/response style system is a repeated alternation between data processing and the presentation of a new screen. The dialogue appears to the user as a sequence of editable screens: the dialogue steps are *screen transactions*. The presentation layer of a system is responsible for a preprocessing of data submitted by the user, the triggering of appropriate business rules, and the presentation of the correct new screen. Given a multi-tier system architecture, there is no requirement that this logic be hosted by

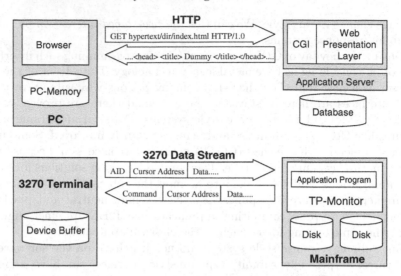

Fig. 2.2. Examples of ultra-thin client based submit/response style systems

the application server tier. In the SAP R/3 system [208], see Fig. 2.3, it is actually hosted by the client tier. The SAP R/3 system architecture is optimized with respect to the notion of commercial off-the-shelf software. In a full version of the SAP R/3 system the vertical architecture depicted in Fig. 2.3 is completed by a horizontal architecture consisting of a production system, a consolidation system, and a development system: the necessary customization of the system is only possible in a defined safe way by deploying new modules via a special transportation system.

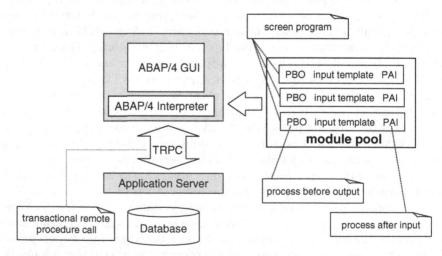

Fig. 2.3. SAP R/3 architecture – a client/server submit/response style system

2.1.2 Cognitive Advantages of Submit/Response Style Systems

Form-based interfaces have clear advantages for the self-explanatory character of a system. The usage of the system is intuitive, since it is guided by a paper form metaphor. However, the importance of the submission process is notable; therefore we want to characterize the metaphor as a *submission form metaphor*. The difference between temporary input and submission, or "sending," is intuitive and fosters the user's understanding of the system. The form-based metaphor has a multi-tier structure of its own, without being fixed to an implementation. The two classes of interactions structure the work of the user into the work-intensive frequent page interactions and the punctual and atomic interactions of the "serious" kind, namely the page changes which also happen to be the conclusion and separation of logically disjoint bunches of work. The submit/response style character puts the user in command of the timing of system usage. It protects the user from irritating disruption of his or her work by incoming information.

In form-based interfaces the submission of a form is an operation that has exactly the semantics indicated by the metaphor. In computer science terms we have compared the submission of an actual parameter list with a method name. The submission form metaphor views interaction with the system as filling out virtual paper forms and submitting them to a processing instance, which represents the core system.

The metaphor has the qualified name submission form metaphor, because other form interface types can be found as well. For example, desktop databases as found in office suites allow form style interfaces, which possess page navigation buttons. Input in this form immediately changes the model. We call such a form style interface a *formlike view*. Applications using formlike views are in principle required to have synchronous views of the data: if two formlike views currently show the same data, and the data are changed in one formlike view, then the other formlike view has to be immediately updated. Many implementations, however, have to stick to polling mechanisms, which leads to latency effects in the update process. Well-known and even worse examples are file managers, which recognize state changes frequently only after manual refresh. It is important to recognize that the necessary refresh in this case is a bad implementation, while the reload mechanism of submit/response style applications is a logically necessary feature.

In desktop databases the model state is the persistent state. Other applications with formlike views have non-persistent states, e.g., spreadsheets.

The submission form metaphor has the advantage of possessing a clear semantics. The two-staged state change due to the two-tiered model is an integral part of the metaphor. This is quite in contrast to, for example, the important desktop metaphor. Consider the important drag and drop feature, which is at the very heart of the desktop metaphor. Drag and drop means regularly either copy or move, and hence can lead to two different effects.

The submission form metaphor is accompanied by the *response page principle* for showing responses of the core system. The submission of a form is a page change, i.e., the page that hosted the form is hidden and a new page is shown. This new page is the response from the server. The response page has three important functions:

- Notifying the user of the immediate status of the submitted form.
- Showing new information to the user.
- Offering new interaction options.

The immediate status of the submitted form is the system's immediate response to the form. Depending on the business logic this may or may not be the completion of the form processing.

- Consider the entry of a new date in a web calendar tool. The response page is the new calendar view with a short notification message. The form has been completely processed.
- Consider the submission of an order in an online brokerage system. The response page is a notification of reception. The execution of the order, however, takes place asynchronously.
- Consider the submission of an e-mail in a mail account on the Web. The response page logically is only a notification of some overall validity of the submitted data, e.g., the recipient's address contains an at-sign. The completion of the intended effect, i.e., the delivery of the e-mail, is not acknowledged at all.

2.1.3 Semantics of Page Change

Each page can contain different forms. A form connects input elements to a page change option, the submit button. Of course the intuition is that only the page edit in the form that belongs to a submit button gives the intended meaning of this command.

This meaning is captured in a message-based model, which we use for the submit/response system. The user interface is considered as a distinct system, which we call the *conceptual session terminal*, or terminal for short. It is very much an abstraction of today's web browser used as a client for an enterprise application. As the name terminal suggests, the terminal is considered to be connected with the unit system, which means that it can communicate by messages and only by messages. The conceptual session terminal has a state, namely the current page shown to the user, optionally including some invisible information within that page, as well as the page edit the user has performed so far on this page. The page edit is kept in the terminal until the user performs a page change, which belongs to a form. Then the contents of the input elements of this form are transmitted as a data record to the unit system. The input elements of this form can contain the page edit of the user, or data which was pre-filled on the page, so-called default data. The transmitted data record is tagged with the name of the form, and together this message is like a remote procedure call. The name of the form is something like the name of the procedure. It leads to an action on the unit system, and this action always produces a result, given as a page description. This page description is a message that is transmitted back to the terminal, and the described page replaces the current page the user has seen before. This gives in effect a page change. We call the new current page the *response page* to the submission, the received message the response message, and if we do not want to distinguish it, we call it the *response*. The page change is therefore the submission of a parameterized command, and the new page is the result. The terminal is locked between send and receive. The remote method call is therefore a synchronous procedure call. This alternation of submissions and responses has of course given rise to the term submit/response.

The parameter of the submission can of course be empty. There is only one type of page change. Each page change can, however, transmit data, which were not rendered on the page.

All page edits that have been performed on input elements which do not belong to the submitted form are therefore lost; the state of the conceptual session terminal after a page change is exclusively the response page.

Of course there are many other possible types of interfaces than the submit/response interface explained so far, e.g., interfaces which support several pages at once. However, the submit/response style system has its advantages in that it is quite expressive yet simple and primarily it is very regular. The strict alternation between the user and system messages yields many advantages for modeling. Therefore it is very suitable for the high abstraction level, on which we want to focus during analysis. A key concept here, which contributes to the whole method's characteristics, is the notion that the user can submit a whole compound data object with each message.

2.1.4 Dialogue Types

We have explained submit/response style interaction as the alternating interchange of messages. We now want to introduce static typing to these messages, and this step alone will lead to a plethora of interesting new properties of our interfaces.

First we want to introduce static types for the response pages. This means that only a finite number of page types are allowed for each interface. It allows us to give a natural yet rigorous meaning to the finite number of pages depicted in screenshot diagrams (sometimes called non-executable GUI prototypes); they simply represent the page types. Furthermore it allows us to give precise semantics to the arrows in these diagrams representing possible page change in the following way.

The current page has a type from a finite number of page types. We conceive the type of the current page as a *finite state aspect* of the terminal. (A finite state aspect is a reduction of the state of a system, which is of interest for the modeler. This is known from finite state modeling in many domains. Consider the finite states a process can have in an operating system. Of course each process can in principle have infinite states, but the finite states are the reduction of interest for the modeler.) The terminal can then be seen as a finite state machine. The arrows are naturally characterized as transitions.

We now turn to the user messages. They are statically typed as well. Therefore there can be only a finite number of possible user messages. Each form on a page must be assigned a single user message type. The page edit on this form prepares an instance of this type. The page change is then used for sending this instance as a method parameter. We identify the concept or the type with the concept of the procedure name. Therefore the type of the message already determines the processing action of the unit system. We call this procedure of the unit system the *server action*. A form on a page is therefore an editable message instance.

For each page type the number of page changes is constant or bound by a constant. Consider a catalogue page which contains a list of books. Each book can be put into the shopping cart with a single click. If we model these interaction options as separate page changes, then the number of page changes is not bound by a constant. We therefore conceive all these interaction options as addressing the same page change, but providing a different parameter every time. In this way the list of interaction options forms a single conceptual interaction.

2.1.5 Conditional System Response

If a message is sent to the unit system, the system's response is conditional, depending on the message and on the system's internal state. Of course the system's response is conditional with respect to the content of the page, e.g., in the case of selecting a book, the shopping cart as the system's response depends on the previous cart state as well as on the chosen book. But the system's response can be conditional with respect to the page type as well. Take a system login dialogue as an example. The business logic says that if a user has never bought anything, then after six months the username will be deactivated and can be taken by another user. The submission of username and password can therefore have a number of different effects.

- If the username belongs to a valid account and the password is valid, then the welcome screen for registered users is shown.
- If the username belongs to a deactivated account and the password is valid, then the user gets a screen informing him or her that the account has been reactivated.
- If the username belongs to a valid account which has been taken over by a user, and the password is the last password of an old user, then the user gets a notification that his or her account has been collected and redistributed. A new account is offered to him or her.

• If the password is invalid, then the user is informed about that, and he or she is offered assistance for forgotten passwords.

The page type as a state of the finite state machine can therefore end up in four different pages triggered by the same page change. We want to have a model that captures both the fact that the user has chosen one single page change as well as the correct page type of the system's response. For this purpose we use a novel bipartite state model. The rationale is that we model the system's processing of the request as a separate state. Therefore if the user triggers a page change, the finite state model of the terminal changes into a processing state, which we call *server action*, and depending on the received response page the state model changes into the respective page type. The state of the terminal therefore alternates between page types and server actions. The server actions are left automatically as soon as the unit system's response is received. In the same way as we identify the page state with the type of the displayed message, we now identify the server action with the type of the message that has been sent from the user to the system and which is processed during this server action. The resulting bipartite state machine is painted as a *formchart*.

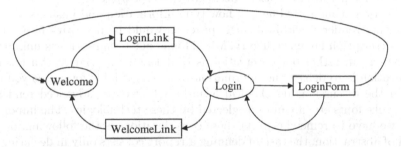

Fig. 2.4. Example formchart for a system login capability

Fig. 2.4 shows a first motivating example formchart for a system login capability. From the system welcome page it is possible to reach a login page via a link. From there it is possible to abort the login dialogue via a link back to the welcome page. Of course the login page offers a login form. The response of the server action representing the login form is conditional: if an error occurs the dialogue flow is branched back to the login page reporting an appropriate error message, otherwise it is branched to the welcome page. The formchart snippet in Fig. 2.4 is taken from the bookstore formchart in Fig. 5.10.

2.1.6 System Messages as Reports

In our definition of submit/response style systems the elements of human–computer interaction are messages from the user to the system on the one hand, and messages from the system to the user on the other hand. We now outline the structure of these messages by giving a first account of a part of the type system for these messages.

Messages from the system to the user are conceived as reports. A report is a structured document, i.e., a document with a fixed format. A typical case would be a simple table: the document can then be seen as a list of data records, each data record being a row in the table. In the viewpoint we want to adopt in our considerations, we consider only the true data as the content of the form. This viewpoint is a little bit tricky, since usually you would require a report to contain some explanatory data, namely first and foremost the header of the table containing the column names. But in our considerations here it is of course desirable to abstract from these requirements in order to concentrate on the business logic. Now, we give one possible solution, which we will use in our following considerations. We assume that the conceptual session terminal has access to the type definitions of our system. This means that the terminal can access type definitions for rendering. This is exactly what we assume to happen with the reports the system sends to the user: the terminal knows the type of the message that is sent. Hence the browser can retrieve the column names, which are nothing more than the role names in the record type, from the user's access to the type system.

We are not interested here in how type information and business data together are rendered within a single page, as would be necessary in a typical page description language like HTML. This is not because this is uninteresting or trivial; rather our observation is that the main priority of a business application is to deliver the information in *some* readable form – as you may see in the discussions on classical form-based systems, advanced rendering topics like fonts etc. are quite neglected by these technologies. The important idea we have to remember from these considerations is the following: on our level of abstraction, the task of defining a report consists only in declaring the information content of the report as a type, and specifying with which data it should actually be filled. Of course reports can have more complex structure than the aforementioned tables. Quite common examples are groups of tables (bestsellers in a category of our bookshop, followed by subcategories), or more complex data structures within a table cell (a table with a hotel in each row, and in one column a list of pictograms for the luxury features in this hotel). In our view we suppose for each report data definition a standard rendering through the abstract browser.

2.1.7 User Input by Forms

As we have said, we see the user input as a message to the system. In our model, in close correspondence to what you will find in current platforms, the user first fills out a form in a local communication with the terminal. The state of the form in preparation is buffered within the terminal. Only at the time when the user submits the form is all the data of the form transmitted to the system. The very notion of a form is that the data within the form adhere to a format, i.e., a data type. Hence the most important part of defining a form is to choose the message data type to which the filled forms will later belong. In our notion of the terminal this information is, moreover, the only thing this terminal needs in order to render the form. The terminal therefore basically uses the type definition itself as a key to the description of a form. Beyond that there will be a possibility to give further specifications in the single form. The bottom line is that a form in our system metaphor is a facility with which the user can construct an instance of a given data type within the terminal, and then submit it or forget it. It has to be said that such a definition of form immediately uncovers some shortcomings of many current form description languages, e.g., HTML again. That is, a straightforward type of form, which we could well need in certain circumstances, is a form where one can input a table, such as a list of records. A good example would be a form for an invoice with many single posts, where each post is mainly described by plain text. At submission you want to transmit the whole invoice to the system. Such a list, which should of course grow as you insert new lines, is a straightforward concept in our view. It is primarily absent in HTML, but it is present in some-tool based form editors from database vendors.

2.1.8 Interdependence of System Response and User Input

A key concept with regard to form-based systems deals with the way the use input can be connected with previous system responses. Forms can contain so-called selection interaction options. The form contains some kind of list, either a list of products, or a list of options or anything else. The user can choose from this list only one object – in which case it is called single selection – or an arbitrary number – in which case it is called multiple selection. The crucial point is here that the user can only choose what was offered by the system beforehand. The offer by the system can well have the status of a report in itself, e.g., in the case of the list of products. Hence the user returns to the system data which he or she had received with a report beforehand. In our model we indicate this by the fact that the report of the system contains not only readable data, but also references to entities in the system. With the selection interaction option of the form the user chooses between these references and sends them back to the system. In our notion, incidentally, this is also the only thing the user can do with these references. They are not human-readable, they are in that sense not even generally machine-readable. We will see in a later section on automated systems communications that in the same way other systems can get such references. They can only use these references in order to send them back to the system. References therefore belong to different reference types. A form field for references has such a type, and only references of this type can be returned in this form field.

2.1.9 Forms and the Bipartite Finite State Machine

The bipartite finite state machine specifies for each page type which server action types the user can submit in this page type. Therefore the forms available for the user in each page type are statically fixed. The formchart as a bipartite state machine gives a model that has an explicit notion of whether the same business functionality is available from two different page states or not. The forms on the page, however, may contain different additional specifications, which may differ from page to page. This will be a topic in the discussion of dialogue annotation in Sect. 5.4.

The best way to characterize the viewpoint which is taken by the formchart with respect to the unit system is the following. The unit system offers a set of server actions, each of which is available for the user depending on certain conditions, especially the page state. The formchart has the task of coordinating the invocation of server actions. It ensures the alternating message interchange through its bipartite structure. Furthermore it makes server actions only available for the user in the way described by the page/server transitions. In the context of interactions between systems we will discuss message communication in general.

2.2 A Message-Based Model of Data Interchange

Many enterprise systems communicate by automated interfaces. Such communication has recently become an area of increased interest in the discussions about Web services. Though Web services aim at being specifically lightweight and try to open up new applications for automated communication, the principle of automated communication is well established within technologies such as EDI. Web services are an implementation technique, not a conceptual notion. The keyword business-to-business refers partly to well-established technology, partly to new initiatives to widen the use of intersystem communication.

In our method we again want to create a homogeneous abstraction level, on which only business logic is modeled. Form-oriented analysis is only concerned with the analysis-level view of such services.

In order to achieve this unit systems can have not only human–computer interfaces, but interfaces to other unit systems as well, namely the service interfaces. In this book we will discuss modeling techniques for such service interfaces, which will have a number of commonalities with the formchart approach. In our method unit systems communicate first hand with messages. The unit system model will now especially support a transactional paradigm. This transactional paradigm offers a convenient approach to model the system behavior with respect to a message. The system response to a message can be specified as if the system can afford to process all messages sequentially, one at a time. In exchange for this it is necessary that the unit system can communicate to other unit systems only after processing the message, by sending new messages.

This can be put into a definition as follows. The *transactional unit system* is a computational automaton with a state. The unit system offers a set of *transactions* it can perform. Each transaction has an associated message type. A transaction takes a message and produces a set of new messages.

An untyped view of *computational automata* is specified by a single *state transition function*:

```
stateTransitionFunction: message × state → state × listof(message)
```

In the statically typed view the state transition function invokes for each message type a different transaction, which is the state transition for this message type. The transition function can provide only a fixed number of message types:

$$\texttt{transaction}_a: \texttt{message}_a \times \texttt{state} \rightarrow \quad \texttt{state}$$
$$\times\ \texttt{listof}(\texttt{message}_{a_1})$$
$$\times\ \texttt{listof}(\texttt{message}_{a_2})$$
$$\ldots$$
$$\times\ \texttt{listof}(\texttt{message}_{a_{n_a}})$$

$$\texttt{transaction}_b: \texttt{message}_b \times \texttt{state} \rightarrow \quad \texttt{state}$$
$$\times\ \texttt{listof}(\texttt{message}_{b_1})$$
$$\times\ \texttt{listof}(\texttt{message}_{b_2})$$
$$\ldots$$
$$\times\ \texttt{listof}(\texttt{message}_{b_{n_b}})$$

$$\vdots$$

In this model, incoming messages are processed in a strictly sequential manner. It may be noted here that this can be seen as one of the major services and achievements of transactional technology to provide serial operational semantics for the application programmer, while behind the scenes sophisticated technology like locking protocols allows for a partially parallel execution. The main task of transactional infrastructures is therefore to provide simple semantics to the application programmer, which would not be scalable if translated directly into an implementation.

Messages in our system view must have a sender and a recipient. There is an inherent network model which takes care of the correct delivery and provision of correct sender information. The static type system is also involved here, in that it requires the outgoing messages to be statically tagged with the correct sender. One of the services which will be provided by the submit/response style interface view is to deal with the need for the sender and recipient of messages in the context of a terminal session where both remain the same during the session. For the terminal the need for a recipient is fully transparent; for the unit system the interesting data are the user ID, not the terminal.

Today there is considerable effort to specify such inter-system interfaces in which a complex protocol has to be observed. Traditional analysis techniques like structured analysis allow for no specification of such complex protocols. Form-oriented analysis offers more specification options for service interfaces through the possibility to specify the actions connected with the messages.

3

Exploring the Online Bookshop

We will use as a running example in our considerations an online bookshop. Such bookshops are familiar from the Web. They show many aspects of general enterprise applications. Note that the industrial transactional web benchmark TPC-W [296] uses a bookshop as an example application, too.

In this chapter we set the stage by defining a minimal yet realistic bookshop. The definition is given by an informal textual description that is accompanied by depictions of the possible screens that show up during usage of the system. Finally a class diagram for the persistent data held by the system is given. Due to its informality the definition is necessarily ambiguous and incomplete. The bookshop comprises the following features:

- Browsing categories.
- Simple search facility.
- Shopping cart.
- Buying.
- Registering a new customer.
- Changing customer data.
- Login and logout.

In our online bookshop the user can explore the books on offer by browsing through a hierarchy of categories as well as searching for particular books by search criteria. Each book has a book page with the details of the book. The user can put books into a shopping cart, which the user can view at every point in time. The user can edit or buy the whole shopping cart. The system allows for the registration as a new customer and the management of customer data. Users that are already registered can log in. Further, a professional bookshop would have additional features like book reviews, wish lists, personalization, or support for the case of forgotten passwords. The data model supported by the example bookshop will turn out to be rather terse. However, the example is already complex enough to encompass the important problems that might show up in modeling a form-based system and furthermore we hope that the example is voluminous enough to convince the reader in the sequel that form-oriented practices really work.

3.1 The Dialogue Model

3.1.1 Login, Registration, and Logout

The customer enters the online bookshop via the welcome page. The welcome page is shown in Fig. 3.1. By choosing links the user can enter the browsing of the bookstore, view the shopping cart, login or register. Furthermore the user finds some recommended bestsellers on the welcome page. For every bestseller the author and the book's title is displayed. Following an appropriate link the user can reach the respective book page, where he or she can view details of the book. Furthermore on the welcome page there is a text field where the customer can enter search items.

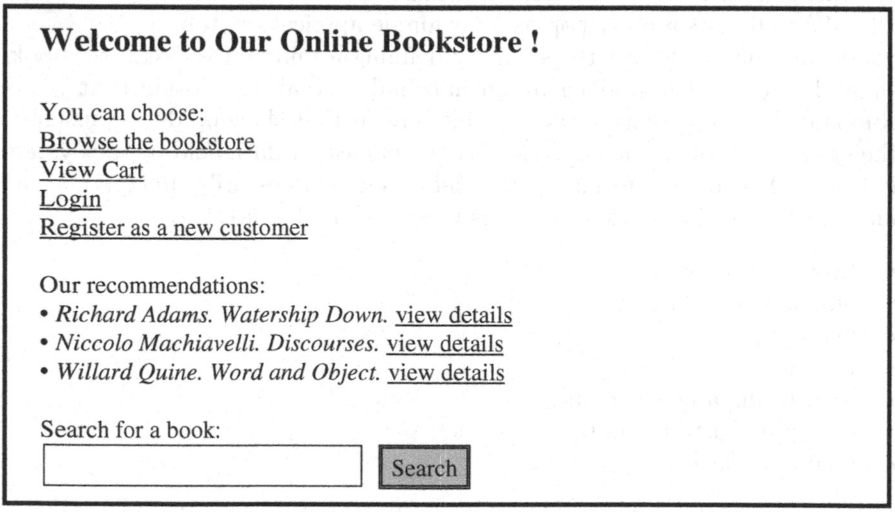

Welcome to Our Online Bookstore !

You can choose:
Browse the bookstore
View Cart
Login
Register as a new customer

Our recommendations:
• *Richard Adams. Watership Down.* view details
• *Niccolo Machiavelli. Discourses.* view details
• *Willard Quine. Word and Object.* view details

Search for a book:

[   ] Search

Fig. 3.1. Welcome screen of the online bookshop

If the customer chooses to log in, the login screen (Fig. 3.2) is shown. The user has to provide his or her e-mail address, which serves as an account identifier, and a password. If no customer with the entered e-mail address exists in the system or if the entered password does not match the e-mail address the system will branch to the login screen again, whereupon an appropriate error message like the one in Fig. 3.2 is given and the entered password is redisplayed. There are other possible mistakes the customer can make, which can be subsumed under the term form field validation. In the case of the login screen the user might forget to provide an e-mail address or a password.

Though these errors can be captured by client-side technology, i.e., without contacting the server, the errors make no difference with respect to a system description from a user's viewpoint. Again, the login screen is redisplayed with an appropriate error message or highlighting the respective formerly error-prone fields. Especially because the user might be stuck in a loop of login screens with error messages, the login screen offers a back link to the system welcome page and a link to the registration page.

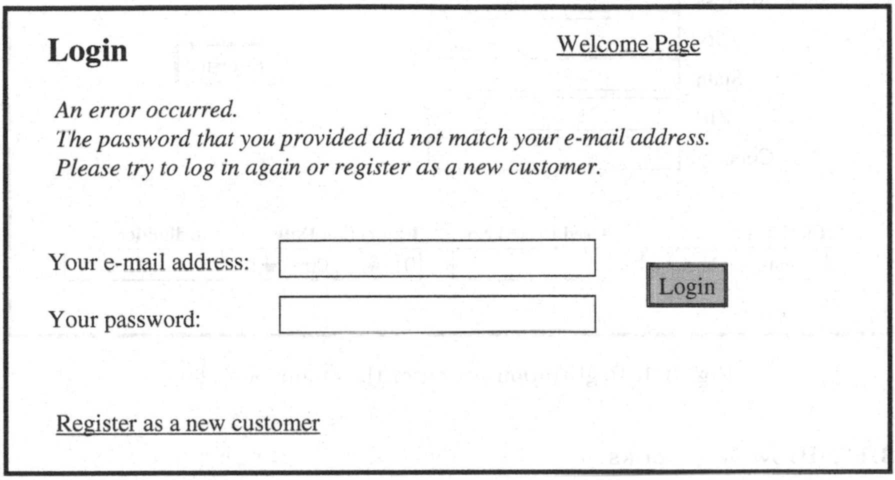

Fig. 3.2. Login screen of the online bookshop

The system's registration page is shown in Fig. 3.3. A customer must fill out a form in order to provide his or her e-mail address, name, address, and credit card information. The customer must choose a password and has to type it twice. Again, if the data provided by the user are erroneous, the page is redisplayed with an appropriate warning. For example, the credit card number is checked and it is checked whether the password matches the retyped password. As a side effect of a successful registration, the customer is logged in.

Consider the welcome page again shown in Fig. 3.1. The figure actually shows the page's version of a system usage where the user is not yet logged in. If the user is logged in, the welcome page might show another headline displaying the name of the user, but more importantly there will be no more links that lead to a login page or a registration page. Instead of this these links will be replaced by a logout button or logout link and a link to a page where the customer account can be edited.

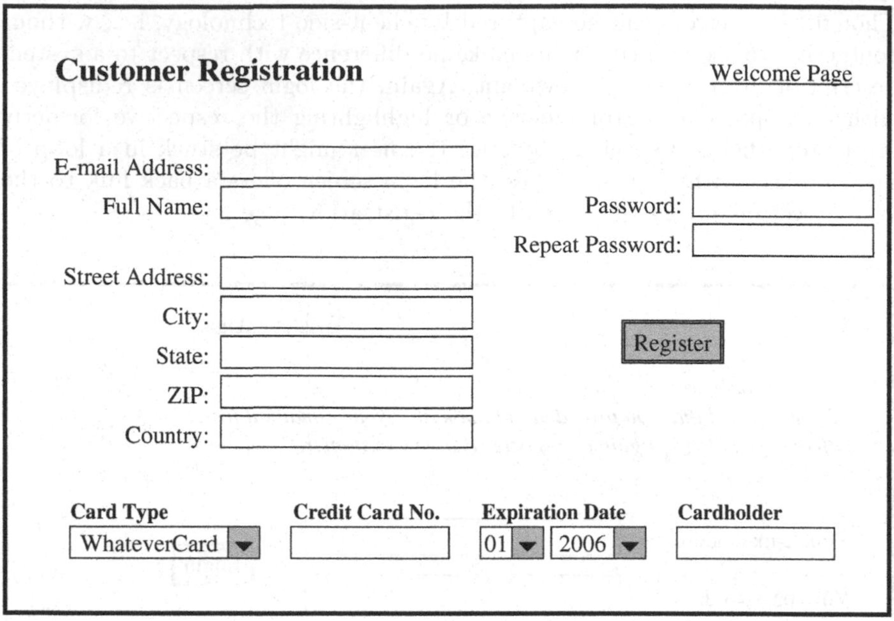

Fig. 3.3. Registration screen of the online bookshop

3.1.2 Browsing Books

Starting from the welcome page the user can browse a hierarchy of book categories. He or she can move from the welcome page to the category of all books, which is shown in Fig. 3.4. As all category pages it shows a list of links to pages of subcategories. This means the user can descend the tree of categories until he or she reaches a category with no further subcategories. Besides the subcategories each category page contains a list of featured books. This is similar to the welcome page, but this time it is possible not only to follow links to the respective book pages, but to put a selection of the featured books directly into the shopping cart by clicking the respective check boxes and leaving the page by the special submit button that is provided for this purpose.

From the category page it is again possible to view the cart. Similar to the welcome page it is possible to the reach the login page and the registration page if the customer is not logged in, and to log out or to reach the account editing page otherwise. It is also possible to search for a book. Furthermore a link to the welcome page is provided. Indeed, a couple of pages of the system support all or a portion of these options; so do the book page, the search result page, the shopping cart, the order information page, and the confirmation page. On these pages the options are always organized in the same way, i.e., the search option at the bottom of the page, and all other options at the upper right corner of the page.

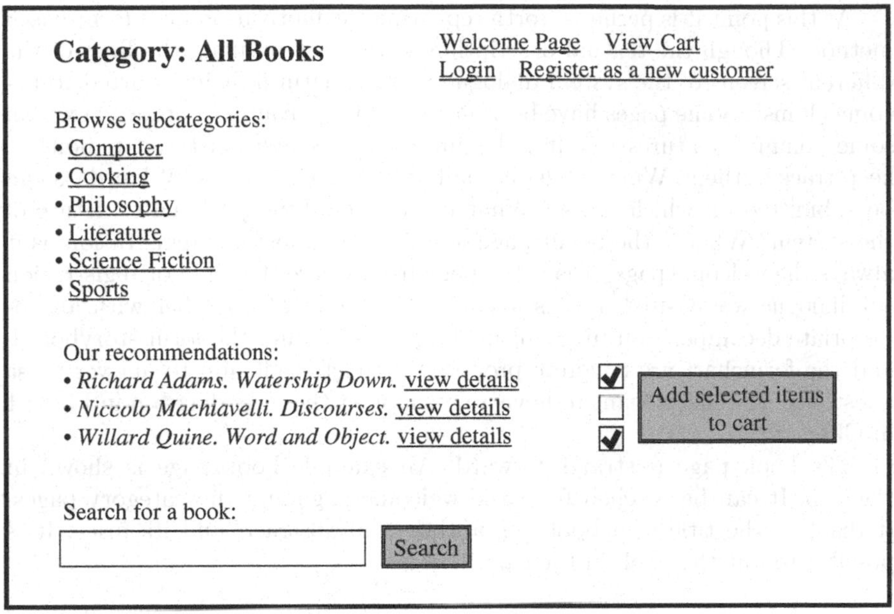

Category: All Books

Welcome Page   View Cart
Login   Register as a new customer

Browse subcategories:
• Computer
• Cooking
• Philosophy
• Literature
• Science Fiction
• Sports

Our recommendations:
• *Richard Adams. Watership Down.* view details
• *Niccolo Machiavelli. Discourses.* view details
• *Willard Quine. Word and Object.* view details

Add selected items to cart

Search for a book:

Search

Fig. 3.4. Category screen of the online bookshop

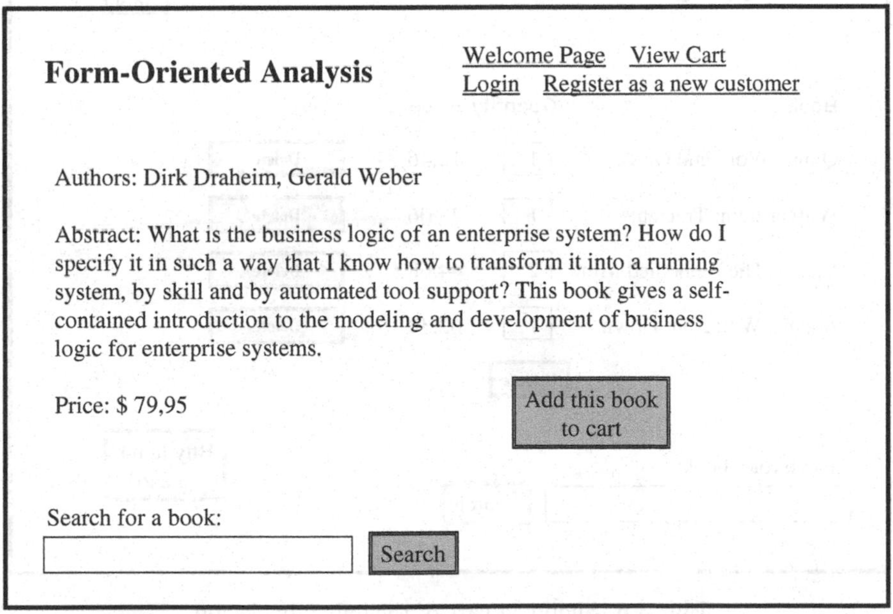

Form-Oriented Analysis

Welcome Page   View Cart
Login   Register as a new customer

Authors: Dirk Draheim, Gerald Weber

Abstract: What is the business logic of an enterprise system? How do I specify it in such a way that I know how to transform it into a running system, by skill and by automated tool support? This book gives a self-contained introduction to the modeling and development of business logic for enterprise systems.

Price: $ 79,95

Add this book to cart

Search for a book:

Search

Fig. 3.5. Book page of the online bookshop

At this point it is perhaps worth repeating the motivation for a form-based method. Though the textual description of the system along the lines of the different screens of the system dialogue is quite natural, it has started to become clumsy. Some pages have been mentioned in advance in order to explain some common features but it is beginning to become hard and tedious to keep track of them. Which pages actually offer which options? What data can be submitted on which pages? What is the overall navigational structure of the system? What is the result page of a successful login or registration: is it always the welcome page or is it the page from where the login or registration subdialogue was visited, i.e., is it context-dependent? Together with an appropriate decomposition mechanism the page diagram, the form storyboard, and the formchart are concrete proposed artifacts that aim to answer these questions. You might want to have a first look at the page diagram in Fig. 4.1 in Chap. 4.

The book page is straightforward. An example book page is shown in Fig. 3.5. It can be reached from the welcome page and the category pages. It displays the title of a book, its authors, an abstract, and its price. It is possible to put the book in the cart.

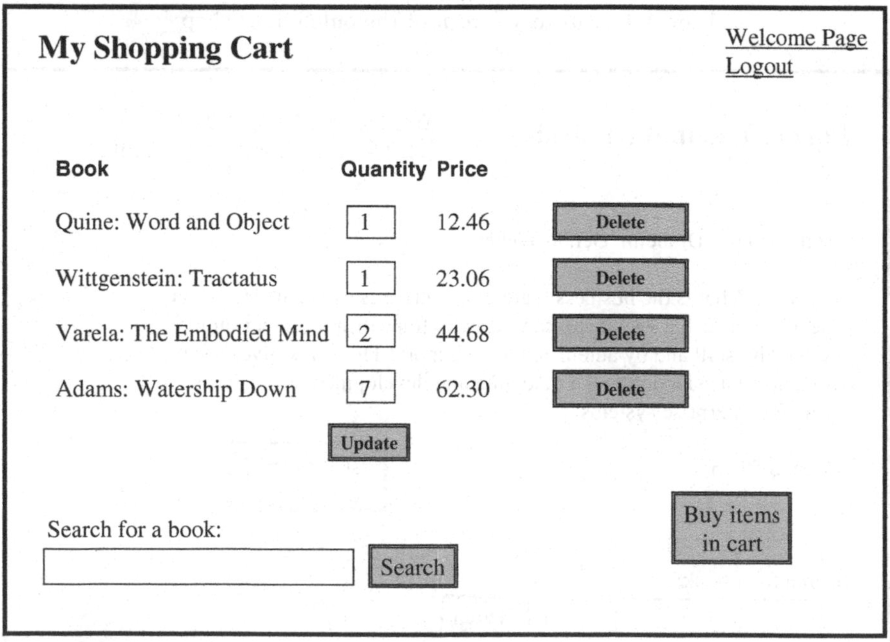

My Shopping Cart				Welcome Page Logout
Book		**Quantity**	**Price**	
Quine: Word and Object		1	12.46	Delete
Wittgenstein: Tractatus		1	23.06	Delete
Varela: The Embodied Mind		2	44.68	Delete
Adams: Watership Down		7	62.30	Delete
		Update		
Search for a book:				Buy items in cart
	Search			

Fig. 3.6. Shopping cart of the online bookshop

3.1.3 Shopping Cart

The shopping cart is a crucial concept in web shops. As in our bookstore it usually not only is used to manage the items the customer eventually wants to buy, but serves as the single entry point to the order subdialogue of the system. The shopping cart page shows a list of selected items with their desired quantities and calculated prices, see Fig. 3.6. The quantities can be edited by the user. Incidentally, as a typical example for the two-staged interaction style of submit/response style systems, the changes to the quantity fields only become valid if the user approves them by pressing the update button. Deleting an item can be done by setting its quantity to zero or using a delete button, which exists for each item in the shopping cart. On pressing the update button or one of the delete buttons the new shopping cart is redisplayed.

3.1.4 Buying

If the shopping cart is not empty the cart page contains a special button for entering the order dialogue. If the user is already logged in, he or she is directed immediately to the order information page shown in Fig. 3.7. If the user is not yet logged in, he or she is directed to the login page that is shown in Fig. 3.2. If the user is new to the bookstore he or she can proceed to the registration page from there. The login page and the registration page have been discussed earlier. However, there is an important difference. This time the user is directed to the order information page instead of to the welcome page after a successful login or registration.

The order information page depicted in Fig. 3.7 summarizes the shipping address, the payment method, and the content of the shopping cart. The user has a last chance to abort the order dialogue. For example, the user might log out to the welcome page. If the user has discovered an error in the displayed order information, he or she can proceed to the account editing page or to the shopping cart page in order to make the necessary corrections. On the other hand, if the user agrees with the displayed information, he or she can finally place the order by pressing the respective button. The order dialogue is completed by a confirmation page that again summarizes the order information.

3.1.5 Managing User Data

A user can change the data on the account editing page. In our minimal bookstore the account editing page is nearly identical to the registration page shown in Fig. 3.3 except for some important differences. Besides a different headline, the account editing page can only be entered if the user is already logged in. Then its customer data are displayed as default values in the form fields of the page. Besides this, the pages behave the same. As in the case of

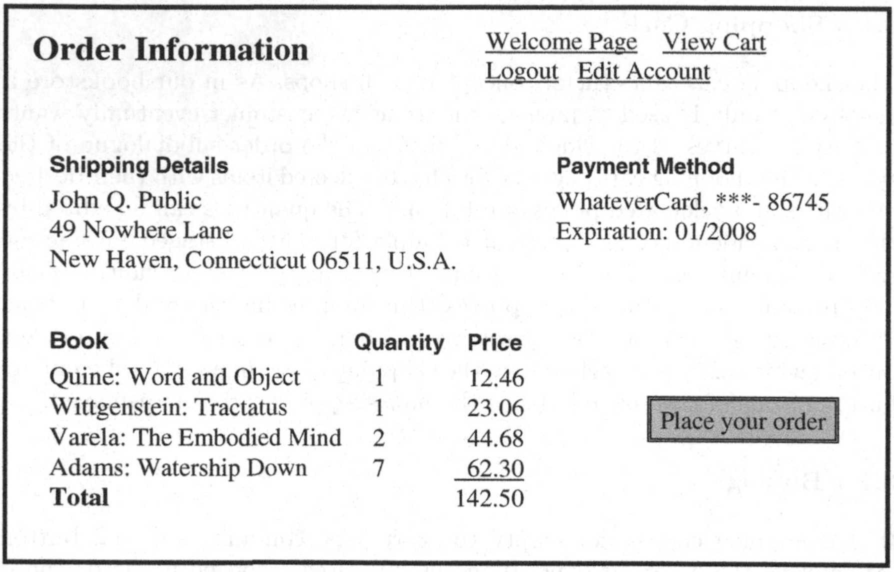

Order Information

Welcome Page   View Cart
Logout   Edit Account

Shipping Details

John Q. Public
49 Nowhere Lane
New Haven, Connecticut 06511, U.S.A.

Payment Method

WhateverCard, ***- 86745
Expiration: 01/2008

Book	Quantity	Price
Quine: Word and Object	1	12.46
Wittgenstein: Tractatus	1	23.06
Varela: The Embodied Mind	2	44.68
Adams: Watership Down	7	62.30
Total		142.50

Place your order

Fig. 3.7. Order information page of the online bookshop

the login page and the registration page, the account editing page is context-sensitive with respect to the targeted page after a successful submission of data. If the page has been entered from the order information page it will direct the dialogue flow back to this page and otherwise to the system welcome page.

3.1.6 Searching for Books

Finally we come to the search feature of the bookstore. This feature is given by the entirety of search forms that are provided by several different pages of the system. If the user submits one or more search items with this form field, the system searches for the most appropriate books. If it finds exactly one book that matches the query the respective book page is shown to the user. Otherwise the dialogue branches to a search result page that is shown in Fig. 3.8. The result screen repeats the search items and presents the book titles found in the same way the featured books of a category page are presented, i.e., with options to view details and add the books to the cart.

3.2 The Persistent Data Model

The persistent data model of the bookstore example is given as a class diagram in Fig. 3.9. The diagram describes the types of master data and transactional data needed and which are gathered by the described dialogues. The master

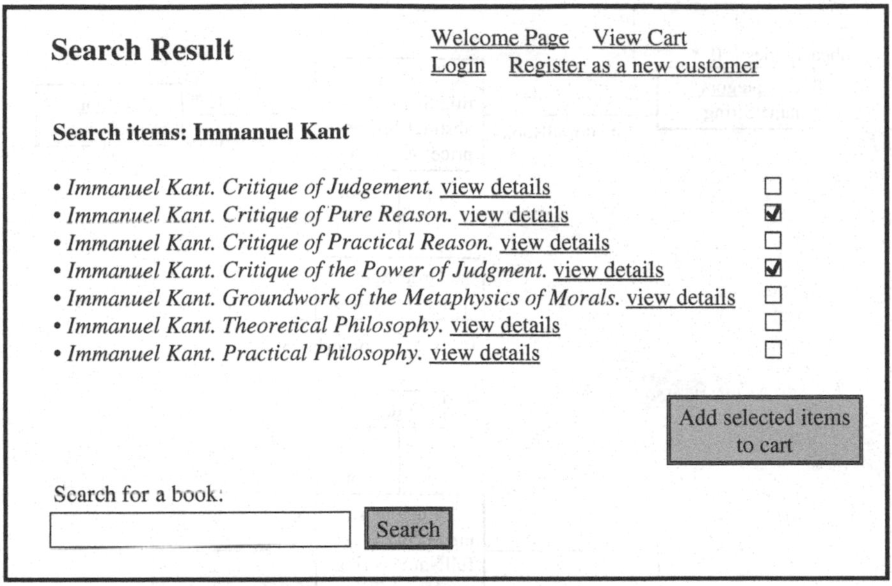

Search Result

Welcome Page   View Cart
Login   Register as a new customer

Search items: Immanuel Kant

- *Immanuel Kant. Critique of Judgement.* view details ☐
- *Immanuel Kant. Critique of Pure Reason.* view details ☑
- *Immanuel Kant. Critique of Practical Reason.* view details ☐
- *Immanuel Kant. Critique of the Power of Judgment.* view details ☑
- *Immanuel Kant. Groundwork of the Metaphysics of Morals.* view details ☐
- *Immanuel Kant. Theoretical Philosophy.* view details ☐
- *Immanuel Kant. Practical Philosophy.* view details ☐

> Add selected items to cart

Search for a book:

[   ]   Search

Fig. 3.8. Search result page of the online bookshop

data (which are rather mid-term master data) encompass information about the books and their categories as well as customer data. The only transactional data modeled are the orders that are placed by web shop users.

Each category has a name and several subcategories. Thus the categories form a structure. Each category features a number of books. Typically, one would like to pose some constraints on this book category structure. For example, one would like to demand that the categories form a directed, acyclic graph, or even a tree – with categories that have no further subcategories as leaves. Furthermore, one would like to require that the books featured by a certain category must also belong to at least one of the leaf categories that are reachable by descending from the considered category. Or, one could require that a category features all the books that belong to any reachable leaf category. It is not necessary to define constraints at this level of detail here. For this reason, we also do not use advanced notational elements, like aggregation, composition, or navigation in Fig. 3.9. We even do not specify all multiplicities in the class diagram.

The data model is pretty terse. It is just comprehensive enough to support the dialogues described in the previous section. At the same time, it is quite self-explanatory because it is derived directly from the dialogues. However, it is necessary to mention the shopping cart. We have omitted it from the data model for the moment. Later, the shopping cart items will be model as part of the data model, too.

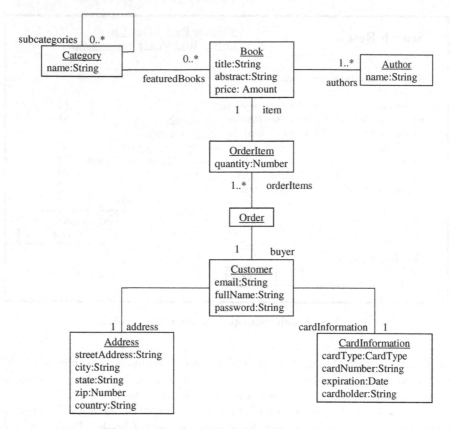

Fig. 3.9. Data model of the online bookshop

3.3 An Exemplary Submit/Response Style System

This example system is already suited to explain the main properties of a submit/response style system and to compare it with other system types. The first important property of submit/response style systems is that they follow a strict two-staged interaction paradigm. Submit/response style systems present to the user at each point in time a page which offers two kinds of interaction options: page interaction and page change. The registration page for our example offers a back link as well as input fields for text input, and a submit button. The back link and the submit button on the one hand and the input fields on the other differ in the effect of input. Input into the input fields is only preliminary until the submit button is pressed; itself cannot change the system state permanently. Links and a submit button change the page with an atomic interaction. They are the only interactions that change the system state permanently. Hence the difference between both kinds of interaction options is that page interaction is fine grained, volatile, and reversible, while page change affects the system state and consists of singular atomic actions.

Suppose the user has chosen to insert a new address record and has already filled out all fields of the new record, but has not submitted the new address. Then in our system there would be no new address record in the non-transient system state up to this time. Only if the user submits the record to the system is the new address record entered into the database. But if the user presses the back button instead, the input is lost.

Page interactions are well understood and can be offered by an application-independent browser, which is able to interpret a declarative page description and provide a sufficiently powerful standard page interaction paradigm. This explains the success story of concrete technologies like the HTML form concept together with the web browser as a standard ultra-thin client. This two-staged interaction paradigm is an important difference between a submit/response style system and other types of systems. Most telling here is a comparison with a system based on a so-called desktop database. Such tools can be found in many office suites. They are typically not multi-user systems, therefore our example is not typical of such an application, but a similar single user application for desktop databases could use a similar screen layout, e.g., for a personal address list. However, in such an application a new database record is created as soon as the user accesses the edit mask. Furthermore, each field entry is entered immediately into the persistent system state. The interaction in these systems is hence single staged. Another important difference is the update policy for pages. In our submit/response style interface, the data shown to the user are not updated until he or she revisits the page.

4

Form Storyboarding

In this chapter we propose some artifacts that are especially advantageous with respect to requirements elicitation for submit/response style systems, i.e., the page diagram, the screen diagram, the form storyboard, and the message storyboard. Each of the proposed artifacts features a new notational concept, which is well motivated. The page diagram is a very lightweight diagram that visualizes the pages of a system and their interconnections. A screen diagram is a special kind of page diagram that visualizes example screens. A form storyboard visualizes both client pages and server actions. Furthermore, in a form storyboard the input elements of forms are visualized. A message storyboard is a refined form storyboard, where the data that are presented to the user are described as well. All the introduced diagrams can be annotated with informal specifications of the dialogue.

The diagrams in this chapter are intended for communication of the main conceptual achievements of form-oriented analysis to domain experts. They are well-suited for requirements elicitation, because they are optimized with respect to communication of form-oriented user interface models. For the same reason they are well-suited for user-manuals. However, the modeler is free to choose when to use the proposed charts, can use different kinds of notations in parallel, and is actually free to create new kinds of charts tailored to the special needs of a running task. For example, adding example screens to a diagram can always be a good idea, i.e., it can be very instructive not only for page diagrams but also for form storyboards. That means we take the descriptive approach as explained in Chap. 9: we do not prescribe a process.

This chapter is rather introductory and therefore it is intentionally informal. The proposed diagrams already express the key elements of the submit/response paradigm. However, questions concerning naming conventions, rigorous typing and data modeling, formal dialogue specification, and so on are deferred to Chap. 5. First, two kinds of analysis models will be defined in Chap. 5, the information system model and the user message system model. It turns out that the different proposed diagrams are just different views on such models – different with respect to expressive power and formality. Second, the formchart is introduced, which has the task of making the analysis models amenable to the writing of formal dialogue specification and coupling to the data model.

4.1 Page Diagrams

Our *page diagram* is intended to introduce the modeler to the notion of submit/response style dialogues in a hands-on fashion. It is especially suited as a starting point for discussion with the domain expert about the intended task of the system. Imagine a first meeting in a web application project. One of the tasks is to define the core requirements of the desired system. How do you proceed? Perhaps it is a good idea to start by just painting the welcome page of the system on a blackboard. Then, you could ask: which important other pages should be reachable from the welcome page? You would paint arrows between the pages indicating connections. Then you would proceed recursively. Perhaps it is possible to group the found pages, to combine some of the found pages, to find new important connections between them. The result is a naive page diagram, showing pages and connections between them. No doubt, such diagrams can help elicitating and communicating system features. Therefore, such diagrams and related techniques like the click-dummy can indeed be found frequently in practice, for example in user manuals. Notably, the web benchmark TPC-W [296] uses in an ad hoc manner a kind of diagram that is similar to the one introduced in this section, in order to give an overview of the system presented there.

4.1.1 Diagrams for Pages and Interaction Options

A page diagram describes a system as a finite set of named pages, each page offering a finite number of interaction options. Please consider Fig. 4.1; in this example client pages are depicted by ellipses and interaction options are depicted by arrows. The example is a partial description of the web shop that we have discussed in Sect. 3. Actually, all of the screens that we have discussed are represented in the figure. It is only a partial description, because it shows only a subset of the possible interaction options offered on the screens. However, we have chosen a crucial subdialogue of the complete dialogue. We tried to select those interaction options that characterize the bookshop example best and to omit rather common interaction options like, for example, search forms or links to the welcome page. Because such basic interaction options are at the same time often quite pervasive, including them into the diagram can easily clutter the visualization. Consider, for example, the shopping cart client page in the center of Fig. 4.1 and compare it to Fig. 3.6. We have chosen to include in the page diagram the item delete option, the items update option, and the option to buy items. We have chosen not to include the link to the welcome page, the logout link and the search form.

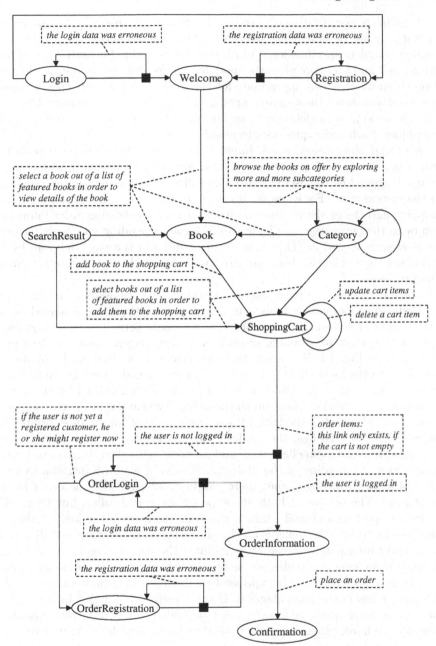

the login data was erroneous

the registration data was erroneous

Login

Welcome

Registration

select a book out of a list of
featured books in order to
view details of the book

browse the books on offer by exploring
more and more subcategories

SearchResult

Book

Category

add book to the shopping cart

select books out of a list
of featured books in order to
add them to the shopping cart

update cart items

delete a cart item

ShoppingCart

if the user is not yet a
registered customer, he
or she might register now

the user is not logged in

order items:
this link only exists, if
the cart is not empty

OrderLogin

the user is logged in

the login data was erroneous

OrderInformation

the registration data was erroneous

place an order

OrderRegistration

Confirmation

Fig. 4.1. Page diagram

A complete specification of a system is often a valuable goal, but in many cases it may not be practically achievable. Our method allows the modeler to create a complete specification, but of course it is usable for partial specification as well and therefore gives the modeler the freedom to choose the degree of precision which seems appropriate for the project. A complete specification that is at the same time clearly arranged, i.e., that stays manageable, requires some kind of model decomposition, model abbreviation and refinement techniques. Such techniques are discussed in Chap. 6.

A crucial observation, which immediately opens the conceptual path to form storyboards, is that system response may be conditional: a single page change triggered by the user can result in different response pages, depending on the system state. For example, if the user chooses to buy the items in the shopping cart, he or she is directed either to a screen showing order information or to the entry page of a login subdialogue, depending on whether he or she is already logged in. This issue is represented in the page diagram by a branching edge. The two branches are annotated with appropriate informal annotations.

The client pages in a page diagram represent sets of possible screens. This comprehension mechanism is used to abstract from the data displayed on a certain kind of screen. However, there is no single correct notion of granularity with respect to grouping screens into client pages. Consider the login client page in Fig. 4.1. If the user provides erroneous login data, he or she is redirected to the login client page until he or she provides correct data. That means initial login screens and error login screens are modeled by the same client page. This works because in the described system the login error screens are actually identical to the initial login screens except for an appropriate error message. Nevertheless, the modeler might want to split the login client page into an initial login client page and an error login client page in order to foster the understanding of the dialogue. Similarly, we have introduced two kinds of login client pages, the "mere" login client page and the order login client page. The screens of both client pages are very similar, but they differ with respect to a crucial point: if the user has entered the login dialogue via choosing to buy the items from the shopping cart, he or she is redirected to an order information screen after login; if the user has entered the login dialogue from somewhere else, he or she is redirected to the welcome page after login. This can be easily expressed by distinguishing between two kinds of login screens in the page diagram. If the screens are mingled into a single client page, appropriate comments must be added to the resulting diagrams that may be harder to understand than the chosen modeling alternative.

4.1.2 Screen Diagrams

Page diagrams do not yet support the notion of typed client pages and server actions. It is the task of the form storyboards and message storyboards in Sect. 4.2 to offer a defined means of visualizing these types. A more ad hoc

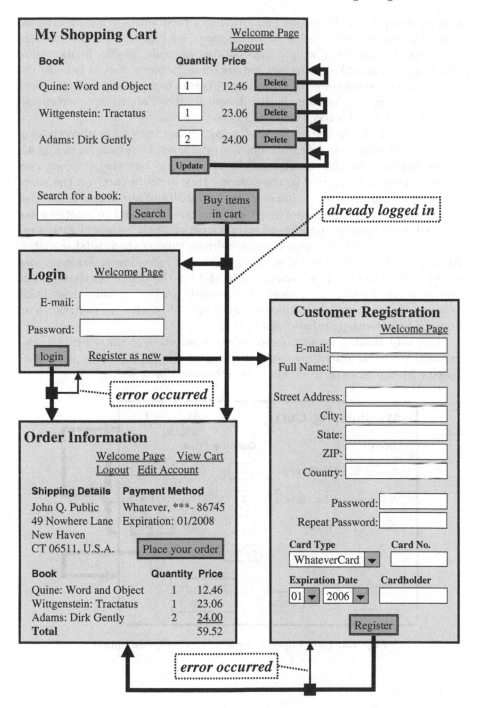

Fig. 4.2. Screen diagram

manner to represent the reports and form input capabilities in a form-oriented chart is offered by the so-called *screen diagrams*, see Fig. 4.2. A screen diagram is a page diagram that simply incorporates example screens in its nodes. Choosing the example screens may require some decisions: should I choose the initial login screen or the error login screen in order to represent the login client page? In screen diagrams a node simultaneously shows an example screen and represents a type of screens employed in the system.

In a screen diagram the source of a page transition can be directly connected to the screen element from which it originates. For example, in Fig. 4.2 the branching edge that is triggered by choosing to buy the shopping cart items is actually connected to the button "Buy items in cart" on the shopping cart screen. In order to improve the readability of our diagrams, further notational elements can be invented and further notational conventions can be fixed. For example, branches of state transitions that represent rather exceptional cases, typically error cases, are drawn thinner than usual branches. As another example we introduce the grouping of related interaction options with a curly bracket, as is shown in Fig. 4.3 for the delete buttons: all the arrows in Fig. 4.2 starting at delete buttons are grouped. A finite description of interaction options is the conceptually preferable notion, in contrast to an unspecified potentially infinite description.

Very importantly, we want to conceive the screen diagram as being a non-executable system prototype. Note that executable prototypes – sometimes called click-dummies or mock-ups – are often used in practice.

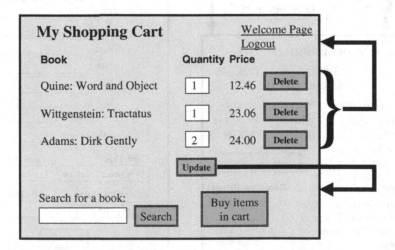

Fig. 4.3. List of options for a single conceptual option

4.2 Form Storyboards

The *form storyboard* [90, 95] takes the understanding of submit/response style applications a step further by introducing into the system model one of the major conceptual cornerstones of form-oriented analysis: in form storyboards the system is seen as a bipartite state transition machine. The basic structure of form storyboards can be seen in Fig. 4.4. Client pages, depicted again by ellipses, and server actions, depicted by rectangles, are strictly alternating. There are transitions from client pages to server actions and transitions from server actions to client pages, both of them depicted by arrows. Unlike a page diagram, a form storyboard never contains branching edges, because a conditional system response is represented by several outgoing edges of a server action. Actually, page diagrams can be seen as the result of shrinking the server actions of a form storyboard to branching points. The resulting page diagram now has branching edges; it is more concise, but still remains a bipartite state transition diagram.

4.2.1 Representing Server Action Signatures

Let us recall the basic viewpoint of form-oriented analysis from Chap. 2. Submit/response style interaction is two-staged: the interaction is divided into page interaction, which is temporary and logically local to the client until a submit is performed, and page change, which is a submit action. Only page change can affect the system data state. Hence the model is already two-tiered on an analysis level. The core system state in this view does not include the client state, which is the conceptual terminal's state. The advantage of this software system paradigm is that the client is well understood independent of the application. Compare this to other types of software systems that may also use form-like interfaces, but are not submit/response style, for example the previously mentioned desktop databases as well as spreadsheet applications found in office suites. These have a single-staged interaction paradigm in which each change is considered directly as a change of the system data state, at least in principle. Form-oriented analysis exploits the following observations:

- It is not necessary to model the fine-grained interaction on one page.
- Submitting a form can be considered a method call. Forms and links can be conceptually unified.
- Messages from the system to the user can be conceived as reports.

Consequently form-oriented analysis maintains strong typing at the system interface. An example of a detailed type system for the two-tiered presentation layer of submit/response style systems is formally elaborated in Chap. 15. In a form storyboard the type of a server action is presented in the server action node with the following notational elements:

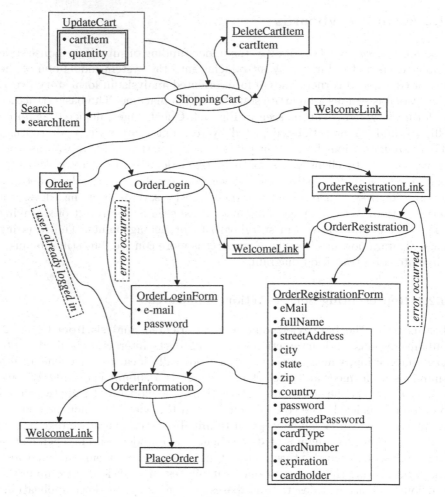

Fig. 4.4. Form storyboard

- *Bullet.* The attributes of a server action signature are given by a bullet list.
- *Border.* Logically connected attributes can be grouped by bordering. Groupings can be arbitrarily nested in order to represent treelike structures.
- *Double border.* A double bordering hints at a possibly repeated occurrence of an attribute or several implicitly grouped attributes. Nesting is also possible.

Consider the server action OrderRegistrationForm in Fig. 4.4. It represents the form that occurs on the screen for customer registration, see Fig. 3.3. This form expects several data items, including the e-mail address, the customer

name, the street. Each of the expected data items is given a name and is
included into the bullet list of the server action in the form storyboard. We
do not specify the type of the parameters further – we only give names to
the parameters. The signature of the server action UpdateCart is more tricky.
On a shopping cart screen, see Fig. 3.6, a list of cart items is shown. All the
items can be updated simultaneously, because there exists an input field for
a new quantity for each of the cart items. Note that the number of presented
cart items is variable, and that is precisely what is expressed by the double
bordering of the quantity attribute. Furthermore, the quantity attribute is
grouped with an explicit cart item attribute by the double bordering. This
is done in the example in order to model the fact that not only a mere list
of item quantities is submitted by the user: each of the quantities is related
to a certain cart item. Of course, the user does not have to type explicitly
which cart item has to be manipulated – the relationship between quantity
and cart item is specified simply by the layout of the screen: the input field
is next to the cart item it belongs to. To express this in a different way, the
cart item parameter of the update operation is a hidden parameter, which is
implicitly provided by the system dialogue. These considerations lead to the
important concepts of opaque identity and opaque reference facade, which are
elaborated in Sect. 5.3.2.

4.2.2 The IT Expert View and the Domain Expert View

Form storyboards are especially well-suited for communication and joint development between domain experts and IT professionals, because they can be
understood differently by members of these two roles. That means the form
storyboard can mediate between the following different viewpoints:

- *IT expert view.* The IT expert understands a page change as an editable
  method call and views server action signatures as method signatures.
- *Domain expert view.* The domain expert views server action signatures
  depicted in a form storyboard as forms.

Of course, the defined viewpoints are not exclusive; they are rather conceptual. The IT expert can further elaborate the informal, incomplete system
specification that is given by a form storyboard. In particular, he or she can
rigorously refine the server action signatures with respect to the concrete type
system of a given technology.

The domain expert view can be fostered by the concept of *page image*. In
the form storyboard each client page together with its accessible server actions
gives a representation of the page with its interaction options, as is shown in
Fig. 4.5. Therefore each such subgraph is called a page image. Page images
can share server actions, as can be seen in the example of the WelcomeLink
server action.

Both screen diagram and form storyboards contain information about the data submitted by the user. However, the form storyboard offers a more systematic approach. At the same time it obviously provides a more abstract view of the system interface than the screen diagram. Despite that, the form storyboard can still be seen as an intuitive high-level prototype of the system – the reader is asked to consider the page images in Fig. 4.5 once more and compare them to the screens in Fig. 4.2.

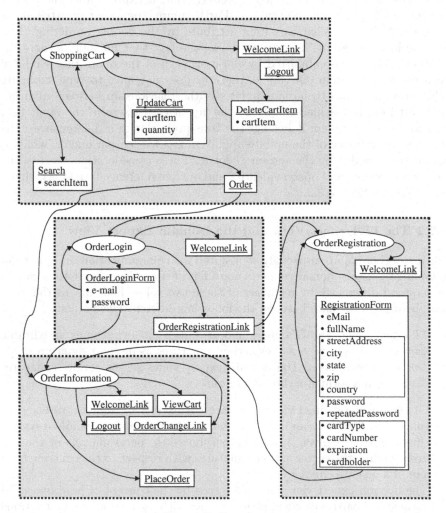

Fig. 4.5. Page images

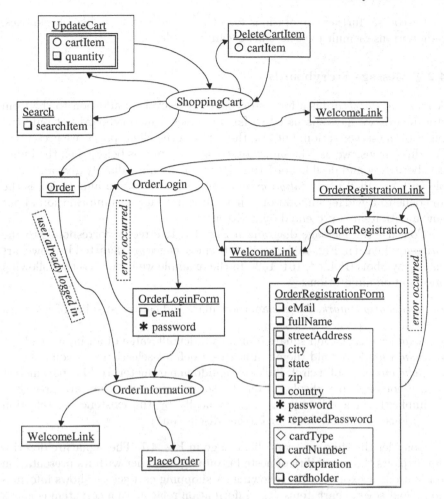

Fig. 4.6. Form storyboard annotated with interaction information

4.2.3 Widget Annotations

Form storyboards can be further supported as a tool for efficient communication with the domain expert if they are annotated with information about the interaction type used for submitting the form parameters. Figure 4.6 shows the form storyboard with such *widget annotation*. It differs from the form storyboard version in Fig. 4.4 in the icons preceding the parameters. In the example, we have used the following icons:

- *Empty square*. An empty square indicates a text input field.
- *Empty rhomb*. An empty rhomb indicates a combobox.
- *Empty circle*. An empty circle indicates a hidden parameter.
- *Star*. A star indicates an input field for hidden texts, i.e., passwords.

Of course, further annotations for other typical widgets like checkboxes, radiobuttons or multiple select fields can be declared.

4.2.4 Message Storyboards

A *message storyboard* is a form storyboard. However, in addition to the form storyboards we have discussed so far, in a message storyboard not only the types of the server action, but also the types of the client pages are presented. For this purpose we use the same notational elements as before, i.e., the bullet list, bordering and double bordering. However, we immediately give an example with so-called *presentation annotations*. A presentation annotation is the analogue to a widget annotation – it is an icon that gives information about how a data item is presented on a screen.

Consider the message diagram in Fig. 4.7. It directly corresponds to the form storyboard in Fig. 4.6 but this time client pages are depicted by flowchart display symbols [154, 84, 161, 162]. In the example we have used the following presentation annotations:

- *Exclamation mark.* An exclamation mark indicates a display of the data item.
- *Solid square.* A solid square indicates a default value of an input field.
- *Solid rhomb.* A solid rhomb indicates a default selection of a combobox.
- *Solid circle.* A solid circle indicates a hidden parameter. Hidden parameters are not explicitly displayed on the screen. However, they are presented implicitly in a different manner, typically by the existence of selection options – see Sect. 5.3.2 for further discussion.

Consider the shopping cart client page in Fig. 4.7. The signature description exploits the possibility of nested grouping; together with its presentation annotations it expresses the following. A shopping cart screen shows information about several cart items. The information relating to a cart item consists of one ore several author names, a title, a pre-selected quantity, and a price – plus a reference to the shopping cart item. Author names, titles, and prices are simply displayed. The displayed quantities serve as the default values for input fields, i.e., the update operation offered on the shopping cart screen. References to shopping cart items, which are needed by the update operation and the delete operation, are not explicitly displayed. However, they are appropriately grouped with the other attributes.

In Fig. 4.7 we can adhere to an easy naming convention with respect to default values. A default value carries the name of the parameter of the targeted server action, preceded by the term "default".

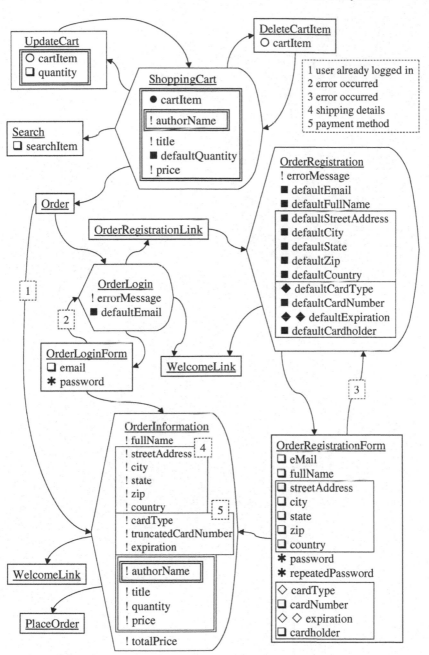

Fig. 4.7. Message storyboard

5

Formcharts and Dialogue Specification

In form-oriented analysis an information system is modeled as a submit/response style system interface that is related to a layered data model. In this chapter we explain the form-oriented view of information system models. We explain the constituent parts of information system models, i.e., dialogue models, layered data models, and dialogue specifications. The notion of a user message system model is introduced, which narrows the modeling of information systems to the exchange of messages between the user and the system. We define the concrete notations which will be used in the examples, i.e., the formchart, a textual class model format, and a concrete dialogue specification language. Finally, the concepts described are used to model our running example – the online bookshop.

5.1 Form-Oriented Information System Models

A form-oriented *information system model* is the description of *user sessions*. A system with a form-based user interface can have an arbitrary number of *open user sessions* at each point in time. An open user session is an ongoing communication with the system. It is the task of the system modeler to choose an appropriate user identification scheme and to model the user session. The user session is assumed to take place on a virtual terminal. If a session is open on the virtual terminal, then the virtual terminal shows a *client page instance*. As long as a user session is open, it alternates between two kinds of states, the *client pages* and the *server actions*.

5.1.1 Components of an Information System Model

In form-oriented analysis an information system is modeled as the user interaction with a submit/response style system interface. It is modeled using a bipartite typed state machine that is tightly integrated with a layered data model and annotated with a dialogue specification [92, 97] – see Fig. 5.1.

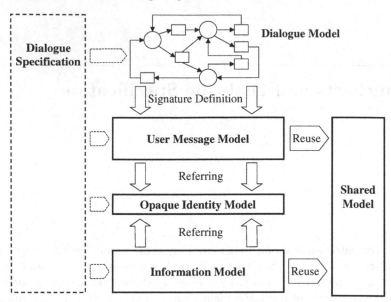

Fig. 5.1. The information system model of form-oriented analysis

The state machine needs to be bipartite because the user interaction with the system, i.e., the dialogue, is a sequence of interchanging client pages and server actions. The state machine part of an information system model is called the *dialogue model* in the sequel. The several model elements of a dialogue model can be annotated with dialogue specification expressions. The dialogue specification narrows the set of possible dialogues, and specifies the exchanged messages and side effects of the system's transactions.

The data model is layered because it describes both the messages that are exchanged during human–computer interaction and the server system state with respect to a well-defined interrelationship. The layering of the data model is oriented towards proven multi-tier system architectures, which target data independence for enterprise applications by exploiting today's mature database technology. The difference between data that are exchanged between the user and the server system on the one hand and data that make up the server system state on the other should not be neglected. On the contrary, in everyday tasks the modeler needs well thought-out concepts to account for the necessary interplay between these two kinds of data. In this chapter, for example, the concepts of opaque identity and cloning are elaborated for this purpose.

The data model, see Fig. 5.1, consists of four packages, i.e., the user message model, the opaque identity model, the information model, and the shared data model. The user message model describes the messages that are exchanged between the user and the system. It defines the signatures of client pages and server actions, i.e., there is a one-to-one correspondence between the user message types and the dialogue model states. The information model describes the server system state. The shared data model is an auxiliary model that serves as a record type repository for the purposes of reuse and the definition of cloning mechanisms. The opaque identity model is used to create a well-defined relationship between the user message model and the information model. Opaque identities does not only make sense as opaque references to complex information objects. They can be used as independent identities, namely in order to identify messages with each other. This leads to the concept of the pure form-based paradigm, which is explained in the next section.

5.1.2 User Message System Models

A *user message system model* is an information system model without an information model. The *pure form-based paradigm* states that it is possible to model a form-based information system solely as the user interaction with a submit/response style system interface. In a *full information system model* some complex persistent data are also modeled. A full information system model is oriented towards ubiquitous system architectures. Furthermore, the existence of an information model can help to structure the system. However, we argue that modeling merely in terms of the messages that are exchanged is also very natural – a completely unsuspecting domain expert is not aware of a database schema; he or she understands the system only in terms of the submitted and received data.

The pure form-based paradigm can be seen as the elaboration of the concept of a paperless office. The only function of the form-based paradigm is to create a container for all documents within an organization. The state of the organization's database is completely expressed as a collection of documents. Important here is that our basic interface metaphor gives us a precise concept for the relation between the user's view and the system. The documents in the system are exactly the screens and forms the user has seen or sent. The screen is what the user sees when he or she initially receives the screen, while the form is the edited screen at the moment of submission. A form in this view has to be imagined as a copy of the client page, with the input fields filled-in as well as a tick mark at one of the submit buttons, indicating that this form was submitted, and hence indicating the user's intention. The term "document" denotes a form or a screen.

The system view is therefore comparable to an archive. It is impossible to change the documents in the archive. Moreover, it is not even possible to see the documents themselves once they are in the archive. If the information is requested, the archive always creates a new screen. By definition these documents are immutable because they represent the information that was on a screen at a certain time. The paradigm supports, of course, the connection between these forms and can offer different ways to see the joint information in the presentation, either as a result of the change, or as the old version beside the change.

The organization of the documents within the archive is fully transparent, as we know from databases. This means that, since we have no direct access, we do not know the organization principle. We have, however, a powerful query mechanism, offering simple as well as advanced searches in the archive. According to our paradigm the query as well as the results are again messages. The user may, however, dislike this inflation of the document base by insignificant and rather informal queries and searches. But there is no need to change the fundamental paradigm, since we can get rid of the garbage. The users simply can write a token "informal" on all unimportant requests. Then we can assume that all queries are augmented simply by the condition neither to return forms containing these tokens nor to return answers to these forms. With this mechanism it is even possible to create arbitrarily elaborate classifications of communications with the system.

The paradigm has been purely untyped so far. Now we again perform the same step as in the case of the form-based interface, we introduce types. We want to view the data model of the untyped case as a treelike semi-structured format. The introduction of types can be seen not as a change in the data model but a change in the query language, or a usage pattern of the query language.

Additionally, we also want to assume that types come with enforcement by the system, i.e., that the system accepts only type correct inputs and only returns type-correct answers. But again this, in a principled approach, can be delegated to the query language. This leads to a new development for the form-based client, which will give rise to an important concept in the next chapter, the so-called client output constraint. In a typed paradigm we want only correctly filled-in forms to be allowed. Such a condition can be enforced by the browser technology. It is, however, also conceivable to have it enforced by the central system.

The pure form-based paradigm fits in well. In such a paradigm the data have a dual status; they are seen as embedded in the forms, but at the same time they are inherently separated by the fact that the forms are style sheets for pure data types. It is a case of an easy and inherent separation of content and representation. They do not usually include the possibility of casual annotation, although this can be added, and there are advantages in this.

One could think that one would need no client pages, but only a mighty search engine. But this would repeat the SQL problem. SQL involved the notion that we would only have data in tables and a natural-language-based mighty search engine. Note that the language designers of SQL originally wanted to give it the acronym SEQUEL – Structured English Query Language [211].

The data model is nothing more than the reuse of the data structure in the various forms in the system. The forms are the views in which the user understands the system. The data model can be understood as doing nothing more than mediating between the different forms in the system. Hence one can see that in principle the data model does not need its own state; its information is contained in the messages.

We want to take a closer look at the central features of the form-based paradigm we have outlined so far. One feature is the archiving of all business communication. Archiving is persistence plus immutability. The second feature is support for types, in the form of server-side checks. The third feature is the structured editor. This concept replaces client-side checks on submission with *local modality*, i.e., at one place in a text only certain interactions are allowed. One natural feature is that the structured editor also supports protected regions, i.e., constant parts of the text. One astonishing fact is that with this notion the formchart can be subsumed under the structured editor; the formchart in its interpretation as a state history diagram – see Sect. 13 – can then be read immediately as the document type, which represents the possible logs of a browser session. The browser can be seen as the application of the structured editor to the document type. The sending of the message has to be modeled as well and this hints at a possible extension of the editor principle: in the future, one wants to understand special purpose editors as library functions for one general editor instead of being separate applications.

5.1.3 Modeling Active Content

It is possible to allow for modeling page updates that are caused by the system, i.e., pushed updates under the umbrella of a single client page state. A typical example is the inbox in a mail system. The inbox page shows the list of received mails. A desired behavior is that incoming mails are immediately shown to the user by appending them to the list. Pages which offer such an update caused by the server we call *pages with active content*. Form-oriented analysis allows only for the augmentation of the currently shown information object. The inbox is an example of a list which receives additional elements. Another example is the disabling of single selection options in a list. The active content does not violate the overall system metaphor of form-oriented analysis: page change is triggered by the user. The active content is conceptually on the level of the page interaction of the user. Page changes cannot be triggered by the system.

Active content can be explicitly modeled, e.g., by indicating it with ampersands at expressions of the dialogue specification. Active content is typically necessary only in a small number of places. A typical system model would put all the active content in separate features. Sometimes a menu feature has an active component specifying a single flag which is visible on all pages, e.g., a flag indicating new mail.

5.1.4 Notations for Information System Models

Different notations – textual, visual or mixed formats – can be defined for the components of form-oriented information system models. Table 5.1 summarizes the components of information system models and the notations that we propose in this book to document these models. The formchart that we introduce in Sect. 5.2.1 will not suffice to describe an information system model completely. It must be accompanied by appropriate documents that describe the layered data model. This is also true for the several diagrams that have been proposed in Chap. 4, i.e., page diagrams, screen diagrams, form storyboards, and message storyboards.

Table 5.1. Form-oriented inormation system models and possible documentations

	Message System Model	Full Information System Model
Model Components	dialogue model + user message model + opaque identity model + dialogue specification	dialogue model + user message model + opaque identity model + information model + shared model + dialogue specification
Exemplary Complete Documentation	formchart + class diagrams: formchart / message types and opaque identities specified in text documents / dialogue specification is typically formal and specified in a separate document	formchart + class diagrams: formchart / message types, opaque identities, information types, as well as shared types specified in text documents / dialogue specification is typically formal and specified in a separate document
Exemplary Partial Documentation	page diagram: client page nodes connected by branching transitions screen diagram: client page nodes connected by branching transitions, representative example screens added to the client page nodes form storyboard: a formchart with form types visualized inside server action nodes message storyboard: a formchart with form types visualized inside server action nodes and report types visualized inside client page nodes *page/screen/storyboard diagrams: dialogue specification is typically informal and is drawn as annotations directly in the diagrams*	

5.2 The Dialogue Model

In this section the elements of the *dialogue models* used in form-oriented analysis are described. We also explain how dialogue models are depicted by formcharts.

A dialogue model is a user interface model. The user interaction with the system is a sequence of interchanging client states and server states. A client state presents information to the user and offers several options for entering and submitting data. Client state and client page are used synonymously. A client page is parameterized. In fact it represents a possibly infinite set of potential client page instances, i.e., the screens that are actually presented to the user. The signature of a client page serves as an abstract description of the information presented to the user. A single screen shows the user a message from the system. A message from the system has two important aspects: on the one hand it is an actual parameter that conforms to the client page signature; on the other hand it is conceived as a report in the sense of Sect. 2.1.6. Beyond the information provided, a client page offers one or more data submission options to the user. Every transition from a client page to a server state specifies that the respective client page has a submission option that calls the respective server action and provides an actual parameter.

By submitting data the dialogue changes into a server state. In the server state, submitted data are processed and, depending on the current server system state, the generation of a new client page is triggered, i.e., the server state is left automatically. Submitting data is conceptually similar to calling a method, the data being an actual parameter. Therefore the server state is often called a server action. The transition to a client page is again considered as the sending of a message, this time executed automatically from the server.

Transitions from a client page to a server action are abbreviated as page/server transitions. Equally, transitions from server actions to client pages are abbreviated as server/page transitions. There may be more than one transition between two given states. Multiple transitions between a client page and a server action are typically used to submit different data to the same server action. A common example found in web-based user interfaces is the capability to select items by following a link out of a list of links. Multiple transitions between a server action and a client page are used to visualize a conditional output in the formchart explicitly.

Each dialogue model state has a unique name. Each transition has a name, which is unique with respect to a given source state and a given target state.

5.2.1 Formcharts

A dialogue model consists of client pages, server actions, and the transitions between them. In the *formchart*, client states are depicted by ellipses, server states are depicted by rectangles, a page/server transition is depicted by an arrow from an ellipse to a rectangle, and a server/page transition is depicted by an arrow from a rectangle to an ellipse. Figure 5.2 shows a formchart that models the dialogue of our bookstore. The formchart corresponds to the bookstore page diagram in Fig. 4.1.

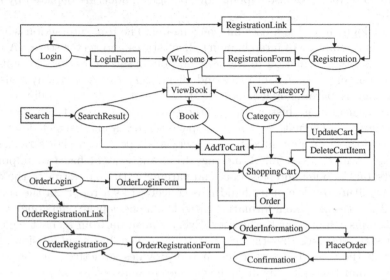

Fig. 5.2. A first formchart example

Every formchart element has a name. Ellipses and rectangles must be given a name by the modeler. Arrows can be given a name by the modeler. If an arrow is not given a name explicitly, it will have a default name that is derived from the arrow's source's name and target's name by an appropriate naming convention that can be given later. With each formchart element a model element of the same name is introduced. In this discussion it is important to distinguish explicitly between chart elements and model elements for the following reason: while the names of the model states are unique and the names of model transitions are unique with respect to a fixed source and target, too, this does not mean that the same model element cannot be painted twice in a formchart. This is because the labels of the formchart elements do not have to be unique. Formchart elements that carry the same name depict the same model element. As a result a dialogue model can be depicted by several different formcharts, distinguished not only by different layout, but also by the number of chart elements. For example, the two formcharts (i) and (ii) in Fig. 5.3 depict the same dialogue model.

Repainting a model element can often improve the readability of a formchart, e.g., it is necessary in order to avoid painting crossing transitions or long transitions, or it can be exploited to focus on a certain concept.

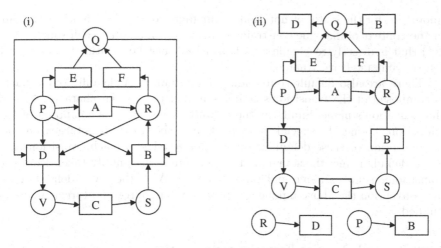

(i)　　　　　　　　　　　(ii)

Fig. 5.3. Two alternative formcharts for the same model

5.2.2 Formchart Naming Conventions

The concrete formchart naming conventions are depicted in Fig. 5.4. An unnamed arrow denotes a transition with a default name. The default name consists of the transition's source's name followed by the keyword TO followed by the transition's target's name. It is required that the transition names are unique with respect to two given states. In order to distinguish transitions globally a unique global default name is derived from the local transition name and the names of the states it connects by concatenating them with the special character > as indicated in Fig. 5.4.

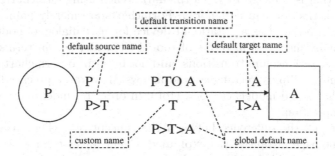

Fig. 5.4. Formchart naming conventions

We introduce the concepts of *transition source name* and *transition target name*, source and target names for short. These names are needed, for example, for writing DCL dialogue constraints, which are introduced in Sect. 5.4.1. The source and target names are similar to association role names found in class diagram notations. A certain uniqueness property is required, which is important for the state set notation of our method, see Sect. 6.5.1, and again in the context of dialogue constraint writing: given a state, each source (target) that is directly reachable by a transition must be identified uniquely by its source name (target name).

There are also default source and target names. A default source name is composed of the transition's source's name, the special character >, and the transition's name. Similarly, the default target name is composed of the transition's name, the special character >, and the transition's target's name. An exception to these default naming rules applies for each transition that has a default name: the source and target names are simply taken from the transition's source's name and target's name. With the given default naming convention the above uniqueness property for source and target names is fulfilled.

5.2.3 Towards Precise Formchart Semantics

In this chapter concrete notations are proposed for the several parts of form-oriented information system models in order to introduce and discuss the most crucial aspects of form-oriented models. The definitions in this chapter aim at being as precise as necessary; however, the definitions of model semantics in the third part of the book will be considerably more precise. For example, Chap. 13 can be used as a reference for the semantics of the dialogue model while reading the current chapter. In this chapter the dialogue model is introduced as a typed state machine. In Chap. 13 a typed state transition machine will be considered as a special kind of class diagram and state visits are represented as object instances of this class diagram.

In Sect. 5.2.1 we have distinguished explicitly between the formchart and the model that is depicted by the formchart. When using formcharts for modeling this distinction can be ignored. Formcharts are merely paintings; they have been introduced as a notational device for user dialogue models. Models are usually discussed in terms of model elements, i.e., in terms of client pages, server actions, and transitions, and not in terms of formchart elements, i.e., in terms of ellipses, rectangles, and arrows. However, a precise distinction between charts and models can be helpful in order to understand aspects of model composition.

In Sect. 5.2 the difference between the concept of a client page and its single client page instances was explained. Client pages form an abstraction mechanism. Once this is understood, the difference can be de-emphasized in the following explanations, because a client page represents every one of its instances. However, as with the formchart's relationship to the represented dialogue model, the distinction always becomes important where model and chart semantics have to be discussed precisely.

5.3 The Layered Data Model

5.3.1 User Message Models

Each state in the dialogue model, i.e., each client page and each server action, has a signature. The state signatures are defined by the *user message model*: for each state there exists a class of the same name in the user message model. A user message model defines the messages that are exchanged between the system and the user.

Messages are immutable; they are merely exchanged between the client and the server, i.e., they are not part of an updatable server system state. The user message model is a class model. Instances of the user message model classes (the messages) must form strict hierarchical structures, i.e., they must be trees. This means that user message model associations must be compositions; see Sect. 15.2.3 for a detailed discussion.

Because complex messages can be built only by composition, it is possible to define a clear notion of deep copying, called cloning, of these messages: cloning of a message yields a complete copy of the old tree as a new tree. An important point is that messages can contain opaque references to data entities of the mutable server system state. From the viewpoint of a message structure these opaque references are treated like objects of primitive type, e.g., the cloning stops at the opaque references. We delve into the topics of opaque references and cloning in the following Sects. 5.3.3 and 5.3.4.

We want to regard triggering a server action as a method call. This view is especially neat, for example, for the conceptual discussions in Chap. 13 and technological considerations in Chap. 11. The signature of a method consists of several formal parameters as labeled components. Therefore the signature of a method is a record type, which can be defined by a class. Similarly the several actual parameters of a method call can be conceived together as one single object, which is sometimes emphasized by referring to such a comprehensive parameter as a *superparameter* in the sequel.

Consequently we refer to data that are exchanged at the system border as messages one time, another time as report or form content, as parameter or superparameter. Each term has its own flavor, emphasizing another aspect of the exchanged data. This richness of terminology helps from the outset to mitigate impedance mismatches between analysis and design on the one hand and between unit system modeling and system data interchange modeling on the other.

5.3.2 Opaque Identity Models

Our approach uses a symbol concept to facilitate communications. Messages between communication partners not only contain primitive data, but symbols. These symbols are a type of primitive data, which only allows for check on identity. Moreover our query mechanism can return result sets with a certain symbol efficiently. The symbol concept is important in reaching a clean high-level model of symbolic computation. Pure identities are not realized as readable primitive data types, but rather as an independent concept, the symbol concept.

In the first place, symbols are pure identities for all communication partners. Each communication partner who wants to use a symbol has to set it in some relation with his or her own information and knowledge base. The challenge which arises is to prevent the homonym problem, i.e., that the same symbol is used for things which are supposed to represent two separate concepts. Once more we use the concept of typing. There is an arbitrary number of symbol types. Communication partners can have their own symbol types, and only they can create new symbols of this symbol type. This concept is such an important concept of symbol use that we give it a different name: *opaque identities*. Symbols do not refer to any information content. However, on the contrary, information content can refer to symbols. But in the case of opaque identities we use symbols in a certain way: the unit system, which owns the opaque identities, uses only one opaque identity for one object of its own data model. This is a pattern for the usage of symbols only. But this pattern allows queries to find an information object using a given symbol. This usage is identical with the concept of primary keys in databases. The primary key concept illustrates quite clearly the concept of symbols. The important artificial primary keys are primitive data type instances without inherent meaning. They obviously do not refer to anything as such. But a primary key can be used to find specific rows due to its use in the primary key row of a table. We view this as an instance of a more general phenomenon. In our view information has only an operational semantics. It is the information processing instance which does the interpretation through its procedures.

Opaque Reference Facades

The information model defines the updatable portion of a server system state. The information model is cleanly separated from the user message model. The only direct connection between the two models is through an *opaque reference facade*, which is part of the opaque identity model. Information entities of the updatable system cannot be part of messages, but they can be represented by opaque identities that may be part of messages. If an opaque identity is used to represent an information entity it is also called an *opaque reference*. The concept of opaque reference is the necessary tool that allows constant data objects like messages to reference instances that are non-constant and deletable. A constant object could not reference such a deletable object by a regular reference, since this reference would be removed as soon as the deletable object is removed. This would obstruct the intended notion of a constant object.

The notion of opaque references works as follows. For every type in the information model there is another type in the opaque identity model, which is called its opaque reference type. The opaque reference types make up the opaque reference facade of the information system model. For reasons of simplicity we assume a default naming convention, where the type in the information model starts with a capital letter as usual, while the opaque reference type has the same name, but starting with a lowercase letter.

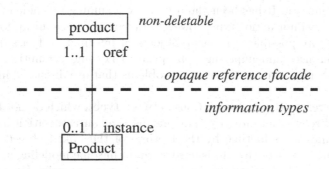

Fig. 5.5. Opaque references in the information model

All information types are connected with their respective opaque reference types through an association according to the diagram in Fig. 5.5, with fixed role names `oref` and `instance` establishing a naming convention as indicated in the figure. Note that each instance of an information type has only one opaque reference instance. Furthermore the following important rules apply:

- *Surrogate mechanism.* Each newly created information type instance receives a fresh instance from the opaque reference type. That is, each opaque reference type acts like a ticket dispenser.
- *Durability.* An opaque reference is unchangeable. Especially an opaque reference is itself non-deletable. If the corresponding information type instance is deleted, the opaque reference remains. It then no longer has an associated information type object, and will never regain one.

The modeler does not have to give the opaque reference type for an information type and the respective association. The modeler can assume that they are implicitly introduced for each information type. The notion of opaque references is particularly strong for modeling submit/response style systems. Opaque references allow information entities to be identified by parts of a message. Without opaque references, it would be difficult to define the semantics for updatable information that is sent as part of a message. This is obvious immediately on the model refinement level of multi-user safe models, which is explained in Sect. 6.7: is an update of the information considered a source of error? Or has it to be understood with respect to an encompassing push model?

The form-oriented usage of opaque references combines on an analysis level the ideas behind two important technology concepts, namely hidden parameters found in web technology and sequencing mechanisms found in databases.

Opaque references can be used by information types, too. This occurs in those cases where user input is recorded in the information basis and the opaque references from the user input are stored as well.

The notion of opaque reference facade just presented is independent of its concrete definition. It has been elaborated by assuming a facade of auxiliary types for every information type; however, alternative mechanisms for defining the concept are possible, e.g., using objects of information types directly as opaque references and imposing appropriate rules and semantics. However, all solutions must circumvent certain problems that are discussed in the next paragraph.

Opaque references are associations between types, which do not follow the principle of referential integrity. This means that an association link should not be bound in its lifetime by the lifetime of the linked objects. This relaxed condition on associations is hard to fulfill in some modeling approaches, since these modeling approaches enforce referential integrity for all associations. The facade approach to opaque references circumvents this problem, by doubling an entity type. Basically this leads to a doubling of the object ID's representing entity instances. One object ID is deleted if the instance is deleted, the other object ID is never deleted. Other alternatives can of course vary here, e.g., using different auxiliary types for different message types etc. The usage of the helper class, which could also be seen as a wrapper class, is especially important concerning collections of opaque references. In the case of single opaque references within a message or part thereof, the deletion of the link could be accepted as an indicator of the deletion of the object. The constant character of the message would then be harder to understand, but it would be feasible. However, as soon as a collection of opaque references is expressed as a simple collection of links within a type, this type can hardly represent a message. The problem here is that the very information over the original collection is lost as soon as an object is deleted, so the constant character of the message would be destroyed.

5.3.3 Information Models

An *information model* defines the updatable portion of a server system state. The updatable portion of a server system state comprises the persistent data as well as the session data. For the duration of the user session the session data as well as the persistent data are part of the server system state. The difference between the two kinds of data is that the session data are ephemeral; they are lost after the user session has ended, whereas the persistent data are not. The loss of session data after the user session can be modeled explicitly; they can be modeled by a further partitioning of the information model as well. However, from a high-level conceptual viewpoint the distinction between session data and persistent data can be neglected. Of course the modeler wants to distinguish between these two kinds of data, but note that the modeler might want to distinguish between other different kinds of data, too. No doubt an information model can be improved if it is divided up for example into core data, transactional data, and inventory data. Furthermore session data are not as frequent as they might seem at first sight. Often typical candidates for session data actually turn out to be persistent data – the shopping cart content is a good example of that. In the following explanations no distinction is needed between session data and persistent data.

The information model contains a classical data model. Note that we abandon use of the term semantic data model. Our information model is about describing data that are stored in a structured way in an information system, not about describing real-world objects. For a discussion of the real-world modeling metaphor see Sect. 9.4.

5.3.4 Shared Data Models

Especially in the case where we have a complex record containing lots of attributes, there is a third useful model: the *shared model*. A shared model contains type definitions that can be used in the user message model as well as in the information model. The task of this model is to allow the maintenance of these signatures on a single spot. The shared model must follow the structural rules of the user message model in order to be used in message type definitions. Instances of the shared model types are immutable if they are part of messages. The shared model fosters reuse; beyond this it enables advantageous cloning mechanisms, so that data can be easily copied from the updatable information state to messages and back via shared types of the shared model.

With respect to reuse the shared model is merely a pattern which addresses common modeling problems and hints at the actual usage of the method. The method of form-based description is designed to support reuse wherever possible. It will be obvious that the message definitions of the formchart and the definitions in the persistent data model will have some lengthy record definitions in common. The shared model is the result of the pattern of singling out pure data record definitions. The shared model types are usually records that are flat lists of primitive data, which are needed in the information model as well as in the dialogue model. It is of course desirable to separate these record definitions and to access them in the user message model as well as in the information model. This enables us, for example, to insert a field for a fax number into an existing person data record resulting in a consistent change of the whole data model.

The other topic directly related with the shared model is the topic of cloning. Cloning is the copying of a data record, i.e., the creation of a new entity instance with the same data content, but with another identity. Cloning is a vital concept in a message-based paradigm, since message sending can

and should mean the sending of clones in many instances. It is a crucial point
of the method that it distinguishes strictly between the concept of sending
a reference, then called an opaque reference, and sending a clone. Often a
modeler hesitates to use a cloning operation, not least because cloning is
not a supported concept within many modeling languages, which implies the
manual description of clone operations and their manual maintenance, which
can easily grow into a maintenance nightmare. In our method it is possible
to support cloning based on the notion of the shared model. Given a used
dialogue specification language, auxiliary semantics for its expressions can be
defined with respect to the shared model in order to provide an appropriate
deep copying mechanism. The usage of cloning is an essential ingredient of
real-life modeling.

The shared data model can be seen as having no state. It has of course
many entities in the running system, but these are always weak entities, i.e.,
part of other composite entities outside the shared model.

5.3.5 Chosen Class Model Notation

The form-oriented data model is given in terms of class models. The concrete
terminology has been chosen for convenience, because it is ubiquitous and
fits current object-oriented technology, on which the more technology related
parts of the book rely. Of course every algebraic data type specification language that supports sum-of-product data types as well as recursive domain
equations can serve for the purpose of data modeling. In any case, i.e., independent of the data specification language used, the semantic differences
between the different data model packages must be defined. In Chap. 7 we
will propose our own stripped-down relational notation for class models.

In the examples presented in this book, only a small data kernel of class
models is used to describe data models. We only use classes with attributes,
navigated associations, and multiplicities. We often do not even use class
diagrams, but a simple ad hoc textual format for class models, which is
indentation-based [190]. Each attribute is written together with its type and
multiplicity on its own row indented below the name of the class to which it
belongs. If an association is navigable from a source class to a target class, its
target role is used as a further attribute of the source class. Role names are
derived from class names unless they are explicitly given by the modeler. It
is the usual convention that a class name starts with an uppercase letter and
a derived role name starts with a lowercase letter.

In the chosen notation it is possible to introduce labels for classes. This way
it is possible to distinguish between different kinds of classes. The labels are
written in front of the class name, separated from it by the special character
>. A label also introduces a new namespace, so that two classes from different
kinds of classes can have the same name – as usual, we use dot notation
to qualify items from different namespaces where necessary. We use these

labeling mechanisms to distinguish the types of the layered data model. For this purpose we introduce the following predefined labels:

- `ServerAction` for server action types of the user message model;
- `ClientPage` for client page types of the user message model;
- `Information` for types of the information model;
- `Identity` for types of the opaque identity model;
- `Signature` for types of the shared data model.

Furthermore we need to introduce the label **class** for class attributes. A class attribute is a global attribute with respect to a given class. Consider the class diagram in Fig. 3.9. The data model depicted by the figure is described in our textual format in the following way:

```
Information > Category
   name: String 1..1
   subcategories: Category 0..*
   featuredBooks: Book 0..*
Information > Book
   title: String 1..1
   abstract: String 1..1
   price: Amount 1..1
   authors: Author 1..*
Information > Author
   name: String 1..1
Information > OrderItem
   item: Book 1..1
   quantity: Number 1..1
Information > Order
   orderItems: OrderItem 1..*
   buyer: Customer 1..1
Information > Customer
   email: String 1..1
   fullName: String 1..1
   password: String 1..1
   address: Address 1..1
   cardInformation: CardInformation 1..1
Signature > Address
   streetAddress: String 1..1
   city: String 1..1
   state: String 1..1
   zip: Number 1..1
   country: String 1..1
Signature > CardInformation
   cardType: CardType 1..1
   cardNumber: String 1..1
   expiration: Date 1..1
   cardholder: String 1..1
```

5.4 Dialogue Specification

A dialogue specification completes the form-oriented information system model.

The concept of dialogue is a rather informal concept. For example, in [165] it is defined as the interaction between a user and a system to achieve a particular goal. A dialogue consists of dialogue steps, but the term dialogue is normally not used for a concrete sequence of dialogue steps but rather for a complete chunk of a user interface, such as the system print dialogue. We use the term both as a synonym for the behavior of a user interface and in the narrow sense of an observed interaction sequence.

We introduce the notion of dialogue specification: a dialogue specification narrows the client page capabilities and specifies server reaction. The overall notion of dialogue specification contributes the concept of different kinds of dialogue specification elements. Each dialogue specification element is annotated to a dialogue model element and has a specific meaning with respect to its kind. The several kinds of dialogue specification elements are summarized in the following:

- *Flow conditions.* The flow conditions determine which page is actually presented to the user after the completion of a server action.
- *Server output specifications.* A server output specification defines the report that is generated by a server action.
- *Client input constraint.* A client input constraint is a condition on the report shown on a client page.
- *Enabling conditions.* An enabling condition specifies under which circumstances a form or link submission capability is actually offered.
- *Client output constraints.* A client output constraint is a condition on the data that can be submitted by a form or a link.
- *Server input constraints.* A server input constraint is a server action's precondition.
- *Side effect specifications.* A side effect specification tells which business logic is triggered by a server action.

It should be possible to write dialogue specifications with respect to dialogue history, i.e., with respect to the states through which a current state has been entered. Accessing the dialogue history can be exploited for reuse. For example, consider two client pages that are identical except for a few input capabilities that depend on the question from which system subdialogue the client pages have been entered. They can be united in a single client page, supposing that the distinguishing parts can be made distinct by appropriate dialogue specifications. Like every good reuse, such proceedings can lead to a better maintainable and readable model.

Note that the notion of *dialogue specification* is independent of the definition of a concrete *dialogue specification language*. It is possible to design a concrete dialogue specification language from scratch; it is also possible to build a concrete dialogue specification language on top of an appropriate existing language. Furthermore, it is possible to provide a dialogue specification language that is purely declarative or a language that has, in parts, operational semantics.

5.4.1 The Dialogue Constraint Language

In the bookstore example model in Sect. 5.5 we will use the so-called Dialogue Constraint Language DCL as the dialogue specification language. DCL is an extension of the Object Constraint Language OCL [237, 238]. For this purpose OCL is enriched by new contexts and keywords with appropriate semantics due to the needs of writing dialogue specifications along the following lines:

- OCL has been introduced to annotate class diagrams. DCL is used to annotate dialogue models. These two viewpoints are unified by the notion of state history diagrams discussed in Chap. 13.
- OCL types correspond to UML class diagram types. In our example we use the textual format of Sect. 5.3.5 for class diagrams. This poses no problems. The textual format used is also a format for core UML diagrams.

DCL follows a declarative approach. The different kinds of specification elements are represented by specialized Boolean expressions. These constraints specify the system by restricting the allowed dialogues and allowed messages. The different kinds of constraints have different purposes, and are different with respect to the points in time at which they must hold. The different kinds of constraints are shown in Fig. 5.6.

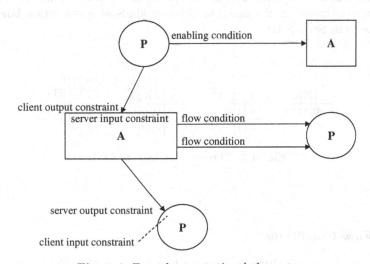

Fig. 5.6. Formchart notational elements

Transitions can host DCL constraints as well as states; in terms of OCL they can be contexts for constraints. Server/page transitions host flow conditions and server output constraints. Server states host server input and side effect constraints. Client states host client input constraints. Page/server transitions host enabling conditions and client output constraints. For constraints and their contexts we use an indent-based syntax again. For each kind of dialogue constraint a new key label is introduced that is written in front of the constraint separated by a colon. For the constraints depicted in Fig. 5.6 the following syntax would be used:

```
P TO A
   enabling: ocl-expression
   clientOuptut: ocl-expression
A TO P
   flow: ocl-expression
   serverOutput: ocl-expression
A
   serverInput: ocl-expression
P
   clientInput: ocl-expression
```

Two other important keywords are added to OCL for the sake of dialogue constraint writing, i.e., source and target. With these keywords a constraint can refer to the actual superparameters of the source and target state of the transition that is annotated with the constraint.

In the subsequent examples it is always necessary to be aware of the fact that OCL is a three-valued logic: the truth tables of the OCL logic operators are summarized in Fig. 5.7. The section proceeds by introducing the different kinds of constraints. A discussion of different kinds of specification languages is taken up in Sect. 5.4.2.

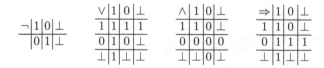

Fig. 5.7. Three-valued logic in OCL

DCL Flow Conditions

Each server/page transition is annotated with a condition. After a server action has processed submitted data the flow conditions are used to determine an outgoing transition. The client page that is targeted by this transition is now rendered. Server/page transitions that are not given an explicit flow condition can be assumed to be annotated with the logical constant true as default. If the flow conditions belonging to a given server action are logically not mutually exclusive it is not possible to determine always exactly one outgoing transition after server action processing. This means that the dialogue specification is non-deterministic with respect to the dialogue flow in these cases, i.e., it is incomplete. It is the modeler's responsibility to ensure that the flow conditions are mutually exclusive for a given server action. As shorthand notation for ensuring deterministic behavior the modeler may number the outgoing transitions to enforce an *evaluation order*. Of course this numbering can only guarantee deterministic behavior if it is unique and complete. However, then the notation is analogous to the case constructs found in higher programming languages.

DCL Server Output Constraints

Each server/page transition is annotated with a server output constraint. This constraint must hold if a server action is left via a given transition. A server output constraint is used to specify the report that is presented to the user on a client page. A natural goal is to specify the report uniquely. It can be achieved, for example, by equating the actual superparameter of the transition target to an expression of appropriate type, or by equating the several attributes of the superparameter to appropriate expressions, possibly conditional in each case.

DCL Client Input Constraints

A client page can be annotated with a client input constraint. This constraint must hold if a client page is rendered. It is used to define properties that must hold for all actual client page superparameters, independent of which server action they are provided with. Each of the relevant server output specifications must not contradict the client input constraint. In a declarative dialogue specification language like DCL a client input constraint is just a shorthand notation for server output specification parts that are common to all transitions targeting a given client page. A client input constraint is logically conjoined to the server output constraints of all these transitions.

DCL Enabling Conditions

Each page/server transition can be annotated with an enabling condition. Omitting an enabling condition is the same as annotating it with the logical constant true. An enabling condition narrows the submission capability that is given by a page/server transition. Only if the enabling condition holds is the link or form represented by the transition actually offered to the user.

Note that, on a certain level of abstraction, it does not matter how a disabled link or form is actually rendered. It may simply disappear from the page, it may be shadowed, or just functionally disabled.

DCL Client Output Constraints

Each page/server transition can be annotated with a client output constraint. This constraint must hold if a client page is left via a given transition. A client output constraint is used to define properties that must hold for all actual parameters that are submitted to a given server action. Actual parameters that are constrained by a client output constraint must not be editable and be correctly provided, e.g., as hidden parameters, or a client-side check must prevent data not fulfilling the constraint from being submitted. An important usage of client output constraints is to relate submitted data to data that are represented on a client page. For example, they can be used to specify that a certain actual parameter must be provided by selection from a data set offered on a page.

DCL Server Input Constraints

Each server action can be annotated with a server input constraint. This constraint must hold if a server action is invoked. A server input constraint can be used to indicate that the system is not yet completely modeled with respect to the system's behavior on violation of this constraint. In a further refinement step the server input constraint can be replaced by flow conditions or client output constraints.

DCL Side Effect Specifications

In the context of DCL we do not prescribe how to specify the data processing associated with a server action, i.e., the side effect on the system data state. Every ad hoc pseudo-code notation may serve for this purpose. For example, an SQL-like data manipulation pseudo-code notation could be used. This pseudo-code would use three types of directives: insert, delete, update. Note, however, that from the standpoint of form-oriented analysis these operations are deliberately informal in contrast to the other DCL constraints.

In DCL we offer a constraint label `sideEffect`, which is used to host OCL expressions or appropriate pseudo-code describing the side effect. If the label hosts an OCL expression, this expression has to be understood as a postcondition, i.e., it must hold after completion of the server action. No extra mechanism for precondition specification has to defined: precondition specifications can be subsumed completely under postcondition specifications given the operator `@pre`.

Annotations for side effects can be made in all contexts of form-oriented analysis, on states as well as edges. A typical context is a server/page transition. Such a side effect specifies the state change under a certain flow condition. The side effect annotation has of course the full transition context, i.e., it can access the source as well as the target. An unconditional side effect of a server action can be specified in the server action itself.

DCL Cloning

In order to support the issue of cloning as discussed in Sect. 5.3.4 we assume an overloaded operator

```
o1->isClone(o2)
```

for each type of the class model. The operator isClone tests if two compared objects have the same attribute values, i.e., if they are clones. The operation is especially useful in side effect specifications to compare data that have been gathered by the dialogue with data that are stored by the server system state via shared data model types.

DCL Accessing the Dialogue History

For the purpose of accessing the dialogue history we introduce the notion of dialogue path expressions and the new property along in DCL.

A dialogue path expression simply consists of transition source names connected by dot notation. It represents a part of a dialogue history, given by a sequence of visited states. Such a path expression can be exploited in DCL expressions only by applying the property along to it. The property along evaluates to true if the current model state has been entered through the states specified in the path to which it is applied. Consider the formchart in Fig. 5.8. The following enabling condition evaluates to true if the states C, R, F, and S have been visited before the client state P has been entered, i.e., if C after R after F after S:

```
P TO A
  enabling: C.R.F.S->along
```

We introduce a wildcard notation that is needed for flexible dialogue constraint writing. A dialogue path expression without wildcards stands for exactly one dialogue history. With the wildcard notation it is possible to define a set of visitable states. The syntax is to put the visitable states in braces, separated by commas. Such an expression stands for the set of all possible dialogue histories consisting of visits to the fixed states. Such a wildcard can be used as part of a dialogue path expression.

Consider the transitions emphasized in Fig. 5.8. The dialogue path expression

$$\texttt{P.\{C,R,F\}.S}$$

represents all dialogue histories that start in S, navigate arbitrarily over the states F, R, C and eventually end in the client state P.

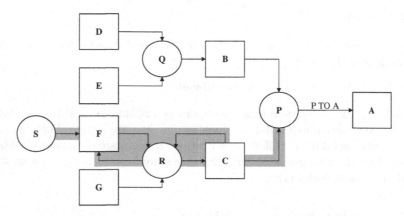

Fig. 5.8. Meaning of path expressions in the formchart

DCL path expressions and their semantics are dealt with in Chap. 13 in more depth. An even more general wildcard notation for path expressions will also be proposed in Chap. 13.

5.4.2 Dialogue Specification Languages

There are a number of languages that would be appropriate for the purpose of elaborating a dialogue specification language. Each concrete specification language has to elaborate precise semantics for the different dialogue specification elements. But before that it has to define the relationship between the specification expressions and the data model. In principle, so-called model-oriented specification languages [148] like Z [171] and VDM [25] can be used as the basis for a dialogue specification language as well as data query languages like SQL [58]. Of course the several possible languages differ with respect to the effort needed for elaboration and must fit or be adapted to the chosen notion of data model. For example, the constraint language OCL already fits the class model approach used in this chapter. There are a couple of query languages that aim at reaching a higher level of data modeling and querying, e.g., [38, 42, 80, 108, 110, 111, 202, 216, 251, 261, 274, 300]. The purpose of the languages DAL and TDAL in Chap. 7 is to provide a parsimonious relation-based notion of data modeling, querying, and constraint writing.

In the concrete dialogue specification language DCL described in Sect. 5.4.1 we have chosen to represent all dialogue specification elements by Boolean expressions. This is an easy and consistent approach. However, at second sight it has its pitfalls. Take the server output specification as an example. It could be simply specified by an appropriate expression of the type of the targeted server action. Specifying it by a Boolean expression has its implications. First, the specification is more clumsy because it has to explicitly equate the output to the desired result. This is actually not the problem. The problem is that that approach is more susceptible to ambiguity. The modeler is free to give loose specifications like stating that an integer parameter is greater than a certain value. The modeler is even free to give constraints that are not at all tight to the server output, constraining for example the side effect of the preceding server actions. This generality can be considered advantageous or disadvantageous. However, it is not obvious in any case how constraints of such a general constraint approach can be exploited with respect to the notion of executable specification. Similar discussions can be held for the server input, client input, and client output constraint. DCL flow conditions and DCL enabling conditions are closer to the notion of executable specification because they are more straightforward transcriptions of the respective dialogue specification elements. Correct DCL flow conditions and DCL enabling conditions can always be reused more or less directly in the implementing code.

DCL is an extension of OCL. OCL is a model-oriented specification language, which is currently widely discussed [53]. For example, there are discussions on how to use OCL as a query language [4] and how to use it for the specification of business rules [81]. OCL is an integral part of the UML specification [237]. The notion of OCL expression is tightly coupled with UML class diagrams. Moreover OCL constraints are used in the UML metamodeling semantics approach in order to specify well-formedness rules for diagrams. OCL has a rich feature set and rich informal semantics. For example, it supports path expressions similar to those found in the Object Query Language OQL [42]. OCL cannot be regarded as a formal language [65]. The semantic ambiguities [125] become even more complex to handle because of the fact that OCL is a three-valued logic. Efforts to give formal OCL semantics are, for example, given in [260, 43]. In [237] the semantics of the declarative language OCL are partly based on operational semantics specified in an imperative pseudo-code.

In DCL we did not conclusively define how to specify side effects. OCL offers means for specifying updates with the postcondition constraint stereotype, which uses a rudimentary temporal logic [254] given by the modal operator @pre. However, this calculus may easily lead the average modeler to non-operational specifications without any need. Take the following example specification for a side effect from [314]:

```
post: customer=customer@pre->including(c)
```

For example, the following is a useful shorthand notation for the above specification:

```
insert customer c
```

We argue that deviating from a purely declarative style of constraint writing can be justifiable. Pre/postcondition specification [247, 217, 218] can be clumsy if the modeler is forced to give semantics over and over again to a basic, i.e., not business-specific, operational phenomenon – like insert, update, or delete. If such an operational phenomenon occurs ubiquitously in the system's functionality then why not extend the specification language by a non-declarative language construct? That is exactly what is done in Sect. 7.3 by the TDAL language by adding a clear-cut operational layer on top of the declarative DAL language.

5.5 The Bookstore Formchart and Data Model

In this section we partially model the bookstore example from Chap. 3 with a form-oriented information system model. We use the textual format for class models defined in Sect. 5.3.5 for describing the layered data model. We use the concrete dialogue specification language DCL defined in Sect. 5.4.1. The section follows the structure of Sect. 3.1. The several formchart diagrams in this section can be considered parts of one whole formchart that completely describes the dialogue model. Figure 5.9 shows a complete formchart for the bookstore. This formchart has a certain normal form: server actions are doubled so often as necessary to entirely decouple the client page nodes from each other in the painting. If we call the painting of a client page with all the server actions directly connected to it its *action set chart*, Fig. 5.9 is an assembly of the action set charts of all the bookstore client pages.

At several points in this section we delve into the details of different modeling alternatives. At other points we choose to prefer concrete modeling alternatives over other alternatives without even explicitly mentioning and discussing the alternatives. This text is concerned with creating a semantical framework for enterprise applications. Every method, just like every programming language, allows for different styles of usage. Fixing a concrete style guide is therefore an important topic in every project, but cannot be the topic of this book. First and foremost, fixing each and everyone would contradict the descriptive approach which we follow in this book. Moreover, if the level of abstraction is too low, the target of elaboration simply becomes unreachable. If we nevertheless discuss modeling alternatives on a detailed level at some points in this section this is not done in its own right, but rather to support the arguments in other, more conceptual parts of the book such as the discussion of complete and executable specification in Chaps. 7 and 14.

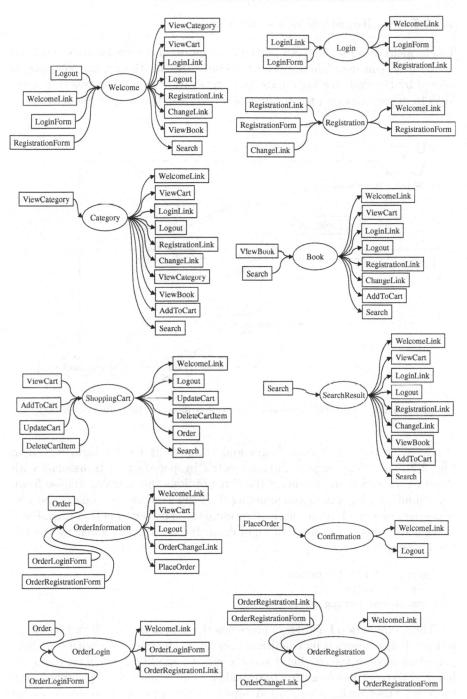

Fig. 5.9. Complete formchart for the bookstore example

5.5.1 Login, Registration and Logout

The formchart in Fig. 5.10 is a partial description of the bookstore's login and registration features. The formchart encompasses all the interaction options offered by the system's login page and registration page. The two respective links from the welcome page to these pages are also taken up in the formchart.

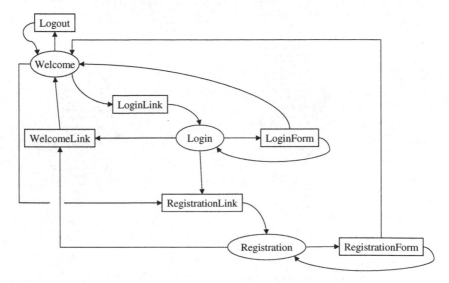

Fig. 5.10. Login, registration and logout feature of the online bookshop

Consider the client page Login and compare it to the login screen in Fig. 3.2. The client page is interconnected by page/server transitions with three server actions representing the three options the user can choose from, i.e., submitting login data and aborting the login process via a link to the welcome page or via a link to the registration page. The server action LoginForm is triggered upon submission of login data. Its signature is given by the following record:

```
ServerAction > LoginForm
  email: String 0..1
  password: String 0..1
```

The server action LoginForm processes the submitted e-mail and password strings. It is connected by conditional server/page transitions with the client page Welcome on the one hand and the client page Login again on the other hand. If the user has forgotten to provide an e-mail address or password, or if there is no user with the submitted e-mail address or if the password does not match the e-mail address, the server action branches back to the Login client page. In this way it sends an appropriate error message and the submitted e-mail address to the client page. The transferred e-mail address is needed as the default value for the e-mail form field. The client page Login must have an appropriate signature as follows:

```
ClientPage > Login
  errorMessage: String 0..1
  defaultEmail: String 0..1
```

Flow Conditions

The conditional branching of the server action LoginForm is specified by the following flow conditions. The type Customer stems from the appropriate class of customer data records in the information model.

```
LoginForm TO Login
  flow: source.email->isEmpty
        or source.password->isEmpty
        or Customer->allInstances->
          select(email=source.email)->
          select(password=source.password)->isEmpty

LoginForm TO Welcome
  flow: not source.email->isEmpty
        and not source.password->isEmpty
        and not Customer->allInstances->
                select(email=source.email)->
                select(password=source.password)->isEmpty
```

The above flow conditions also cover cases where there is more than one customer in the system with a certain e-mail address. Though these cases are considered wrong in our bookstore example, because the e-mail address should serve as an identification of the customer, the above flow conditions are not concerned with this problem. The restriction is enforced somewhere else, typically within the scope of the specification of the registration error handling or by an appropriate class invariant as a static alternative. For example, consider the flow condition from the server action LoginForm to the client page Welcome. With respect to the password mismatch problem it requires only that there exists at least one customer with the given e-mail address that has the given password. The flow condition relies on the fact that there is at most one customer with the given password, i.e., that this is enforced somewhere else.

Server Output Constraints

The data transferred from the server action LoginForm to the client page
Login are specified by the following server output constraint:

```
LoginForm TO Login
  serverOutput:
    if   source.email->isEmpty and source.password->isEmpty
    then target.errorMessage="forgotten e-mail/password !"
    else
      if   source.email->isEmpty
      then target.errorMessage="forgotten e-mail !"
      else
        if   source.password->isEmpty
        then target.errorMessage="forgotten password !"
        else
          if   Customer->allInstances->
               select(email=source.email)->isEmpty
          then target.errorMessage="no such user !"
          else target.errorMessage="email/password mismatch !"
          endif
        endif
      endif
    endif
  serverOutput:
    if   source.email->isEmpty
    then  target.defaultEmail=""
    else  target.defaultEmail=source.email
    endif
```

Consider how error messages are handled in the above example. One could
argue that from a conceptual modeling viewpoint it is not appropriate to use
real message strings as flags for the several errors. In a real project you would
like to model the type of the error message attribute abstractly as a type –
even in coding you would introduce error codes and separate them from the
error messages. However, the selected solution is appropriate for the purpose
of a compact example. The default data transferred from the server action
LoginLink to the client page Login are specified by the following server output
constraint:

```
LoginLink TO Login
  serverOutput:
    target.errorMessage=""
    and target.defaultEmail=""
```

Because the transition from LoginForm back to Login covers all the possible errors, the output constraint is a nested conditional construct. As an alternative it is possible to exploit an evaluation order annotation for flow conditions. Compare Fig. 5.11 with Fig. 5.10: the single transition from LoginForm
to Login is replaced by a couple of new transitions.

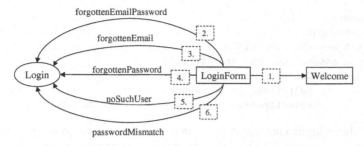

Fig. 5.11. Conditional server/page transitions

In Fig. 5.11 each of the different possible errors is represented by an own server/page transition that is named after the respective error. It is a matter of taste which of the two solutions is considered the better. In the latter solution the need for more transitions is in opposition to the decreased complexity of the resulting flow conditions. The case differentiation for the errors is mapped to the flow conditions of the several server output constraints:

```
LoginForm > forgottenEmailPassword > Login
  flow: source.email->isEmpty and source.password->isEmpty
  serverOutput: target.errorMessage="forgotten e-mail/password !"
                and target.defaultEmail=""
LoginForm > forgottenEmail > Login
  flow: source.email->isEmpty
  serverOutput: target.errorMessage="forgotten e-mail !"
                and target.defaultEmail=""
LoginForm > forgottenPassword > Login
  flow: source.password->isEmpty
  serverOutput: target.errorMessage="forgotten password !"
                and target.defaultEmail=source.email
LoginForm > noSuchUser > Login
  flow: Customer->allInstances->
        select(email=source.email)->isEmpty
  serverOutput: target.errorMessage="no such user !"
                and target.defaultEmail=source.email
LoginForm > passwordMismatch > Login
  flow: true
  serverOutput: target.errorMessage="email/password mismatch !"
                and target.defaultEmail=source.email
```

Server Input Constraints

The above described way of how errors of submitted login data are handled by the system is only one of several possible alternatives. If the modeler has already identified the possible mistakes, but does not want to decide how they are handled, the server input constraint is the right place to specify them. Consider the following input constraint for the server action LoginForm:

```
LoginForm
  serverInput:
    not source.email->isEmpty
    and not source.password->isEmpty
    and not Customer->allInstances->
            select(email=source.email)->
            select(password=source.password)->isEmpty
```

The above input constraint introduces the assumption that the submitted login data are correct. That is, the server action LoginForm can rely on them and the special error handling can be dropped from the specification. This means that the transition back to the client page Login can be deleted with all its constraints and that the flow condition of the transition to the client page Welcome can be set constantly true, too: actually the new server input constraint is identical to the flow condition that formerly led to the welcome page. The system specification has become incomplete in the sense that it has to be refined in a further refinement step by describing an error handling, which is sketched in Fig. 5.12 for yet another possible example refinement. However, at the same time the system specification remains robust in the sense that knowledge about the incompleteness is encapsulated in the server input constraint.

This means that introducing a server input constraint for a server action can be considered as giving it the status TBD, i.e., "to be defined", in the sense of [158].

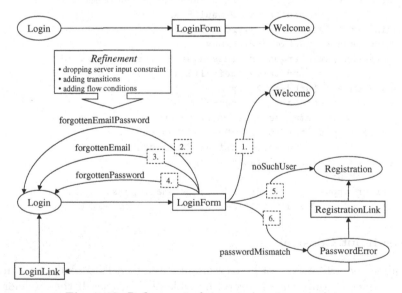

Fig. 5.12. Refinement of a server input constraint

As an abbreviation for the above server input constraint it is possible to define a signature with more constraining multiplicities for the attributes of the server action LoginForm:

```
ServerAction > LoginForm
  email: String 1..1
  password: String 1..1
LoginForm
  serverInput:
    not Customer->allInstances->
        select(email=source.email)->
        select(password=source.password)->isEmpty
```

With the new signature the server action can assume that an e-mail address and a password are provided. This means that we can subsume the concept of multiplicity of a server action's attribute under the concept of server input constraint. This is an arbitrary choice. Equally well one could define such constraining of a multiplicity as a shorthand notation for client output constraints. This would be in accordance with the more general observation that a type is a data restriction, that each server action signature is a restriction on the data submitted to the server, and that each client page signature is a restriction on the data sent to the client.

Client Output Constraints

The question whether an error is actually handled by server-side or by client-side processing can be considered as too low-level from an analysis viewpoint. However, if it is desired to distinguish between client-side and server-side handling, client-side handling can be specified, for example, by employing a client output constraint. This way, it is possible to specify client-side processing for the pure form field validation of our login form:

```
Login TO LoginForm
  clientOutput:
    not target.email->isEmpty
    and not target.password->isEmpty
LoginForm
  serverInput:
    not Customer->allInstances->
        select(email=source.email)->
        select(password=source.password)->isEmpty
```

Now, it is required that the targeting client pages are "responsible" for really providing data. We delve into the technological issues of this topic in the Sects. 11.1.3 and 11.1.5.

Server Output Constraints

If the data submitted to the server action LoginForm are correct, the dialogue
flow is branched to the client page Welcome. The welcome page displays the
name of the logged-in customer, therefore it has the customer name as a
parameter. Actually the page Welcome exists in two versions. Depending on
whether the customer is logged in or not, it offers different interaction options
and displays different headlines. Therefore the page has a further Boolean
parameter to indicate whether the user is logged in:

```
ClientPage > Welcome
  loggedIn: boolean
  customerName: String 0..1
  featuredBooks: FeaturedBook 0..*
```

Compare the above signature with the welcome screen in Fig. 3.1. The
welcome screen shows a list of recommended bestsellers. Therefore, the signature Welcome has an attribute of type FeaturedBook, which is given in the
following Sect. 5.5.2.

The server output constraint for the transition from LoginForm to Welcome
ascertains that the loggedIn bit is set and the correct customer name is displayed on the welcome page:

```
LoginForm TO Welcome
  serverOuptut:
    target.loggedIn=true
  serverOuptut:
    target.customerName=Customer->allInstances->
                        select(email=source.email)->
                        asSequence->first.name
```

As discussed for the flow conditions of the server action LoginForm, the
above constraint is written for the general case where there might be more
than one customer with the given e-mail address. The server output constraint
allows us to select an arbitrary customer matching the e-mail address because
it assumed that there is exactly one such customer. Similarly the matching of
the password is not a concern for the server output constraint because this is
already ensured by the respective flow condition.

The effect of the server action Logout is modeled by the following server
output constraint:

```
Logout TO Welcome
  serverOuptut:
    target.loggedIn=false
  serverOuptut:
    target.customerName=""
```

Enabling Conditions

If the user is not yet logged in, the links to the login page and the registration page are offered. If the user is logged in, a link to logout is offered. In order to specify this, the concept of enabling conditions is used in the following way:

```
Welcome TO LoginLink
    enabling: not source.loggedIn
Welcome TO RegistrationLink
    enabling: not source.loggedIn
Welcome TO Logout
    enabling: source.loggedIn
```

Modeling a Dialogue Status

The loggedIn bit in the signature Welcome does not have to be understood as being actually displayed. It is used to model a status of the dialogue. With respect to the current status the welcome page is rendered differently, in the simplest case distinguished through the welcome headline. A user is logged in or logged out. A lot of pages depend on it. As a matter of course there are alternatives to model these two basic dialogue states. Some modelers would perhaps like to introduce session data indicating if a user is logged in and which user it is.

```
Information > CurrentUser
    class > customer: Customer 0..1
```

Then constraints can be written with respect to these session data instead of the actual message parameter. This way of modeling makes the notion of login more explicit; moreover it is closer to the actual implementation.

Link Signatures

The server actions WelcomeLink, LoginLink and RegistrationLink represent mere hyperlinks. No data are submitted by following the links. The server action Logout expects no data, too. Therefore all of these server actions have the empty record type:

```
ServerAction > WelcomeLink

ServerAction > LoginLink

ServerAction > RegistrationLink

ServerAction > Logout
```

Server Action Side Effects

We consider the registration page shown in Fig. 3.3. The server action Registration Form provides input capabilities for the e-mail address, the customer name, the password and its repetition, the address, and the card information. The client page Registration displays an error message and the data gathered by RegistrationForm as default values except for the password. The interplay of RegistrationLink, RegistrationForm, and Registration is analogous to the interplay of LoginLink, LoginForm, and Login. The user message model types RegistrationForm and Registration reuse the signatures Address and CardInformation from the shared data model:

```
ClientPage > Registration
  errorMessage: String 1..1
  defaultEmail: String 1..1
  defaultFullName: String 1..1
  defaultAddress: Address 1..1
  defaultCardInformation: CardInformation 1..1
ServerAction > RegistrationForm
  email: String 1..1
  fullName: String 1..1
  address: Address 1..1
  password: String 1..1
  repeatedPassword: String 1..1
  cardInformation: CardInformation 1..1
```

The side effect of the server action RegistrationForm could be specified with the following pseudo-code:

```
RegistrationForm TO Welcome
  sideEffect:
    insert Customer x
      x.email = source.email
      x.fullName = source.fullName
      x.password = source.password
      x.address->isClone(source.address)
      x.cardInformation->isClone(source.cardInformation)
```

We want the above pseudo-code to have the following meaning: if the server action RegistrationForm is left via the transition to the page Welcome, a new information object x of type Customer is generated. This new object has the data gathered by RegistrationForm as attribute values.

5.5.2 Browsing Books

The formchart in Fig. 5.13 encompasses the browsing feature of the bookstore. It is possible to visit more and more subcategory pages, to view detailed book information, and to add books to the shopping cart.

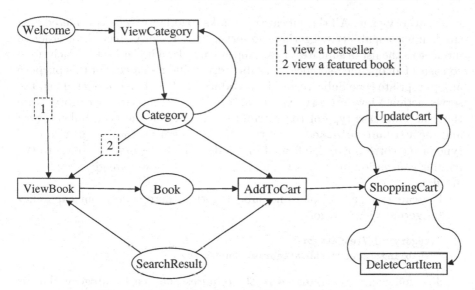

Fig. 5.13. Browsing feature of the online bookshop

Consider the example screen of the client page Category shown in Fig. 3.4. The following types are introduced in the layered data model for the client page and its neighboring server actions:

```
ClientPage > Category
  currentName: String 1..1
  subcategories: Subcategory 0..*
  featuredBooks: FeaturedBook 0..*
Signature > Subcategory
  category: category 1..1
  name: String 1..1
Signature > FeaturedBook
  book: book 1..1
  authorNames: String 1..*
  title: String 1..1
ServerAction > ViewCategory
  selected: category 1..1
ServerAction > ViewBook
  selected: book 1..1
ServerAction > AddToCart
  selected: book 1..*
```

The category page shows the name of the current category. It shows a list of subcategories and a list of featured books. Consider the list of subcategories first. This list shows the names of the subcategories of the current category. But the list is not just pure information to the user. For every subcategory there is a link or a button the user can select in order to reach the respective new category page. All the subcategory links together can be considered as a single input capability triggering the server action ViewCategory. In order to model this the list of subcategories is represented by a list of tuples. Each tuple consists of an opaque reference to a subcategory and its name. For this purpose an appropriate type Subcategory is introduced in the shared model. Then the server action ViewCategory expects an opaque reference to a category. Note that the lowercase type of the attribute `category` in the type Subcategory and the attribute `selected` in the type ViewCategory is the opaque reference type of the corresponding information model type Category, according to the naming convention in Sect. 5.3.2. The subcategory names are given by String attributes.

If a category page displays no subcategories, there is no input capability for triggering ViewCategory:

```
Category TO ViewCategory
   enabling: source.subcategories->notEmpty
```

The following constraint correctly requires that each category that is passed to the server action ViewCategory stems from the set of offered subcategories:

```
Category TO ViewCategory
   clientOutput:
     source.subcategories.category->includes(target.selected)
```

Now it has to be specified that the correct name of the current category is displayed and the correct subcategories are offered with their correct names. This is done by the following server output constraints. Note again that the notation convention in Sect. 5.3.2 is used and the opaque references are dereferenced and referenced with the predefined role names `instance` and `oref`:

```
ViewCategory TO Category
   serverOuptut:
     target.currentName=source.selected.instance.name
     and target.subcategories.category
        = source.selected.instance.subcategories.oref
     and target.subcategories->forAll(
          name=category.instance.name
        )
```

The above constraint is interesting with respect to the relationship of subcategory references and subcategory names. It is specified that a reference to a category is encapsulated with the corresponding category name in a tuple. Following the discussion in Sect. 2.1.6 this is a conceptual description for the fact that the reference and the name are rendered together in some way. However, an opaque reference is not really visible. So the grouping can be exploited to specify that a concrete selected opaque reference actually stems from a button or link that is correctly labeled with the corresponding name.

A similar discussion as for the list of subcategories applies to the featured books of a category. It is possible to view details of featured books and to add books to the cart. However, in the case of adding books to the cart, it is possible to select not only a single book, but a couple of books. This multiple selection capability is realized with a list of check boxes on the page in Fig. 3.4. Appropriate signatures have been introduced for the server actions ViewBook and AddToCart; the respective constraints are the following:

```
ViewCategory TO Category
  serverOuptut:
    target.featuredBooks.book
    = source.selected.instance.featuredBooks.oref
    and target.featuredBooks->forAll(
          authorNames = book.instance.authors.name
          and title = book.instance.title
    )
Category TO ViewBook
  clientOutput:
    source.featuredBooks.book->includes(target.selected)
Category TO AddToCart
  clientOutput:
    source.featuredBooks.book->includesAll(target.selected)
```

Now we give the types for the states Book and SearchResult:

```
ClientPage > Book
  detailed: book 1..1
  title: String 1..1
  abstract: String 1..1
  price: Amount 1..1
  authorNames: String 1..*
ClientPage > SearchResult
  featuredBooks: FeaturedBook 0..*
```

5.5.3 Shopping Cart

Consider the shopping cart page in Fig. 3.6. With respect to the dialogue displayed in Fig. 5.13 two actions can be triggered, i.e., to update the cart with new item quantities and to delete an item from the cart. The following types are appropriate:

```
ClientPage > ShoppingCart
  cartItems: ShoppingCartItem 0..*
Signature > ShoppingCartItem
  cartItem: cartItem 1..1
  authorNames: String 1..*
  title: String 1..1
  defaultQuantity: Number 1..1
  price: Amount 1..1
```

```
ServerAction > UpdateCart
  update: UpdateCartItem 1..*
Signature > UpdateCartItem
  selected: cartItem 1..1
  newQuantity: Number 1..1
ServerAction > DeleteCartItem
  selected: cartItem 1..1
```

The shopping cart content is modeled merely by a type CartItem in the information model:

```
Information > CartItem
  item: Book 1..1
  quantity: Number 1..1
```

Deleting a cart item is actually an update operation on the cart. This yields a modeling alternative. The server action DeleteCartItem can be discarded if a new transition from ShoppingCart to UpdateCart is introduced, which is depicted in Fig. 5.14. This time the client output constraint of the delete transition must explicitly express that only one opaque reference is selected by the customer. It must further express that the selected quantity equals zero.

```
ShoppingCart > delete > UpdateCart
  clientOuptut:
    target.update->size=1
    and source.cartItems.cartItem->
        includesAll(target.update.selected)
    and target.update.newQuantity=Set{0}
```

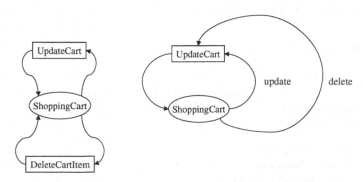

Fig. 5.14. Shopping cart feature of the online bookshop

5.5.4 Buying

The feature of buying books comprises the means of placing the shopping cart content as an order and offers the user a subdialogue to log in and register. The feature is sketched in the formchart in Fig. 5.15.

Consider the server action Order. It is merely a link, and is only activated if the shopping cart displays items; it directs the user to the client page OrderInformation if the user is already logged in, otherwise it directs the user to the page OrderLogin:

```
ServerAction > Order
ShoppingCart TO Order
   enabling: source->cartItems->notEmpty
Order TO OrderInformation
   flowCondition: CurrentUser.customer->notEmpty
Order TO OrderLogin
    flowCondition: CurrentUser.customer->isEmpty
```

The client page OrderInformation, shown in Fig. 3.7, and page Confirmation need the following signatures:

```
ClientPage > OrderInformation
   shippingDetails: ShippingDetails 1..1
   paymentMethod: PaymentMethod 1..1
   desiredBooks: Signature.OrderItem 1..*
   totalPrice: Amount 1..1
ClientPage > Confirmation
   shippingDetails: ShippingDetails 1..1
   paymentMethod: PaymentMethod 1..1
   boughtBooks: Signature.OrderItem 1..*
   totalPrice: Amount 1..1
Signature > ShippingDetails
   fullName: String
   streetAddress: String 1..1
   city: String 1..1
   state: String 1..1
   zip: Number 1..1
   country: String 1..1
Signature > PaymentMethod
   cardType: CardType 1..1
   truncatedCardNumber: String 1..1
   expiration: Date 1..1
Signature > OrderItem
   authorNames: String 1..*
   title: String 1..1
   quantity: Number 1..1
   price: Amount 1..1
ServerAction > PlaceOrder
```

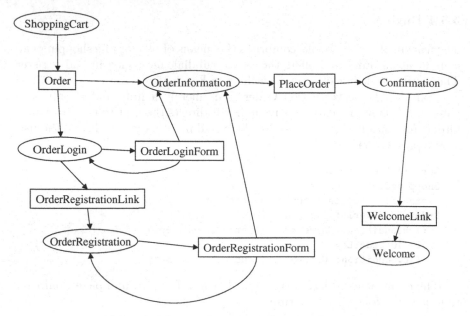

Fig. 5.15. Buying feature of the online bookshop

Now we wish to consider the subdialogue for login and registration in the formchart of Fig. 5.15. The subdialogue is identical to the login and registration dialogue discussed in Sect. 5.5.1 except for its exit points. For the order subdialogue it is important that finally submitting login data or registration data results in the client page OrderInformation and not in the client page Welcome. Therefore new model states are introduced for the order subdialogue, tagged with the leading term Order. Types, transitions, and constraints can be copied from Sect. 5.5.1 and adapted with respect to the differences mentioned. It would be desirable not to copy but to reuse the common dialogues in such a case. This is an example where accessing the dialogue history can be exploited as will be shown in the sequel.

Consider the formchart in Fig. 5.16. This is the result of merging the formchart in Fig. 5.15 and the formchart in Fig. 5.10 into a single formchart. The two corresponding states of the core login and registration subdialogues have been amalgamated to form a single new state, as indicated by the leading term New.

Consider the server action NewLoginForm. It has a transition to the page Welcome derived from the state LoginForm in Fig. 5.10 and a transition to the page OrderInformation derived from the state OrderLoginForm in Fig. 5.15. The path to the page OrderInformation must be followed if the login dialogue has been entered from the order dialogue the last time it was entered; otherwise, the path to the page Welcome must be followed. This can be specified by the following flow conditions:

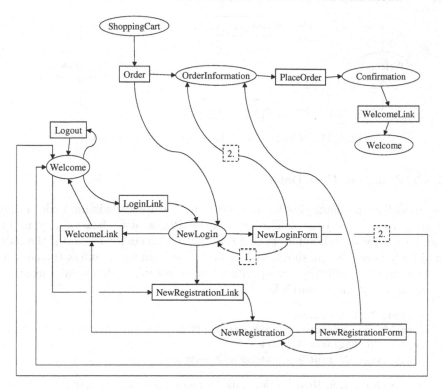

Fig. 5.16. Reuse of the login and registration subdialogues

```
NewLoginForm TO OrderInformation
  flow:{NewLogin,NewLoginForm}.NewLogin.Order->along
NewLoginForm TO Welcome
  flow:{NewLogin,NewLoginForm}.NewLogin.LoginLink->along
NewLoginForm TO NewLogin
  flow: source.email->isEmpty
      or source.password->isEmpty
      or Customer->allInstances->
         select(email=source.email)->
         select(password=source.password)->isEmpty
```

In the flow conditions we have used dialogue path expressions, the `along` property, and the wildcard notation for dialogue path expressions, which were introduced in Sect. 5.4.1. A similar discussion applies to the server action NewRegistrationForm. It is debatable which of the above two modeling alternatives, i.e., the one represented by Figs. 5.15 and 5.10 or the one represented by Fig. 5.16, is better. The latter reuses model elements but needs more complex constraints.

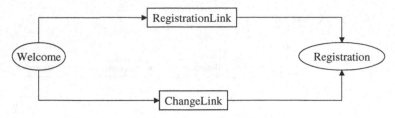

Fig. 5.17. Managing user data in the online bookshop

5.5.5 Managing User Data

For modeling the change feature for user data the already existing registration page can easily be reused. The client page Registration has already input parameters for default values that can be filled with customer data if the user is already logged in. As shown in Fig. 5.17, a new link that offers the change feature must be added to the specification, to complete the already existing server action RegistrationLink:

```
Welcome TO ChangeLink
  enabling: CurrentUser.customer->notEmpty
Welcome TO RegistrationLink
  enabling: CurrentUser.customer->isEmpty
```

The server action RegistrationLink has to send constant default values to the page Registration, and the server action ChangeLink has to send user data. Before turning to the respective server output constraints, recall from pages 65 and 84 that both the type Registration and the type Customer reuse the types Address and CardInformation from the shared data model. Therefore the DCL cloning notation can again be exploited in the following server output constraint:

```
ChangeLink TO Registration
  serverOutput:
    errorMessage=""
    and defaultEmail=CurrentUser.customer.email
    and defaultFullName=CurrentUser.customer.fullName
    and defaultAddress->isClone(CurrentUser.customer.address)
    and defaultCardInformation->isClone(
        CurrentUser.customer.cardInformation
      )
```

The server ouptut constraint for the transition from RegistrationLink to Registration must specify all parts of the message parts explicitly. Note that it is assumed that the type CardType is supported by an advanced widget type, see Sect. 11.1.8, and therefore can be handled as a basic type with respect to the definition of the type Registration:

```
RegistrationLink TO Registration
  serverOutput:
    errorMessage=""
    and defaultEmail=""
    and defaultFullName=""
    and defaultAddress.streetAddress=""
    and defaultAddress.city=""
    and defaultAddress.state=""
    and defaultAddress.zip=""
    and defaultAddress.country=""
    and defaultCardInformation.cardType=CardType.Default
    and defaultCardInformation.cardNumber=""
    and defaultCardInformation.expiration=""
    and defaultCardInformation.cardholder=""
```

5.5.6 Searching Books

The search feature of the bookstore is visualized in Fig. 5.18. Searching a book by a given search item in general results in the client page SearchResult. If the search yields a unique result, the detailed book page is presented rather than the search result page. With respect to some offered capabilities, the page SearchResult is quite similar to the page Category. A list of books is offered: in the case of the page Category a list of featured books; in the case of the page SearchResult a list of books found by a system search functionality. In both cases it is possible to choose a single book, in order to view its details, or to choose a couple of books, in order to add them to the shopping cart. To give some idea of this similarity the page SearchResult has already been displayed in Fig. 5.13.

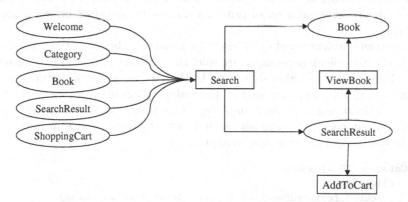

Fig. 5.18. Search feature of the online bookshop

The formchart in Fig. 5.18 contains all client pages of the bookstore example that offer a search capability. A useful shorthand notation for such kinds of features will be introduced in Sect. 6.5.1 by the so-called state set notation. Not only is the page SearchResult reachable uniformly from a couple of other pages, but actually so are most of the other dialogue states, too, e.g., the pages Welcome, Login, and Registration. In this section, the interesting core dialogue of the bookstore has been discussed. Menu-like capabilities, i.e., capabilities offered uniformly on many pages, have been represented once and dropped on other occasions. The client page Login is a typical example. In order to explain its transitions to and from the page Welcome it has been contained in the formchart in Fig. 5.10, but all the other transitions from the other states have been dropped from the charts presented.

5.5.7 Representation of Widget Types

Form-oriented analysis abstracts from concrete layout questions in the modeling of submit/response style systems. Therefore it is important to understand how we can ascend from layout-centric widgets to an abstract representation of interaction. In this section we analyze a typical interaction pattern and discuss how it is represented in client output constraints.

Widgets can be editable fields for primitive types, check boxes, or radio button lists. Since we deal with the analysis level, the differences between functionally equivalent widget types are of minor interest. Therefore a list of submit buttons is equivalent to a single submit button and either a radio button list or a selection list. Hence single selection lists, radio button lists, as well as submit button lists are conceived as particular presentations of a single abstract interaction option, which we call single selection. Check box lists as well as multiple select lists are considered accordingly as multiple selection. Whether using single or multiple selection, the user can choose from an offered collection, which must be part of the client page signature. In case the user has to choose between a set of primitive values, these values are wrapped as objects.

Selections in formcharts give rise to a constraint between the offered collection in the client page signature and the selected items that are part of the addressed server action signature. In that server action signature the parameter that has to be provided by the radio button list must be part of the offered collection in the client page signature from which to choose. Such a client output constraint written in DCL was discussed above in Sect. 5.5.2 where it was used in our example application.

```
Category TO ViewBook
  clientOutput:
    source.featuredBooks.book->includes(target.selected)
```

For simplicity we now consider the following simplified types and constraint:

```
ClientPage > Category
  featuredBooks: book 0..*
  name: String 1..1
ServerAction > ViewBook
  selected: book 0..1
Category TO ViewBook
  clientOutput:
    source.featuredBooks->includes(target.selected)
```

In the type Category the collection of opaque references to featured books is now the top-level part of the client page signature. The above constraint can be graphically shown as in Fig. 5.19. In graphical user interfaces, different widget types offer different possibilities for the user to provide information within a form. In form-oriented analysis, each widget type gives rise to characteristic client output constraints, which describe the semantics of the respective widget type. We can therefore speak of *widget constraints* in form-oriented analysis. A widget constraint is a part of a client output constraint that specifies one imagined widget of the addressed form. Figure 5.19 shows what implications such a widget constraint representing a single selection would have. The class diagram represents a client page and a server action together with parts of their message types. We consider one of the opaque reference types passed from the client page to the server action. In order to specify that this should be a single selection there are two conditions which have to be imposed. The first condition is that the chosen items – their number is not yet specified – must indeed be a selection of the offered items. For this purpose we introduce the intuitive keyword **selection** as a generic constraint. The formal definition of this selection constraint is not of interest here; it can best be given by making use of a novel constraint concept, the concatenation constraints introduced in Chap. 7. The second property is the specification of the number of items to choose. This is done by the multiplicity indicated in the figure. A multiplicity of 1 here specifies a single selection. The multiplicity * would specify a multiple selection.

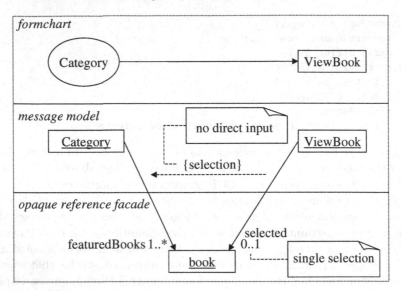

Fig. 5.19. Graphical representation of a client output constraint. The subset constraint specifies that the chosen information must have been on the page

6

Model Decomposition and Refinement

Models quickly become large. We need a method of partitioning them in order to manage their complexity and to be able to discuss them with colleagues. In this chapter we discuss questions relating to the composition and decomposition of the different types of models introduced so far. We propose concrete notational elements that help to organize large models. The composition mechanisms for the model are especially simple and flexible. A notation for state sets is introduced that allows for weaving transitions. A notation for state specialization is introduced that can be used to express dialogue history dependency. Furthermore this chapter deals with model refinement. Different detailed refinement stages for form-oriented information system models are defined. The findings of this chapter are independent of the concrete notation employed.

6.1 Model Union

The topic of composition is a very important one for the application of a method. It is here that we meet another very central concept of our modeling method, the *model union*. This concept will be of great help in giving clarity and lightweightness to our whole modeling method. The concept of model union we describe is extremely simple yet extremely versatile; it is indeed versatile to the degree that all the composition methods we discuss in this book will be basically reduced to it! We will discuss a number of example problems in detail, especially in the area of the decomposition of the formchart, but all these discussions will be based on the powerful concept of model union. We first discuss the concept of model union in general; we then go on to discuss its application to formcharts.

The Intuition Behind Model Union

Model union is best understood using the following thought experiment: consider you have been modeling for some time, and your model has reached a considerable size. You start to realize that it is now too big, and you identify two rather separate topics, say, end-user interface and administrator interface. Hence you want to partition your model. But the user management turns out to be necessary for both topics, and you want this part in both models, not in a separate submodel. So you now decompose the model into two non-disjoint parts, both containing the user management. This partitioning can be done, because you know how to compose the parts again, namely by a union which is basically a graph union, i.e., the common part is only taken once. The operation follows the idea of set union.

Monotonic Modeling

Specifying can be conceived as describing constraints on a system. Even the definition of types has an obvious constraint character. Types enforce type safety. Moreover they create a vocabulary for the constraints to speak about.

In our modeling we have taken care that all model elements add new constraints. Semantically, therefore, the system specification is the conjunction of all model elements. The associative, commutative nature of the "and" operation ensures that the model elements can be considered in every ordering. Their interconnection is not realized by their ordering, but by the identifiers which they share.

The *monotonic* nature of the "and" operation together with associativity and commutativity may be seen as the enabling semantic foundation of our general composition mechanism, the model union. These properties mean that a model is a set of modeling elements and its natural composition is the set union.

6.2 Formchart Decomposition

Formchart decomposition can be used to represent, for example, a refinement step, a generalization, or a specialization. Actually we have already used formchart decomposition throughout Sect. 5.5, where all the discussed features have been submodels of Fig. 5.9.

In Sect. 5.2.1 we have stated that a chart element with a given name can occur several times in a chart. Model elements have unique names. Chart elements with the same name denote the same model element. Therefore, given two charts these can be understood as a single chart immediately. Decomposition can be discussed solely in terms of formchart elements in the sequel. This is possible because the relation between the chart and the state machine it denotes is given canonically. For example, it can be made precise by introducing a graph-based metamodel for paintings. In such semantics charts are conceived as graphs, too, and differ from the state machine they denote only with respect to the possibly multiple naming of graph elements. Then the relationship between charts and state machines can be formalized as a factorization of chart elements with respect to identical naming.

A *formchart decomposition* consists of only two operations:

- *partitioning into submodels;*
- *optional naming of submodels*

A formchart decomposition selects arbitrary subgraphs of the formchart and optionally names them. The first interesting thing about this mechanism is that the partitioning is really unconstrained. For example, it is not required that the resulting submodels are connected graphs. It is also not required that the partitioning is unique; that is, the several partitions may overlap. It is further not required that the partitioning is complete; that is, some of the formchart elements do not have to belong to any of the partitions given explicitly by the modeler. This freedom in choosing partitions is needed for a feature-driven approach – see Sect. 6.4. In Fig. 6.1 the partitions of a formchart are defined by bordering. A submodel name is given inside a document label.

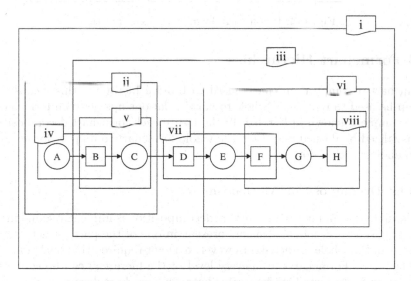

Fig. 6.1. Named partitioning of a formchart

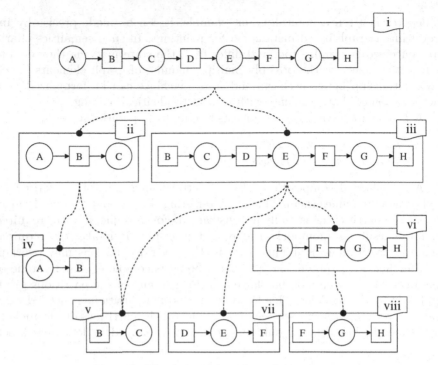

Fig. 6.2. Hierarchical formchart decomposition

6.3 Formchart Hierarchies

Formchart decomposition can be used to build a hierarchy; this means that it can be used to represent "whole to part" relationships between formcharts. An example is shown in Fig. 6.2. In the figure each formchart decomposition is visualized by dashed lines from the whole formchart to its part formcharts, each ending with a dot.

A Flat Decomposition Mechanism

A hierarchy stemming from formchart decomposition is implicitly sound in the following sense: all model elements present in one of the part formcharts are present in the whole formchart. However, it is not required that such a hierarchy be strict. Formcharts from every level of the hierarchy can be composed into a new formchart. This is possible because formchart decomposition (partitioning and naming) is a *flat decomposition mechanism*. This means that it is not hierarchical on its own, because the composition of formcharts is not an abstraction mechanism: a formchart is itself not a model element! The naming of a formchart does not introduce a higher level kind of model. This is the crucial difference from common packaging or leveling mechanisms. Management of models is kept orthogonal to models.

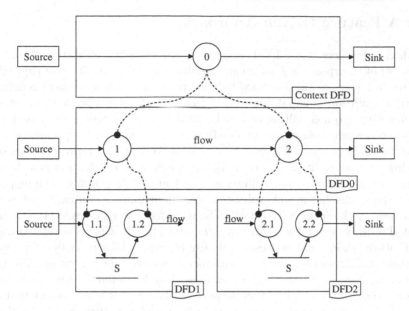

Fig. 6.3. Structured analysis: leveled data flow diagram

Consider the leveled data flow diagram in Fig. 6.3. The notational conventions for this diagram stem from structured analysis, as presented in [79]. Processing elements are numbered uniquely, and a dot notation is used to represent the decomposition of processing elements. We again use the dashed line notation in Fig. 6.3 in order to visualize chart element decomposition. The leveling of the data flow hierarchy introduces a strict hierarchy. The composition of processing elements of one level is really an abstraction: it is used as a processing element again on a higher level.

A flat decomposition mechanism fosters the viewpoint that one is interested in only the complete model. The information given by formchart partitioning, naming, and building hierarchies is merely information for the purpose of managing and communicating the formchart. It can be dropped without loss of specification completeness: for example Fig. 6.1 is the result of flatting Fig. 6.2 by dropping the hierarchy. Figure 6.4 is the result of further dropping the decompostion information. Formchart decomposition allows for maximum flexibility. For example, several, even overlapping, strands of hierarchy can be built without conflict on top of the complete system formchart.

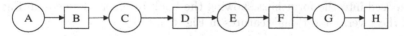

Fig. 6.4. A flat formchart

6.4 A Feature-Driven Approach

Gathering features is a helpful activity for requirements elicitation [180, 157, 299]. For our purposes, a *feature* can be defined as: (i) a condition or capability *offered to* a user, or (ii) a defined behaviour. In [157] a *requirement* is defined as: (i) a condition or capability *needed by* a user to solve a problem or achieve an objective, (ii) a condition or capability that *must be met* or possessed by a system or system component to satisfy a contract, standard, specification, or other formally imposed documents, or (iii) a documented representation of a condition or capability as in (i) or (ii). This means that a feature is a slightly more general notion than a requirement. A feature is a potential selling point of a system; whether it adds value to a system or fulfils a contract [158] is not addressed by the term *feature* itself. The term *feature* is a completely product-related term, whereas the term *requirement* is already a process-related term.

Features should not be described only in terms of formcharts – for example, succinct textual feature descriptions are essential for a good specification document. Not all features can be expressed by formcharts; this particularly applies to non-functional system properties. However, it is important that every subgraph of a formchart can be used to model a feature. A submodel can represent a system subdialogue. Of course there should be an agreement between the stakeholders that a certain subdialogue actually represents typical system usage.

It is necessary to point out that certain important interaction capabilities can be modeled easily with submodels of a complete system formchart. An interaction capability that is offered similarly on different occasions, in different contexts, by several client pages consists of a set of typically loosely coupled or even uncoupled model states and transitions. In our bookstore example we find lots of such features:

- login, logout, and registration;
- search functionality;
- back link to the welcome page;
- viewing the shopping cart content.

The notion of use case can be subsumed under the notion of feature, but not vice-versa. A use-case-driven approach fosters understanding a system as a set of exemplary interaction sequences. Therefore a use-case-driven approach does not encourage the modeler to describe a feature like, say, the following: the user wants to reach an overview page from everywhere.

See how the complete formchart of our bookstore in Fig. 5.9 can be decomposed into the formchart showing the bookstore core dialogue in Fig. 5.2 and the several additional features in Fig. 6.5.

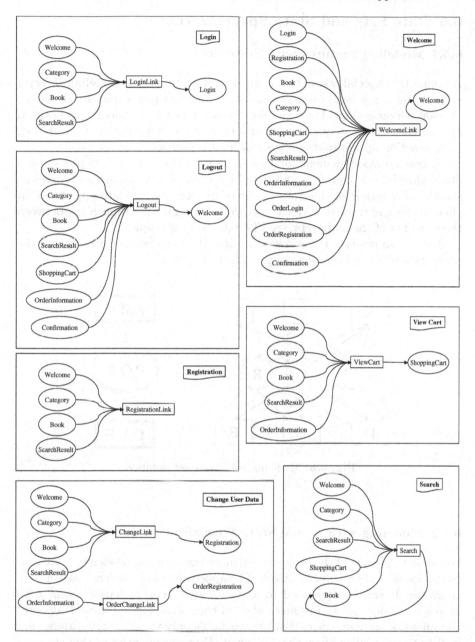

Fig. 6.5. Additional features of the bookstore

6.5 State Sets and State Specialization

6.5.1 Modeling Features with State Sets

An important special case of formchart decomposition is the modeling of server actions that are present on many pages and of client pages that are the result of many server actions. For example, without using formchart decomposition appropriately you can quickly clutter a diagram with a menu-like option, i.e., an interaction option that is offered on many, perhaps even all, pages.

A new notation element for this purpose is the *state set*, depicted by a double-lined state icon. It is annotated by a list of state names and serves as shorthand notation for these states. An edge between two state sets of, say, m client pages and n server actions represents the complete graph $K_{m,n}$ between the elements of the state sets, see Fig. 6.6 for an example.

Fig. 6.7 shows how the mechanism described can be used to improve the presentation of the bookstore features from Fig. 6.5.

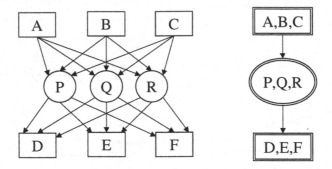

Fig. 6.6. Modeling with state set notation

6.5.2 Modeling with Visual State Specialization

Formchart elements of the same name denote the same model element. We now introduce *visual state specialization*. The apostrophe is considered as a special character. It can be appended to a state name. A formchart element with such a name denotes an *instance subset* of the corresponging state. It denotes the subset of *state instances* that are reachable only via those transitions that lead to the specialized formchart element. Precise semantics of this notation are given in Sect. 13.4.

Consider the example in Fig. 6.8. A system is described by two semantically equivalent formcharts (i) and (ii). The system has two major features, A and B. Feature A comprises all states having a name starting with an A or starting with an S. Feature B comprises all states having a name starting with a B or

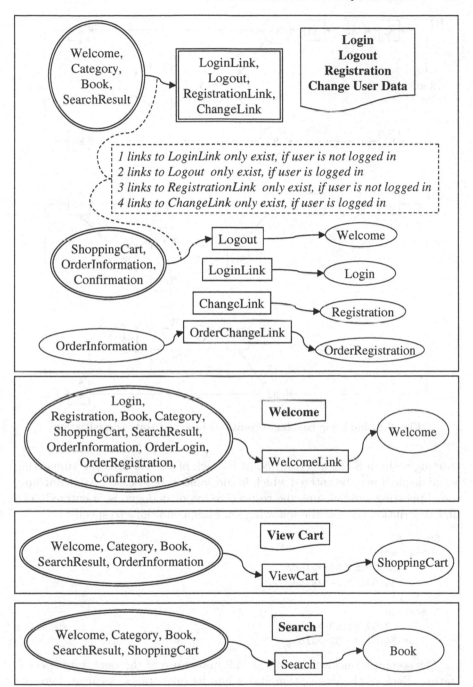

Fig. 6.7. Using state set notation for the bookstore features

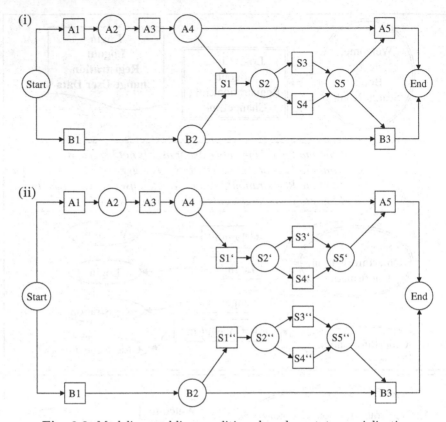

Fig. 6.8. Modeling enabling conditions based on state specialization

starting with an S. At a certain point in each of the features the supporting
subdialogue S may be entered which is the same in both cases. After finishing
the supporting subdialogue, the respective major dialogue is re-entered. The
first description (i) uses the following enabling conditions to specify this:

```
S5 TO A5
   enabled:
        S3.S2.S1.A4->along
   or S4.S2.S1.A4->along
S5 TO B3
   enabled:
        S3.S2.S1.B2->along
   or S4.S2.S1.B2->along
```

The second formchart (ii) in Fig. 6.8 makes use of the new state specialization. Each of the description styles has its advantages because there are
tradeoffs concerning global and local complexity and ease of understanding
with respect to the whole diagram and a single diagram state. The new notation can be used in the example bookstore to model the reuse of the login

and registration subdialogue by the order feature along the lines discussed in Sect. 5.5.4.

6.6 Decomposition of Page Diagrams and Form Storyboards

In addition to its use with pure formcharts, formchart decomposition can be used for the page diagrams and form storyboards discussed in Chap. 4, because all of the diagrams are considered simply as different views or different visualizations of form-oriented information system models. Of course, the state set notation and the notation for state specialization can also be used for the other form-oriented charts.

However, if visual decomposition is applied to page diagrams and form storyboards some care must be taken with respect to consistency of the several chart elements, because these diagrams are based on merging different kinds of model elements into one document. Take dialogue specifications as an example. They can conflict if they are directly annotated in a chart. It has to be considered that a model element can be painted more than once in a chart. If a transition is painted twice there is a potential conflict with respect to the annotated comments. What if the comments are different? A brute-force solution would be to simply forbid it. Another solution would be to consider the comments as logically conjoined. Though this is possible in principle, as one might check for the different kinds of dialogue specification elements introduced in Sect. 5.4, we in general consider it as an antipattern to make use of this option – it seems too easy to overlook one of the transitions that plays a part in a constraint. This discussion leads on to the syntax model approach in Chap. 12 that provides the conceptual framework to overcome notation-related problems like these.

6.7 Model Refinement

Form-oriented analysis allows for different grades of detail. It does not require complete specification. We do not confine form-oriented analysis to a single process model in this book. Instead we provide a set of well-defined incomplete abstraction layers called refinement stages. Refinement can be defined by using the notion of feature: a model B is a refinement of a model A *iff* A is a submodel of B. We now explain the most important refinement stages:

Signature Model

The *signature model* contains the complete data model and the complete formchart, but no constraint annotations in both diagrams. This model is valuable as the bare metal model giving the complete structure of the user interface and the data.

Server Input Declared Model and Server Input Safe Model

Server input constraints have been explained as being related to user input that does not meet the requirements, e.g., the user enters a sum above its limit. Server input constraints have to be replaced in later stages by branches from their server sates or by client output constraints. For example, sometimes the details of processing erroneous data are of minor interest, therefore it is helpful if their full specification can be deferred. A *server input declared model* is a model that contains server input constraints. A *server input safe model* is a model where all server input constraints are replaced.

Multi-User Abstracted, Declared, and Safe Model

Typically, submit/response style applications are multi-user systems. Therefore one has to consider many clients acting on the same data model. Each client has its own instance of the finite state machine. These instances are completely independent and interact only via the data model. Single executions of the server action of different instances of the formchart are considered as mutually exclusive and not interfering with each other, i.e., the data model is seen as accessed in a virtually serial manner. This is a helpful viewpoint for the specification phase, and is fully compatible with later development stages of typical form-based applications. However, only the single server action is executed atomically in this sense. Hence subsequent interaction of the same user with the system can be influenced by the interaction of other users. Such effects are therefore called multi-user exceptions. These exceptions are due to the fact that submit/response style systems are typically based on an optimistic business logic approach. Well-known examples are systems with shopping carts. A typical strategy is that the items in the shopping cart are not reserved for the customer. It is assumed a rare event that the item has been sold by the time the customer finally wants to buy the contents of the shopping cart. This assumption is exactly the optimistic assumption, and vice versa the multi-user exception occurs whenever the optimistic assumption fails. For many purposes the modeler may want to use a model that abstracts from such multi-user problems, and therefore does not contain the exceptions of this type. Such a model, which will be the *primary working model*, we call the *multi-user abstracted model*. The *multi-user declared model* is the model in which all multi-user exceptions are excluded by server input constraints. The *multi-user safe model* is the model in which these constraints are replaced by branches leaving server states.

   The definition of the multi-user abstracted model is indeed a precisely defined term if we make use of the decomposition mechanism. A multi-user abstracted submodel is a model in which each flow condition can be fulfilled without interaction of another user. Take the submodel which ends after buying a book. If there is only one user using the bookshop, then no book he puts into the shopping cart can be bought by another user in the meantime.

7

Data Modeling

Our aim in this book is to develop a precise notion of business logic for submit/response style enterprise systems. Therefore we are looking for a modeling approach that singles out business logic. This will encompass business data modeling and business logic programming. There are many general purpose modeling languages around. We have seen that these modeling methods can be used within the fundamental principles of form-oriented modeling. But they support transactions poorly, a crucial element of an enterprise business logic paradigm. The aim of general purpose modeling languages is to present a unified format for all modeling purposes from the outset. Our goal is in contrast more specific. We want to provide a modeling language optimized for high-level business logic. If the method turns out to be applicable in other areas, then this is of course even better! But for now we discuss its use for business logic. In the case of the data modeling language we are of course concerned with business data. Later we introduce the access language for these models, which is then used to define business logic as functionality.

A data model describes the static structure of the state of a system. The well-known conceptual modeling languages like ER and UML happen to be similar with respect to their underlying semantics, which are relational. ER and UML are nevertheless sometimes considered more conceptual than the simple relational calculus. This can be seen by the fact that naive waterfall processes for database development proceed from conceptual modeling to relational modeling. There is certainly a demand for an explanation why this upgrade for the mentioned languages to the conceptual class is justified. The ER and UML communities appeal to intuition.

We, however, look for scientific arguments that a modeling language offers an important abstraction concept beyond the relational model. We call our modeling language the *parsimonious data modeling language*. Its models are called PD models for short. The language for accessing these models is called DAL (Data Access Language). PD and DAL abstract from an important implementation aspect, the implementation of relation types. A PD model can be translated into different relational models, using one of a set of known standard relational mappings of the relation types. They are explained in Sect. 7.2.2. Our modeling language abstracts from these mappings because all of these mappings can be used for the implementation of DAL queries.

In Chap. 5 we developed the form-oriented modeling method, and we pointed out that the main contributions of this method are independent of the underlying data modeling method. We demonstrated how UML and OCL can work in this context. The main disadvantage of the UML/OCL combination is that OCL does not foster executable specification in our terminology it is not a high-level programming paradigm. This is a drawback since for the specification of form-based enterprise applications, high-level programming is a very natural specification paradigm. DAL is designed as a high-level programming language, which can be easily translated into standard platforms for transactional enterprise applications. The PD modeling language is a convenient data modeling foundation for DAL.

Concepts behind DAL

Since the PD modeling language is designed to be a business data modeling language we need a data access language which is equally fitting for business logic, and which will be called DAL. This language will also address an issue that is even more general than business logic programming, and this is high-level programming. High-level programming is a specification of business logic which is known to be executable. What is allowed in concrete high-level programming can be said to depend on the current state of technology. In our case one of the crucial contributors for providing a high-level programming language on the given abstraction level is the relational database technology with their mature relational model.

The PD model is accessed through DAL. This access language has the task of defining queries and updates on the PD model. In principle both types of operations, queries as well as updates, are characterized as functions. That is, the updates are state transition functions. If updates are viewed as state transition functions, then the type of the return value must contain the new system state. This state transition view will be present only in a very implicit manner in the update expressions. The update expressions rather will have the form of commands, namely the commands update, insert, delete. Besides the new state they always return a result, i.e., the affected part of the object net. The information content of this result is always sufficient to reconstruct the state before the update. Queries in contrast do not affect the system state.

It is important to set these properties of the access language in relation to the definition of transactions as state transition functions. First of all one should distinguish those transactions which never change the system state, and those which may change the system state. Note here that we talk about static properties of code, not about a single execution event. This distinction is omitted in many discussions on the matter. In a particular execution an update command can of course remain without affecting the system state.

The property of being an update refers to the fact that it is deployed as an update, i.e., all code is divided into updates and queries. We will discuss such static properties under the notion of style formats. This distinction can be statically checked by looking at the primitives used in the code.

7.1 The Parsimonious Data Modeling Language

As we have indicated, the PD models can be seen as simplifications of UML and ER models. A PD model in our approach is described by a mathematical object, its so-called model graph. Because we conceive PD model graphs as mathematical objects, the visual representation is not prescribed. We prefer a visual notation which is similar to graph notation. Furthermore we use the textual notation introduced earlier as well. The reader is, however, free to choose his or her own visual representation. The set of all PD models of course forms a language, we call it the PD modeling language.

7.1.1 The PD Model Graph

A PD model consists of *entity types*, *relation types*, and *roles*. An entity type has entity instances. A relation type is a predicate which says whether a number of entity instances are thought of as being connected. Each role *role(a, t)* is connected with one relation type a and one entity type t. The *model graph* is defined to be a tuple (E, P, R, e, p), where E is the set of entity types, P is the set of relation types, and R is the set of roles. $e : R \mapsto E$, $p : R \mapsto P$ are the functions giving for each role its entity type and its relation type.

The number of roles of a relation type is called the *arity* of that relation type. The entity types of the roles of a relation are called the entity types *connected by* the relation type.

The data model of our example bookshop is presented in Fig. 7.1 as a PD model. For example, the entity types Book and Category are connected by a relation type. The role featuredBooks is the role of Book in this relation. Each PD model is a kind of bipartite graph, where the roles serve as edges. However, there can be multiple edges between two nodes: roles have an identity.

The relation types with arity 2 are the most common in data models. We call data models which use only binary relation types *binary PD models*, BPD models for short. We strongly favour BPD models in practice. However, in this fundamental discussion we also introduce higher arities, since they virtually come at no cost, and they will be exploited in the semantics part. In the following we will discuss only binary relation types for the sake of simplicity.

Between two entity types there can be an arbitrary number of relation types. Especially for the cases where the relation type is between an entity type and itself (which is allowed), we need roles to model the connections of the relation type with entity types.

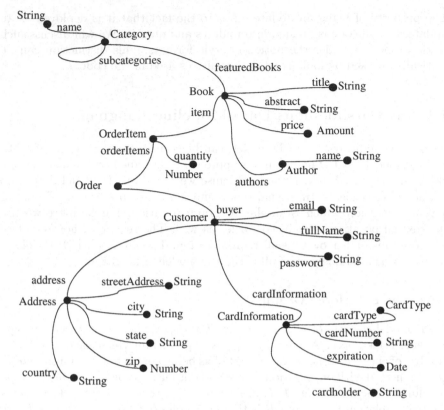

Fig. 7.1. The data model of the bookshop as a PD model

In the PD model the entity types, relation types, and roles are identities; nevertheless we will use names to refer to them. However, in PD diagrams, these names are not part of the formal apparatus. They are just a kind of comment, while we identify concepts by their identities. This aspect will be elaborated in Chap. 12.

The *static semantics* of a PD model are the set of all the possible *states* of this model. An entity type represents the collection of all *entity instances*. Entity instances are opaque identities. Each entity type is assumed to be a *repository*, i.e., a countably infinite set of entity instances. We call an entity instance that has never been used before a *fresh entity instance*.

In each state a relation type is represented by a finite relation between the connected entity types. A relation type can be viewed as a relation which changes through time, which means the relation type can represent a different relation in each state.

The relation consists of tuples of entity instances from the connected entity types. These tuples are called *links*. Two entity instances of the connected entity types which appear in a link are called *linked*. If $(s, t, \ldots, x)$ is a tuple in relation type a, then we say s is a partner of t along a and vice versa. The entity instances in the tuple are called the *targets* of the link at the specific role. The relation type between Book and Category can, for example, be used in a query about which books are in a given category. The relation type itself allows every book to be connected with possibly every category. If the modeler decides that each book should belong to only one category, he or she can use a *multiplicity*. A multiplicity is a special *constraint*. Constraints are an independent concept themselves, which is explained in Sect. 7.4.

The *dynamic semantics* of a PD model describe the possible updates on the state of the PD model. Updates are the transition from one state to another. As one can see from this definition, updates make sense only in the context of a typed automaton model of the system. Then the system changes its state through updates, while the PD model remains the same. There are three important notions of updates: primitive updates, DAL updates, and transactions. The *primitive updates* are simply the insertion or the deletion of a single link between two entity instances. The operation *insert of link l on relation type a, insert(a, l)* means that a becomes $a \cup \{l\}$. The *delete of link l on relation type a, delete(a,l)* means that a becomes $a \setminus \{l\}$. Whether an insertion or deletion takes place depends on the previous state. The *DAL updates* will be the updates that are the effect of a single expression in DAL. The *transactions* are complex updates which are still executed atomically.

An entity type can represent a record type. In this case associated entity types represent the attributes of the record type. The main purpose of the entity type within the method is that different entity types are separated. The rationale behind the PD model is that a record is not represented as an entity instance alone, but as the entity instance together with a number of links that connect it to entity instances of other entity types. A typical operation in the business domain is the insertion and deletion of a complete data record. This deletion is also modeled as a deletion of links, i.e., there is no special operation necessary for the deletion of the entity itself. The operation of deleting a record is realized as the deletion of all incident relation type links which belong to its state.

An *relation type path* is a path of relation types in the PD model. A relation type has two *directions*, each in the opposite direction of the other. Each direction has a *forward role* and a *reverse role*. A direction path is a directed path of directions. Two direction paths are *isoterminal* if they have the same initial and terminal entity type.

7.1.2 Textual Notation

The textual notation can be used for PD models as well. All class definitions of the bookstore example can be read as entity types. The attributes represent associations. Their role name is the attribute name in one direction and the record type name in the other direction. Note that in the following pseudo-code examples we are very informal with respect to names since these names are only placeholders for identities. In that sense our textual formats are deliberately informal because we want to concentrate on the abstract representation behind it.

7.1.3 Primitive Types

Primitive types are entity types, but have additional available operations. Primitive types are part of the language definition; in other words, the language comes along with a set of primitive types. It is very useful to make a distinction between those properties of the language that are independent of the set of primitive types and those that are not. In the case of our modeling approach, as well as in many other languages, the language is in principle conceivable with different sets of primitive types. Therefore this set of types is in a sense like a parameter of the language definition. We often use primitive types of SQL 99 as primitive types.

7.1.4 Submodels

A model B is a *submodel* of model A if the entity type sets, relation type sets, and role sets are subsets accordingly. All relation types in A which connect at least one entity type from B, but are not included in the relation set of B, are called *external* relation types of B in A. If an external relation type has one connected type not contained in B it is called *outgoing*. An external relation type can, however, have all connected entity types from B, but still not be contained as a relation type. It is then called a *detouring* relation type.

A direction of a (binary) relation type is simply identified with a role of that relation type. The role itself is also called the targeted role of the direction; its counterpart is called the role from which the direction *starts*.

A *subsystem* is a submodel with a set of directions on external relation types, the *external references set*. All directions contained in this set must start in the subsystem. Only one direction of each detouring relation must be contained in the external references set.

7.2 The Data Access Language DAL

We present here the Data Access Language for our PD model as a modification of SQL. Given that this turns out to be a viable option, we see it as a favorable solution and an added value to the reader since it simply applies a well known and well understood language instead of defining a new one from scratch without need, like other methods may do. We want to point out that this is not an endorsement of the rather old-fashioned syntax of the SQL language. The syntax of SQL is debatable, but this debate is simply a different one from that discussed in this book. Note that we do not claim that the data modeling approach presented here is proven to be highly intuitive; we assume here that the well established language SQL is sufficiently understandable. The real aim of our approach to the data access language is to deliver benefits to maintainability in case the model changes. For the following we assume some familiarity with SQL [170].

In DAL it is allowed to use entity type names instead of roles. This is very convenient for unnamed roles. In the case of the textual notation for data models we have typically one named role on a binary association. We want to agree on a naming convention for the other roles so that we have an alternative to the pure entity type name for ambiguities. This is quite a convenient approach because we then have a very consistent naming scheme. The association itself is named like the role from the textual format with suffix "Rel". The opposite role of e.g. buyer in Order is named orderAtBuyer. This reminds us that we leave the entity type at the role buyer and go to the entity type Order. With this naming scheme the textual notation becomes a simple and efficient tool for rapidly creating PD models.

7.2.1 Understanding SQL Queries

SQL queries are very similar to the expressions of relational calculus. They can be seen as having a certain normalized form. In an SQL query we first specify a so-called labeled product of an arbitrary number of tables. The labeled product (also called dependent product) is similar to a Cartesian product, except that the elements are not tuples, but records, i.e., functions from an index set to elements according to the type of the index. Then we perform a selection on this structure according to a Boolean expression. Finally we use a combination of a projection and the computation of new rows, giving the so-called result clause. In the case of the use of aggregate functions there are additional steps, which we will discuss later.

The syntax of the SQL query is as follows:

SELECT (result clause, written with colons) FROM (labeled product, with colons) WHERE (Boolean expression for selection)

We call the labeled product of the tables the *initial selection base*.

The concept of structural joins is not explicitly addressed in SQL, but it is helpful to consider it for our own deliberations. Within the selection expression (the WHERE clause) there are expressions which define *structural joins* beside the other parts. Structural joins are expressions which equate foreign keys with the primary key of the referenced table.

It is helpful to look at the difference between the case where all tables are connected through structural joins and cases with different groups of tables where each group is connected within but the groups are disconnected between them. In the first case each element of the selection base is a structurally connected set of table rows. In the latter case a full Cartesian product is only formed between the joint selection bases of the single groups.

The result set of an SQL query is a single table. It is implicitly clear that this table is in first normal form since the whole PD model of SQL databases is first normal form. But together with the fact that the result of an SQL query is always only one table it implies that the table often violates the second normal form. This will be overcome in DAL.

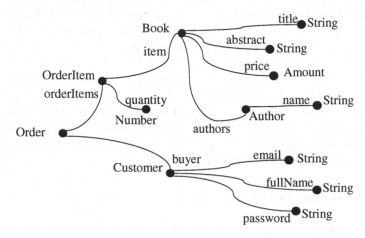

Fig. 7.2. A submodel of the bookshop

7.2.2 Mapping Parsimonious Data Models to Relational Models

SQL can be used for specifying queries, updates, and constraints on the data model. We propose a minimal modification of SQL for our purposes. Each PD model can be mapped onto a relational database schema in the SQL data description language SQL DDL. There are two important mappings of this kind, the *direct mapping* and the *compact mapping*, yielding the direct model or the compact model. The direct mapping maps every relation type to a table and every role to a row. We do not need tables for entity types. This is almost a mere syntactic transformation since it follows simply the straightforward semantics of the PD model. Note that the direct model has no NULL values in the tables. The entities could be represented by an arbitrary type suitable for artificial keys, we choose the type Number. We will assume an unlimited set of new data types for this purpose.

The compact mapping merges relations based on multiplicities. As an input it takes a combination of a PD model and a set of major multiplicities on this model. It maps each such combination onto a relational model. For any entity type MyEntity with at least one single attribute it creates a table MyEntity with an artificial primary key myEntityId. All single attributes become rows named after the roles of the attribute. If a lower multiplicity is 0, then the row can contain NULL values. We call the star-shaped group of entity types which is mapped to such a table a *record*. We call the central entity the *record entity type* of the record. The table on which it is mapped is called the *record table*. The information on 0..1 to 0..1 relation types (and stricter combined multiplicities) is contained in two tables. Each table has a row with a foreign key to the other table. Each of these rows is called the *sibling row* of the other. The fact that the relational model is a so-called first normal form is of course expressed in the compact mapping. Fig. 7.2 shows a cutout of the example bookshop. The compact model for this cutout contains the following tables. They are given in a peseudocode for relational schemata.

```
Book(        bookId: Number primary key,
             title: String,
             abstract: String,
             price: Amount)
authorsRel(  authors: Number references Authors.authorId,
             bookAtAuthors: Number references Book.bookId)
Author(      authorId: Number primary key,
             name: String)
OrderItem(   orderItemId: Number primary key,
             quantity: Number,
             item: Number references Book.bookId,
             orderAtOrderItems: Number references Order.orderId)
Order(       orderId: Number primary key,
             buyer: Number references Customer.customerId)
Customer(    customerId: Number primary key,
             email: String,
             fullName: String,
             password: String)
```

In this example the compact model contains only one table from the direct model, namely the table authorsRel. If we want to get a quick overwiew over the relational structure, the compact model can be represented in the textual format but with single attributes only, either 0..1 or 1..1. This can be seen as the first-normal-form translation of the textual notation. We use a new label Table in order to avoid misunderstandings.

```
Table > Book
    title: String 1..1
    abstract: String 1..1
    price: Amount 1..1
Table > authorsRel
    authors: Author 1..1
    bookAtAuthors: Book 1..1
Table > Author
    name: String 1..1
Table > OrderItem
    quantity: Number, 1..1
    item: Book 1..1
    orderAtOrderItems: Order 1..1
```

```
Table > Order
   buyer: Customer 1..1
Table > Customer
   email: String 1..1
   fullName: String 1..1
   password: String 1..1
```

The direct mapping delivers the conceptual advantage of the PD model to the standard SQL DDL schema. One important part of this conceptual advantage is that all combined multiplicities are subtypes (special cases) of the 0..* combined multiplicities. Given a statically valid SQL SELECT statement s over the direct model of PD model p; given some role r with a multiplicity x in p; then s is also valid in the direct model of each PD model p' that results from p by replacing x by a stronger multiplicity. The considerations here are reminiscent of the Barbara-Liskov principle [196].

This is not true for the compact mapping, because as soon as a * upper multiplicity is narrowed to a 1 upper multiplicity, the compact mapping changes.

In principle the direct mapping is sufficient for writing constraints with SQL. It requires, however, many joins. The compact mapping avoids certain joins because of the way it combines tables.

We offer a possibility of combining the convenience of the compact model with the maintainability of the direct model which is inherited from the PD model.

For this purpose we define the *standard mapping* and the standard relational model of a given PD model. The standard relational model is the union of the direct model and the compact model. The standard mapping contains redundant information. All tables from the direct model, which are also contained in record tables, are called *redundant tables*. The important property that allows this concept to remain executable is that all redundant tables in the direct model can be seen as views on the compact mapping. This means, they are in fact not stores, but computed from the direct mapping. Furthermore a crucial observation is that these views do not have to be updatable because, as we will see later, the redundant tables are actually never updated. Technically, the sibling rows can not be seen as view, but we assume that they are kept consistent with a trigger mechanism. It should be mentioned that there are other possible models which could be used like the compact model in the following discussion.

Realizing Joins

Preferably, joins should be realized by using the table from the direct mapping. A join is a Boolean expression. For example, if we take the relation type order-ToOrderItem (theOrder, orderItems), then a possible select statement would be SELECT Order, OrderItem FROM Order, OrderItem, orderToOrderItem WHERE Order=theOrder and OrderItem=orderItems.

Updates

In SQL updates we use the tables from the compact model. Of course in the case of many-to-many relation types they are part of the direct model as well. All update commands of SQL DML on the compact model can be interpreted directly on the PD model, and are consistent with the combined major multiplicities used for the definition of the compact model.

We have said for queries that narrower multiplicities are subtypes of wider multiplicities. Of course, this principle extends to the query part of update commands – the update commands in SQL DML have WHERE clauses as well. It has to be pointed out that for the types affected by the update the subtype relation is different. For inserts, a wider multiplicity, especially the * multiplicity, is a subtype of a narrower multiplicity. For example, the insertion of arbitrarily many links is only possible with appropriate multiplicities. The different behavior of insert and queries has deeper reasons arising from the phenomenon of contravariance.

However the limitability is a generalization of all upper multiplicities. If a function adheres to limitability, then it is able to cope with the fact that at an arbitrary current number of links the capacity is reached, and it has provisions for this case. For deletes and updates we have the additional problem that the interpretation is not obvious. Does a delete on an formerly 0..1 attribute that is now a 0..* attribute mean "delete one link" or "delete all links"?

Definition of DAL

Each DAL operation lives in the context of one composite object. The composite object can be written with a CONTEXT clause. For the DAL operation, the content subsystem of the context appears as the complete data model. Here we use the fact that a composite indeed keeps a whole subsystem. This inconspicuous rule is in fact the central enabling concept which allows us to combine the modeling of one system with the modeling of a net of systems. This is not an obvious thing if we use a relational language. Recall that the union of two valid states over a data model again gives a valid state over a data model. The problem is though that all classical relational queries change their result because relational queries take the whole extension of a type. With our CONTEXT clause we can limit the query to one system. All outgoing relation types can be queried and set by the DAL operation.

Later, in the case of DAL operations in transactions, this context is given implicitly. The whole transaction lives in the context of one single composite object, a unit system.

Seamless Integration of Result Sets

We can use SQL INSERT statements for queries. Given an intended SELECT query, one can easily define a table for holding the query results and use an insert instead. If we use such an insert clause for querying then we replace the INSERT with an alternative keyword, namely REPORT, in order to state our intention. Moreover, we restrict the REPORT statement to the row=value syntax for the insert statement. This mechanism is not order sensitive and fits much better into our paradigm. The REPORT statement is accompanied by the possibility to mark a subsystem as volatile. Such a subsystem will be deleted automatically at the end of a transaction. Reports that go into a message type will be delivered after the end of the transaction, while reports which go into a volatile entity type serve only as intermediate results. Our REPORT and INSERT statements do not support the SQL ORDER BY concept, since this does not fit to the fundamental data model, where entity sets are not ordered.

The following example REPORT statement creates a new search result for the bookshop. It delivers all books with the author "Immanuel Kant". We suppose that the local variable `result` contains a new object of type SearchResult.

```
REPORT
  INTO FeaturedBook
    searchResultAtFeaturedBooks = result
    book = Book.bookId
    title = Book.title
  FROM Book, Author, authorsRel
  WHERE Author.authorId = authorsRel.authors AND
        Book.bookId = authorsRel.bookAtAuthors AND
        Author.name = "Immanuel Kant"
```

Normalization

The result table of an SQL query can be de-normalized, i.e., the information can be repeated in some rows. If we would like to normalize the result, we have to distribute it over different record tables. In principle, it is semantically easy to allow simultaneous insert into different tables: therefore we allow this in both the INSERT and the REPORT clause. The one additional necessary change is that we have to allow one GROUPBY statement for each such insertion.

We prefer a different solution, which computes the denormalized result first.

The key concept necessary for performing normalization is the GROUPBY clause. For example, in order to receive treelike data structures for the representation of an order, one may use a query for the OrderItem record table, and then use the same query for the Order table, but with "GROUPBY orderId" this time. If the treelike structure has even more levels the GROUPBY clause must be used in a different form for the different records.

7.2.3 User Rollbacks: Nontransactional State

Parts of the PD model can be annotated as nontransactional. Then the state of those parts is never rolled back, neither by roll backs nor by aborts. This is used, for example, for modeling session states and represents the situation in current application server technologies, where such a nontransactional state is used.

7.3 The Transaction Data Access Language TDAL

TDAL (Transaction Data Access Language) is similar to an embedded language like PL/SQL.

We give in the following the abstract syntax of TDAL. We have extended the usually known concept of abstract syntax a little bit in order to make it even more self explaining. In the abstract syntax, we denote identifiers by an identifier type followed by a ^ or &. This concept allows us to incorporate some non-context free aspects about definitions into the grammar itself. The ^ stands for a place, where an identifier is defined. The & stands for a place, where an identifier is used. The scope is the TDAL procedure. By using only abstract syntax we want to point out that the syntax is not the focus; we will elaborate this thought in Chapter 12.

```
procedure  := RPROCEDURE procedurename^
              context& entitytype&
              LEVEL isolevel
              program
isolevel ::= 0..3
program ::= program program
          | report | insert | update | delete
          | SAVEPOINT label^ program
          | ROLLBACK label& | COMMIT label&
          | IF boolexpression THEN program ELSE program
          | empty
          | WHILE boolexpression DO program
          | FOR entitytype& ORDER BY role& DO program
```

In defining the transactional language we have been a little bit more reductionist than in the customization of SQL DML. We explain here the essentials of our transactional language.

The entity type in the **transaction** nonterminal is the message type. The *context* is the separated composite object which serves as the context for all DAL operations in the transaction. The syntax of the DAL clauses is not included; we have discussed DAL earlier as minimal modification of SQL. The

discussed DAL clauses appear in the followin abstract syntax as nonterminals
`report`, `insert`, `update`, and `delete`.

All TDAL procedures are similar to database triggers ON INSERT, but
with so-called detached execution. This means that if one transaction has
performed a REPORT into a message type, then all procedures related to
this message type are called, each in a new transaction. The inserted entity
instance is called the superparameter. It is available within a procedure. One
can imagine every SQL clause in the procedure as being augmented by appropriate clauses that add this record to each element of the selection base. We
can have multiple procedures attached to each message type. This concept
is an improvement over dynamic binding. In TDAL the different procedures
attached to one message type are not necessarily mutually exclusive. The fundamental concept of a transactional language is the sequence of statements,
which allows the consecutive execution of TDAL statements. Local variables
can be defined by defining a volatile entity type, for example a whole record.
This can then be updated at will. Embedded Languages typically have iterative loops, the FOR loops. Such loops are needed only in some cases, since
the relational queries themselves have an iterative structure and have the
conceptual advantage that they express concurrent execution of the request.
The FOR loop in contrast has the feature that each execution of the body
can transmit results to the next execution in local variables. The FOR loop
considers all instances of an entity type ordered according to the chosen role.
Concerning the WHILE loop one has to be aware that the system abort is
a firm part of the TDAL semantics. A WHILE loop will never run forever,
but will be aborted sooner or later. The Boolean expression syntax in the IF
statement is simply the syntax of the where clause. Messages are sent using
REPORT statements to write in the message types. These message types are
typically transactional, i.e., a message is sent only if a transaction is commit-
ted. Non-transactional messages can be used for exceptions to be transmitted
in the case of an abort. Therefore there is no separate exception concept. Note
that there can be an arbitrary number of transactions per message type.

7.3.1 User Rollbacks

Savepoints are used to create subtransactions (nested transactions). A savepoint clause is a block named with a label and has the form `SAVEPOINT label`
`program`. The block in the savepoint clause is the subtransaction body. The
COMMIT acts as an exit to the specified subtransaction which conserves the
changes. A user rollback is performed by the operation ROLLBACK. This
operation performs an undo on all changes since entering a certain savepoint
block in the program. The rollback can specify an arbitrary enclosing savepoint. The DAL language takes a block-oriented approach here in order to
ensure statically the correct usage of rollbacks. Outside the block the label
cannot be used for rollback. The programmer therefore has to take care not

to leave the savepoint block as long as he or she intends to roll back this part of the transaction.

7.3.2 System Aborts and Guaranteed Execution by Queuing

This section is an excursion concerning the implementation of the access language. Transactional applications are implemented on transactional systems. The transactionality is enforced by the transaction monitor. Databases can be used as stand-alone transactional systems. Multi-tier platforms use a separate transaction monitor as coordination instance for the transactions. Note that earlier in the development of transactional platforms, whole multi-tier systems were called a transaction monitor, since they formed monolithic products. As indicated, we now call this term transactional system. Today, the term transaction monitor usually refers only to the transaction service within such a transactional system.

Transaction processing systems enforce the ACID properties of transactions. This is molded into the ACID concept of transactions. The letters of the acronym mean:

- **(A)tomicity.** A transaction is either executed completely or it is not executed (rolled back).
- **(C)onsistency.** A transaction leaves the declarative integrity constraints intact.
- **(I)solation.** A transaction is executed virtually seriallly. It appears as a protected region.
- **(D)urability.** The completion of a transaction, as one of the possible outcomes of the atomicity, means that the transaction is performed on persistent data, or in other words, the changes are persistent.

The definition of atomicity already relates to the concept of a system abort of a transaction. In order to achieve the virtual serial view the transaction processing system uses an optimistic strategy. In some cases the optimistic assumption fails. For these situations it is necessary to roll back transactions. These cases are system aborts. The applications which participate in the transaction have to be able to cope with this case.

In typical transactional systems today, the necessity to deal with system aborts has been alleviated by the system architecture. In these architectures there are inbuilt repetition structures, which repeat the transactional code until the transaction has performed without system abort. The execution of transactions in these loops can only fail for other reasons, such as the transaction is too resource-consuming. We call this transparent ACID, or simply TACID. The difference between ACID and TACID transactions is: in the case of a failing TACID transaction, a repetition makes no sense; in the case of the ACID transaction it does.

Hence in the specification there is no need to specify the repetition of a transaction in case of failure.

The virtual system model for TDAL can be described as a serially executing system with a waiting bag at the front. A waiting bag is needed in contrast to a FIFO waiting queue, since the order of queries may be changed especially when transaction aborts occur. The right order could be guaranteed with respect to each client's requests only. This virtual machine behaviour can be achieved by transactional platforms.

We have explained how TDAL is primarily used to specify transactions, i.e., operations, which are atomic as a whole. It can, however, be used for specifying non-transactional operations as well.

Purpose of Transactions for the Business Logic

The transaction service in a system has primarily the task of providing the basic machine model on which multi-user business logic on shared data becomes possible. The transactions provide the consistent foundation on which to build more complex business logic. Transactions are the business logic equivalent to atomic operations in operation systems design. Business logic features which resemble mutual exclusion are not expressed by transactions. For example, if a customer consultant wishes to lock a certain set of data in order to perform some changes, these changes are not realized as a single transaction. Instead the act of reserving the data, the so-called check–out and the corresponding check–in are programmed as transactions. One has to say that this type of reservation is rare in large systems since it often turns out to be too inflexible.

7.3.3 Decomposition

TDAL procedures can be used for functional decomposition. We make use of the savepoints for this purpose. Procedure names are valid labels for savepoints. Using the name of a procedure as a label for a savepoint means that this procedure is executed attached at the time of the commit of this subtransaction. The subprocedures can leave their results in local variables of the caller.

7.3.4 Application of the Data Access Language to Form-Oriented Modeling

DAL can be used as a dialogue specification language in form-oriented modeling. TDAL can be used to write server actions. A TDAL procedure which specifies a server action receives the message from the user message model, but with an additional attribute, the *user identity*. The user message model is a submodel of the message model used in TDAL. This is an application of the model decomposition mechanism. The TDAL procedure must send under any condition exactly one message with the same user identity and containing a new client page. If one wants to ensure statically that the constraints annotation match with the implementation of the server action, then one can use a TDAL template which guarantees that. The body could look as follows. The templates <dosomething> can have side effect. This TDAL template can statically ensure, also thanks to the TACID principle, that always exactly one client page is sent – see Sect.7.4.3.

```
<dosomething>
IF flowcondition1
THEN <dosomething1> <send client page content1>
<here server output constraint1 must hold>
ELSE IF flowcondition2
THEN <dosomething2> <send client page content2>
<here server output constraint2 must hold>
ELSE <dosomething3>
<here server output constraint of the default transition must hold >
```

7.4 Constraints

Constraints are based on Boolean expressions in the PD model, which are used in certain *constraint contexts*. If they are denoted formally, we will use Boolean DAL expressions. A constraint has a *constraint expression* and a context, where it is located.

There are three contexts which are in principle global to the model, and one context class. The global contexts are the *transactional invariant context* and the *structural invariant context*, and the *deployment context*.

Static constraints are Boolean expressions which refer only to the current state of the PD model.

A *transactional invariant* is a Boolean expression on the PD model that must hold after each transaction. A *structural invariant* is a Boolean expression in the PD model that must hold after each basic DAL operation, i.e., even within transactions. They are called structural because the intuition is that they refer to structure in the PD model, which goes beyond the PD model semantics. A typical example is given by structural 1..1 multiplicities for attributes. They express the conception that the attribute must always be there.

A constraint can be given between every two TDAL operations. If a constraint is given at such a place we call it a *checkpoint*. The pre- and postconditions often found in modeling languages represent simply the checkpoints at the beginning and the end of a transaction.

7.4.1 Generic Static Constraints

Generic static constraints are frequently occurring types of constraints. The catalogue of generic constraints is like a library; they are not part of the language definition. The use of generic constraints is just the use of prede-fined Boolean expressions. Theoretically they are understood as parametric polymorphic expressions, since they use type variables. The following static constraint definitions apply specifically for binary relation types unless stated otherwise.

Multiplicity

A *multiplicity* is a constraint that refers to a role. Let a be a relation type connecting T and S. Then the multiplicities at $role(a, T)$ restrict for each element of S the number of partners from T along a. These multiplicities are called multiplicities of T from S (along a). There are two types of multiplicity constraints, *lower multiplicity* and *upper multiplicity*. The lower multiplicity gives the minimum number of partners; the upper multiplicity bound gives the upper bound. The upper multiplicity can be simply the true condition, namely the *trivial upper multiplicity*, also called *many* or denoted by an asterisk. A lower multiplicity on *role(a, t)* has a *lower multiplicity number*. A non-trivial upper multiplicity has an *upper multiplicity number*. The *major multiplicities* are the upper multiplicities *, ≥ 1 and the lower multiplicities $= 0$, ≤ 1. The combination of a lower and an upper multiplicity on a role is written two dotted points, where many is represented by an asterisk, e.g., 0..1, 2..4, 1..*. We call such a combination a *combined multiplicity*.

Note that multiplicities in our method are constraints, not principally distinguished from other constraint types. This is a major difference to other modeling methods like ER and UML. Each association end can therefore have multiple associated multiplicities.

7.4.2 Limitability

An *upper limitability* on a role is similar to a non-major upper multiplicity. It requires that inserts must be able to deal with the case that the limit has been reached. The limit is not constant however. An upper limitability has special favorable properties with respect to maintainability. Formally speaking all upper multiplicities are special cases of the upper limitability for inserts as well as for queries. The concept of limitabilities is a critique on non-major multiplicities because it discourages for example expressing "a soccer team has 11 players" as an upper multiplicity. Take for example "A certificate requires 2 audits". What if these rules are changed and 3 audits are needed? If the old rule was given as a non-major upper multiplicity, then some parts of the business logic may rely on the exact number 2. Suppose the rule for granting the certificate was written as "if the first audit is sufficient and the second audit is sufficient, then grant certificate." Obviously, the new third audit is not tested after the change. A non-major upper multiplicity should be used only if the consistency of the business logic necessarily depends on the multiplicity. The same holds for lower multiplicities as well. An upper limitability states that the programs must be able to cope with every capacity limit. The upper limitability applies information hiding; the threshold of the upper multiplicity is hidden. Logically there exists a corresponding concept for the lower multiplicity, the *lower limitability*; it states that the business logic must be able to cope with the case that a certain number of entries is required. The business logic is not able to query the value, it only receives an exception. Again, a business logic respecting a limitability is more general than a business logic which depends on querying the current threshold.

Attributes

A frequent question arising from the fact that the PD model is based solely on relation types, is the question about attributes. Indeed an attribute of entity type e is just another entity type f connected via any relation type. The multiplicity at the primitive type is arbitrary. A *unique attribute* is an attribute with a 0..1 multiplicity at the entity type. The term unique is of course not used for primitive data. A *single attribute* is an attribute with upper multiplicity 1 at the attribute. An *optional attribute* has lower multiplicity 0. A *required attribute* has lower multiplicity 1.

Relationships

Relationship constraints are more a pattern. They can be seen as materializations and then generalizations of relation types, see Fig. 7.3. A *relationship* constraint has one entity type R, the *relationship entity type*, and several with R connected entity types, which are called *correlated* entity types. The defining condition of a relationship is that all correlated entity types have multiplicity 1..1 from R. The relationship can be seen as an entity type which models the links of a relation type as an entity type. Accordingly, each tuple of a partner across the correlated relation types can have more than one relationship instance, which connects them. If only a part of the entity types connected to the relationship is correlated, then other connected entities can be seen as attributes of the relationship. A classical example is the relationship between employee and employer. Every employee can in multiple cases be employed by an employer, with different time spans. The advantage of the PD modeling method is that the semantics of relationships is fixed, but versatile. A true constraint on relationships is the *relationship uniqueness*. It relates to the relationship partners, and states that each tuple of relationship partner instances must have a unique relationship instance as a connection.

Because of relationships there is no need for something like an associative class. The semantics of the associative class in UML are not uniquely defined [271]. Given a relation between employer and employee with contract as associative class; it is not clear whether there can be only one contract between each employer and employee or several contracts. If there can be more than one, then it is not clear whether they can have identical attributes.

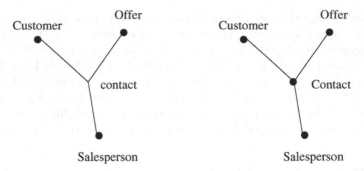

Fig. 7.3. A relation of arity 3 and an alternative model with a relationship

Moreover it is not specified how an associative class behaves under deletion of the link. The straightforward semantics would be that the class is deleted as well. Curiously, the associative class is then in a kind of composition relation to two (or more) instances, since the deletion of either instance leads to the deletion of the link and hence to the cascading delete of the associative class instance. Similarly it is not clear, whether an associative class instance can be transferred from one link to another.

This is a telling example of the kind of serious troubles one can encounter if one introduces prematurely a modeling element solely following an appeal to intuition.

Higher Multiplicity

Higher multiplicities are a generalization of multiplicities to relation types of higher arity as well as for relationships. They are structurally identical as simple multiplicities. Their semantics are, however, that they specify the number of partners, if all other partners in the higher multiplicity remain fixed.

Subset

A *subset constraint* between a subset relation type and a superset relation type states that the subset relation type is a subset of the superset relation type.

Nand

A *nand constraint* is a constraint between a set of relation types starting at a central entity type t. It states that an entity instance of t has at most one link to one of the relation types.

Xor

An *xor constraint* is a *nand* constraint where an entity instance of the central entity type must have one link to one of the relation types.

If

An *If constraint* is a constraint that connects a relation type and a Boolean attribute of an entity type. It states that the Boolean expression is true if the relation type has a link. There is no need for a separate if/else constraint, since this can be realized by using an *if* constraint and an *xor* constraint.

Partial Order

A *partial order* is a constraint on a group of directions on relation types. It states that all links of the involved directions of relation types must form a directed acyclic graph. If each link is seen as an edge in the direction which participates on the partial order, then these links must form a directed acyclic graph. The *partial order diagram* is the directed graph formed by entity types and the directions participating in the partial order in the class diagram itself. It is important to notice that the partial order diagram can have cycles, because the partial order constraint demands a cycle-free state, not a cycle-free PD model, as shown in Fig. 7.4. Furthermore, a partial order constraint only introduces a non-trivial constraint if the partial order diagram has cycles. For a partial order every cycle in the partial order diagram must contain one relation type a, for which the multiplicity at the entity type targeted in the participating direction of a has a lower multiplicity 0. Every such relation type part of a cycle c is called a *forward ring terminal* of c. A partial order p has an *inverse order* inverse(p). For a cycle c The forward ring terminal of inverse(c) is called the *backward ring terminal* of c.

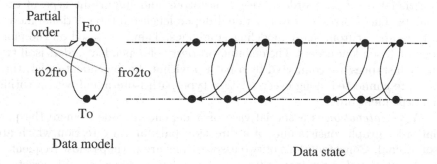

Data model

Data state

Fig. 7.4. A partial order in the data model and a valid state of this model

Entity types as well as relation types can participate in different partial orders.

An example of a partial order is the tree of categories in the online bookshop. The main tree is modeled by the entity type `category` together with the self-relation type `parent`. This constitutes the smallest possible cyclic partial order. Accordingly, both directions of `parent` have lower multiplicity 0. Since the upper multiplicity of the forward direction of `parent` is 1, this partial order characterizes a tree. Note that these constraints alone do not mean that there is only one category tree in the system. In order to enforce this, we need another constraint, which states that there is only one entity instance, which has no parent.

There is another self-relation type of category, namely the relation type category link. This relation type models whether a category is listed within another category, which is not its parent. Such listings are called links, and they are used to make browsing the catalogue more convenient. If we were to put no constraint on category link it would be possible to mention a category in every other category. But we prefer to give the relation type other more restricted semantics, i.e., it is intended that the relation type may be used only to mention a category in another one, which could serve as an alternative parent. We can capture this intuition by including it in the partial order of the parent relation type. As a result, the graph of parent relations and links must form a directed acyclic graph. This example hints at an important property of partial orders: every subset of the participating relation types forms a partial order in itself.

Entity types can participate in different partial orders, and these partial orders do not have to be compatible.

The defining property of a *treelike partial order* is that for each entity type in the partial order all outgoing directions within the partial order have a *nand* constraint.

Functional Dependent Orders

Functional dependent orders are a ubiquitous and important type of constraints. They correspond to functional dependencies in the relational model, but are absent from many modeling languages. They are based on the more general dependent orders. The defining property of dependent orders is: if two entity instances are connected by a path p within the dependent order, then they are connected along every relation type path isoterminal with p within the dependent order.

A *concatenation* is a special case of a dependent order, where the partial order graph consists only of a direction path and a direction which are isoterminal. Concatenations of two associations are perhaps most frequent.

A *functional dependent order* is a dependent order where all targets of relation types in forward direction have multiplicity 1..1. Hence a functional dependent order is cycle-free since it has no ring terminals.

The partial order diagram of functional dependent orders is a commutative diagram, and we call it the *commutativity diagram*.

A dependent order is *maximal* in PD model d, if there is no dependent order in d, of which it is a subset. This is a property of a dependent order with respect to a data model, since of course the maximality may hold in a submodel, but may be lost in a greater model.

Composition Constraint

A *composition constraint* is a constraint on a single *composite entity type* and a subsystem, the *contents subsystem*. Every entity in the contents subsystem must have a *master relation type* to the composite entity type. A common case is that this relation type has a 1..1 combined multiplicity at the composite entity. This expresses that every weak entity type instance belongs to only one composite entity type instance. This is one valid possibility of a general condition concerning master relations, which we will explain later. The defining property of the composition constraint is that for every link in a relation type in the contents subsystem, both partners must belong to the same composite entity instance. A composition therefore assigns whole substates to a single entity instance. We call this instance the composite entity and the substate with this entity the composite object. An entity type in a contents subsystem is called a *weak entity type*. The contents subsystem as a PD subsystem is part of the definition of the constraint, as shown in Fig. 7.5. Like every other subsystem, a contents subsystem can have detouring relation types. Note that the defining property for the composition constraint does not apply for these relation types. These detouring relation types can therefore have links between different composite objects.

One entity type can have multiple master relations. Consider the case where one entity type A is again part of another entity type B. Then the weak entity types of A are also weak entity types of B. Furthermore, consider types representing data records that appear in different compositions. Then one such record type has several master relations of other composite types. The composite constraint then only requires that every instance of this data type belongs to only one of these composition constraints. Accordingly, a composite entity type can have a master relation to itself. This is a typical situation in treelike data structures.

The general condition concerning all the master relations of one weak entity type is now the following. All master relations must form a single partial order.

The composition constraint offers an interesting advantage for of the PD model, namely that the PD model does not need a reflection step in order to capture states of PD models as substates. A composite entity type instance has a complete associated data model, and therefore each entity instance of the composite type has a complete state associated with itself. In this way dumps of a state can be easily modeled.

Each weak entity type has one *immediate master* relation type. The immediate master relation types form a treelike partial order. Note that such an

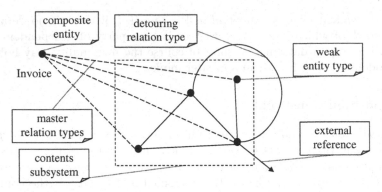

Fig. 7.5. A composition constraint with composite entity and contents model

order does not have to be tree-shaped in the data model. All master relations form the transitive closure of the order of immediate master relation types. In a *typewise* composition each entity type must have only one immediate master entity type. That means that the immediate master relation types form a treelike partial order, which is even treelike in the data model. A *firm composition* is a composition, where the master relation must not change during the lifetime of the weak object instances. The weak object instances can not change the composite where they belong. A *separated composition* has no detouring relation types.

An entity is deleted from a composition by deleting its immediate master relation link. This operation is the basic notion of deletion of entity instances in our method, as we have hinted at earlier. This operation forces all links along contained relation types to be deleted because this is demanded by the composition constraint.

Multivalued Dependencies

Multivalued dependencies are directly analogous to the notion in relational database theory. A multivalued dependency is a relationship. A multivalued dependency is a constraint concerning one entity type called the *join entity type* and two other entity types called *multidependent entity types*. The join entity type can be understood as representing a join. The constraint demands that the multiplicity of the multidependent entity types is 1..1. The join entity type can then be understood as being a single relationship, where in fact two relationships should be used.

Absolute Number and Singleton

If we want to define the *absolute number* of instances of an entity type t in the system, then we use a relation type of this entity type to the system entity type, the so-called master relation type (see Sect. 7.4.2). The multiplicity of t on this relation type bounds the number of instances. A common usage is of course the multiplicity 1..1; then the entity type is called a singleton type.

Isomorphism

The identities in the data model can be said to serve only as anchor for the links between identities. An exchange of an identity in the whole state leaves the semantics the same. This is equivalent to the concept of understanding the identities as opaque. Moreover, this consideration motivates the concept of *isomorphism*. This notion is what is called in mathematics an equivalence relation, which means it is a weaker notion of equality. Therefore there can be several definitions, differing in cases which are still considered as structurally similar. We single out here one especially important concept, which is rarely defined precisely in modeling methods, namely the concept of cloning. A *clone* constraint is a constraint on a 1..1 to 0..* relation type between two entity types the clone type and the cloned type (which are often the same type). For both a group of associations should be defined, the so-called *clone parts*, similar to compositions. Indeed a typical case will be that one of the types is a message and therefore a composition. The constraint holds, if all linked entity instances of the composite entity types have the same number of clone parts. Note that in our modeling approach this means for hierarchical data structures like trees that both trees must be a deep copy of each other.

Inheritance

The PD model does not use inheritance, also known as generalization. Inheritance for the sake of expressing alternate information content is expressed by the *nand* constraint. Inheritance may seem a superficially intuitive approach to modeling specialization of classes. A look at examples shows that a solution with inheritance is not flexible enough. Consider a class BusinessPartner with subclasses Customer and Supplier. Some business partners may be sometimes customers and sometimes suppliers. Inheritance would require now a case-by-case formation of multiple inheritance relations. In the data model proposed here one sees that one has simply to drop the *nand* constraint. The *nand* constraint should only be demanded if it is really required.

In many cases, the nature of the inheritance relation may even be a composition relation. The specialization entity types like customer and supplier are composites to business partner. This by the way contains another hint that metaphorical arguments are often outright misleading. The object-oriented metaphor appeals to intuition: wouldn't it be so intuitive to say that a certain business partner is a supplier? This kind of argument discourages a look for other equally plausible alternatives. In the case here, for example, an at least equally plausible viewpoint is to see the specializations as similar to attributes in our language. The Supplier is then a supplying business partner. And, lo and behold, there is from the outset no problem in having a supplying and buying business partner. Moreover this enables us to discuss the problem of really contradicting attributes, which can come up of course, like say fixed and mobile (which simply means we want to use the *nand* constraint), in greater clarity than if it is mixed up with problems introduced by a wrong metaphor. In that sense one could call our approach an attribute-oriented approach in contrast to an object-oriented approach. There is no problem at all in the fact that the attribute-oriented approach is moreover form-oriented.

Network Messages

A *network message* is a composite entity type that is a weak entity type of several unit systems. Each message entity is either a received message or a sent message. A sent message has a remote association to a recipient, which has another unit system u (belongs to another unit system). A sent message has always a clone, which is a received message and a part of u. A received message has an external relation type, each instance has a link to the sender, which has a reference to the sending unit system. We model messages in such a way that both external relations, sender and receiver, are also cloned. In the sent instance as well as the received instance, one of the unit systems associated via these external associations is also the composite entity. A received message can be either executed or pending. For the unit systems representing terminal nodes of the network, all messages received by these nodes can be seen as being immediately executed. (But not the messages sent by these systems.) The sent and the received clone of one message are connected by a so-called *transport* relation type, which is directed from the sent to the received instance. The execution of a message at a unit system through a TDAL command creates a list of sent messages. These sent messages are connected to the received message by so-called *production* associations; these associations are directed from the executed received message to the generated messages. Only an executed received message can have outgoing production associations. Each message type can have several production associations, and each production association can have multiple links outgoing from a single instance of an executed association.

All transport and production associations in the model form a partial order, expressing the flow of messages. The nondeterminism of the message model is expressed in our view how the message model evolves through time. In a certain state, some received messages are pending, some are executed. One message sent from a terminal node is called an *inbound message*. Each such message can trigger a set of messages, crossing the model. These messages are called the *cascade* caused by the incoming message. A system in which the cascade can be infinite must be considered erroneous, because it would basically lead to an uncontrolled and meaningless system load. A cascade should be finite. An infinite cascade is an unsuitable method to realize active behavior. Active behavior is the case that a system part creates a message at a certain time without a user request. We model active behavior by a dedicated network node, which is modeled as a terminal node. This terminal node can receive time requests which are messages consisting solely of a time and an identifier. The terminal node then will sent a message with only the identifier back at the requested time.

Of course there are interesting aspects that involve the inclusion of this timing behavior into the model, but for the kernel network model this aspect is an external aspect, which is realized on top of the basic messaging model.

Sender and recipient modeling for messages is done in the definition above in an abstract fashion: the sender and recipient have been characterized in a way that is at a closer look an abstract data type definition: the sender and the recipient are only said to have a unit system, not to be the unit system. Hence each sender and recipient is supposed to have a function senderUnit (recipientUnit), which gives the appropriate unit system. In fact at least on the recipient side it is more natural to connect the message with transactions, as we will do now. If we put these considerations in other words, we can say a unit system can be said to model freely its sender and recipient structure.

7.4.3 Generic Temporal Constraints

Temporal constraints are Boolean expressions which compare different states of the PD model with each other.

In this section we will introduce generic constraints, which are in fact temporal constraints. Even such simple properties like being immutable are in fact a temporal constraint – a point which is often overlooked. We will introduce the generic temporal constraints in this section informally.

We have introduced checkpoints as the places between two DAL operations, including the beginning and the end of a transaction.

Timestamp

A *timestamped relation type* is a relation type with a role timestamp of primitive type timestamp. The defining property is that a new relation link always carries the current time as timestamp. A *log relation type* is a permanent timestamp relation type.

Full Immutability

Full immutability is the concept that a part of the model has a state from the start of the model, and this state is constant. A *full immutability* constraint follows from a certain combination of other constraints, e.g., from two permanent associations that are combined by an *xor* constraint. A primitive operation in the DAL INSERT and REPORT statements is the NOW() function, which returns the current timestamp. It returns the same timestamp for all applications in the current operation. The timestamp is provided by the clock of the transaction context.

Immutability Constraints

The notion of immutability comes in two quite distinct flavors. These are expressed in the two types of immutability constraints discussed here, namely permanence and immutable composition. Permanence is in some sense the simpler constraint, since it expresses a notion of immutability as a property of a single link. A relation type is permanent, if each link is never removed once it is inserted. The other immutability constraint, the immutable composition, expresses the concept of a to a composition content model. The content model of one composite identity must not change as long as the write lock is in place. There are many possible implementations of this constraint.

A *permanence* is a constraint on a relation type, which states that no deletion of links of this relation type is possible.

In an *immutable composition* the content must not change during the lifetime of the composite object. The creation therefore has to be completed in a single transaction.

Notes versus Immutable Composition

The immutable composition is used to express a immutable content associated with a model part. There is an important modeling alternative to immutable composition, namely the *notes* concept. The composition constraint requires the composite object to be single-hosted by a composite entity. One purpose of this is to allow the composite object to have sole control over the updates. Since these updates are not possible with immutable composition, the composition is not used for this purpose in this case.

The immutability of the immutable composition enables an alternative modeling approach, where one such object can be part to many entities, which are then of course not composite entities any more. Such a shared immutable object is called a *note*. A model with a immutable composition is transformed into a model with a note by introducing a separate note entity type. The note content is a composite object of the note, while the old composite entities have only an association to the note. There is a computable bidirectional translation between a model with immutable composition and a model with notes. This translation we call the note/strong-composition alternative. In the form-oriented user interaction model we use for example strong immutability. Strong immutability has the advantage of having more identities, which represent the different places of usage of the note. This is indeed in some cases necessary. This possibility is of crucial importance at one place within the form-oriented user interface modeling, namely for the modeling of single selection. This is expressed by a constraint which requires that only one object from a list within a message can be included in the user request. This constraint is expressed as a 1..1 multiplicity. But if the same message object could be used several times, then this constraint would not be correct. The identity of the message encodes not only the content but also the position within the object net. A more complicated constraint would be needed for a note-based model. On the other hand, the note-based model may in other cases express exactly the desired thing. For example, if one has different documents, and one wants to compare them. The note concept is more flexible than, e.g., requiring outright a set semantics on an entity type, i.e., that each instance of the entity type is structurally different.

A generalizing concept, which is motivated by the note/strong-composition alternative is the concept of the *noteanchor* constraint. If we want to use both approaches in one model, we can connect both submodels with the noteanchor constraint and express in this way that the targeted model parts must be in the note/strong-composition relation. The name noteanchor is derived from the fact that the note is connected with the anchor, where a clone of this note is hooked into the data model. The noteanchor concept is an instance of the concept of a view, which we have taken from the important database concept. This application of the view concept has however an important very special focus. It serves as a way to give path-dependent usages of data, giving the notes an identity.

Deeds

We can apply the note/strong-composition alternative to the messaging paradigm. Messages are sent by cloning. We can avoid the cloning of messages, and try to view messages as data truly shared between different unit systems. Messages are immutable compositions. The notes in the alternative model are called *deeds*. All deeds form the *dccd model*. We call this alternative approach deed-based in contrast to the message-based approach presented so far. The use of deeds requires the replacement of the notion of unit system given above with a different notion; we call it the *house system*. The house system has access to deeds in transactions. The house systems share state, namely the deed model.

The basic idea of viewing data as being shared between different unit systems is clearly an instance of the so-called concept of distribution transparency. The deed-based approach uses the concept of distribution transparency only in a very special case, namely for immutable data. Usually distributed programming with distribution transparency or remote writing has a number of peculiar consistency problems. In the special case of using deeds they do not occur because of the immutability of deeds. This is of course desired.

Unit Systems

A *unit system* is a firm composition. The defining property is that all TDAL procedures accessing the unit system state are either in the context of the unit system or in a context within the unit system content model. This means no transaction spans across the unit system content model boundary. It is, for example, impossible to create a join in a query that spans across the unit system specification boundary. The communication across the boundary is exclusively message based. As a consequence of this, different unit system instances have states protected against each other and the outside. This will be used in the component notions presented in Chap. 8.

The effect of the unit system specification is therefore not to enforce the transactionality within the unit system; since the transactions within the unit system are always free to send messages to other transactions within the same unit system, they can always create multistep, non-transactional functionalities. The purpose of the unit system is rather to separate its instances from each other and from the outside. It is the creation of a membrane. The unit system specification fits to our decomposition mechanism. The notion of unit systems fits to our main considerations about good composition mechanisms, because in a given modeled system we can remove all unit system specifications and the system functionality remains the same. It has effects only with respect to future changes of the model. Hence the unit system specification can be translated into a style format. The unit system is however not a decomposition, but an assertion about properties of its parts. A unit system specification can clash with a transaction specification. The counterpart to a unit system is a *transactional system*. A transactional system is a firm composition where the state can be fully accessed by transactions. The combination of both notions is a transactional unit system.

There are two natural purposes for defining a unit system. These purposes are encapsulation and distributed design. Their relationship takes up the discussion on the net as an analysis-level concept. The encapsulation aspect represents the analysis view on the net, and this is our primary interest here. When we first mentioned unit systems, we emphasized that each unit system is a black box, i.e., a single unit of abstraction, conceivable as a single *abstract data object.*

There is a crucial difference to the encapsulation concept of many object-oriented languages, like Java. In Java, the classes are the encapsulation boundary. The operations of a class can access the private state of all instances of the class. This is counterintuitive, since it violates the initial intuition in object orientation. The unit of encapsulation should be the instance. Vice versa this is another hint why metaphorical approaches like object-orientation easily run into difficulties. In contrast, in the notion of unit systems the boundary protects the instances from each other.

Let's consider an entity type representing accounts. If an account would be a unit system type, then a transfer would be modeled by a message flow, which is dealt with appropriately within the different account instances. If however we want the composite objects to collaborate in joint DAL expressions, then we use a unit system which contains all accounts. Then a transfer could be performed in a single DAL query. This situation would then resemble the situation in many object oriented languages. The question which solution is better depends on the application.

The relation types within one unit system are called local relation types. The external relation types are called remote relation types. Entity types can be part of different unit systems. Important is the case where a composite entity, e.g., a message, is a weak entity type of several unit systems, and has in these unit systems the same contents subsystem. Due to the definition of the master relation, the instances of these entity types must belong to different unit systems. In each unit system, the type can have different relation types. One subset of the unit system set is the terminal set which contains terminal nodes. These unit systems have no data model besides the model for the network messages. They represent the boundary of the network model of the data model.

A TDAL procedure of a unit system can be only executed if the superparameter is part of the unit system. Our message based network model assumes that the network infrastructure copies each message from the producing unit system to the receiving unit system. Later we will discuss an alternative model for messaging based on so-called deeds, which will work without the copying process.

Asynchrony and Distributed Systems

Our data manipulation model has a layer above the transaction layer described by TDAL. We call it asynchrony. Asynchrony is a model of programming operations, which as a whole do not require transaction isolation. The layer of our execution model, which enables the modeling of distributed systems, is the asynchrony layer. It is not primarily dealing with distribution, but with asynchronous execution.

As a matter of fact, the simulation of a distributed system on a transactional system is immediately possible. From the viewpoint of the transactional system the messages of the distributed system are messages from itself to itself. Note that the transactional system uses the messaging service, but only for these messages from itself to itself. These messages are put into the waiting bag. If a transactional system executes a distributed system, then all TDAL transactions of the unit systems in the model become transactions of the single transactional system. The distribution style format then implies that there is no isolation between such cascades of transactions. Note that this simulation of a distributed system on a transactional system uses the messaging service, but only for those messages from the transactional system to itself. These messages are put into the waiting bag, and the waiting bag delivers the desired non-deterministic behaviour.

Each received message must refer to a transaction on the unit system. The transaction identity must be part of the message. A message can be pending for some time, and will then be executed. The TACID principle, explained in Sect. 7.3.2, defines a policy which makes technical issues concerning transaction processing as transparent as possible.

On a message the corresponding TDAL operation is executed. The semantics of the TDAL operations is given in a separate chapter.

Remote Subscriber

The remote subscriber constraint is the way to realize remote publish/subscribe event notification. It is important to mention at this point that the observer pattern as a local implementation pattern is not necessary in our modeling approach, since it is on a lower abstraction level. It is rather an implementation of the virtual machine. Between different unit systems, however, this concept is necessary. The subscriber concept is about allowing an entity instance to keep track of changes without actively observing. So calling this an observer by saying it appears as if it would observe is purely a matter of taste. A *remote subscriber constraint* is a constraint which refers to

- an association between the so-called remote subscriber entity type and the *remote publisher* entity type, where the association is an opaque reference to the subscriber hold by the publisher;
- the so-called *notification entity type*, which must be a message;
- a query on the publisher's unit system, which takes an entity of the publisher's type as a superparameter.

Subscriber entity instances associate themselves to publisher entity types. A message of the notification entity type must be sent to each subscriber by each transaction, during which the query changes its result for a publisher as a superparameter.

Reduced Consistency

The virtual serial view of the execution of operations is a costly paradigm. In a system there are often transactions which are not dependent on a perfectly accurate isolation from different transactions. Therefore the implementation platforms offer the possibility to execute business functionality on lower isolation levels. In order to offer such a feature in a still precise specification paradigm, we must be able to specify lower isolation levels, so that the implementation can make use of these relaxations. The definition of the isolation levels is not the focus of this book. It suffices to know that the shortest way to represent the modeler's intention is clearly to assign an isolation level to the appropriate functionality. According to our source code principle, each isolation level is identified by a single identity.

We do not want to introduce formal semantics of isolation levels here. However, we can derive the overall structure of the isolation-level semantics. The main principle which has to be taken into account is the following. A relaxed isolation level cannot be specified as a constraint on a model which has semantically a higher isolation level, if this constraint is not used. Therefore an isolation level l can only be specified if there are basic semantics of the model, which implies a lower isolation level than l. Note that the isolation levels adhere only to a partial order. Hence we see that every functionality must receive an explicit isolation level, and a relaxed isolation level is expressed as the fact that the functionality under consideration does not receive the highest isolation level.

7.5 Style Formats

A *style format* is a constraint on the syntax model, not on the data model. Style formats are also annotated on the data model. The style format's constraints on the syntax model demand that wherever this style format is annotated a certain condition x holds on the syntax model. The annotation of a style format to an instance within the syntax model is a link of one relation within the syntax model, the annotation relation. The style format's constraints on the syntax model have usually the form: "for each link of the annotation association, x must hold on the annotated part of the model." The semantics of a style format is much different to a data model constraint. The data model constraint would not be evaluated statically. Complex data model constraints need for their definition a style format as well for the following purpose. A data model constraint may target different data model parts in different roles, e.g., the composition constraint as exactly one composite entity type and arbitrarily many weak entity types. The typedness problem here, i.e., the question of whether the application of the data model constraint matches statically with the constraint description, corresponds to a style format.

Later we will give DAL queries semantics by interpreting them as parts of the model, thus eliminating to a considerable extent the need to have a separate formal basis for the model and the manipulation language. In this interpretation DAL queries and TDAL programs will be parts of the model, which fulfill a style format. The virtual machine that executes our high-level program searches for applications of these special style formats, i.e., the DAL and TDAL queries, and can then interpret them directly. As we have said, the virtual machine will not be able to interpret arbitrary constraints.

In the same way a virtual machine interpreting a form-oriented specification would work. The dialogue specifications have to be given according to style formats. They are constraints in the general constraint language, but have to adhere to the structure defined by the style format. The virtual machine for form-oriented analysis then takes the constraints according to the style format and can immediately interpret them.

The concept of style formats recognized by the executing infrastructure is a major contribution of the high-level programming approach outlined here. It indicates a novel way of defining special-purpose languages. They are defined as a set of style formats recognized in a semantically defined framework.

7.5.1 Fulfilling Style Formats and Guaranteeing Constraints

A constraint is just a Boolean expression on the model. Such Boolean expressions we may want to use in several circumstances. The Boolean expression is referring to a state of the system or, in the case of temporal constraints, to the history of the system. Constraints are part of the model, i.e., they are themselves static objects, like the other model parts and the whole model. Let us consider those cases where the constraint is satisfied at any time. What are these cases? In general, such cases are usages of the system. We could say, if the system is used according to some non-automatic guidelines by disciplined people, that the constraint is fulfilled, otherwise it is violated. So it depends on the usage, whether a constraint is fulfilled or not. Constraints are fulfilled by system usages. They can however be *guaranteed* by models. This means it is not possible to violate the constraint in a given model. It can be that if a style format is fulfilled, then a constraint is guaranteed. A typical example is multiplicities. A multiplicity is a constraint on a role, let's consider an upper multiplicity of 1. Let's say that there is exactly one transaction that would violate the multiplicity, if called, e.g., by inserting two links. If in the system this transaction is never called, then the constraint holds. Hence the system fulfils the constraint. This cannot be checked statically, because the fact of whether a transaction is called or not is in general not statically checkable. Often we want to ensure statically that the multiplicity holds. Therefore we demand that no transaction may contain an operation that could possibly violate the condition. Therefore it is a style format. It is an enforced programming style; a static checker can keep track of compliance to this style format. That is what happens semantically to some extent with programming languages through the concept of the array type and the corresponding single type. In an array type one can insert a new element. Into a single element one cannot even possibly insert two elements – the program would be rejected by the type checker. The shortcoming of common programming languages is, however, that a single type cannot replace an array in read access. This is overcome in our modeling approach, as we have outlined earlier.

7.5.2 Implication Relation Between Style Formats and Constraints

A style format can be used as a result of a translation of a declarative constraint. The translation involves making decisions, i.e., the resulting constraint can be stronger than the original declarative constraint. This means that we have to consider an order that expresses an increasing strictness of constraints, which connects declarative constraints with statically checkable style formats. A style format S guaranteeing a constraint A is then stricter than A, but less strict than every constraint B that is not guaranteed by S.

On the relationship with the strictness order of style formats we can say: it is compatible with the style format strictness order, i.e., a stricter style format never guarantees fewer constraints.

7.5.3 On the Choice of Style Formats

The use of style formats is almost always intricately combined with parts of the model, where a selection from a plethora of possible designs had to be made, and therefore a certain clearly defined amount of arbitrariness played a role. This kind of arbitrariness is unavoidable in principle. Style formats are in this way a classical example of where our discussion of descriptiveness versus prescriptiveness has to be applied. By using the term style, we intend to make the arbitrariness explicit. One example of the underlying phenomenon will be the discussion on asynchrony. Asynchrony will turn out to be the semantic basis of a distributed paradigm. But there will be a number of different yet equivalent ways to introduce the concept of asynchrony. One question in this regard will be the application of another well-known alternative, the note/strong-composition alternative.

We call such choices positive rules (from Latin positum = placed). The classic example of positive rules is traffic rules. Even if it may appear more intuitive, left-hand traffic is at a closer look an arbitrary choice and there are cultures where indeed right-hand traffic is practiced. Therefore the definition of the high-level programming paradigm as well as the related message-based network paradigm will include such positive choices.

7.5.4 Mutual Implementation of Constraints

Constraints can be implemented by other constraints. A simple example is the implementation of the *xor* constraint by other constraints. We can implement the *xor* constraint by a *nand* constraint combined with an or constraint on the same relation types. Such implementations are therefore a decomposition method on the constraint language. In our operational semantics the executable language is a subset (a number of style formats) of our declarative constraint language.

Style formats are static constraints on models, i.e., the structure. Constraints are constraints on the model states. Sufficient realizations are translations of constraints into model parts and style formats that fulfill the constraints. Necessary realizations are translations of constraints into model parts and style formats, which are the only possible realizations for fulfilling the constraints.

7.5.5 The Relation Between Different Specification Styles

The following discussion of different specification styles for different purposes will be based on a basic business case for the development of software for our system. The customer is the one who requests a software system from the software supplier; he or she has therefore the right to express its requirements freely.

Formally we use only a single notion of data model for different purposes, which in other methodologies may be considered different abstraction layers.

A *requirements-driven model* is a model that is the result of translating requirements into a model. In our business case for software, where we assume that a customer orders a software system from a software supplier, the requirements-driven model expresses the wishes of the customer. Therefore there are no restrictions on a requirements-driven model. This implies that a requirements-driven model can contain non-executable declarative constraints, because the customer is free to formulate his or her request. It can, however, of course contain high-level programs as well.

For constraints, which are in their nature declarative, we can define a standard translation process, which translates them into executable specifications that satisfy the declarative constraints. These executable specifications may not necessarily follow from the declarative constraints, i.e., the translation result is stricter. That means in choosing this translation we make a decision on how to implement the declarative constraint.

By accumulating such translations, we can translate more and more declarative constraints into executable specifications. There are three possible results of translations of a declarative constraint into an executable constraint:

- A style format instance. We have said that such style format instances are statically checked. This happens, for example, to an immutability constraint. The constraint is translated into a style format, which makes sure that no updates take place that could violate the immutability. This is an example of a case where the original constraint is translated into a sufficient, but not necessary constraint.
- A high-level program part. Again, the high-level program part may be stricter than the declarative constraint. It is worth noticing that in some cases the constraint is hardly translated at all, but is used as a check in some part of the system. Many of the dialogue constraints are translated in this way into the Boolean expression of conditional statements within a TDAL query.

We understand the DAL and TDAL expressions simply as constraints on the data model. Being a high-level program, i.e., containing only executable specifications, is a style format, and even a very simple one. It implies that only the DAL and TDAL expressions are used as constraints on the data model.

In our methodology the transition between models of different abstraction levels is smooth.

Relevance for the Constraint Language

The considerations about the translation of declarative constraints into other constraints are also of relevance for our subsequent presentation of common generic constraints. It is quite natural to understand such generic constraints as first of all declarative. An example is a multiplicity. Such a multiplicity will be intuitively defined as a constraint that restricts the number of links that may be connected to instances of a certain entity type. It will turn out however that in the application we want to translate such multiplicities into static checks, so-called style formats, which ensure on the model itself that the constraint can never be violated.

Our general approach prefers the definition of constraints as declarative constraints, so that different translations into style formats can be used.

8

Message-Based Modeling of Data Interchange

In this chapter we discuss a form-oriented model for communication between automated systems, which is fully integrated and compatible with the form-oriented user interface model. The user interface is an immediately tangible access to enterprises systems. But enterprise systems also communicate with each other. If this communication is between organizations, then the actual content of the communication becomes an analysis-level concept. It is about what one organization says to another, in most cases surely in the context of mutual commitments. We turn therefore to our network model of servers which communicate with messages. In this chapter we introduce modeling methods, which represent these networks according to this fundamental system view. The model developed here not only is easy to employ in the system specification, but also maps naturally on many implementation platforms, including EDI and Web services.

8.1 Connectivity of Enterprise Systems

The automated communication between systems is one of the cornerstones of an efficient IT infrastructure within or between organizations. The challenges here are not just the different technologies used by different organizations and the agreement on the semantics of the exchanged messages. A further important issue is related to system stability. An organization participating in automated communication wants to make sure that the use of the automated interface does not endanger the stability of its own system. But also within a single organization very similar stability demands for system communication appear, since the desire is to decouple the systems with respect to failures so that no single event can endanger the whole IT infrastructure.

8.1.1 Message-Based Middleware

An established best practice for the implementation of data interchange between different system units is the use of message-based middleware. In using message-based middleware, systems can send information asynchronously to other system parts. The delivery can be configured to follow different quality of service (QoS) levels. A particular high-quality service can be obtained by the use of persistent messaging. A crucial element of the message-based infrastructure and a key difference to simple remote method invocation is the existence of queues, which store the messages until they are retrieved by the receiver. The queues fulfill two intertwined purposes. First they provide a buffer for bridging temporal load peaks; of course this means that the queued requests experience a delay in response time. Secondly they provide a means of secure intermediate storage; in the case of persistent messaging this is a transactionally safe storage. Asynchronous messaging services are used to build synchronous request/response services on top of them.

We recall that the transaction service enables consistent multi-user business logic on shared data. Persistent messaging now is attractive, since it allows combining independent transactional systems in a transactionally safe manner, without creating the considerable overhead of a distributed transactions framework. The use of a global distributed transaction service based on two-phase commit has not prevailed as a viable infrastructure. The two-phase commit protocol has the disadvantage of requiring the `prepare` command, which has a considerable footprint on the respective database where the `prepare` is performed, since it requires the database to remain in this state until the commit message is received. The persistent messaging service here has the advantage that after sending the messages to the service the local resources are immediately freed. We can imagine the local networks, each serviced by a true two-phase commit distributed transaction service, as islands. These islands can be connected by persistent messaging services, so that transactionally safe cross-island processes can be performed, without slowing down the local transaction services.

The message-based paradigm is the foundation of our network model. The consistent use of this paradigm not only provides a simple and adequate model for specification purposes, but also ensures that the specification is directly translatable in many current architectures, including persistent messaging and Web services. Our message-based network paradigm is part of the high-level programming paradigm.

8.1.2 Electronic Data Interchange

Message-based data interchange is used in many mature technologies. EDI is an implementation technique for business message interchange [109]. EDI allows communication with high QoS, which can furthermore be customized. The interchange is traditionally on dedicated networks, so–called value–added networks. EDI furthermore defines industry-wide message types, which can be seen as one of the most important examples of domain models, i.e., common models for an application domain. A system based on EDI can easily be modeled with form-oriented techniques, and the form-oriented description can be seamlessly mapped to a design for a system communicating with EDI.

8.1.3 Web Services

Web services [8, 51] are an implementation technique for message communication. They use XML as the format for messages; XML Schema is the basic type system [295, 24]. Notations for distributed systems based on Web services are called Web service orchestration languages. The currently most discussed Web service orchestration language is BPEL [291], also called BPEL4WS. It is a joint effort by IBM, Microsoft, and BEA. BPEL4WS is technology-dependent. It describes only Web service communications. It is not appropriate for modeling at the design or analysis stage. Structurally BPEL combines a data flow approach with a process model based on pi-calculus.

Web services use a type system given through the XML Schema concept. XML Schema is only implicitly a type system. Conceptually, XML Schema is a memory mapping schema for a type system. The memory model is a tape with the ASCII alphabet. Deployed Web services are described by the Web Service Description Language WSDL. This language allows the specification of configuration information, i.e., about the data transmission options chosen.

8.1.4 Integration of Legacy Systems

A major application area of middleware is the integration of legacy systems with added systems or the interconnection of previously unconnected systems. All kinds of middleware are used, while no single type of middleware can be used as a one-size-fits-all solution. CORBA is a well-known middleware for legacy integration, which offers a synchronous remote procedure call mechanism among other services.

8.1.5 Component Orientation

Message-based technologies are used by component frameworks as well. These component infrastructures started in cases with proprietary communication paradigms; now they include message based interfaces as well. The notion of component orientation has become a much overloaded concept in recent literature. We want to single out two different aspects and consequently use two different terms, namely shelf components and plug components, for these two different notions. They should be kept separate, since there is no necessary interconnection between them.

There is one aspect in the notion of components which concerns the stability of a component. This is usually mingled with other aspects of component definitions. Components are intended to be stable and self-sufficient units of code, but these notions are generally not made precise. We are looking for a precise capture of this notion and want to call it the concept of shelf components. The motivation for a notion of this kind can be found in the vision of complex infrastructures created by commercial off-the-shelf (COTS) building blocks. In this vision the independence and stability of components serves as a warrant for the viability of stable architectures built in that style. The appropriate functional specification to use for shelf components is the concept of a unit system, beause unit systems have a protected state. In doing so we ensure that shelf components have only one way of communicating, namely the messaging paradigm. The communication across the unit system boundary is exclusively message based. An analogy may be drawn to the separate address spaces of operating system processes. Are all transactional systems shelf components? The answer is no, since not every transactional system represents a whole unit system. A transactional system may be only a subsystem of a unit system. Two transactional system within one unit system may interact with each other through updates on the state.

The second aspect of component notions is a special composition concept which we call the concept of plug components. They are supposed to communicate with the outside world over connections for which they provide a port. They should be plug-and-play enabled by so–called glue to arbitrary other components which match under certain matching criteria. The most natural matching criterion, however, simply uses typed ports. Ports have a type and usually a direction with respect to this type. Ports with equal type and opposite direction match, other ports do not match. The concept of plug components is related to architecture description languages, ADLs. In our approach, plug components can be mapped to unit systems as well. Outgoing ports of a unit system are the message receivers of the outgoing messages of this unit system. They are left abstract in the unit system definition and can be changed by the glue. Ingoing ports are the transactions of the unit system.

8.2 The Message-Based System Viewpoint

If we work in today's system landscape, the scope of our analysis goes in many cases beyond a single organization. We want to analyze a network of organizations, always open to include new organizations. There is one important point we have to realize: the system landscape we are interested in in this case is already distributed on the analysis level. Our whole view of this scenario is necessarily one of a net, not only for technical reasons! This is very important, since it is a good point to train our skills in sensing the different abstraction layers. Think of the concept of a very integrated service provider. That is a company that offers a computing center to its corporate customers. The companies using these services have the majority of their computing infrastructure on the provider's servers and work only with thin clients. It is the natural extension of typical webmail accounts, and it was indeed one of the visions at the start of the Java era. Java started as a language for applets, and the net computer was the vision. This vision did not prevail, for a number of reasons we know or we can at least guess on ex post. Today different companies typically have their own servers, and communicate over the net. But would we have to abandon our style of working completely, if the service provider vision worked out? Would it then be outdated, or even impossible to think of the companies as distinct players in a net? Certainly not, because even in this case the companies would of course be strictly different entities and their systems would have to be strictly protected from each other! It would be the service provider's responsibility to enforce this. It is certainly not impossible to do so; webmail accounts are a good start. The companies would still send messages by email or similar services to each other. The boundaries between the organizations and the messages which they send to each other are hence not a haphazard product of the underlying technology, but a concept of the analysis level, of the business model itself. If we change the implementation, this must not change the status of a message between organizations, let's say an order or contract. This idea is of course easily blurred by the fact that indeed the technical possibilities may lead or even force us to change the business processes; the availability of mail has changed over time the way we do business. But we still have to distinguish between the technology and the processes we use it for. This is why it is an important step for the reader to understand that it is not a concrete technology, like Web services, which is the new business model. The concrete technology is replaceable, even if the fervent advocates of such technologies would not like to hear this. The particular technology makes only a difference with respect to the quality of service it is able to deliver, because this is important for the question of whether the respective information channel can be used for a certain business communication; in this regard we will later see that not always the newest and hottest technology does the best. E-mail, for example, has today a serious problem with spamming, while alternative services for business-to-business, such as EDI, do not suffer from these problems at all. The generic analysis model of our world of interacting organizations is hence our business network. The organizations have a corporate identity and unity; they are the nodes. They communicate with messages, which have meaning to the users, and which are not artifacts of our chosen technology. These messages are semantically what we call asynchronous messages. This basic network model has therefore unit systems, which communicate with messages, and is a hierarchical model. Of course one asks immediately: Can we make this model hierarchical, and offer the possibility that the nodes, which are now unit systems, can themselves be constructed as such a network? We therefore will present the message-based paradigm in full generality as a hierarchical model.

8.3 Data Interchange Model

The data interchange model captures the message-based interaction between systems in a network. It is based on the interface description of the systems in the network.

An important aspect of our modeling approach, which will play a role in the data interchange modeling, is related to our typed approach to unit systems. Unit systems are compositions, i.e., a single unit system is represented by an instance of a type, and all data types of its content model are related by a master relation type. We therefore have the notion of a unit system type and a single unit system of this type. Several servers, which run the same software would be modeled as several instances of the same unit system type. The *data type interchange model* considers the unit system types and their communication.

8.3.1 Interface Descriptions

We call the set of all transactions of a system the *business interface* of the unit system. We can of course create subgroups of the transactions offered by a system. We call such a subgroup a *business subinterface* of the unit system. The server actions of a formchart are transactions as well. They comprise a business subinterface of the system and are part of the business interface. The business interface without server actions is the *automated interface*. A business subinterface of the automated interface is a service interface. Building subinterfaces is a special case of model union, the decomposition mechanism of formcharts.

We recall the automaton model of transactional unit system types. A transactional unit system has a finite number of business transactions, which are triggered by ingoing messages. The business transaction is defined using TDAL. Each business action can provide a list of outgoing messages at the end of its operation. We call the description of the message types involved with each transaction the *bidirectional transaction signature*, and they will form the building block of the model we describe here. Each such signature is a pair consisting of the input type and the collection of output types of the transaction. Note that the list is a static property and therefore contains exactly the message types, for which producing code is contained in the transaction. Taking all transactions of a unit system together, we define the *bidirectional system interface* simply as the collection of those bidirectional transaction signatures.

The unit system addressed by a message has a type and a unit system identifier, which is simply the entity instance representing the unit system. This identifier is part of the message.

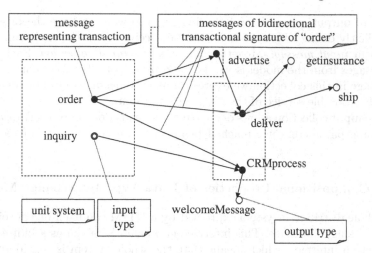

Fig. 8.1. An example data type interchange diagram showing all the notational elements

8.3.2 Data Type Interchange Models

A *data type interchange model*, DTIM for short, represents a distributed system consisting of unit systems by representing the involved types of messages and systems. It is a directed graph with message types as nodes, plus an output collection and input collection described later. An example showing the notational elements is shown in Fig. 8.1. Each message type m in the model is the superparameter of one transaction of one unit system. A directed edge leads from message type m to message type a, if the transaction with superparameter m is producing an outgoing message of type a. The outgoing edges from message type m therefore represent all the outgoing messages of A. Therefore we find the bidirectional transaction interfaces represented in the DTIM. A message type can have many ingoing edges as well, coming from all the transactions that can produce such a message. A message type represents outgoing messages as well as the receiving transaction at the same time. Another aspect we want to express is the association of transactions to the unit system they belong to. The transactions are represented by their superparameter message types. So we can conceive all transaction superparameters belonging to one unit system as a group within the graph, and we call such a group a *model subsystem*. However, in the DTIM these model subsystems are rather only comments; it is one of the properties that these subsystems do not play a crucial role in the semantics of the diagram. There is a certain asymmetry in this diagram between ingoing and outgoing edges. The system can in principle receive inputs of any message type. However, in order to indicate that the system is producing output to the environment, it has to have message types which do not represent specified transactions, but outgoing messages. These message types form the *output collection*, each one called an output type. In the following we also want to have the possibility to explicitly define which messages can be received from the environment; we call them *input messages*, together forming the *input collection*. Each choice of messages from the model is valid as the input collection. By not including a message in this collection we express that this message does not relate to a publicly available service of the distributed system.

The input collection allows of course for a dead code analysis. Transactions with superparameters not reached from the input collections can never be called.

8.3.3 Compositional Properties of Data Type Interchange Models

The whole distributed system expressed by a DTIM can itself be conceived as having a single interface. This interface can again be given as a bidirectional transaction interface, which means that the whole system is considered as a single subsystem in a larger system. For each input method we choose those messages from the output list which are reachable in the directed graph.

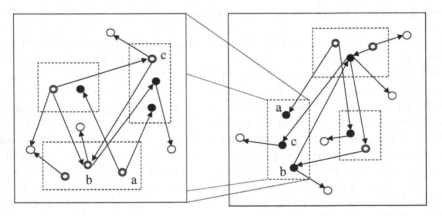

Fig. 8.2. Similar to functional decomposition, a model subsystem in one DTIM can be defined by a whole sub-DTIM

Together this information has the desired form of a bidirectional system interface. In this way we can use one DTIM *a* as a model subsystem in another DTIM *b*. This is shown in Fig. 8.2. The relation between the two diagrams shows that this is a compositional concept. We can form larger diagrams, by modeling subsystems and connecting them with a diagram on a higher level. This is similar to functional composition. The subsystem can be said to be called over its interface by the higher level system. Of course this concept also gives rise to an operational notion, namely for the procedure of inflation of such a node, by which the node is replaced by the full DTIM. This operation is a composition operation; the inverse, i.e., the inflation of a part to a node and the creation of a separate DTIM, is a decomposition operation. Besides these operations one can use feature composition, the general composition method for source code as well.

We call the edges between two messages from the same unit system *self-edges*. There is an interesting aspect concerning self edges: in principle, such edges could always be omitted. This is shown in Fig. 8.3. The DTIM with self-edges contains more information than the DTIM without, since the latter can be straightforwardly obtained. But this information is internal information about the subsystem, hence we usually want it to be removed in favor of higher abstraction.

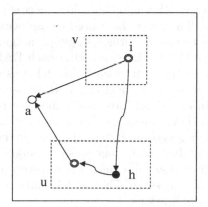 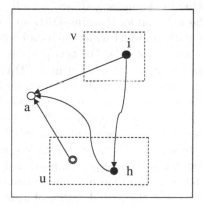

Fig. 8.3. Edges between actions within the same model subsystem can and should be replaced

There is, however, a crucial semantic difference between an interface obtained this way and the analogous interface for a unit system. While in the case of the unit system the parts of the bidirectional system interface represent transactions, this is not the case in the newly constructed interface.

The grouping of several unit systems in one distributed system has a striking intuitiveness. However, a closer look leads to an even more basic view of the underlying compositional structure. In fact one can see the true compositional operation as being performed on bidirectional transactional signatures only, giving rise to the general concept of bidirectional signatures. A bidirectional signature can be composed with a signature of one of its outgoing messages to form a new bidirectional signature. The former composition concept for data type interchange diagrams can be explained by this operation. If two bidirectional transactional signatures are composed in this way, the resulting operation is not transactional in general. This motivates the possibility to explicitly specify such a composed operation as transactional. Such a specification means that on the implementation level it has to be ensured that the transactionality is observed. The usual solution to this is that both operations are performed under a distributed transaction mechanism. We call the operation, which is triggered by an ingoing message into a system, in general the action. If the system is a unit system, this action is a transaction.

8.3.4 Message-Based Modeling of Data Model Access

So far the role of the unit system is a minor one in the data type interchange diagram. This role can nevertheless be enhanced by integrating the data model access into the message-based paradigm. The transactions serving as the building blocks in the data type interchange diagram participate in two interaction paradigms. On the one hand they communicate with each other in the message-based paradigm; on the other hand they have access to the data model by using DAL operations. There may be a need to use occasionally a model which offers a certain reduction towards a single paradigm, as far as possible. For this purpose it should be pointed out that each DAL operation, which is used in a TDAL transaction, can itself be modeled as a transaction. Therefore a natural message-based refinement of a DAL transaction is a system where the control flow in the TDAL program is modeled in a message-based manner, while the single DAL operations are performed as message-based communication with a different system. We call this system the *database node*, because it is basically the database with analogous precompiled statements. These precompiled statements receive only actual parameters at each call, and then deliver the result set as a message. This model represents fairly well the actual design of multi-tier applications.

8.4 Data Interchange Specification

The DTIM enables us to discuss characteristic specification patterns in full analogy to the dialogue specification within form-oriented interface modeling.

8.4.1 Flow Conditions

In DTIM a flow condition is a specification on an edge between two message types s and r, which specifies the conditions under which such a message will be sent. It is therefore analogous to the flow condition for formcharts. A crucial difference arises nevertheless, since one transaction can send multiple messages, even of the same type. The flow conditions therefore do not have to be exclusive in any way. A flow condition is meant to specify whether any message of the given type is sent at all.

8.4.2 Output Specification

The output specification on an edge between two message types s and r specifies the set of messages of type r that has to be sent. There are two approaches, giving it either as an output query, which actually has the message set as a result set and is therefore a high-level programming directive, or as an output constraint, which is a Boolean condition on the result set and is in general a non-executable specification.

8.4.3 Side Effect

The side effect specification is simply the TDAL program that represents the transaction. This side effect specification is primarily designed for messages representing transactions. But it can be used for a node, which represents a distributed system itself, as well. It is then used to specify the overall functionality with respect to this message. Of course one has to pay attention here to the transactionality. In a typical project this can take different forms. One common case is that one starts with a side effect specification in TDAL, which is understood as not being transactionally atomic. During replacement of the node with a distributed system, one reaches a functionality which has weaker but still sufficient transactional properties. This is a very economic method of using the formalism at hand. On the top level the transactional specification with TDAL is the simplest way to sketch the functionality.

8.4.4 Synchronization Specification

Synchronization is a notion from concurrency models, specifically from Petri nets. If each transition in a Petri net is annotated with a type, then the synchronization must be replaced by a program that performs a composition of the messages as well.

Synchronization can appear in purely automatic processes as well as in processes that involve user interaction. In the DTIM formalism the distinction can be made either transparent or abstract.

In our framework a synchronization construct is a constraint. If n message types have to be synchronized, the unit system has to possess n transactions receiving the message type. Each of these transactions has an outgoing transaction of a single compound type. Some data flow approaches avoid the synchronization concept, because it is indeed restricted. It favors synchronization between statically distinguished message communications over synchronization between homogeneous messages. For example, if a synchronization event requires that all members of a team have to send an acknowledgement, this cannot be expressed with the usual static synchronization constraint of, for example, activity diagrams, since all these notifications follow the same transition.

Instead the synchronization constraint has to be modeled on the non-static data content, like is done in our data interchange specification. The data interchange specifications hence express our view that just evading the problem is no solution. A synchronization specification targets several transactions.

8.4.5 Additional Targeting of Edges

Flow conditions, side effects and output specifications are so far described as targeting not the ingoing edges of the transaction they refer to. In all these cases it could be argued that one can give meaningful semantics if they would also be allowed to target ingoing edges. The straightforward semantics is that of a path expression that is connected with an **and**. As an example, consider a side effect specification on transaction receiveFlawReport, which has the task of receiving reports about books with missing pages, etc., and of initiating action, if this seems to be repeated for the same edition. A flow condition could say that a notification is sent to customerRelationship, if this report is from a customer. It could be that the messages from customers come along a different ingoing edge than the messages from an employee. Therefore we could express this by targeting the incoming edge of customers by our flow condition. The flow condition body could actually be empty in this case, since the flow condition is expressed solely by targeting the appropriate edge.

8.4.6 The Operational Semantics of the Data Interchange Specification

The data interchange specification is a special case of the data model for a network. It is a feature of the network model. A DTIM does not have to contain DAL and TDAL operation specifications. It contains however connectivity specifications, which can be in the whole model combined with DAL and TDAL specifications.

One can say that DTIMs discuss the partitioning of a model into a network. A DTIM restricts the possible paths on which messages can be sent. Note that we do not say it defines the paths on which messages are sent. It can be that for a declared message there is never a message that flows. Usually one will require that a DTIM contains only message flows for which there is a transaction that sends it.

The key notion in the operational semantics of the network model is the effect of a single external message. The message goes to a transaction on a node, then the transaction may trigger new messages, and so a message cascade is started, which is supposed to terminate. Messages going out of the network have in this view no subsequent effect; they are outputs of the network.

The second aspect of this operational semantics is that it is concurrent, i.e., in the semantics we have to be aware that the state of each node, which can be targeted by two messages, may have changed in the meantime due messages from other message cascades that are taking place concurrently.

The fact that messages going out of the system could cause new messages within the neighboring system is dealt with under the notion of the union of systems. The message cascades in the unit system form a single message cascade in the whole system.

The notion of coordinating the messages within one cascade is what is dealt with, e.g., in the notion of Web services orchestration. It is one of our results that we see here two major alternatives for dealing with this kind of coordination. The orchestration approach is rather the approach to establish coordination patterns on the message graph level. We prefer the semantic approach, which achieves consistency results by making the individual nodes consistent against non-deterministically incoming messages by classical semantic invariants on the internal model. The coordination approach is only used where necessary.

The concept of the cascade is where the network model goes somewhat beyond the notion of the TDAL program itself. Our network model is however based on one fundamental principle concerning the relationship between distributed and local systems. The distributed systems are in our approach a special case of local systems, not vice versa. Distribution is a style format on a model that prevents certain DAL and TDAL operations that would be allowed on a local model. However, with the concept of distributed transactions, these operations could be allowed again.

A distribution scheme is a graphical description of the distribution in a system model. Within a system model one can use distribution schemes in different layers. The data type interchange diagram is in principle a distribution scheme. A distributed transaction service for example would appear as a unit system in the system description. The distribution scheme which considers this distributed transaction service as an opaque unit, is the distribution scheme that catches the distributed semantics of the system. One has to keep in mind that a distributed transaction scheme behaves like a local system. If one is interested in the physical distribution, however, one may want to consider the unfolding of the unit system in the bigger diagram. Both diagrams are connected by a generalization of the concept of elision.

8.4.7 Application of the Data Interchange Specification to Form-Oriented Modeling

DTIMs can be used to specify server actions. The mapping of user messages from Sect. 7.3.4 applies here. Again, it has to be ensured that always exactly one client page is sent back. The terminal client where the dialogue according to the formchart takes place is usually one subsystem. All client sessions are instances of this unit system.

Within a server action modeled in a DTIM it is possible to query a remote system and to forward the response to the user. Take a look at the example in Fig. 8.4. In this example we assume that the user authentication service is on a remote system. The example shows a cutout of the bookshop formchart with one server action LoginForm. Note that this cutout is exactly the neighborhood of the LoginForm server action. The two solutions below show two different specifications of this formchart cutout with DTIMs. The interface of

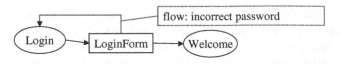

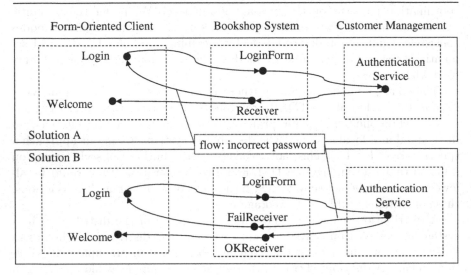

Fig. 8.4. Example DTIMs describing how the login dialogue accesses a remote authentication service

the remote customer management determines which alternative is the right one.

All client pages are in the leftmost unit system, the form-oriented client. The transitions between the leftmost unit system and the bookshop subsystem represent all ingoing and outgoing transitions of the server action LoginForm in the formchart. The node LoginForm in the bookshop subsystem represents the actual message type LoginForm from the user messsage model. The submitted form goes to this transaction. The bookshop subsystem queries an external customer management system about the authentication. This system answers to a receiver transaction. There are two natural variants for the interface of the authentication service. In solution A it sends back one message type containing the statement on the validity of the user request. In solution B it sends an error message in the case of an invalid request. The bookshop then has to offer two receivers for the respective message.

8.5 The Relation to Data Flow Diagrams

The DTIM is naturally derived from the information at hand in the modeling method. We want to discuss the relations between the DTIM and Data Flow Diagrams (DFDs) used in methods like structured analysis.

8.5.1 A Reconstruction of Data Flow Diagrams

We can also represent a form of DFDs within our data modeling method, which is similar to DFD notions in other modeling approaches like structured analysis. A DFD can be obtained from a DTIM by reducing the information content. An example of two equivalent diagrams is shown in Fig. 8.5. This reduction is best explained for a unit system u. In a DTIM the neighborhoods of the messages associated with u represent the bidirectional transaction interface of u. In a DFD the outgoing messages are not drawn from the particular action of the unit system, i.e., not from a particular ingoing message. Each bubble in a DFD depicts simply the list of ingoing and the list of outgoing message types of a unit system, and is therefore obtained from the bidirectional transaction interface by omitting the information about the relation between incoming message type and outgoing message types.

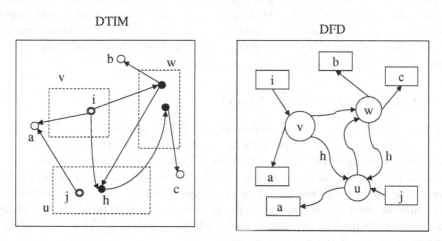

Fig. 8.5. A DTIM and an equivalent DFD

The bubbles are connected by edges, which are annotated by message types. At this point one has to say that there are two principal modeling alternatives concerning message types. Either one can assume a message type is bound to a certain unit system. Then messages with the same information content but going to different unit system types are built by creating new message types. This notion can be seen as including the recipients address in the message. It is in accordance with the semantic situation in the underlying type system. The other alternative is to allow the same message type to go to different unit systems. We call such a type a message body type. Both approaches can be used for annotating DFDs, but it is important to choose one in advance. The advantage of using message body types is that it usually does not double the information contained in the diagram.

The use of the message body types implies that it is more consistent to allow one message body type to enter a bubble multiple times. We call each of these occurrences of a message body type a port. The ports are distinct. A DFD must have model elements for ingoing and outgoing messages connecting to the environment, called terminators. The collection of terminators has the same structure as the input and output port collection of the bubbles. The decomposition of DFDs works therefore in the same way as in DTIMs.

In DFDs one message input port cannot be addressed by multiple senders. This concept has been sacrificed for the sake of a simpler syntax model. It has to be modeled by its own bubble, which has to be redefined each time a new producer is added. There are of course a number of obvious solutions to support this concept. Note here that the graphical representation is not the interesting point. Whether one chooses to draw arrows with multiple sources, flowing together in the middle, or special generic processes, which have always one exit and arbitrarily many input ports of the same message body type, does not make any difference. A notable difference can be found if we choose ports sitting on the bullet periphery, which can be addressed by multiple arrows. The difference here is that the port is always there, even if only one arrow goes in. This is already some kind of bipartite diagram!

8.5.2 Bipartite Interaction Model

A bipartite interaction model following the DTIM approach is the *data pool model*. It is a bipartite graph with one node set being actions and one node set being message body types, called pools here. Given a mapping from messages to message bodies, a data pool model can be obtained from a DTIM by replacing each edge in the DTIM by two edges, one from the sending action to the message body type and one from the message body type to the receiving action. A data pool model contains less information than a DTIM, since static information about the receiver is lost.

8.6 The Interplay of Formcharts and Data Interchange Diagrams

8.6.1 The Mailbox Interface – a Web Services Browser

Another useful interface concept besides the session terminal is the mailbox client we have mentioned before, which is basically an e-mail account for sending typed forms and receiving typed reports. The mailbox client can be addressed as a recipient by any unit system in the network. One difference between the mailbox and terminal is that in the mailbox the sender and recipient within the messages are visible. The inbox can be sorted by time as usual, or partitioned according to the types of ingoing messages first. Each type of message then has a separate inbox. For the conceptual discussion, which is our main focus, it is not important to have lots of features for mail organization, therefore we just assume that the messages are kept forever, in order of their receipt.

The message composer, with which the user can create new messages, again follows the type system, i.e., first the user chooses which message type he or she wants to create. If a message type can contain opaque references, the user can fill in opaque references from all messages he or she has previously received. The only constraints here are the types of the opaque references. With respect to multiplicities there are two approaches: either the mailbox client enforces multiplicities, or it does not. These approaches therefore yield in some sense to two subtypes of the mailbox client, but we do not want to overemphasize this aspect.

The mailbox client is intended to represent the maximally non-modal client as the opposite concept of the modal client which is represented by the form-chart. The two interface concepts are designed to serve different specification demands.

8.6.2 The Different Roles of Terminal and Mailbox

The terminal defined by a formchart in some sense represents the more immediate user's view of the system. The form-oriented user interface model as provided by the terminal client is the interface model which allows the user interface to be specified directly as a black-box model of a system, but nevertheless includes such advanced concepts as the direct manipulation of opaque references. The user interacts directly with the black-box interface; there is no complex mediating technology. In fact this is another facet of our observation that you can abstract from page interaction. In some sense you can say that we use here one of the basic assumptions that today's basic interface metaphor, graphic screen, and pointing device are indeed a *direct manipulation* technique. It is a good thing to realize that such terms like direct manipulation always contain a hidden premise, and perhaps the form-oriented approach has a nice incidental contribution in allowing the explication of this assumption.

The other interface model, the mailbox client, is in some aspects similar and in other aspects a complementary model. The mailbox client is designed to be a good interface for the system model.

If we want to verify whether a system according to the specification fulfills the demands of the users and the domain experts, the formchart is the most appropriate tool. Now only with a formchart specification does the system become tangible and amenable for discussion and negotiation. If the system is only given as a set of transactions, it is not easy to say, let alone to achieve agreement about, whether the system achieves what it is meant to achieve. The system architect, who is not specifically considering the design of the user interface, may on the other hand consider using the mailbox client. Somehow this is compatible with some intuition about user interfaces. Specially trained personnel could be said to be *power users.* Power users prefer non-modal dialogues, since the guidance by modal dialogues is for them of little or no value, whilst the impediment through the modality is a serious drawback.

While the formchart represents the end user's view of the system, the non-modal terminal represents not only the power user's view, but also one of the software engineer's views. If the software engineer wants to explore the business method interface, then he or she can use the mailbox client. The mailbox client allows the most general interaction with the system.

8.7 Topic Bundles

The simplest way of topic bundling happens through business transaction identities. In classical communication we know headlines like "your mail from 2004-03-04." The date is supposed to establish a unique reference; it is a natural key. Order numbers are artificial keys. In our framework we use opaque keys. These keys represent the activity itself. Based on this we give a descriptive, not prescriptive process model. We define the process simply as the set of all communication referring to the same key. We call such a set for a key k the *topic bundle* of k. If a process or dialogue is triggered by an initial message, this message is a natural choice to represent this process. It may however be advisable for reasons of code architecture and separation of concerns to provide an independent type that subsequently serves as the business transaction identity type.

The instances of business transaction identity types can be seen to represent process instantiations. The fact that this concept lives on the level of coding guidelines adds a considerable amount of flexibility to the process support offered by the fundamental DTIM framework, and shows also that process paradigms live on a different conceptual level than process-enabling technology. Each process paradigm is a different topic-bundling approach, and since the possibilities for different topic-bundling technologies is not bounded, there is no limit to the possibilities of process technologies.

As an example, a concrete process technology could support the branching into subprocesses and their later reunion, another paradigm could only allow for processes that follow a finite state machine paradigm. In a third process paradigm the one subprocess could split from one main process and later rejoin a different main process, and so forth. The fundamental insight, which could perhaps even help the process modeling area to consolidate their modeling paradigms, is that a specific process model should be a module, implemented on top of a general model that enables processes, but which does not restrict the process notion in itself.

9

A Descriptive Approach

Concrete software management differs in different projects due to the problem domain, project scope, and business culture. This has to be taken into account if concrete software development activities are discussed. We do not prescribe a software process in this book. Instead we propose artifacts and argue how they can be exploited to improve system development activities. Of course, the different degree of formality of the different artifacts as well as the proposed composition mechanism hint at a process like intuitive succession of diagrams from informal to formal, but it is important to realize that this is by no means necessary. Since the semantics of the diagrams is completely independent from any process definition, the diagram is basically neutral with respect to its use in a process of whatever kind. Therefore we coin the notion of *artifact orientation* that can be exploited for empowering developers and improving the agility of software projects.

This chapter discusses several topics that are related to software process in one sense or another. In Sect. 9.1 we discuss two possible viewpoints to software processes: descriptiveness vs. prescriptiveness. In Sect. 9.2 we discuss problems of metaphors in software engineering. Sect. 9.6 introduces artifact orientation and explains how it can be considered as the core of an ultra-lightweight software process. Visual modeling has been a widely recognized concept in the recent past. We explain our position to this concept in Sect. 9.5. Model-based software development has been a central topic within the software engineering community; this is documented by terms like complete specification, executable specification, forward engineering, reverse engineering, and recently model-driven architecture. High-level programming is our defined viewpoint with respect to all this, which is further discussed in Sect. 9.7. The chapter finishes with a discussion of advanced systems modeling approaches in Sect. 9.8.

But before all this we first have to explain our general notion of descriptiveness, our opinion about modeling in general, and our opinion about the role of knowledge in modern software engineering organizations.

Descriptiveness in General

It is not obvious how to discuss *applied sciences* against the background of established philosophies of science [47]. Nonetheless each applied scientist has the challenging duty to define his or her personal working moral. Is an applied scientist a person who uses scientific knowledge to solve practical problems? Is he or she an inventor, an innovator, a troubleshooter? Aren't these the tasks of an engineer? So what is the difference between an applied scientist and an engineer?

We assume that in applied sciences an object of investigation has a practical problem side and a practical solution side. However, an object of investigation should be a family of problems and solutions that are dependent on several driving forces rather than a single completely defined problem and its best solution. Then, given an object of investigation, a descriptive approach ideally targets the systematization of the problem domain and solution domain under consideration as completely as possible – a challenging demand, admittedly. If it is possible to identify a problem domain, overemphasizing a single problem is considered an antipattern by the descriptive approach, though in practice rather concrete problems – accompanied by hype – are often the subject of major interest. For example, a particular notation like the XML Query Language is not abstract enough, and a discussion too close to the syntax would be considered unsatisfactory or too low-level from a descriptive viewpoint. Compare this, for example, with the notion of first-order logic, which is for mathematicians a class of logics, rather than one particular syntactical representative.

We have tried to apply this principle, for example, in the definition of the form-oriented artifacts. First, the identification of the two-staged interaction paradigm, as well as the notions of the form-oriented information system model and the user message system model are considered the real contributions of form-oriented analysis. Though very important, the several concrete proposed diagrams, i.e., the formchart, the form storyboard, the page diagram etc., are considered secondary concepts. From the viewpoint of descriptiveness, form-oriented analysis should not be used to restrict the modeler. If desired, he or she should even be free to design – on the basis of the proposed artifacts – new artifacts that fit his or her tasks best. We should only try to convince a developer to learn the details of a complicated artificial language if this language has an observational behavior and is capable of completely describing the required product.

Quality of Models

It is sometimes said that abstraction is the core characteristic of modeling. In this context abstraction is explained as the omission of details. However, this is an unsatisfactory explanation that needs elaboration – in many cases it just misses the point. For example, a mathematical model of an airplane abstracts from its internals, i.e., the seats, the coffee machine, and even its engine. The mathematical model may allow to calculate the flight characteristics of the airplane. However, this is really not due to the omission of the details of the internals, it is due to the mapping of the airplane's basic characteristics into an appropriate algebra. This means that modeling is sometimes not in the first place abstraction but targeted translation. The mentioned details are not on a finer granularity in this case, but without relevance to the problem. Consider a scaled wooden model of the airplane. Is the different size an omitted detail or is it a translation into a different medium? Assume we would only model the wing, be it as a mathematical or scaled down physical model, because, say, only the wing matters for some questions, e.g., the produced lift. Would we call it still a model of an airplane? We loosely identify the following different kinds of models – the list is not comprehensive:

- *Specifying models.* Models representing the result of requirements elicitation: amortization plans, building plans, class diagrams, formcharts.
- *Insight models.* Informal models encapsulating system theories that cannot, at least yet, be otherwise expressed formally:
  - Lasswell's formula of mass communication [193]: "Who says what in which channel to whom with what effect?"
  - Brook's law [32]: "Adding manpower to a late software project makes it later."
- *Statistical models.* A survey is a model of the population: measures on the random sample, e.g., the arithmetic mean, serve as estimators for population parameters, in the example the population mean.
- *Simulation models.* Models you can calculate with in order to predict system characterics: Monte Carlo simulation, linear programming, Markov chains, queuing theory, free-body diagrams, fluid dynamics.

Software modeling is on the level of specifying models. Software models are models of the software, since the software is the specified object. Prominent software metrics like COCOMO (Constructive Cost Model) [27] and FPA (Function Point Analysis) [159, 183] lie in a gray area somewhere between insight models and simulation models.

Software Engineering Knowledge

A core asset of software engineering organizations is knowledge [101]. This is true not only for software engineering organizations but for engineering organizations in general. The knowledge of an engineering organization is a body of distributed individual know-how. But organizational knowledge has another very important aspect that is a *dynamic* aspect: organizational knowledge is a permanent process that is kept alive by social interaction. Knowledge is communicated between individuals, some individuals are learning, others are teaching. This means engineering organizations are learning organizations, even without the need for adaptation to a changing environment. Traditional learning in engineering organizations has two main characteristics:

- ad hoc word-of-mouth;
- hierarchical tendency.

The vast majority of knowledge is communicated ad hoc word-of-mouth. Ad hoc means that the knowledge is transferred on demand whenever it is needed to get a given task done in the midst of a running project. Modern knowledge management approaches make concrete proposals on how to overcome this state of learning in action. But for some concepts a word-of-mouth knowledge transfer may be the significantly most efficient way. Consequentially, an ad hoc word-of-mouth knowledge transfer is sometimes deliberately chosen, i.e., it is not in place just because of a lack of maturity. It is more challenging to characterize the conceptual level needed to make knowledge permanent and communicable than to propose document file formats and process formats for such knowledge transfer. Despite systematic knowledge offensives like the SWEBOK [3] guide to the software engineering body of knowledge or the Software Technology Review [115], it cannot be neglected that important areas of software engineering, like software/system architecture or software/system performance are still far from a systematic understanding, and that existing know-how in these areas is still not amenable to systematization.

9.1 Descriptiveness, Prescriptiveness, and the Software Process

As a starting point for this discussion, consider the following quote from Winston W. Royce, in the introduction of his seminal paper [266]:

> I am going to describe my personal views about managing software development. I have had various assignments during the past nine years, mostly concerned with the development of software packages for spacecraft mission planning, commanding and post-flight analysis. In these assignments I have experienced different degrees of success with respect to arriving at an operational state, on-time, and within costs. I have become prejudiced by my experiences and I am going to relate some of these prejudices in this presentation.

A software process can be intended to be descriptive or prescriptive. A software process can actually be used in a descriptive or prescriptive manner in a concrete software project. Consider a purely stagewise software process model [21]. Such a stagewise software process model defines the software project as a sequence of phases, i.e., the process model does not encompass notions like iteration or preliminary program design. Applying this stagewise process model naively to a software project would mean: it is forbidden to do any design during the analysis phase; it is forbidden to do any coding during the design or analysis phase. Such a process can indeed be sensible, e.g., if the process captures special knowledge about a repeatable project in a concrete application domain. However, in general a project managed in such a strict stagewise way can hardly be successful, because in general there is a need for early design and early coding accompanying other activities. But the stagewise process model is not a hypothetical process; it is used successfully in everyday software projects. How is this possible? Because it is not used in a prescriptive manner. It is used rather as the project manager's viewpoint on the project in these cases; it is simply not understood as a device to reduce the developer's activities. However, it is used to control the activities: the end of the phases are milestones that represent the important project estimation and planning efforts.

If a stagewise model is applied successfully, it allows developers to do things differently as long as the milestones are fulfilled: of course the developers are allowed to consider design and to code early on, if they feel that it is necessary to improve the quality of the product or to speed up the project. Now, the project management might want to take control of the observed proven activities in a project, in order to exploit best practices and to avoid common errors. For this reason the project management will refine the process model. Now the delivery of product portions at fixed dates is negotiated between the project management and the developers, as is the compliance to work patterns. The usage of a refined process model only makes sense if the practices contained are actually employed, i.e., if their accordance is controlled.

However, even with a refined process model it would be wrong to prevent developers doing things differently if necessary. The project management that might want to take control of all activities in a software project may ends up in planning tasks with a granularity of an hour. In the resulting process there is no longer any space for using ones own initiative any more and the process has become prescriptive again. We use the term *micro management* for this.

A software process can be intended to be descriptive or prescriptive. A descriptive software process encapsulates observations about practices that worked. A truly descriptive software process is really a software process *model*. A prescriptive software process is designed from scratch to be used as a normative reference in a software project. Both a descriptive and a prescriptive software process can be used in either a descriptive or prescriptive way. A descriptive model should not be used without need in a prescriptive manner.

Using a process model as a normative reference makes sense for such prescriptive processes that are accompanied by an assessment model and available assessment mechanism. This is true for the Capability Maturity Model (CMM) [244, 245] and ISO 9001 [164, 166, 243] as well as for the IT Infrastructure Library (ITIL) [44, 239] – to give an example from the domain of IT service management. It is possible to get a judgment from a certified consultant that states if a concrete process is in accordance with the defined practices. We call such process models *employable process models*.

Batteries not included: without an assessment mechanism it is hard for project managers to decide if their project really follows a given process. Still, in our opinion a merely prescriptive process can be exploited as a knowledge base of good practices. But care should be taken as there is another source for learning about good practices: a competitor's successful project [311]. In opposition to verbose process models, *strategic benchmarking* is really used in practice. It has to be noted that the introduction of a new process model sometimes actually does not have the purpose to improve process quality but to take control of an otherwise rather chaotic process.

9.2 Metaphor A Posteriori

Worse than prejudices that are the result of project experience – see the quotation at the beginning of Sect. 9.1 – are prejudices that are *not at all* the result of experience.

In the discipline of software development metaphors are pervasive: engineering, architecture, design, objects, agents, actors, contracts, services, desktops. The metaphors used in software development are proportional analogies: the application of the name of one thing to another is based on proportion [13]. A metaphor can be a brilliant learning device [14]:

> *Accordingly, it is metaphor that is in the highest degree instructive. It follows, then, that for style and reasoning alike, that in order to be lively they must give us rapid information. What we like are those that convey information as fast as they are stated – so long as we did not have the knowledge in advance – or that our minds lag only a little behind. With the latter two kinds there is some process of learning.*

However, sometimes metaphors are not used merely as cognitive devices. Sometimes a metaphor is used as the justification, driving force, and – last but not least – as the benchmark of a whole scientific community or subcommunity.

Metaphors are used in poetry [13] and rhetoric [14]. Using metaphors in systematic science is risky. Sometimes a metaphor is more invented than constructed. Sometimes a metaphor is much too plausible. Sometimes the proportion established by a metaphor is too weak: the two related things are only loosely coupled by the metaphor. An example for a metaphor that is both rather invented and too weak is the rhapsodic reference of the design patterns community to the architecture pattern language of Christopher Alexander [6]. We quote from Christopher Alexander's keynote speech at the OOPSLA conference in 1996 [7]:

*"Now – my understanding of what you are doing with pat-
terns...It is a kind of neat format and this is fine. The pattern language that we began did have other features, and I
don't know whether those have translated into your discipline. I mean there was a root behind the whole thing – a
continuous mode of preoccupation with under what circumstances is the environment good. In our field that means
something."*

Actually the design patterns approach has been partly misleading. Basically design patterns target software maintainability and reusability by foster-
ing high cohesion and low coupling. The problem is that the allowed solution
domain is narrowed to the world of mere software components. In practice, design activity is different. Design targets the solution of a lot of non-functional
system requirements like performance, scalability, system maintainability, security and so on. Subject to design activity are systems consisting of hardware
and deployed software. This leads directly to the architecture metaphor of
software engineering in general. It is sometimes said that the software system
designer crafts a system blueprint, and that therefore software system designers correspond to architects, because architects craft building plans. We
wonder if the latter is true. What is actually the task of an architect? What
is the task of a civil engineer and what is the task of a structural engineer?
Is the proper task of an architect – compared with software development –
rather similar to requirements elicitation than to system design? We do not
want delve into this topic, this means we do not want to improve or refine the
software architecture metaphor. We just want to point out its weakness.

Similarly, we often observe that a justification for a concrete software technology is plausible at first sight but is actually spurious. We provide a common
misconception about LDAP as a concrete example. The plausible motivation
for why the usage of Lightweight Directory Access Protocol (LDAP) should
bring the added value is consolidation of business data, derived from the X.500
standard. But it is only a vision, and for this envisioned application LDAP has
no unique selling points above other technologies, instead it has clear drawbacks, e.g., no relational query language. However, one important situation
in which the decision to use LDAP is made is when choosing LDAP as an
alternative to NIS+, because LDAP is compatible with SSL. The decision is
made by technical staff, and the integrated data are account metadata. This
decision is based on a hard reason, a technical feature missing in alternative
technologies. LDAP is also used as a naming service for configuration data.
Even if there are projects that use LDAP for the consolidation of business
data, it is not clear whether in these cases the choice is good.

The origins of an exaggerated claim are not always as easy to detect. If
the origin of a concept is industry, a claim sometimes stems from a market-
ing strategy. If the origin of a concept is academia, a claim sometimes stems
from a silver bullet [33] vision. Invalid claims lead to misconceptions. A mis-

conception has its impact. In industry a misconception is rather immediately observable: *project delay*. In academia the misconception has rather longitudinal implications: (i) job transition traumas with respect to education, and (ii) starvation of scientific subcommunities with respect to research.

9.3 On Desktop Metaphors

Desktop metaphors do not necessarily support ownership for the user, they rather provide a virtual world for the user – under ownership of work products, in our case information, we understand the idea that the user is in charge of manipulating the work products freely. It is certainly no exaggeration to say that metaphor-heavy approaches, involving animated and talking cartoons [221], bring applications a step nearer to computer games. And computer games are a proof by example that non-modality does not at all imply ownership or empowerment. Indeed computer games have gone a considerable way towards non-modality of their interfaces, expressing options by physical or behavioral metaphors like grabbing things in three-dimensional space etc. Yet the essence of the game is, of course, that the user is nevertheless challenged by the virtual environment. Some metaphor-driven office tools are no less challenging to the user than these games.

At this point we want to anticipate our discussion about an integrated source code model in Chap. 12 and to state our opinion that the use of physical metaphors in professional programming languages does appear implausible. Metaphors originally targeted the computer illiterate. A programmer using a professional programming language should be assumed to be a power user. The power user needs semantic transparency as is offered by ownership of information. Catchy phrases covering some of these aspects might be:

* *The power user does not need metaphors.*
* *The power user needs ownership of his or her work products.*

We try to empower the reader by providing an ownership-oriented paradigm here, and we do this with the aim that the reader will be better able to provide appropriate metaphors to the end user. Therefore our approaches target the power user as the reader, and do not primarily present metaphors.

That said, it may of course be no wonder that the form concept in form-oriented analysis, which may be conceived as being similar to a metaphor, tries to reconcile these aspects. The form-oriented metaphor presented in this book is a metaphor not for the power user, but for the end user, which is supposed to be rather the reader's customer. The form-oriented metaphor can indeed be seen as being especially suited to provide ownership of work products even to the end user. This is indeed a rare property of a metaphor and makes the form-oriented metaphor especially valuable.

Drag and drop as such and object orientation as such do not support ownership of the work product. This difference can be tied to the fact that the form-oriented metaphor keeps information as information, adding only intuition about interaction and persistency questions. The object-oriented metaphor and the drag and drop metaphor in contrast want to build a virtual world for manipulating information, but rather end up in a mix between virtual physics and visualized information. This intermediate virtual world is fully arbitrary and therefore differs in all elaborations of the paradigm. No two object-oriented paradigms are the same. If it comes to the details, therefore, the novel user simply cannot rely on intuition, since he or she has no intuition of this novel environment.

9.4 On Real-World Modeling

Semantic data modeling [49, 152] and object-oriented analysis [279] are centered around the same basic notion, so-called real-world modeling. The real-world modeling approach proposes that data modeling should find and describe real-world objects. It is assumed that this way modeling becomes easier and leads to more stable models.

In this section we want to argue that a data modeling approach can be successful without referring to a real-world modeling metaphor. In the first place we want to pursue a focus shift with respect to data modeling: it is not the task of data modeling to describe a real-world cutout; it is the task of data modeling to describe data stored in an information system. A concrete model does not have to be judged with respect to undisputable facts of the real world; it must be judged with respect to its appropriateness for the tasks of the relevant information system.

Software models, if seen as specifying models, are models of the installed system. The latter was defined as the system running the software. We specify the functionality of the running software and not, like in object-oriented analysis, the functions of the things which are managed with the software. The models which we call in compliance with widespread terminology data models are at the first instance specifications of a data base as a running system. The specification can then be seen as specification of the business data, which has to comply with the data model in order to be processed. The specification is defined as the specification of the running software in contrast to the software as pure information. It is a valuable, cost saving fact that we can assess the compliance of a proposed system before this system is online or even running. But this fact does not force us to change the definition of specification. The data model is sometimes part of the running software, like in databases, where it is often called metadata. Concerning the relation of data and data model, it is correct to say that the data model is the *type specification* of the data or, in a more reductionist terminology, the model is a single compound type, the type of the data. An analysis model is in our terminology a pure black box model of the system functionality whereas a design model would be a white box model.

Risks of Real-World Modeling Approaches

A real-world modeling metaphor is not an undisputable precondition for data modeling. On the contrary, it is necessary to mention that a real-world metaphor has its risks, too. On the one hand, a data modeler might be confused about the concept of real-world object, resulting in bafflement rather than guidance. On the other hand, a modeler might find data structures that are less appropriate for a given task, which is a risk that actually follows the risk mentioned above.

If a real-world modeling metaphor is to add value to data modeling by providing guidance for finding appropriate data structures, it has to mitigate risks like the ones just mentioned. Therefore elaboration of a real-world metaphor must face two problems: the problem of conceptual basis, where it must define and discuss its notion of real world; and the problem of recommended action, where it must provide detailed explanations on how the notion of real world can actually be exploited in the everyday tasks of a data modeler. It is not enough to state that objects are all around and just have to be picked up. Equally perilously, the elaboration might run into severe difficulties with respect to the conceptual basis: important theoretical questions may arise that have been discussed by philosophers for 2300 years. Moreover, there are several risks with respect to these questions. They simply might not be recognized. They might be neglected. They might be discussed without appreciation of their discussion in other disciplines.

Key Argument Against Real-World Modeling Approaches

A real-world modeling approach is an approach that is based on a real-world modeling statement. A real-world modeling statement claims that the model captures facts in the real world. The real-world modeling approach is naive since it does not refer to the well established discussions and critiques concerning the classic correspondence theory of truth [12]. If the real-world modeling statement is not exploited strictly in the subsequent parts of the method, the real-world argument has to be considered as flawed, because if the real-world statement is omitted the subsequent apparatus of the method does in effect not change.

The real-world modeling approach deals with the question of the relation between data and the objects described by the data. Note that in form-oriented analysis this question is finely separated from core parts of the methodology. The central analysis notion of form-oriented analysis, the form-oriented user interface, is an information technology concept and deals not with this question at all. Form-oriented user interface modeling does not necessarily refer to concepts outside the information technology area. The same is true for the message based network model. The question of how to model the facts in the so-called real world is in the case of enterprise systems the question of how to model an enterprise. It is in our view naive if one does not take into account the abundant experience of other scientific communities regarding the question of business modeling. In today's working environment everybody should be a generalist to some extent. Software engineers are often involved in areas of business modeling due to their general skills. This does still not mean that these activities belong to the core area of software development. It only means that even a software developer has to be open for interdisciplinary topics.

9.5 Visual Modeling De-emphasized

The modeling method presented in this book is not a visual method, because visual methods do not scale to the system sizes under consideration here. If you imagine a system consisting of 5000 business classes, you quickly realize that the whole system cannot be depicted in a single diagram. Decomposition may appear to be the solution to the problem, but in practice conventional decomposition mechanisms cannot be used because of the need for readability. The decomposition has rather to provide a modularization that is adequate for the functionality under consideration.

Visualization alone yields no abstraction. For example, visualizing classes using boxes and references between classes using arrows does not yield a more abstract class model than a textual equivalent in an appropriate programming language that uses curly braces instead of boxes and further attributes for the references between the classes. Sure, if operations are involved, a visual class diagram typically omits the operations' implementation, but such obvious abstractions are not a unique selling point of visual modeling techniques or visual modeling tools, they are, for example, also achieved by integrated development environments, even without roundtrip engineering metaphors in the latter case. Sure, the notion of class is an abstraction mechanism – a class abstracts from its many instances – however, the visualization of a class does not add to the already achieved level of abstraction.

If visualization does not support abstraction, it could still be justified for cognitive reasons: visual models are (i) easier to grasp, (ii) easier to understand, and (iii) easier to communicate. Although this is not proven, we do not ignore that, to some extent, especially for small models, this is actually true – we also use visualizations for our models in this book – see Sect. 5.1.4. It's simple: if we feel that a visualization can foster understanding or communication, we visualize the model, otherwise we don't. A comparison with mathematical textbooks might be instructive; there, mathematical objects – graphs, sets, categories – are visualized by little ad hoc paintings wherever appropriate, because they often really help understanding, but it is not at all a question whether these paintings are more than mere learning aids. At the same time, using a vizualization for a mathematical object does not commit the author to use visualizations consistently throughout the book for all mathematical objects of the same kind.

- The artifact of interest is always the model, not the diagram that visualizes the model.
- During modeling, visualization itself must not be subject to investigation.

Actually, visualization has also its risks. First, visualization can raise new, typically *marginal* but bothering questions: is it allowed to paint a model element more than once? Is it allowed to paint crossing arrows? Should class names have a different font size than attribute names? What is a nice distance between two classes? What colour for the classes? At least if more than one developer are involved, visual models demand for style guides in the same way that textual representations do. Furthermore, as already mentioned, large diagrams can quickly become unmanageable. However, the most serious problem is that visualizing models can be too time-consuming, resulting in an overhead that can not be justified. Even small visualized models are not automatically better than their textual counterparts. For example, if a class model has a critical mass of associations, experience is needed to lay out the diagram in a clearly arranged manner. A developer might be tempted to spend too much time laying out or even embellishing diagrams. Among software engineers, separation of content and layout is a generally accepted best practice, e.g., for content management of complex web sites. So, separation of content and layout should be an issue in modeling, too.

All this said, we argue that the leading paradigm for the management of the model must be a logical, non-visual method. This distinction also helps in clarifying that this discussion is about a syntactical issue, i.e., that the visual concepts under discussion are syntactical notions as well. We will discuss the problems involved here in Chap. 12 on the integrated source code model. There we will argue that artifacts can be seen as instances of ordinary data types. This means we can subsume the concept of syntax under the concept of data types. This approach shifts the priorities in choosing the syntax of a language, sometimes also called the metamodel, from visualization concerns to semantic concerns as well as to questions of modularization and automated processing. This favors parsimonious syntax models. The visualization of artifacts in this approach is therefore identified as a purely separate layer above the syntax model itself. This supports the use of various visualizations, according to the needs and preferences of the user.

9.6 Artifact Orientation

Software processes comprise artifacts and activities. In software projects the work is often planned along activities, the project is often tracked along the improvement of artifacts. Software processes view artifacts as the input and output of activities, and are described as artifact flows with activities as processing elements. A tight coupling of artifacts and activities arises naturally: there is a need for initial planning and the result of that initial planning is a stop-or-go report; the final product of a software project is code, and code is the result of coding. But it is not enough to introduce one producing activity for each artifact and to describe the software process as a flow of artifacts through activities. Reality is more complex. Take design as an example. Design is sometimes conceived as a blueprint for subsequent coding. However, if there is no compelling standard architecture in the project, i.e., if design alternatives have to be considered, design is rather the quality of software than its building plan. It is improved throughout the project. This notion of design is the basis of the design strategy of Extreme Programming [20].

Recognizing problems that arise from a coupling of artifacts and activities is as old as writing on software processes. Software processes implicitly address the decoupling of activities from artifacts, e.g., by iterations [266], spiral models [26], or two-dimensional process architectures [188]. Artifact orientation shifts the focus. It stands for explicitly decoupling artifacts from activities from the outset. Artifact orientation is a descriptive pattern and is independent of any software process. Artifact orientation proposes to ask throughout the project the following question:

How do we improve quantity and quality of the artifacts?

Artifact orientation can be taken as a directive for project planning and tracking. In the extreme, artifact orientation can be taken as the basis of an ultra-lightweight method for small projects and small teams:

- *Vision.* The desired product is described by a vision document.
- *Activity follows artifacts.* At project start the desired artifacts are defined. Activities are triggered by the need to improve artifacts.
- *Simultaneous improvement.* Artifacts of the several artifact sets are improved simultaneously.

The objectives of artifact orientation are similar to the objectives of the work product orientation of the experience-based approach to object-oriented software development [153]. This is the software development method of the IBM Object-Oriented Technology Center, which emphasizes work product definition in order to ensure that the mutual dependencies of work products, activities, increments, and project phases are transparent and manageable.

9.7 The High-Level Programming Viewpoint

High-level programming is the encoding of business rules, as they are stated by the domain-level experts. The programmer's job is not to change these business rules according to his or her own intuition. The task of the high-level programmer is again not to change the business processes until they fit best to the preferred system. It is rather the task of the business programmer to implement the demands of the users.

We also should not confuse high-level programming with business process integration (BPI), a totally orthogonal concept. BPI is intended for an organization in which different parts follow different business processes for similar tasks. BPI is the endeavor to unify these different rules of procedure, of course with the aim of creating synergies or enabling rationalization, i.e., cutting the costs of creating an enterprise information system, or improving the cooperation between organizational units. A BPI initiative is intended to result in a single business model, where previously many different business models have been in place. BPIs have as a matter of fact mixed results in practice. However, BPI is totally orthogonal to high-level programming. The notion of high-level programming describes the way we want to model business logic, regardless of whether it is integrated across an organization or not. High-level programming expresses an approach of focusing on the business logic. In high-level programming we separate the business logic from technical IT information, like configuration data, technical error messages, host addresses, etc. In short, business logic is our notion of analysis, separated from design and implementation. This approach brings added value, regardless of whether a BPI does not take place, or it has been tried but failed, or it has succeeded. Especially if the business logic is very complicated – because the organization is heterogeneous and stays so – the high-level programming approach is more important than ever.

Of course in our view the introduction of a new IT system is an excellent point in time to perform a BPI, to justify it within the staff, and to reap high benefits from it. Nevertheless a decision maker should recognize that it is by no means a good thing to have essentially a coupling of two major projects, the change in the IT technology as well as the BPI projects.

We have to be aware, of course, that with the use of an ERP system there is often the necessity to do exactly this, namely the coupling of the IT rollout with a BPI. This is of course due to the fact that an ERP is not a freely programmed system, but a fixed system that allows basically only for customizations. The use of such a system and the customization is not what we understand under high-level programming, since it lacks the generality that we want to see in high-level programming and that we can deliver with our approach.

Business programming is the generalization of high-level transactional programming to general architectures, including desktop databases. It is clear that there are other paradigms on the same abstraction level as high-level transactional programming. Our representative of business programming is high-level programming. The approach of understanding a concept through a representative is explained in Sect. 14.2.3.

We present business programming as a counterproposal to conceptual "real-world" modeling. The latter leads to a calculus with peculiarities that certainly offer no benefit to maintainability; for example, it requires strict bipartiteness of otherwise extensionally identical concepts, namely relations and entities. Compare this with the justification of the bipartite modeling approach in the form-oriented paradigm. In this approach the two concepts, client page and server action, are different and the bipartiteness is based on the understanding of the system type.

This becomes clear in the assessment of a given ER diagram. You can assess its well-formedness which will include a check for bipartiteness. However you can not check formally whether the relationships are indeed relationships since this is subject to opinion. Now, perhaps this dilemma is the origin of the claim that the ER diagram expresses undisputable facts. How such a view deals with the mere existence of higher-order ER diagrams is not clear at all.

We see two important motivations with respect to maintainability, which are addressed but not fully solved in conceptual modeling languages. In contrast, our modeling language and system view are designed as solutions for these clearly stated maintainability issues of relational database schemata.

One maintainability issue is that the business logic should be as tolerant as possible to changes in multiplicity of relations. For example, assume an account currently could have two contact persons, but in future is required to have only one. Then all old queries should still work, since they should have worked if *by chance* every account had only one contact person. Old updates obviously may not comply, like "insert another contact person".

The second issue is that the model should allow only consistent updates. Normalization theory is one operational method for this purpose which does not argue metaphorically. Normalization theory tries to change the model in such a way that the generic update commands on tables lead to consistent state changes. Many proponents of conceptual modeling stress some connection between conceptual modeling and normalization with statements like: the canonical database design from an ER diagram is automatically in third normal form.

Our analysis comes to a different result. We argue that there is a canonical system model, but it is a de-normalized one. This model is the message model; it contains only the input messages, their timestamp of execution, and the output messages. The output messages can be removed if the system model is made deterministic. Note that in the message model *system* updates are possible, although message updates are not possible. The system state is in fact updated by each input message.

Why do we not stick to the message model; why do we do data modeling? Something like normalization may be a good candidate. But normalization is not a goal in itself. In our view, one motivation is to restrict updates to consistent updates. The system designer wants to deliver a set of consistent system update operations. He or she wants to avoid update anomalies. Relational normal forms avoid some update anomalies, but the capabilities of normalization theory are limited to the alternatives which can be gained by schema evolution, and the focus of normalization theory is narrowed to one peculiar type of constraint, the functional dependency. The generic state change commands a relational database is supposed to offer are inserts, updates and deletes. The only generic constraint on the schema, which results in denial of update commands, is the referential integrity: a row with a primary key which is used elsewhere as a foreign key must not be changed. By the way some aspects of normalization are strongly intertwined with the concept of compound keys; in a concept based purely on artificial keys these questions do not arise.

There is one intuitive operational concept that improves the consistency of updates, which we call the *one place principle*: each information unit is stored in one place only. This is achieved to some extent by normal forms for relational database schemes. One can argue that this is the most that a method the normalization theory can achieve. The one place principle cannot solve every consistency demand. We argue that data modeling together with constraint writing is the right general framework for achieving the desired consistency.

This deliberation allows us to give a general and abstract definition of a normal form for a relational model. A relational model for an application domain is in normal form if every generic update allowed by the database is a consistent update, in other words if it makes sense in the business. If a business model can be brought into normal, form then each information unit is only stored at one place and can be changed independently from all other information units. The concept of referential integrity shows that this is not even possible in data models, which are in normal form.

This however states the problem very clearly. Logically, there are only two possibilities. On the one hand is a model of the state where each information unit can be changed independently and still leads to a consistent state. On the other hand is a model with constraints telling us which updates are possible. The first case would certainly be a unique model even if we would not say indisputable. It would achieve full orthogonality. Alas, we at least do no know how to do it. Hence we need constraints. Type specifications are constraints, multiplicities are constraints.

9.8 Advanced Systems Modeling Approaches

One has to be aware that the system modeling techniques we have introduced in this book are designed for project sizes as found in a professional environment on a reasonably large scale. Such projects can be major strategic ones for the company involved, and they require a considerable financial investment, which is expected to deliver return on investment. Furthermore a new IT project nowadays always has a precursor system at the intended workplace. And the new IT system often coincides with a change in the way the users do their business. In other words, the social systems may change as well. Furthermore the transition to the new system has to be well planned.

9.8.1 Systems Analysis

Our notion of analysis is dedicated to these necessities, and differs therefore from other analysis approaches, which focus more on establishing novel ontologies. In our view a proper systems analysis has to have the following parts:

- An analysis and description of the existing system. This should of course be based on the documented rules of procedure of the organization.
- A workload metric.
- A model of the proposed system.
- A feasible plan for the transition between the systems.

Domain experts play a crucial role in the provision of these parts. Note, further, that our discussion of analysis is tailored to projects for enterprise systems within an organization. A somewhat different scenario is software projects for creating off-the-shelf software, e.g., for whole industry sectors. In the latter case the method works best if the sector has a high degree of uniformity of processes, e.g., through benchmarking.

Analysis of the Existing System

The systems analyst, who has to provide the analysis of the existing system, has a crisp and clear first task: to gather all existing documentation of the system, and to review it. Documentation does not mean the user manual of an IT system. It refers to the processes and workflows in the organization which are most likely documented, since many organizations have undergone streamlining and re-engineering in the past which aim at clear business processes [269]. The review includes the following tasks: classification of the paradigms of the documentation, assessment of completeness. The most difficult part is probably to check whether these processes have indeed been followed. This also makes clear that the system analyst will easily reach the limits of his or her resources. The existing systems analysis does not have to mean a rewriting of the documentation; this may be reserved only to the case where a direct comparison with the proposed system is needed.

Workload Metric

For finding the appropriate solution for the proposed system, one has to assess the workload with which the system is confronted. The estimation of future workload has of course to be provided by the strategy makers who are aware of the vision for the business, and know on which scenario to base the estimation.

Model of the Proposed System, Benchmarking

In modeling the proposed system again, the systems analyst has a clear and primary task, which one may rarely find in textbooks on software processes:

the central task is industry benchmarking (which is something different from the notion of benchmarks in performance measurements). The systems analyst has to look at what others do, what benefits they achieve, how his or her idea compares with theirs. The proposed system does not really have to have a novel approach, it should rather follow a proven approach. One can consider best practices from industry as safe. If one takes a new approach, one should know exactly why it is going to work, or make appropriate tests.

A Transition Model

The transition model has of course to be interconnected with the planning of the software development project, e.g with the delivery date. The transition model must also contain plans for the case of malfunction, e.g., projecting realistic times for bug fixes. One important part of the transition model is the plan for when and how the users start working with the new system.

9.8.2 A Game Model for Systems Analysis

In large projects, a thorough planning process should involve intensive testing and review of the proposed system. This may also include a simulation of the new system in order to test the appropriateness of the system and to find loopholes early on. Such a simulation can be more or less automated in itself.

In systems analysis, it is important to be aware that not just the IT systems are relevant. The social and technical systems are important for a thorough understanding of the problem domain as well. Therefore a thorough analysis must also model the social and technical systems. We therefore need a modeling paradigm for these systems, and we need an easy to understand metaphor, which helps us to verify the appropriateness of our models.

A straightforward approach would be to try to develop a single vocabulary for socio-technical systems, which seems appropriate, and to define it for all upcoming projects. However, we will present a more open basic approach, which may be even more convincing with respect to its appropriateness.

We look for a modeling approach for systems analysis which empowers a team of systems analysts to effectively perform the following activities:

- Discussion of a proposed model.
- Discussion of a certain example scenario, and examination of what may happen according to the model.
- Reaching agreement on whether certain developments are possible or not according to the model.

The basic approach, which we follow in order to ensure the principal possibility of such activities of the modeling team, is a kind of game-theoretic approach. A given proposed model can be taken by a systems analyst. We could envisage this analyst as arguing to his or her colleagues: "Look what could happen if truck A arrives before the processing order X is in place." This could lead to the recognition that the model does allow for a basically impossible event, thus showing that the model has to be changed. But it could also show that a certain feature of the IT system, being part of the model, does not in any cases fulfill the purpose it is supposed to fulfill, thus giving rise to a change in the IT system. This system modeling approach is therefore quite a powerful tool, which is actually even suitable for requirements elicitation, as we will see in due course.

9.8.3 Non-functional and Embedding Specifications

Non-functional specifications certainly have from a modeler's viewpoint their own troublesome features. The question of a suitable formalism is especially difficult for non-functional specifications. We want to discuss non-functional specifications in the context of the so-called *embedding specifications*, since there are some natural relationships. Some non-functional specifications, such as privacy, have a close correlation to embedding specifications. It could perhaps be overstated to say that embedding specifications are all that is needed to define privacy, but certainly this connection should be kept in mind. It seems to be say at least something important about the nature of such non-functional requirements.

Embedding specifications take up the reflections on software specification as the specification of a system running the software in question. An embedding specification defines how an information system specification has to be read as a factual system specification. It fixes the abstract system at least qualitatively in space and time. An abstract system specification without an embedding specification is just a mathematical object. One can even say that an abstract system specification cannot have a state at all, even such a thing as a finite automaton. It can only have a structure, which reminds us of a state-based system, or which is traditionally read as a specification of a state-based system, but usually it is just some mathematical set. Only by using an embedding specification does this state-like something indeed become a state. The embedding specification ties the software system, which up to this point is just a definition, to a system installation. The space in which the embedding takes place is more a social than a physical space. The embedding places systems in organizations and gives access to persons. Concerning the notion of time, however, this embedding can be seen as being very physical. The embedding with respect to time mostly takes place in the same way, since in complex system models like the data modeling we have introduced, it may be hard to imagine how to interpret the model differently than in the usual way. This can, however, be treacherous. In using this embedding, the model dimension which created the state that changes through time gets its intended semantics. The embedding specification is related to the territoriality of enterprise systems. One standard embedded specification states, that there is only one installation of an enterprise system for a certain organization.

The distinction between type and instance remains meaningful: a single installation is an instance, but many installations can belong to the same type. These considerations are crucial for a deeper understanding of enterprise applications, because installations of enterprise systems are by far more important notions than installations of many other software products like, for example, office applications. The form-oriented interface itself is a type specification; it specifies a terminal session. Each enterprise system installation will of course have numerous terminal sessions during its lifetime.

The remarkable connection between non-functional requirements and embedding specification is the following. A straightforward embedding specification of an enterprise system automatically states the maximal non-functional requirements. So just stating that a system according to a typical specification is supposed to be installed at a certain place means literally that there is a perfect, faultless system. In fact it states unrealistically high requirements. A simple embedding specification requires service without downtime, absolute privacy, failure-free infinite persistency. This means that, from the standpoint of an embedded system specification, non-functional requirements are not stated as demands, but as relaxations. We have to specify that the specification is not supposed to hold 100%. Similar aspects have been encountered in the case of transactions. There we have seen that naive semantics produce a specification which demands the highest isolation level. And with respect to distributed transactions, we have seen that there is no problem at all in specifying a global transactional network with the highest isolation level; in fact there is almost nothing to explain. The problem is to implement it!

Relaxations can be specified quantitatively, qualitatively, or prescriptively. The isolation level specification is a qualitative specification. A specification of mean time between failures is a quantitative specification. The demand to use SSL is a prescriptive specification, since it does not state the intended goal, but the solution. This is a relaxation in the sense that it concedes that – absolute security being impossible – SSL is seen as fully sufficient. Quantitative relaxations are necessary for professional high-profile projects, but sadly enough they remain often restricted to them. In some regards quantitative relaxations are difficult to achieve.

Part II

Tool Support

10

Forward Engineering and Reverse Engineering

In this chapter we decribe a prototypical forward and reverse engineering tool suite – see Fig. 10.1. The tool suite exemplifies how the form-oriented approach to information systems can be exploited in model-based development. Angie [100] is a textual format for formcharts with message types and a forward engineering tool. JSPick [94] is tool for revovering models from the source code, whereas Revangie [103, 102] is a tool that recovers a model by monitoring a system. The models recovered from Angie are intended to be used by a model-based load test tool.

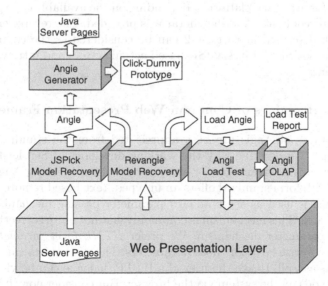

Fig. 10.1. The Angie language related tool suite

10.1 Forward Engineering

In this section we describe the language and tool Angie for the type-safe specification of web presentation layers and the subsequent generation of an executable interface prototype. A textual description of a web-based dialogue can be directly expressed in the proposed language and is then automatically mapped onto a system structure in compliance with currently discussed web design patterns like the Model 2 architecture. The Angie tool bridges between the specification and implementation level. The proposed language directly supports the system metaphor of form-oriented analysis, namely the system model as a bipartite state machine.

Web interaction based on HTML forms is untyped. In many common web presentation frameworks this leaves the programmer with a considerable number of tasks like type conversion, which are moreover error prone. Angie frees the programmer from these tasks by introducing a clean abstraction layer and offering a generator tool based on this abstraction layer. Moreover, Angie supports the recommended Model 2 architecture. For this purpose the language Angie uses the system metaphor of form-oriented analysis, in which the system is modeled as a bipartite state machine. A description of a web interface in the Angie language is independent of particular target languages or even particular frameworks for this architecture. Angie rather focuses on the principles of the HTML interaction model itself, not the platform for generating dynamic HTML. An Angie document allows the generation of web presentation layers for arbitrary platforms, depending on the available code generators for the Angie compiler. A Java generator is provided. The reverse engineering tool JSPick described in Sect. 10.2 can be considered as the counterpart of Angie, because JSPick takes a JSP-based actual system and retrieves a typed specification.

10.1.1 Shortcomings of Common Web Presentation Frameworks

The advantages of Angie are best appreciated from the standpoint of the design phase. We describe why the working developer of Servlet-based web interfaces can gain advantages for everyday problems by using Angie.

The HTML form standard offers an untyped, text-based remote call mechanism, which is used as the standard parameter passing mechanism for dynamic web sites. This mechanism is commonly, but not quite correctly, referred to as CGI parameter mechanism. We prefer *HTML form parameters* in the following as precise term for those parameters. The mechanism can be used in HTTP links as well. Hence the user of a HTTP dialogue can be viewed as invoking methods on the system via the browser. But consider now, for example, Java Server Pages (JSPs) and Servlets [248]. Servlets and JSPs give access to HTML form parameter passing through an object-oriented mechanism, yet still in the style of the original CGI (Common Gateway Interface). Commonly accepted documentation and testing concepts, when used naively in the context of developing a Servlet-based ultra-thin client tier, may consider only the purely technical HTTP parameters instead of the parameters significant for business logic. In the formal language called Angie each Servlet or JSP is seen as a method with the form parameters as parameter list. Such a method is called a dialogue method. Each result page offers the user the choice between different calls to dialogue methods as the next step in the dialogue. Dialogue methods can be called by links or forms. Forms can be seen as editable method calls offered to the user. Angie allows specifying the links and forms contained in a page. From each specified method declaration and call the generator will produce appropriate code templates as described below. The Model 2 architecture is a recommended good practice for web presentation layer design. A detailed discussion of the Model 2 architecture can be found in Sect. 11.2.1. In the Model 2 architecture, the user request is directed to a so-called front component, which executes business logic. Dependent on the outcome, the front component redirects the request to other dialogue methods, the result pages. Note therefore that one JSP will potentially yield as many different result pages as it has redirect directives.

10.1.2 The Language Angie

The language Angie is a specification language for HTML dialogues. Its type system and syntax are oriented towards Java. Angie allows the specification of an HTML dialogue as a textual representation of a message storyboard. A whole web interface is specified in Angie in a single source file. The Angie compiler performs static type checking on this specification and the code generator generates JSP templates, containing protected regions. The JSP templates can be completed by inserting custom code into the protected regions. Each dialogue method has a fixed parameter set. The method construct in Angie is again similar to the method syntax in Java. The type checking requires that the signatures of method definition and invocation is matching, i.e., that the parameter list matches and that the single parameters have the same type. We present a simplified Angie syntax in Fig 10.2, which defines a superset of the Angie language. In the body of Angie's method construct, the programmer has to specify all links and forms which will be offered by the result page of this method. Since links and forms enable calls of dialogue methods, their declarations resemble method calls. They start with the keywords link or form, they get a label, and finally they have a method call syntax. For links, the actual parameters are names of variables. In form declarations each actual parameter is a pair of the widget type that will be generated and a variable name. The values of these variables are used to provide the default values within the widgets.

```
link myLabel calls myMethod(myActPar1,..,myActParN)

form myLabel calls myMethod(WIDGET1 myActPar1,..,WIDGETN myActParN)
```

```
syntax   ::= <LOCATION> <EQUALS> <LOCATOR> methods ( menu )?
methods ::= ( method )*
method  ::=
 ( <ACTION> | <PAGE>  )? <IDENTIFIER> <OPEN> parameters <CLOSE>
 <CURLYOPEN> ( calls  )? <CURLYCLOSE>
parameters ::= ( parameter ( <COMMA> parameter )* )?
parameter  ::=
 ( ( <BOOLEAN> <IDENTIFIER> )
   |( ( <INT> | <STRING> )
       ( ( <ARRAYOPEN> <ARRAYCLOSE> <IDENTIFIER> )
         |( <IDENTIFIER> ( <ARRAYOPEN> <ARRAYCLOSE> )? ) ) ) )
calls    ::= ( call ( <OR> call )* )
call     ::= ( link | form | redirect )
redirect ::=
  <REDIRECT> <IDENTIFIER>
  <OPEN> actualLinkParameters <CLOSE>
link ::=
  <LINK> <IDENTIFIER> <CALLS>  <IDENTIFIER>
  <OPEN> actualLinkParameters <CLOSE>
actualLinkParameters ::=
   ( <IDENTIFIER> ( <COMMA> <IDENTIFIER> )* )?
form ::=
  <FORM> <IDENTIFIER> <CALLS>  <IDENTIFIER>
  <OPEN> actualFormParameters <CLOSE>
actualFormParameters ::=
  ( actualFormParameter ( <COMMA> actualFormParameter )* )?
actualFormParameter ::=
  ( <TEXT> | <TEXTAREA> | <CHECKBOX> | <RADIO> | <COMBOBOX> |
    <MULTIPLELIST> | <HIDDEN> ) <IDENTIFIER>
menu ::=
   <MENU> ( <IDENTIFIER> (<COMMA> <IDENTIFIER>)* )?
   <CURLYOPEN> calls <CURLYCLOSE>
```

Fig. 10.2. Grammar of the language Angie

Two-Staged Request Processing

Angie directly supports the system paradigm established in form-oriented
analysis: the typed bipartite state machine. The action and page declarations
in Angie enable a two-staged request processing. Angie offers two method
modifiers, action and page, which qualify the respective method as corresponding to a server action or client page.

The Menu Construct

Angie also supports a menu construct. This construct may contain link and
form declarations, which will be included on every result page of a specified list

of page methods. The menu construct is the Angie notation for the concept
of state sets (with respect to client pages), which has been introduced in
Sect. 6.5.1.

Generation of Code

The language Angie serves as a formal specification language, but also as input
to the Angie tool, a type checker and generator. The Angie tool performs the
following static checks:

- It checks whether all calls to methods (in the result pages of other methods) have correct parameter sets. This is important, especially for forms.
  Here the tool checks whether the widgets chosen in each actual parameter
  matches the type of the corresponding formal parameter.
- It checks *syntactically* whether every action calls only *page targets* via
  redirect declarations, and whether every page calls only *action targets* via
  link or form declarations.

For correct input, the Angie generator produces the following output code:

- For each method it produces one JSP with the same name. Within that
  JSP it produces code which performs runtime type checking whether the
  method is called with the correct parameters, and converts the parameters
  to local variables with the same name as the formal parameters in the
  Angie file. Subsequently it creates a protected region which can be used
  as a method body for the Java code.
- For every link or form declaration in the Angie method body it creates
  HTML code, giving a form or link which offers a correct call to the corresponding method. Within that HTML code, the Angie tool again creates
  protected regions for each HTML parameter, defining where to insert Java
  code which produces actual parameters. Similarly, it creates redirect directives for the redirect declarations in the method body.
- For every menu declaration, Angie weaves the contained link and form
  declarations into the specified page methods.
- The Angie tool produces comments, structuring the generated code.

10.1.3 The Online Bookstore in Angie

We now give Angie code for the running example, the online bookstore. We
only specify a cutout of the system, which is visualized in Fig. 10.3. The menu
construct is used to specify the back link from the login page to the welcome
page.

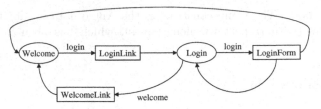

Fig. 10.3. Bookstore login capability

```
page Welcome(String customerName){
  link login calls LoginLink()
}
action LoginLink(){
  redirect Login(errorMessage,defaultEmail)
}
page Login(String errorMessage, String defaultEmail){
  form login calls LoginForm(
                  TEXTFIELD email,
                  PASSWORD  password
               )
}
action LoginForm(
  String email,
  String password
){
     redirect Welcome(customerName)
  or redirect Login(errorMessage,defaultEmail)
)
menu Login {
  link welcome calls WelcomeLink()
}
action WelcomeLink(){
  redirect Welcome(customerName)
}
```

10.1.4 The Position of Angie Within Related Technologies

In comparison with other tools Angie can be seen to be on the declarative side, while other tools typically fall on a rather operational side. We can see that if we compare Angie with web presentation frameworks; Angie does not prescribe architecture or design, even if it goes very well with concrete technologies. This is our very aim in making an abstraction; we want to have added value for the concrete technology, yet we do not want to be tied to that. The current Angie tool output is consistent with SUNs Model 2 [248] as a JSP design pattern. Due to the generative approach of the Angie tool it is however quite possible to support advanced and more flexible system designs as well.

In comparing tools like Angie one has to be aware of the precise task this tool is designed for. It has nothing to do with, e.g., web authoring tools, which are more related to content management systems, another important technology class. Such tools typically also achieve a certain abstraction level, but this targets questions of information modularity, as expressed in description languages like WebML [45]. It is interesting to compare Angie with interactive Tools, e.g., Wizards [29] and graphical IDE's. From the software engineering standpoint the important advantage of Angie is that you have a formal specification in form of the Angie source code, while in the case of Wizards you have only the resulting system. The functionality of Angie is different from tools like [230], which provide an interconnection between different language paradigms like HTML and SQL. Angie takes one signature specification and generates code in the different paradigms, Java and HTML, according to this signature specification. Angie consequently performs static type checking and ensures that the resulting system is statically well typed.

10.2 Reverse Engineering

In this section we introduce a notion of design recovery tool for presentation layers. The concept is described along the lines of the concrete tool JSPick. JSPick is a reverse engineering tool for JSP-based web presentation layers. JSPick allows for automatic generation of documentation of the whole system interface in an easy to read specification language. The section proceeds by describing how the tool supports the recovering of form types and the recovering of page signatures. The formal semantics of the tool based on the pseudo-evaluation technique are provided in Chap. 15.1.

Consider javadoc, the standard Java documentation tool. Javadoc would not be applied to the Java Servlets code that is generated by a JSP container. However, the considerations concerning javadoc foster the understanding of the JSPick concepts. Javadoc is not suitable for documenting Java Servlets, because applying javadoc to the customized server script classes leads only to the documentation of the technical parameters HTTPRequest and HTTPResponse. The documented technical signatures are not amenable for a application of reasonable specification techniques. The interesting parameters, which are significant for the functional requirements and business logic, namely the HTML form parameters provided by the forms or links calling the page, cannot be documented automatically. All this amounts to saying that javadoc is a pure redocumentation tool in the sense of [50]. The generated code documentation adds no value to the semantics that can be read directly from the code, only a visualization is created.

In contrast, JSPick is a design recovery tool in the sense of [50]. JSPick exploits the NSP concepts (Chap. 11) in order to infer from the code a meaningful documentation at a higher abstraction level. JSPick extracts from a system interface all pages with their signatures together with the contained links and forms. JSPick generates a GUI browser for a given system. With that browser the developer can examine source code, abstract syntax trees, type information, warnings, and the linkage structure of the system under consideration from several different viewpoints.

The tool presented in [144, 143, 142] analyses source code and pages of a web application and generates an architecture diagram that visualizes the interactions between static pages, active ASP or JSP pages and other software components by arrows. The same support is offered by the tool WARE (Web Application Reverse Engineering) [199] for ASP- and PHP- based systems. A technique for recovering navigational structure and a conceptual model from a web application without tool support is described in [11]. An example of a tool that can track the change history of a web site is given in [34].

10.2.1 Recovering Form Types

As a basic feature JSPick encounters violations of the combined Java/XHTML block structure: Java and the markup language block structure should be compatible as described in Sect. 15.2.4.

For every form information about the dynamically provided form input capabilities is created. The information inferred with respect to a given form is called its form type in the sequel. Consider the JSP example page in Listing 10.1. The most succinct JSPick presentation of the web signature and the form type that is extracted from the code in Listing 10.1 is the following:

```
jsp examplePage.jsp( []x, z, y){
  form calls http://www.foo.net/targetedPage.jsp(
    TEXT a, TEXT[] b, TEXT[] c, TEXT[] d, TEXT e, RADIO f,
    RADIO[] g, SELECT h, SELECT[] i, HIDDEN j, VARIOUS k
  );
}
```

For a form each targeted formal parameter is given. We use the following terminology in the context of JSP: (i) a *formal parameter* is a name that is requested in a server page, and (ii) a *formal parameter targeted by a form* is the name-attribute of a possibly generated control contained in the form. If it is sure that always exactly one control is generated for a certain parameter then it is given as a single parameter. Otherwise it is given as an array parameter.

Note that a collection of radio buttons is one single control: a set of radio buttons offers the user one capability to select one single data item and is therefore conceptually equal to one single select menu. A multiple select menu is considered as a collection of controls. A multiple select menu is conceptually equal to a set of check boxes: each of its options offers the user the capability to select or deselect a data item independently of the other menu options. The conceptual view of radio buttons and multiple select menus is summarized again in the informal equation (10.1).

$$
\begin{aligned}
\text{mulitple radio buttons} \\
\equiv \quad \text{one single select menu} \\
\not\equiv \text{one multiple select menu} \\
\equiv \quad \text{multiple check boxes}
\end{aligned}
\tag{10.1}
$$

As further information the control kind of each targeted formal parameter is given. If it is possible that a parameter is targeted by different kinds of controls it is given the various-control , which is a pseudo-control that has been introduced merely for this purpose.

Listing 10.1 Java Server Pages: example input to the JSPick CASE tool

```
01 <html>
02   <head><title>Example Page</title></head>
03   <body>
04     <form action="http://www.foo.net/targetedPage.jsp"
05           method="get">
06       <input type="text" name="a">
07       <input type="text" name="b">
08       <input type="text" name="b"><%
09       for (i=0;i<2;i++){%> <input type="text" name="c"><%}
10       if (cond){%> <input type="text" name="d"> <%}
11       if (cond){%> <input type="text" name="e"> <%}
12         else   { if (cond){%> <input type="text" name="e"> <%}
13                    else   {%> <input type="text" name="e"> <%}
14                 }%>
15       <input type="radio" name="f">
16       <input type="radio" name="f"><%
17       for (i=0;i<2;i++){%> <input type="radio" name="f"><%}
18       if (cond){%> <input type="radio" name="g"> <%}%>
19       <select name="h"><option>A<option>B</select>
20       <select multiple name="i"><option>A<option>B</select>
21       <input type="hidden" name="j"><%
22       if (cond){%>
23         <input type="radio" name="k">
24         <input type="radio" name="k"><%
25       } else {%>
26         <select name="k"><option>A<option>B</select><%
27       }%>
28     </form><%
29     v1=request.getParameterValues("x");
30     v2=request.getParameter("y");
31     v3=request.getParameterValues("z");
32     if (cond) { v4=request.getParameter("z"); }
33     %>
34   </body>
35 </html>
```

Summing up, a form type maps each formal parameter targeted by the form to a type consisting of a control kind and a possibly array annotation. The presented form types already provide the developer with valuable debugging information. The second kind of information is extracted page signatures.

10.2.2 Recovering Page Signatures

The JSPick page signatures are crucially motivated by an insight into the specific interplay between HTML/XHTML forms and JSPs: the method request.getParameter of the request-object should only be used for a parameter if it is sure that the parameter has at most one value. This is clearly stated in the online API documentation of the Java Servlet technology 2.2. The reason for this is obvious: the getParameter-method only returns the first value if it is applied to a string parameter [76]. More seriously in the older Java Servlet [75] version 2.1 this behavior is just proposed and the return value has been implementation dependent in such cases. Formulated in another way, if a parameter might have more than one value the getParameterValues-method should be used. This guideline motivates the way JSPick infers the web signature. If in a page a parameter is only requested by a getParameterValues-method, it is a formal array parameter. If in a page a parameter is possibly requested by a getParameter-method, it is a formal single parameter. Based on inferred form types and web signatures, JSPick can detect potential violations of the guideline described above and can generate an appropriate warning.

The information extracted by JSPick can be analyzed with respect to several classes of potential sources of error. For example, it is easy to implement reports on the following non-mutual exclusive indicators for a flawed design:

- A parameter is requested by a getParameter-method, but it is not provided by a targeting form.
- A parameter is provided by a form, but it is not requested in the targeted JSP anywhere.
- Forms targeting the same JSP may target different formal parameters.
- A form targets a non-existing form.
- A parameter may be requested by both a getParameter-method and a getParameterValues-method.
- A formal parameter that is targeted by a password control may be targeted by another non-password control.

10.3 Source-Code-Opaque Reverse Engineering

This section describes source-code-independent reverse engineering of dynamic web sites. The tool Revangie builds a form-oriented analysis model solely from the usage of a web application. The recovered models can be, for example, exploited for the purpose of requirements engineering and load

test development. Revangie can explore a given web application fully automatically or can passively record its usages. The collected data, i.e., data
about screens, server-side programs, and system responsiveness, are analyzed
in order to build a user interface model. We present several adequate screen
classifications, which are utilized to yield significant models.

Revangie is a tool that is able to recover the model of a dynamic web
interface without looking at the source code. Revangie recovers models independent of source code because of the manifold of languages, platforms and
architectures a dynamic web site can be implemented in. The source-code-
independent approach is a straightforward one, because it is much easier to
analyze HTML code than the generating code. It is an essential claim that the
analysis of the generated HTML is sufficient to recover sophisticated models.
It is not only easier to analyze HTML code than the generating code, but
more convenient too, because the HTML code can be explored through the
single point of access of an HTTP port, whereas the generating code can have
a complex deployment structure. In the case that the source code is inac-
cessible, analysis must be source-code-independent anyway, as is the case in
typical product benchmarking efforts.

We explain the motivation for Revangie by describing its role in the Angie
tool suite. Please consider Fig. 10.1. Revangie is used to recover form-oriented
models from a dynamic web site. The textual description of this model in
the language Angie can be subsequently used for forward engineering of click
dummies, as they are conveniently used for requirements engineering, or customizable systems, which can help in migrating to model-driven architecture.
In addition to this, Revangie can collect data about user behavior that can
be used for load testing. It is further work to provide the load test tool Angil
that simulates real users on the basis of an annotated version of the Angie
language.

Revangie automatically classifies screens to pages in order to construct
adequate models. Different equivalence relations can be used for screen classification – see Fig. 10.4. Figure 10.4 uses a modified formchart diagram, where
single, completely unclassified screens are drawn instead of client pages. The
equivalence relations together with the subset relationship form a lattice.

- *Trivial identity* is the coarsest possible equivalence relation. All screens are
  equivalent. It is practically unimportant, but forms the top ($\top$) element
  of our lattice.
- *Screen identity* is the finest possible equivalence relation for screen classification and consequently forms the bottom ($\bot$) element. Each screen that
  is received by a web client gets its own page, even when two screens have
  the same HTML code.
- *Textual identity* groups screens with the same HTML code into the same
  page.
- *Source identity* groups screens into the same page that were generated by
  the same action.

- *Targets identity* groups screens with identical *targets signature*, i.e., the same set of server action signatures targeted by a screen. Targets identity can be coarsened to *form targets identity* by excluding the signatures of links from the targets signature, or orthogonally, coarsened to *internal targets identity* by excluding forms and links that target external actions, like links to other web sites.
- *Title identity* groups screens with identical HTML titles.
- *Pattern identity* groups screens that match a user-defined pattern. This may be a textual pattern, a purely syntactical pattern or a mixture of both; regular or, at most, context-free patterns are usually sufficient.
- A *conjunction* $A \wedge B$ groups those screens that are equivalent by both A and B, yielding a refinement of both A and B.
- A *disjunction* $A \vee B$ groups those screens that are equivalent by A or B, yielding a coarsening of both A and B.

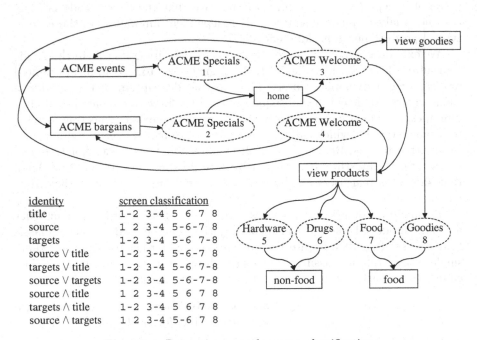

identity	screen classification
title	1-2 3-4 5 6 7 8
source	1 2 3-4 5-6-7 8
targets	1-2 3-4 5-6 7-8
source ∨ title	1-2 3-4 5-6-7 8
targets ∨ title	1-2 3-4 5-6 7-8
source ∨ targets	1-2 3-4 5-6-7-8
source ∧ title	1 2 3-4 5 6 7 8
targets ∧ title	1-2 3-4 5 6 7 8
source ∧ targets	1 2 3-4 5-6 7 8

Fig. 10.4. Revangie: example screen classifications

11

Typed Server Pages

In this chapter a strongly typed server pages technology is proposed. Server pages technology is a state of the art in the field of web technology. The proposed technology is seamlessly integrated with form-oriented analysis. There exist canonical mappings from formcharts to the proposed technology. The core type system of the technology is given as a convenient Per Martin-Löf style type system in Chap. 15. This enables precise reasoning about the concepts introduced. The formal semantic basis provided for type safety is also a contribution to form-oriented analysis in general, because it renders more precisely the interplay between server actions and client pages of a submit/response style system.

Web applications are ubiquitous. For every company that wants to stay competitive it is not a question whether to deploy Internet technology, but how to deploy it [252]. Highly skilled workers are needed to operate e-commerce technology [315]; indeed a research study [124] conducted by the Gartner Group has shown that more than three-quarters of the cost of building an e-commerce site is labor-related. Consequently web technology is worth looking at.

Ultra-thin client based enterprise applications benefit from scalability and maintainability. Server pages technologies are widely used in the implementation of ultra-thin client applications. A drwaback of these technologies is that the low-level CGI programming model [57] shines through, especially when user data are gathered in a completely untyped manner. In this chapter a strongly typed server pages technology is designed from scratch. The contributions target the stability and reusability of server-pages-based systems. The findings are programming language independent. The results are formalized. The following concepts are combined:

- Parameterized server pages. A server page possesses a specified signature that consists of formal parameters, which are native typed with respect to the type system of a high-level programming language.

- Support for complex types in writing forms. New structured tags are offered for gathering arrays and objects of user-defined types.
- Exchanging objects across the web user agent. Server-side programmed objects may be actual form parameters and therefore passed to client pages and back, either as messages or virtually as objects.
- Higher-order server pages. Server pages may be actual form parameters.
- Statically ensured client page type safety. The type correct interplay of dynamically generated forms and targeted server pages is checked at compile-time.
- Statically ensured client page description safety. It is checked at compile-time if the generated page descriptions are always valid with respect to a defined client page description language.
- No unresolved links. It is statically ensured that all generated forms and links point to existing targets within the system dialogue.
- Active controls. NSP direct input controls are dynamically type-safe; that is, dynamic type checks with respect to data entered by the user are statically ensured. Equally checks with respect to required data are statically ensured.

The proposed server pages technology NSP (Next Server Pages) both overcomes drawbacks of current CGI-based technologies and helps the developer immediately to code cleaner, reusable, and more stable systems. The NSP approach is oriented towards improved web application architecture and improved development techniques from the outset:

- Enabling technology for improved web-based application architecture and design. In NSP a server-side call to a server page is designed as a parameter-passing procedure call, too. This enables functional decomposition of server pages and therefore helps decouple architectural issues and design patterns.
- Reverse engineering. The NSP concepts are exploited by the fully implemented reverse engineering tool JSPick, which recovers web signatures and form types from JSP-based presentation layers. The formal semantics of the tool are given in pseudo-evaluation style.

11.1 Type-Safe Interplay of Forms and Scripts

The above concepts aim to overcome certain drawbacks of CGI-based technologies, which today provide the single most important means to build presentation layers of web-based systems, as explained in the sequel. A web-based system consists of a set of server-side scripts. A script is a code unit that is called across the Net by the user by submitting a form or selecting a link. On behalf of this the script triggers business logic and eventually produces a client page that is sent back to the user. The client page is coded in the client

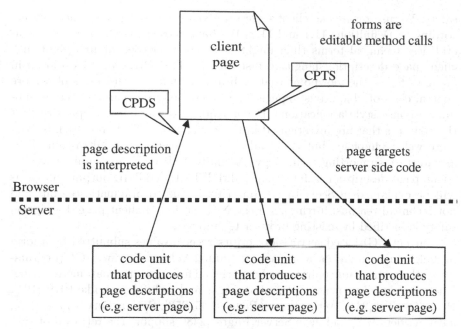

Fig. 11.1. CPDS and CPTS

page description language HTML or XHTML. The client page description is interpreted by a browser. A page presents information to the user and offers him or her one or more forms and links. Every form and every link target one of the server-side scripts; that is, the user gets explicit control over the dialogue flow. For the NSP approach it is crucial that a form may be viewed as an editable method call, gathering actual parameters from the user. A form may have preselected actual parameters, hidden parameters in more technical terms. It follows that links can be subsumed conceptually under forms.

We coin the two terms *client page description safety* and *client page type safety* for two desired properties of web applications.

Definition 11.1 (Client page description safety, CPDS). *A web application has the property of client page description safety if its server scripts always only produce valid page descriptions with respect to a defined client page description language.*

Definition 11.2 (Client page type safety, CPTS). *A web application has the property of client page type safety if the client pages generated by the server scripts always only contain such forms and links that provide exactly those actual parameters that are expected by the respective targeted server scripts.*

Figure 11.1 shows the interplay of server-side scripts and the browser and visualizes the notions of client page description safety and client page type safety. We use terms like client page type error, correctness, or checking according to Definitions 11.1 and 11.2. We have chosen to use some more general, less technical terms than might actually be needed at first sight, like client page description language instead of HTML/XHTML. We did so in order to foster the viewpoint that web applications are instances of a more general class of ubiquitous applications, which may be characterized as submit/response style applications. Furthermore we wanted to emphasize that the concepts that are investigated in the context of NSP do not stick to concrete web technology, but could add value to every future ultra-thin client architecture supporting technology. Actually NSP guarantees only a weaker client page description safety than valid HTML/XHTML output safety, as will be explained in Sect. 15.2.4, but this is due to pragmatic reasons and not technical reasons: furthermore the NSP notion of client page description safety is justified by existing browser technology.

Current CGI-based server-side scripts receive values submitted by a form or link conceptually as a stream of named values. In raw CGI programming, the name/value pairs must be retrieved from an input parameter string. The several well-known scripting languages and technologies, like PHP [194], Perl [308], Tcl [241], Active Server Pages [195, 253], Python Server Pages [10], Java Servlets [76], and Java Server Pages [248], support the retrieval of submitted values with appropriate data structures. But beyond this, these technologies do not support any appropriate notion of a server script signature, i.e., the interesting types of the received string-valued parameters with respect to a business logic or, in more code-oriented terms, with respect to a high-level programming language type system, are not supported.

In contrast, NSP offers appropriate tags to define a complex server page signature. Based on this Definition 11.2 of client page type safety obtains a precise meaning in the context of NSP, because parameters that are expected by a server page are just the parameters specified by the server page's signature. NSP provides both client page description checking and client page type checking. From the viewpoint of an NSP type system the generated client pages are the actual code which has to be considered. The generated code is naturally not available at deployment time, therefore NSP defines coding guidelines in Sect. 15.2 for writing the server pages which are

- non-prohibitive: all reasonable applications of scripting are still allowed;
- sufficient: client page description and type safety are ensured;
- convenient: the coding guidelines target the NSP developer. They are natural and easy to understand. The coding guidelines provide the informal definition of the NSP type system.

It is necessary to mention the debatable important opinion [242] known as Ousterhout's dichotomy. A division is made between system programming languages for programming components from scratch and scripting languages for programming component glue. It is argued that the typeless nature of a scripting language is crucial – a property that enables rapid development. The objectives of the present work contradict this core argument of Ousterhout's dichotomy.

Conservative Amalgamation

The NSP concepts are programming-language-independent results. They are reusable. They must be amalgamated with a concrete programming language. For every such amalgamation a concrete non-trivial language mapping must be provided. The NSP concepts are designed in such a way that concrete amalgamations are conservative with respect to the programming language. That is, the semantics of the programming language and especially its type system remain unchanged in the resulting technology. The NSP concepts are explained through a concrete amalgamation with the programming language Java. As a result of conservative amalgamation the NSP approach does not restrict the potentials of JSP in any way; for example, its state handling facility, the Servlet API session concept, is available as a matter of course. Formal semantics of an NSP core type system are given with respect to an amalgamation with a minimal imperative programming language.

Integration with Form-Oriented Analysis

NSP-based systems benefit from type safety. But beyond this NSP's capability for server pages' functional decomposition suggests reconsidering web application architecture and design. In the NSP approach a server-pages-based presentation layer is characterized as a closed collection of typed dialogue methods, an abstract viewpoint that is shared by form-oriented analysis. Based on functional decomposition it is possible to find canonical mappings from formcharts to NSP technology. Consequently NSP becomes an integral part of form-oriented analysis.

Next Server Pages Preliminaries

The NSP technology [93] is presented by the concrete amalgamation of NSP concepts with the programming language Java [127]. In the NSP approach a server page is considered to be code of a programming language with defined syntax and defined type system. In contrast, JSP code is just a convenient notation for Java Servlets. It is essentially a mix of HTML and Java code, which may occur inside special opening and closing scriptlet signs. Actually, beyond being a convenient notation, JSP technology offers some sophisticated mechanisms like tag libraries [78] and JSP actions, especially for supporting the integration of Java Beans into a server page. Furthermore JSP is intended to foster techniques for separating content from layout. But all these issues are incidental to the current discussion. The semantics of a JSP server page are given by the effect of a preprocessor that yields a Java Servlet by placing the HTML parts of the server page into output statements and adding these statements to the Java code that occurs inside the scriptlet signs.

11.1.1 A Motivating Example

The improvements of the Servlet API over raw CGI programming (support for retrieving values and a session mechanism) are available to JSP developers as a matter of course; besides JSP technology has the same disadvantages as other CGI-based technologies, as described in the introduction: JSP-based systems may lack client page description and type safety. JSP does not offer a natural server-side call to server scripting code. However, the combination of the JSP actions `jsp:include` and `jsp:param` does not provide a usual type-safe parameter-passing mechanism, it just provides a convenient notation for the low-level Java Servlet include mechanism.

Listing 11.1 Java Server Pages: counter example – form definition

```
01 <html>
02   <head>
03     <title>Registration</title>
04   </head>
05   <body> <%
06     int j;
07     boolean c;
08     // computation of the variables j and c
09     for (int i=0; i<j; i++) { %>
10     <form action="http://localhost:8080/NewCustomer.jsp"> <%}%>
11       Name: <%
12       if (c) { %>
13           <input type="text" name="customer"><br> <%
14       } %>
15       Age: <input type="text" name="age"><br>
16       <input type="submit">
17     </form>
18   </body>
19 </html>
```

As an instructive example consider the system that comprises the two server pages given in Listing 11.1 and Listing 11.2. The first server page generates a registration client page that contains a form for gathering a customer's name and age. This form targets a server page that stores the received data in a database and forwards the request to another server page. Several dynamic errors may occur. First of all, the opening form tag in line 10 of Listing 11.1 occurs inside a loop body. Only if the variable j has value 1 before the loop is entered is a valid HTML document sent to the browser. The input capability for the customer name occurs underneath a control structure in line 13. Only if the Boolean variable c evaluates to true will the input capability actually occur on the registration page. Listing 11.3 shows the result page for the case

Listing 11.2 Java Server Pages: counter example – targeted page

```
01 <html>
02   <head>
03     <title>NewCustomer</title>
04   </head>
05   <body> <%!
06     import myBusinessModel.CustomerBase; %> <%
07     String customer;
08     int age;
09     String foobar = request.getParameter("foobar");
10     customer = request.getParameter("customer");
11     try {
12       age = Integer.parseInt(request.getParameter("age"));
13     } catch(NumberFormatException e){
14       // error handling
15     }
16     CustomerBase.createCustomer(customer,age);
17     // further business logic %>
18     <jsp:forward page="Somewhere.jsp"/>
19   </body>
20 </html>
```

Listing 11.3 Java Server Pages: counter example – generated client page

```
01 <html>
02   <head>
03     <title>Registration</title>
04   </head>
05   <body>
06     <form action="http://localhost:8080/NewCustomer.jsp">
07     <form action="http://localhost:8080/NewCustomer.jsp">
08     <form action="http://localhost:8080/NewCustomer.jsp">
09       Name:
10       Age: <input type="text" name="age"><br>
11       <input type="submit">
12     </form>
13   </body>
14 </html>
```

when variable j has value 3 and variable c evaluates to `false`. The fact that the form tag occurs three times in the client page is actually tolerated by some of the ubiquitous web browsers, nevertheless it must be considered a dynamic client page description error. For example, in the case when variable j has value 0 even a tolerant browser cannot recover from the error, because together with the form tag the vitally information about the targeted page is missing.

As an example of a dynamic client page type error, assume that the customer parameter of the business logic method in line 16 of Listing 11.2 must not be a null object, i.e., the targeted server page relies on the reception of a customer name. However, it is not guaranteed that an input capability for the customer name is offered to the user by the registration page. If no such input capability occurs as in Listing 11.3, no respective value is sent on submitting the form and consequently the effort to retrieve such a value in line 10 of Listing 11.2 will result in yielding a null object.

Even more obviously, the developer would like to have a tool that gives a warning with respect to line 9 in Listing 11.2, because a value bound to name foobar will never be provided by a form of the registration page. However the JSPick tool presented in Chap. 10.2 is able to detect such sources of error.

Another kind of dynamic type error may occur with respect to the customer age parameter. A user may enter a value that is not a number, which is an event that must be caught by the developer. Appropriate error handling code, either through client-side or server-side scripting, must be provided, which is a tedious and error-prone task.

11.1.2 The NSP Document Structure

NSP modifies and augments XHTML [304] due to the special needs of developing parameterized strongly typed server pages. Very importantly, an implementation of NSP will always only send XHTML to the browser, and consequently NSP technology can be used immediately with existing standard browsers, i.e., no plug-ins are needed.

Though NSP is an XML document that is interlaced with imperative code, its objectives must not be confused with that of Extensible Server Pages (XSP) [209], a dynamic XML technology. XSP is an integral part of the XML publishing framework Cocoon, which targets separation of concerns between content, logic, and style of web publishing applications. In contrast, the NSP approach is not oriented too much towards building information architectures [262] for the time being, but towards improving the stability of enterprise information systems [181] with a tiered ultra-thin client architecture.

The name NSP/Java is used for the concrete language that results from merging NSP concepts with the programming language Java. If it is obvious from the context that not just the entirety of NSP technology concepts is meant, the term NSP is used for NSP/Java, too. An NSP consists of a signature definition, a Java definition block, and a core document. There are NSPs that may be called across the net by a form or a link, while others may be called by another NSP on the server side in order to be included. For NSPs that may be called across the Net the core document consists of a head and a body; for the other kind of server page the core document content is enclosed in include tags. A first example is given in Listing 11.4 and Listing 11.5,

which show the NSP counterpart of the customer registration system, which
was discussed in Sect. 11.1.1.

Listing 11.4 NSP: form definition

```
01  <nsp name="Registration">
02    <html>
03      <head>
04        <title>Registration</title>
05      </head>
06      <body><java>
07        boolean c;
08        // computation of the variable c </java>
09        <form callee="NewCustomer"><java>
10          if (c) {</java>
11            <input type="String" param="customer"></input><java>
12          } else {</java>
13            <hidden param="customer">"DefaultName"</hidden><java>
14          } </java>
15          Age: <input type="int" param="age"></input><br>
16          <submit></submit>
17        </form>
18      </body>
19    </html>
20  </nsp>
```

Listing 11.5 NSP: targeted page

```
01  <nsp name="NewCustomer">
02    <param name="customer" type="String"></param>
03    <param name="age" type="int"></param>
04    <java>import myBusinessModel.CustomerBase;</java>
05    <html>
06      <head>
07        <title>NewCustomer</title>
08      </head>
09      <body>
10        <java>
11          CustomerBase.createCustomer(customer,age);
12        </java>
13        <forward callee="Somewhere"></forward>
14      </body>
15    </html>
16  </nsp>
```

The signature of a server page is defined with appropriate parameter tags. Attributes are used for specifying the name and the type of a formal parameter.

Definition 11.3 (Web signature). *A web signature is a record type which consists of the specified formal parameters of an NSP as labeled components.*

We coin another term for the concept of web signature, namely formal superparameter. Analogously, an actual superparameter is the entirety of actual parameters provided by a form or a link targeting an NSP with respect to a given formal superparameter.

Definition 11.4 (Web server page). *A web server page is an NSP that may be called across the Net by a form or a link.*

Definition 11.5 (Include server page). *An include server page is an NSP that may be called for inclusion in another NSP.*

The web server pages are the front components of a tiered system's presentation layer, therefore we use the term dialogue method synonymously for such server pages, especially to distinguish them from business methods. Similarly we use the term dialogue submethod for NSP include server pages.

In NSPs Java code is placed inside java tags. Some Java code may be placed between the signature definition and the server page core. It is called a Java declaration in accordance with JSP terminology and hosts code that is intentionally independent of the single server page invocation, such as import declarations or a definition of state that is shared by all the several sessions. Java code that occurs in the server page core is executed upon invocation of the server page. The server page parameters are accessible in the inline Java code. In addition to the tags it is possible to use Java expression tags as a controlled variant of direct, i.e., Java-coded, writing to the output stream. Note that a static type system cannot prevent such dynamic errors that result from using the output stream to send computed description languages tags directly to the browser. Generally, using the output stream for sending description language is considered bad style and may lead to dynamic errors. It is an NSP rule that the output stream must not be used in a way that corrupts the otherwise type- and description-safe NSP system. For example, if a corrupted form that is caused by a prohibited use of the output stream contains invalid input capabilities or a wrong number of input capabilities, this is considered just as a dynamic error, like division by zero.

In NSP no special non-XML syntax for expression scripting elements like the JSP <%= and %> signs is available. Accordingly it is not possible to generate NSP tag parts, and attribute values especially may not be generated. Element properties that may have to be provided dynamically are supported by elements instead of attributes in NSP. As a result an NSP is a completely block-structured document and therefore it is possible to give a precise convenient definition for the syntax of NSP, which is the essential basis for the detection and exploration of further concepts of syntax analysis and syntax manipulation. Moreover, an NSP is a valid XML [31] document. Therefore NSP will benefit immediately from all new techniques developed in the context of XML. In particular, NSP can be used in combination with XML style sheet technologies [322, 222].

NSP Forms and Hyperlinks

An NSP form specifies the targeted dialogue method via a callee attribute. Somewhat similar to the parameter-passing mechanism in ADA [298], a targeted formal parameter of a called method is explicitly referenced by its name. For this purpose the tags in lines 13 and 15 of Listing 11.4 have parameter attributes.

In the present simple example the form provides actual parameters exactly for the formal method parameters, either by user input or by hidden parameters. In general the overall notion of type-safe calls of NSP methods demands sophisticated guidelines for writing forms presented in Sect. 15.2 and a new innovative widget set presented in Sects. 11.1.3 through 11.1.7.

The syntax of NSP hyperlinks follows the NSP form syntax; Listing 11.6 provides an example. Therefore the NSP hyperlink syntax is very natural, i.e., no low-level, tedious handling with special characters is needed in order to use hyperlinks with parameters. An NSP link element must not contain any other code than hidden controls and one link body element that gives the link text. In fact it must contain exactly one hidden control of the correct type for every formal parameter of the targeted dialogue method.

Listing 11.6 NSP: hyperlink

```
01 <link callee="NewCustomer">
02   <hidden param="customer">
03     "John Q. Public"
04   </hidden>
05   <hidden param="age"> 32 </hidden>
06   <linkbody> underlined link name </linkbody>
07 </link>
```

A Motivating Example

All the code of lines 7 to 15 in Listing 11.2, which is needed for the reception of parameters, becomes a two-line web signature declaration in Listing 11.5.

In Listing 11.1 the opening form tag is a loop body, which may lead to dynamic errors. In NSP this is prevented from the outset by NSP syntax. An element may only occur as a whole, i.e., with both opening and closing tags underneath a control structure.

There is no assurance that the registration page generated by Listing 11.1 offers an input control for the customer name. In contrast, in the NSP code in Listing 11.4 it is for example not allowed to omit line 13 without violating the NSP coding guidelines, i.e., without provoking an error message at compile-time.

Obviously faulty requests to non-existent parameters as in line 9 of Listing 11.2 are not possible in NSP code, because NSP is strongly typed and all formal server page parameters have to be declared.

Furthermore, in an NSP system it is statically ensured that data provided by the user are dynamically checked. That is, a server-side dynamic error like the one described for the age parameter in Listing 11.2 would not be possible in an NSP system because of the concept of active controls, which is introduced in Sects. 11.1.3 and 11.1.5.

11.1.3 NSP Active Direct Input Controls

NSP supports the usual HMTL/XHTML controls, but they are refined and elaborated further due to the special needs of a type-safe server pages technology. Each control is supported by its own element. Each control has a param attribute, which is used to directly specify the name of the targeted formal parameter. That is, the param attribute replaces the name attribute of HTML/XHTML controls. Another usage of the param attribute is specifying a field of a complex actual parameter of form message type as explained in Sect. 15.2.3.

In HTML/XHMTL the input tag is used for a couple of conceptually unrelated controls, like direct text input, radio buttons, check boxes, etc. Every of these controls has its specifics; especially the behavior of non-direct input controls differs fundamentally from the behavior of direct input controls. Therefore in NSP every control type becomes a markup language element.

The input tag is used in NSP for a direct input field only. NSP provides different direct input fields for different programming language types. That is, NSP is already typed on the level of controls. Compare this to HMTL/XHTML again, where controls always yield only text, i.e., pure string data. In HMTL/XHTML the type attribute is used to specify a widget kind. In NSP the type attribute is used to specify the type of a direct input field. The direct input controls of NSP are active input controls in the following sense. A form that contains a direct input field cannot be submitted if the user has entered data that are not type correct with respect to the field's type. Instead, an error message is presented to the user. Furthermore, in NSP a formal parameter can be specified to be required by the developer. Then a form that contains a direct input field that targets this formal parameter cannot be submitted if the user has entered no data in this field. Again an appropriate error message is presented to the user. Dynamic type checking of data provided by the user and dynamically ensuring data entry are ubiquitous problems in web interface development. The developer must provide solutions by either client-side scripting with one of the ECMAScript [107, 169] derivatives or server-side scripting, a tedious and error-prone task. With the NSP notion of active direct input controls it is possible to statically ensure the desired dynamic checks.

In NSP/Java the Java types int, Integer, String, and the type Date of the JDBC API [316] are supported by direct input fields. If data entry for a formal parameter is optional and no data are entered by the user, a null object is passed as the actual parameter on submit. The single exception to this rule is the type String: if no data are entered in a field for an optional parameter the empty string is sent instead of a null object. For formal int parameters data entry is implicitly required. The type int is a Java primitive type and no null object is available for signaling that no data have been entered. Alternatively it would be possible to select a certain int value to take over the role of the null object, most probably zero. But then the receiving dialogue method could not distinguish between actually entered data and the event when no data have been entered.

There are two further direct input capabilities for the type String, namely a text area and a password field.

The XForms standard [106, 105] allows for specifying constraints on data gathered by a form. In order to address parts of XML data in expressions XForms relies on XPath [52]. Type correctness and entry requirements are important instances of possible XForms constraints. But the XForms approach goes beyond these. It is possible to specify arbitrary calculations and validations on the gathered data. An event model allows for the appropriate reaction on the violation of the given constraints. The technology allows for sophisticated constraints, but the notion of NSP active controls is different. In XForms constraints can be given with respect to a form. But it is not ensured that all forms targeting a critical server-side action actually prevent the same errors from occurring. In contrast, in NSP, strictly based on the typing of server pages, the constraints are given for formal parameters of dialogue methods. In this way it is possible to statically ensure the desired dynamic checks; that is, NSP active direct input controls are dynamically type-safe in the sense that they make NSP-based systems type-safe with respect to dynamically entered data. A programming language is dynamically type-safe if untrapped errors are prevented [39].

11.1.4 Actual Object Parameters

In HTML/XHTML only text, i.e., string data, can be passed as a hidden parameter, an item of a select menu, or the value of a radio button or check box. The JSP expression scripting element supports implicit coercion for data that are convertible to String in order to send them to the user agent. However, the data are received as string values by the targeted server pages.

In the NSP approach arbitrary objects can be passed virtually across the Web, i.e., passed to the user agent and passed to a dialogue method on submit in the sequel. An object can be passed in this way as a hidden parameter, an item of a select menu, or the value of a radio button or check box. A value of primitive type is just copied to the user agent and to the dialogue method on submit. The present type is preserved. But NSP supports passing of objects of arbitrary non-primitive types. Somewhat similar to the RMI parameter-passing mechanism [285], two different parameter-passing semantics are supported. First, as a default, a reference to the object in question is passed to the receiving dialogue method. As an alternative, if the passed object is serializable [286], the object is copied and a reference to this copy is passed to the receiving dialogue method. Based on the semantics of serialization, arbitrary deep copies of object nets can be passed as parameters.

A hidden parameter, select menu item, radio button, or check box value must be given as a Java expression. This expression must have the type of the encompassing control. The encompassing tags implicitly switch to a Java expression modus, i.e., no additional expression tags are needed in order to explicitly signalize a Java expression. Furthermore this rule applies whenever appropriate in order to give a Java object as a certain desired property of a control. For example, a default value may be given for direct input fields. In HTML/XHTML the tag's value attribute is used for specifying the default value. In NSP input field tags may contain a type correct Java expression for this purpose. Again the input field tags implicitly switch to a Java expression modus. The default value of a direct input field must match the input field's type or it must be the empty String.

11.1.5 NSP Active Single Select Controls

NSP supports single select menus and multiple select menus, which are distinguished as usual by a multiple attribute. A select element has option content elements. The NSP option element has no value attribute, but instead of this it has a value content element and a label content element. The value tags contain a Java expression for a selectable data item. The label tags contain a Java String expression that is displayed in the select menu control and denotes the respective data item. In NSP the radio button is supported by an element.

Single select menus and radio buttons are conceptually equal. If a single select control targets a formal parameter that is not an array parameter, it must be ensured that the user actually chooses one of the items. Therefore NSP select menus and radio buttons are again active: a form encompassing such a control cannot be submitted unless the user has finally chosen one of the items.

Both NSP radio buttons and NSP select menu options have checked attributes. Instead of employing activity for radio buttons and select menus the NSP approach could rely on the request for comment document on HTML [22] that specifies: if no radio button or select option is checked, the user agent chooses the first one as preselected. Regrettably many ubiquitous browsers do not implement this behavior. For this reason even the HTML specification [257] differs from [22] in this point. As a result a set of radio buttons or a single select menu may yield no actual parameter. But exactly this must be prevented if a formal parameter is targeted that requires data entry. There are two more solutions to this problem other than active controls. First, an NSP container could dynamically ensure that a checked attribute is added when needed, i.e., it could simulate the behavior demanded by [22]. Secondly, the NSP type system could be extended by checks that force the author to ensure that checked entities are always provided. Besides, single select capabilities with no preselected items are desired.

11.1.6 Auxiliary NSP Interaction Controls

NSP supports hidden parameters. Hidden parameters offer a way to overcome the stateless nature of the Hypertext Transfer Protocol [113], because they allow for maintaining state between client/server exchanges. However, there are other opportunities for this, i.e., techniques based on client state persistence [187] and URL rewriting. Anyway today's APIs offer high-level session-tracking mechanisms. Therefore the more interesting aspect of hidden parameters is the following. Hidden parameters enable arbitrary reuse of a dialogue method in contexts where only a part of its web signature data should be determined by user interaction.

NSP distinguishes between two check box concepts that reflect the two different ways in which the HTML/XHTML check boxes are used. First, the check box element yields an actual Boolean parameter, true for a checked check box, false for an unchecked check box. Secondly, a set of value check box elements can be used to offer the user a choice of items. In the value check box tags a selectable data item is given as a Java expression. Assume a set of value check boxes that target the same formal parameter. Such a value check box set is conceptually equal to a multiple select menu, because the user may check a couple of the alternatives offered. A value check box set yields a value array on submit.

11.1.7 NSP Submit Button

In HTML/XHMTL the submit button can also specify a name/value pair. The submit button is subsumed under the input element. A form is allowed to have several submit buttons. This is an important facility that is used in web applications to offer the user a choice between different functionalities for the same form. For this purpose the values that represent different functionalities must be defined and the targeted script must switch to the correct alternative on submit. The respective code quickly becomes fault prone; its design suffers an "ask what kind" antipattern. Note that we take a generalized view of "don't ask what kind" that is explained in Sect. 11.4.1. In contrast, in the NSP approach it is possible to specify a targeted dialogue method for each submit button. The NSP submit element has an optional callee attribute for this purpose. If no callee attribute is given for a submit element, the callee attribute of the encompassing form is inherited. Furthermore a submit element can contain hidden parameters, so again NSP gains from its solid theoretical basis: a form can target a variety of different dialogue methods providing different functionality and possessing different web signatures. This allows for flexible and at the same time robust design.

11.1.8 Towards an Improved Widget Set

Further improved widget sets are easily imaginable: for example, widgets that are tailored to gather data of complex, user-defined type, or widgets that allow drag and drop in the interaction within a page. That is, there are advanced form and widget concepts, which are not ubiquitous in current types of submit/response systems, but which show that form-based interfaces can have a comfortable appearance and functionality. However, a discussion of these issues does not undermine the submit/response-style interaction paradigm but rather supports it.

Direct input widgets are in the first place textual input fields. Strongly typed input widgets would allow only input of correct primitive type. Strongly typed widgets are directly related to formatted widgets. Examples are fixed length, integer, fixed point, date, and IP numbers. Certain special formatting widgets can be seen as widgets for complex data types, e.g., IP address widgets can be built from four integer widgets. In this case it is desirable that the framework allows us to define the dot key as an alternate key for focus shift: hence, if the user enters the IP address in the keystroke sequence with dots, the IP address is correctly placed across the four widgets.

If the user is required to enter a selection from a large set, neither radio buttons nor select lists are suitable. An example is the input field for a train station. Here an adequate input widget would be an auto complete widget. If the user enters a character sequence, a list of all choices with this sequence as a prefix is offered.

11.2 Functional Decomposition of Server Pages

In this section we provide a discussion of important current approaches to web interface programming based on the Model 2 architecture [96]. From the results we show how to improve web presentation layer architecture. The enabling technology for this is the NSP concept of typed server-side calls to server pages. The concept of higher-order server pages is introduced, which enables even more flexible design. It is demonstrated how the improvements integrate with form-oriented analysis. Furthermore we provide a comparison of proven and current web technologies, i.e., technologies that are related to the web presentation layer or web-enabled access to information systems.

In HTML/XHMTL only plain unidirectional links are possible. Though a limited number of different link behaviors are available, important simple notions such as a desired page decomposition are not defined for HTML/XHTML. XLink [82] overcomes these limitations in a general XML setting. XLink has been influenced by [168]. XInclude [204] improves XLink with respect to document decomposition by defining a processing model for merging documents.

The central architectural questions concerning web-based system interfaces are located on the server side. We review current web application frameworks for building dynamic web pages. Web application frameworks consider only the presentation layer in a multi-tiered web application. Our considerations are based on an analysis of the problem addressed by these frameworks. Special attention is paid to proposed composition mechanisms. In that comparison we can analyze the technological contributions as well as the shortcomings of these approaches.

11.2.1 Model 2 Architecture

In practice the tight coupling of code with layout has become a drawback for server pages technology. Therefore, separation of business logic processing and presentation generation, called processing/presentation separation in the following for short, became a goal.

In the discussion on how to reach processing/presentation separation, Sun has become influential by proposing several server-side architectures, such as the "redirecting request" application model – later coined the Model 2 architecture [248]. This model has become commonly known as following the Model View Controller paradigm. We will in due course outline that it is a misconception about Model View Controller if the Model 2 architecture is subsumed under this pattern. We therefore give an evaluation of the Model 2 approach without relying on the MVC argument.

The Model 2 architecture uses a threefold design in which the request is first directed to a front component, typically a Servlet, which triggers the creation of a content object, typically a Java Bean (Fig. 11.2). The bean is then passed to a presentation component, typically a scripted server page where the data within the bean are embedded in HTML/XHTML. The server-side objects are considered as the model (M), the front components as controllers (C), and the presentation components as views (V), because for Model 2 architecture some good practices are established on how to partition the request processing between the three parts. The most important recommendation is related to the use of the server pages: the server pages should be used only for presentation purposes. Model 2 architectures can achieve a reuse of presentation components. If several front components generate the same output page under certain conditions, this page can be used from both components. Model

2 also allows separate maintenance of totally different response pages that may be generated from the same front component under certain conditions.

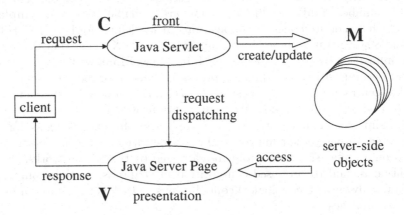

Fig. 11.2. Model 2 architecture

The Struts [77] framework is widely accepted as the open source reference implementation of the Model 2 architecture. Struts proposes functional decomposition based on a proprietary composition approach in which business processing units inform the controller object about the next processing step. Parameter passing between processing units is not established by the Java method parameter-passing mechanism, but by emulating a parameter-passing mechanism through transferring bean objects.

It is important to clarify a serious misunderstanding in architecture proposals for web site development. The web application frameworks following the Model 2 approach do not follow the MVC paradigm. This paradigm [186] was introduced in Smalltalk and is a completely different concept. It only has superficial similarities in that it has three components from which one is related to the user interface, another to the application. However, the problem solved by the MVC paradigm is totally different. MVC is related to event notification problems within a GUI that provides different views of the same data, which have to be synchronized. MVC was renamed within the pattern community as observer pattern [119] and became an accepted general pattern for event model design problems. For example, the Java Beans component model relies on an observer-pattern-based event model. As another example the GUI event model of the first Java version 1.0 followed the "chain of responsibility" design pattern [128], but today it follows the observer pattern. The misnomer is even more astounding if one considers that the property of GUIs which makes MVC necessary, namely view update, i.e., push technology, is known to be absent in the pull-based approach of HTML/XHTML browsers.

The fact that web application frameworks rely on a misconception of the MVC paradigm does not necessarily imply that these frameworks have a bad design. But the argument for this architecture, namely that it follows a proven good design, is flawed. Only by recognizing that this argument is invalid is the way free for a new evaluation of the architecture and a recognition of advantages as well as drawbacks.

The Model 2 architecture defines a fixed decomposition combined with an intended separation of concerns. The incoming request is performed on the business model, then data are presented to the user in response. The difficulty with the approach lies not in the proposals for separation of concerns, but with the composition mechanism offered. The question is which semantics govern the interplay between the components: after you know how to divide, you have to know how to conquer.

The Model 2 architecture offers a complex communication mechanism based on the passing of beans. Beans are attached to a hashtable by the generating unit and retrieved from the hashtable by the target unit. In that way data are transmitted from the Servlet to the scripted page. This mechanism is nothing more than a parameter-passing mechanism, but without static type safety. The semantics of the composition paradigms of presentation and business logic are only conceivable by direct reference to the components found in the running system. In contrast, we will later use our NSP approach, where simple method call semantics are sufficient and allow for a sound architecture. Hence in the Model 2 architecture a considerable part of the architecture redefines a parameter-passing mechanism which delivers no added value beyond method invocation. The Model 2 architecture therefore is still interwoven with a legacy-technology-driven design pattern that is far from creating a clear-cut abstraction layer.

11.2.2 Server-Side Calls to Server Pages

NSP is open with respect to architectural decisions. It distinguishes between server pages that may be called across the Net by a form or a link and server pages that may be called by another NSP on the server side in order to be included. The latter server pages have been termed dialogue submethods earlier. The NSP call mechanism for dialogue submethods has identical semantics as the Java method call with respect to parameter passing. It is the only composition feature that is needed to build sound and well-understood web application architectures. NSP does not force the user into a specific design. With NSP no early decision between Model 1, Model 2, or other architectures is necessary.

The NSP approach to design can be seen as a generalization of another proposal of the JSP specification, named "including requests" [248].

In order to call a server page from within another server page, the call element is used (Listing 11.7, lines 8–11, lines 14–16). The opening call tag has a callee attribute. Upon call the targeted server page generates a document fragment that replaces the respective call element in the calling document. The output of the dialogue submethod must be a valid content element with

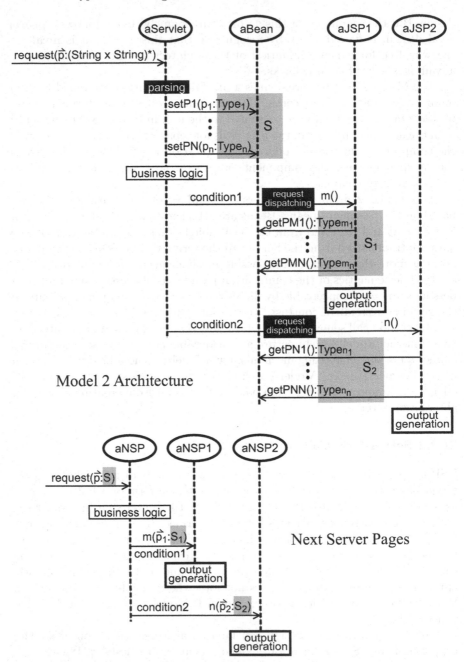

Fig. 11.3. Model 2 architecture versus NSP functional decomposition. The figure shows a typical control and data flow in a Model 2 architecture system except for details of request dispatching and the improvement of a counterpart system build on NSP technology by an interaction diagram

respect to the context of the respective call element. Actual parameters are given to the called dialogue submethod by actparam elements. The opening actparam tag has a param attribute, which has the same purpose as the param attributes of the NSP control elements. For each formal parameter of a dialogue submethod exactly one actual parameter must be given in every targeting call element. Call elements may only contain actparam elements; especially they cannot contain dynamic code. The call element provides the NSP equivalent of the JSP request dispatching include mechanism. Analogously NSP supports redirect and server-side redirect, i.e., forward, by appropriate elements in the same way as the call element.

The example in Listing 11.7 consists of a main page and two dialogue submethods. The first dialogue submethod receives a String parameter and an int parameter and produces a message with respect to these parameters. The second dialogue submethod is called inside a table element and receives an array of Article objects. An Article object has three String properties x,y, and z. The dialogue submethod generates a table row for each object. A row contains three table data cells, one for each object property.

In the JSP technology parameter passing to a JSP differs fundamentally whether the JSP is called across the Net or called on the server side. In the first case, parameters come as raw string data, as the data are inherited from the old CGI mechanism. However, if a server page is called locally, it is established coding practice to pass the parameters by a bean object attached to the request parameter. Hence, a page must be designed either to be callable from the Net or to be callable from the server, and in both cases the developer has to face a parameter-passing mechanism different from any reasonable parameter-passing mechanism. In the Servlet request dispatching mechanism, it is possible to attach new name/value pairs to the request object URL before invoking another Servlet. The JSP technology provides a JSP standard action, i.e., the param action, for attaching new arguments for included server pages. However, both of these are not parameter-passing mechanisms, because only string parameters can be attached in an uncontrolled manner. In NSP, in contrast, parameter-passing is identical whether the page is called over the Net or within the server. In both cases the parameter-passing mechanism is essentially identical to the parameter passing encountered in Java. The parameters of a page in NSP behave identically to local variables in the Java code; in fact they are local variables initialized by the actual parameters. The difference is visualized in Fig. 11.3. This transparency in the parameter-passing mechanism comes at virtually no additional cost compared to the approaches in web application frameworks.

NSP allows for arbitrary application architectures based on functional decomposition. NSP frees the developer from considering the implementation details of the parameter-passing mechanisms. Hence all special runtime entities that are needed in NSP to deliver the method call semantics are hidden from the developer. Processing/presentation separation is in the first place a pattern for source code organization. NSP allows the challenges in process-

Listing 11.7 NSP: functional decomposition with dialogue submethods

```
01 <nsp name="mainPage">
02   <html><head><title>Some Page</title></head>
03     <body><java>
04       String customer;
05       int age;
06       Article[] articles;
07       // get data for variables customer,age and articles </java>
08       <call callee="prelude">
09         <actparam param="customer">customer</actparam>
10         <actparam param="age">age</actparam>
11       </call>
12       <table>
13         <tr> <td>X</td> <td>Y</td> <td>Z</td> </tr>
14         <call callee="tableContent">
15           <actparam param="articles">articles</actparam>
16         </call>
17       </table>
18     </body>
19   </html>
20 </nsp>
21
22 <nsp name="prelude">
23   <param type="String" name="customer"></param>
24   <param type="int" name="age"></param>
25   <include>
26     Hello Mr. <javaexpr>customer</javaexpr> !
27     <!-- other ouptut with respect to customer and age -->
28   </include>
29 </nsp>
30
31 <nsp name="tableContent">
32   <param type="Article[]" name="articles"></param>
33   <include><java>
34     for (i=1;i<articles.lentgth;i++) {</java>
35       <tr>
36         <td><javaexpr>articles[i].getX()</javaexpr></td>
37         <td><javaexpr>articles[i].getY()</javaexpr></td>
38         <td><javaexpr>articles[i].getZ()</javaexpr></td>
39       </tr><java>
40     }</java>
41   </include>
42 </nsp>
```

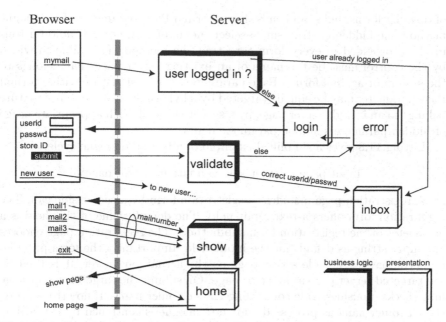

Fig. 11.4. Example interaction diagram. The figure shows the login dialogue of a web-based mail account. The user logs in and views his or her inbox. If the stores a password for a certain time no login is necessary

ing/presentation separation to be solved without referring to system architecture. In contrast, in NSP the functional decomposition mechanism allows for the desired separation of concerns. In Fig. 11.4 we give an interaction diagram which shows the login dialogue of a web-based mail tool. The user logs in and views his or her inbox. If the user stores a password for a certain time no login is necessary. In the given example the depth of decomposition is adapted according to the complexity of the respective functionality. The login screen is used for the initial login screen as well as for the login screen after an invalid login attempt. Viewing a mail is realized as a simple server page call. The example demonstrates the openness of NSP for different architectures.

11.3 Higher-Order Server Pages

NSP formal server page parameters may receive server pages again. This introduces the notion of higher-order server pages. The higher-order server pages concept can be exploited to foster system maintainability and system part reusability.

NSP introduces the Page type as a single proprietary type to be used for a formal parameter in addition to the types of the amalgamated programming language. Formal parameters of Page type may be used as callee attributes of opening forms, links, and calls. For a formal Page parameter of a dialogue method one hidden control, single select menu, or at least two radio buttons must be provided in every form targeting the method. The value provided by the control must be the name of an existing server page that belongs to the system or again a formal Page parameter. A web signature with a formal Page parameter may be equally targeted by a hyperlink or, if the web signature belongs to an include server page, by a server-side call, with appropriate usage of hidden parameters and actparam elements.

Listing 11.8 gives a simplified example of a typical dialogue cycle:

input page – server-side validation – error page

A registration page includes a registration form by a server-side call. The registration form offers a text input field. The default value of this field is a parameter of the registration form submethod. The registration page chooses an empty string as default for the input field. Importantly the form provides its encompassing include server page as the actual parameter. It is used by the targeted server page as an error page. On submit the targeted server page first checks a business rule concerning the customer name. If no error occurs, the customer name is processed and the dialogue is continued by forwarding to another server page. Otherwise the form that targeted the server page is redisplayed and serves as a simple error page. This time the last user's input for the customer name is the default value for the input field. The example given in Listing 11.8 is an instance of a more general, common design problem that can be given a reusable, flexible solution based on a higher-order server page concept. Consider the case where several forms target the same dialogue method, which processes the data and branches the dialogue flow, and the next page in the dialogue depends on the form that triggered the server page. Without higher-order server pages the developer must explicitly keep track of the dialogue and must switch to the correct next page accordingly, which is an instance of a design that suffers an "ask what kind" antipattern in the sense of our view of "don't ask what kind," which is discussed in Sect. 11.4.1. Figure 11.5 shows a feature containing three registration pages similar to the one given in Listing 11.8. The feature is visualized as a formchart. The server action for processing new customer data validates submitted user entry and presents an error page to the user if necessary. In the case where the action has been triggered by the first or third registration page, the respective page is redisplayed. Note that the dialogue constraint language of Sect. 5.4.1 is used to express the flow conditions in Fig. 11.5. In the case where the action has been triggered by the second registration page, a specific error page is presented to the user.

Listing 11.8 NSP: higher-order server pages

```
01 <nsp name="Registration">
02   <html>
03     <head><title>Registration</title></head>
04     <body>
05       <call callee="RegistrationForm">
06         <actparam name="defaultCustomer"> "" </actparam>
07       </call>
08     </body>
09   </html>
10 </nsp>
11
12 <nsp name="RegistrationForm">
13   <param name="defaultCustomer" type="String"></param>
14   <include>
15     <form callee="NewCustomer">
16      <input type="String" name="customer">defaultCustomer</input>
17      <hidden name="errorPage">RegistrationForm</hidden>
18     </form>
19   </include>
20 </nsp>
21
22 <nsp name="NewCustomer">
23   <param name="customer" type="String"></param>
24   <param name="errorPage" type="ServerPage"></param>
25   <java>import myBusinessModel.CustomerBase;</java>
26   <html>
27     <head><title>NewCustomer</title></head>
28     <body><java>
29       if (CustomerBase.validate(customer)) {
30         CustomerBase.createCustomer(customer);</java>
31         <forward callee="Somewhere"></forward><java>
32       } else {</java>
33         <call callee="errorPage">
34         <actparam name="defaultCustomer"> customer </actparam>
35         </call><java>
36       }</java>
37     </body>
38   </html>
39 </nsp>
```

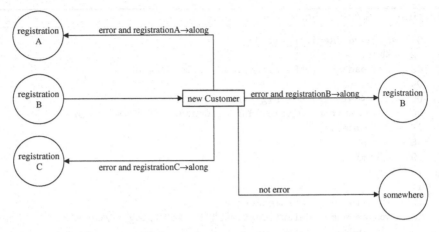

Fig. 11.5. Higher-order server pages design example

11.4 A Comparison of Web Technologies

11.4.1 The "System Calls User" Approach

The domain-specific language [83] Mawl (Mother of All Web Languages) [16, 17, 189] is a server script approach with a sophisticated concept for form presentation. The definition language for forms is an HTML dialect. The scripting language is oriented towards the programming language C. Form presentation to the user is done in a "system calls user" way, i.e., a procedure is called in the server script. The actual parameters that are passed to the procedure are the data presented to the user; the return value of the procedure is the data entered by the user. In this way, Mawl allows for seamless integration of a script organizing session concept. The input type and output type of a form must be declared. Mawl supports static type checking of these types. Iterator tags, indexing for list data, and a dot notation for record data are available in the form description language for data presentation. Mawl separates between service logic code and markup language from the outset. Based on this device independency [35] is introduced to a certain extent: forms cannot be described just in the aforementioned HTML dialect [15], but in the Phone Markup Language (PML) [258], too. PML allows for describing documents that are served over a telephone by special telecommunication portal middleware. PML is one of the precursors of Voice XML [210]. In the "system calls user" approach the overall control flow is prescribed by the server script code, because the return point of a form presentation is fixed. Form presentations are treated like procedure calls: after form processing the control flow returns to the call point. This abandons the core paradigm of hypertext, where a page may encompass several links and forms each targeting different locations. In order to add flexibility, Mawl supports multiple submit buttons. In the case where a form should be able to target different server actions, the receiving script can analyze which submit button has been pressed, and can branch the control flow appropriately [68]. That is the purpose of the usual HTML multiple submit buttons, too. However, the resulting designs relying on such control flow branching must be considered flawed. These systems seriously suffer an "ask what kind" design antipattern resulting in high coupling and low cohesion. The situation is even worse if multiple forms target different server actions. These multiple forms must be emulated by one single superform and several submit capabilities. The output type of the superform must encompass the output types of all emulated forms, which has to be considered a further design flaw. We use the term "ask what kind" as an antipattern name in a generalized sense. Assume that a form containing several submit capabilities is to be reused. Then every scripting code that reuses the form is responsible for branching the control flow correctly – high coupling. This is an error-prone pattern. Furthermore, consider a change to the submit buttons in the forms. Now it is necessary to be aware of all the distributed hard-wired case structures and to fix them accordingly – low cohesion. The term "don't ask what kind" [55, 56] has been coined in the object orientation community for the use of polymorphism as a basic pattern of assigning object responsibilities [192] for similar reasons.

11.4.2 Web Application Frameworks

The NSP approach must not be mistaken for a variant of architectural approaches. These web application frameworks target separation of presentation, content, and logic to different extent. Web application frameworks follow an approach that has become known as MVC architecture or Model 2 architecture. Further objectives of these web application frameworks can be integration with enterprise application frameworks, rapid development by providing an integrated development environment, support for internationalization, support for security, or support for dynamic form field validation. A prominent commercial MVC web application framework is the Sun ONE Application Framework (JATO). The most widespread application servers according to [256], namely Oracle9iAs, IBM WebSphere, and BEA WebLogic, come along with MVC web application frameworks, too. WebMacro is an early open source project that allows the separation between Java and HTML. Other prominent open source web application frameworks are Struts [77] and Cocoon, both hosted by the Jakarta project.

11.4.3 Functional and Logic Programming Language Approaches

The mature, comprehensive WASH project offers two technologies WASH/CGI [294] and WASH/HTML [292, 293] for web authoring based on the functional programming language Haskell [150]. WASH/CGI offers static checks for user interface type safety, and WASH/HTML offers static checks for weak user interface description safety. WASH/CGI is a domain-specific language for server-side web scripting. Dynamic generation of HTML output is monad-based. The form presentation concept encompasses a callback mechanism that allows for full design flexibility. WASH/CGI programs are dynamically type safe: untrapped errors cannot occur, because necessary server-side reaction to user-entered data that cannot be parsed is enforced. A compositional approach to specifying form elements is offered. WASH/HTML defines a Haskell combinator library for dynamic XML coding. In [293] four levels of XML validity are defined. Well-formedness is the property of correct block structure, i.e., correct matching of opening and closing tags. Weak validity and elementary validity are both certain limited conformances to a given DTD. Full validity is full conformance to a given DTD. The WASH/HTML approach can guarantee full validity of generated XML and guarantees weak validity with respect to the HTML SGML DTD under an immediate understanding of the defined XML validity levels for SGML documents.

There are a couple of other projects for dynamic XML generation that guarantee some level of user interface description language safety, e.g., [138, 212]. We will delve further on some representative examples.

A Haskell library for CGI scripting is proposed in [212]. There is also a server pages technology available for Haskell [215]. Haskell Server Pages guarantee well-formedness of XML documents. The small functional programming language XMλ [273] is designed to ensure full XML validity [214]. XMλ is based on XML documents as basic data types. The approach given by [212, 215, 273, 214] comes along with a client-side scripting technology for Haskell [213].

Yet another project in the context of Haskell is [312], which investigates two different approaches. In the first approach a library for XML processing arbitrary documents is provided, and well-formedness of XML documents is ensured. The second is a type-based translation framework for XML documents with respect to a given DTD, which guarantees full XML validity.

The LAML (Lisp Abstract Markup Language) project [234, 235] proposes web programming based on Scheme. Two other Scheme-based web publishing systems are proposed in [255] and [129]. Beyond this it is shown in [129] how the features of a Scheme extension can be exploited for an efficient web server implementation. A conceptual basis for the continuation style of functional web publishing technologies is given by [151] as a generalized notion of monads.

In [138, 139] a comprehensive CGI programming library for the functional logic multi-paradigm language Curry is proposed. A notion of submit button event handler is introduced and enables in effect a callback-style programming model. A specific abstract data type is used for references to input fields, which enables compile-time checks with resepct to input field naming. Pillow [37, 36] is a CGI library for the CIAO Prolog system. LogicWeb [198] is a toolkit for even improved amalgamation of logic programming and web programming. Neither the Pillow approach nor the LogicWeb approach offer user interface type safety.

Part III

Semantics

12

The Integrated Source Code Paradigm

In this chapter we discuss the domain of so-called collaborative work, which is at first hand separate from the area of enterprise applications but which has as it will turn out a strong connection to enterprise applications; indeed this connection will deliver important synergies. Collaborative work is a typical activity of employees in a modern organization, separate from the use of enterprise applications. If we use office applications not only for us alone, but in the context of an intensive teamwork, this activity becomes collaborative work. Computer supported collaborative work is the vision of performing this team work with the support of a powerful software that supports us in versioning and project management, we call it the *team server*. The basic paradigm of collaborative work is also different from work on an enterprise application. The work product of a single unit of work is more a document and less a filled-out form. More generally, the result is a incremental change of a document, we call it a *delta* of this document. The basic model of collaborative work is that team members reserve documents for their exclusive write access, called *check out*. The entering of the changed document is called *check in*.

12.1 Towards Structured Collaborative Work

There are many examples of collaborative work where the team server uses whole documents as the smallest unit of interest. The team server keeps basically versions of documents. In concrete technology, the team server keeps often deltas of documents. The system CVS is a classical example, for which ASCII files are the single unit of interest. But there is an important class of collaborative work which asks for a more elaborate approach. It is this the case that the documents produced by the collaborative work are structured documents. Software development and CAD are examples. In the case of software development the document structure is given by the programming language. The structure recognized by the team server can include the syntax, the static semantics including the type system, and parts of the dynamic semantics.

Currently, many software projects are managed with CVS. The CVS system in itself is not aware of the programming language structure. The team server hence does not enforce or support correctness according to the structuring rules of the document type. Another modern form of collaborative software usage however uses a team server which compiles every version that is checked in and may even perform automatically unit tests on this code. Such unit tests can be developed from the programmers and added to the unit test base. This approach would even allow to reject check-in for deltas which fail compilation or unit testing.

The aim of this chapter is to develop a high-level theory of such potentials for a team server for structured documents. This discussion of collaborative work stays in a twofold connection to enterprise applications. On the one hand, as we have seen in the chapters before, the creation of enterprise applications involves a plethora of formats for structured documents. Not only are the artifacts which comprise the executable enterprise software of an increasing number of formats – HTML, Java, C#, SQL, WSDL, XML. Also in the modeling process of enterprise applications there is a huge demand for powerful special purpose languages like the modeling methods presented in the previous chapters, formcharts, dialogue constraints, data models. It is therefore intuitive that an advanced tool base for the development and maintenance is a powerful asset for leveraging the full potentials of such a special purpose approach.

But we will see that there is also a very natural way in which our considerations on data modeling can help in obtaining a semantically rigid yet simple model for collaborative work on structured documents. The key idea is of course here once again a courageous and somewhat reductionist thesis. In this case it is the statement: documents are just data. Why should we not use our powerful concepts for persistent data in order to create persistence for documents? Moreover, for our aim of understanding collaborative work on structured documents, we will use a second powerful identification of terms. The fact, that we have structure in documents and type systems in our data model as a tool, fosters the following immensely far-reaching statement: a document format definition is just a data type definition. We now make this insight operational and propose the following approach to collaborative source code development: we use our data model to represent structured documents, and we define document types by creating data types. This so far is the core concept of the integrated source code paradigm presented in this chapter.

However, we will also offer one further conceptual step. This final third step will be that we even use our interaction and operation model for the manipulation of the documents, or even more generally speaking, of the team server. Hence we use the well understood interaction paradigm of form-oriented analysis for source code manipulation. The result is then a form-based description of collaborative work. The virtual machine which is defined by our paradigm, serves as the basis for defining source code manipulation. The business machine is hence used here as a collaborative machine. In some sense it will turn out that for collaborative work a very generic business logic is the best tool. This generic business logic can be informally described as allowing all possible changes to the data model. Now this final step is at the first place a conceptual step, i.e., it is a thought experiment, which is supposed to help our understanding. It does not necessarily mean that we work with this form-based interface for creating our programs. Currently one could see a certain tendency of interactions with editors becoming more and more form-based. This is also due to the fact that structured editors are increasingly fashionable, a well known concept but little used in the past. The main idea of this third step is however to have a reference interface to the team server which allows us to fix semantic questions, even if this reference interface may not be the one we use. This is in parallel with many other systems, like databases, which have one reference interactive interface, while most of the time the database access will happen with other interfaces through application server. There are different aims and priorities of collaborative work on the one hand and OLTP (Online Transactional Processing) work on the other. One important service of the data model to the source code paradigm will be simply the concept of opaque identities itself, one of the main elements of our machine model. This concept does provide the quantum leap of this source code paradigm over the ASCII-based paradigm of many languages, especially because of the fact that we can make use of a machine model that is a model of a global network, and therefore supports immediately the notion of a global collaborative network.

It is not our aim in this chapter to reconstruct all the artifacts we have introduced so far once more within the integrated source code paradigm. On the contrary, we have presented artifacts which are easy to use within the fully conventional framework of ASCII editors. For example, we have provided ASCII representations of many concepts like class diagrams, which are usually today only presented as visual artifacts, only accessible by dedicated tools. Note that this points on one property of the integrated source code paradigm; it has to be seen in the context of dedicated tools. The goal is here to get a tangible access to the reader. As soon as we fully apply the integrated source code paradigm, we get a fully self-referencing, but also circular paradigm: the data model defines the language; the language defines the data model. This is from the practical side indeed wanted, because it ensures a maximum in integration, reuse and consistency. Yet from a reflective and critical standpoint there is an argumentative circle. These concepts are indeed old. In programming languages a similar approach is called bootstrapping. A language translator is first provided manually or in another language, then a language translator is written in the language itself and translated with the initial translator.

The aim of this chapter is not to execute this bootstrapping procedure. Our aim is rather to pinpoint on certain potentials in languages like DAL, which are accessible through the use of such an advanced integrated source code paradigm. This approach should enable the reader also to understand the importance of this integrated source code paradigm. By looking at artifact types like formcharts and DAL specification, we find well understood artifacts, for which we can judge the potentials of such a modern source code paradigm. We therefore will exemplify throughout the chapter, where one of the new ideas of the integrated source code paradigm is especially applicable to our method. However this new source code paradigm is also an exciting and fundamental achievement in its own right, based on our form-oriented system view and data model.

This approach is also very fascinating from the standpoint of theory building. In the way we use our data model for modeling documents, we obtain a neat and clean theory of documents and document manipulation almost for free, whereas in the conventional approaches the whole theory of compiler construction is needed. We therefore call this paradigm the integrated source code paradigm.

12.2 Structured Artifacts

We start our deliberations from the traditional view of source code. In different areas of computer science we encounter various notions of program code and therefore different approaches to formal languages. In the following we list some traditional concepts of source code, ranging from low-level to high-level models, which are motivated by their respective application areas.

- In constructing standard compilers for ASCII text files a program code is a word over a subset of the ASCII alphabet. In that form the source code is processed by the initial process of lexical analysis.
- After lexical analysis the source code is tokenized. For the subsequent stages, i.e., the parser, source code is a stream of tokens, where each token is a semantic unit in itself. Particularly the identifiers, which denote methods or variables, for example, are single tokens. The purpose of the identifiers is solely to denote an identity; they are already opaque in this sense, in contrast to literals of basic data types. The syntax has among others the purpose to describe how to obtain a treelike data structure, the parse tree, from the linear stream of tokens.
- In discussions on the semantics of programming languages one often uses the concept of abstract syntax, as we have done by introducing DAL in Chap. 7. In this concept a piece of code is a tree; the syntax has only the purpose of describing the structure of the tree. Each non-terminal represents a node type, and the right side of the rule denotes the structure of the code. In abstract syntax we can use iterations in the rule. The difference between abstract syntax and concrete syntax is that abstract syntax does not have to care about delimiters, which are used to create the treelike structure.

For our purposes the important property of formal languages is that they are structured artifacts, amenable to automated processing. We introduce in this chapter a notion of formal languages which integrates better with this method than the notions introduced above. We call formal documents like programs *structured artifacts*. The essence of our approach is that structured artifacts are modeled as ordinary data objects in our PD model defined in Chap. 7. We define a formal language by ordinary types in our data model. We call the data model which describes a formal language in this way a *syntax model*. Since in this way the descriptions of formal languages are integrated into the data model, we call this approach the integrated source code paradigm. This integration extends therefore to the level of instances as well, where structured artifacts are ordinary entity types besides other entity types.

The integrated source code paradigm is intended to support the programmer as a typical power user. A power user has different demands of his or her tools than the naive user. Ease of use in the long run and even for complex tasks is the priority. One group of power users has traditionally stuck to ASCII-based terminals and command-line tools. Their demand obviously does not lie in sophisticated visual representation. If a new source code paradigm sets out to convince those power users that the emphasis must not be laid on visualization, but on the superior structural properties of the typed source code paradigm presented here, then this makes it more easily accessible to powerful tools.

Our approach abstracts from one part of language processing altogether, namely parsing. The most difficult task in understanding this approach may therefore lie in the process of understanding that these parts of language processing can be eliminated from the discussion by keeping the discussion on one level of abstraction. It is also important to realize that many discussions on semi-structured data like XML take place on this lower level, which does not have to be considered here. Semi-structured data as well issues of parsing can be seen at the same level of abstraction as memory organization in programming languages and the physical layer in databases. In language theory the memory model is basically a tape over an alphabet. It is one of the strengths of modern type systems that the programmer does not have to care about the actual memory layout of types used in the programming language. In the same way our integrated source code paradigm gives us direct access to the structure of artifacts, without having to worry about the representation.

12.3 The Syntax Model Approach

We said earlier that the first step in the integrated source code paradigm is to view the structured artifacts as data in the data model. The traditional role of the grammar, which expresses the syntax, is taken over by a data model. One composite entity type from the data model is considered as representing the language. All instances of this type are considered as words in the language. Having understood the difference between this integrated source code paradigm and traditional languages we still want to use the term syntax. Hence we call the data model describing a language the *syntax model* of this language.

Syntax Model for the Parsimonious Modeling Language

The syntax model of the PD modeling language is very condensed, as can be seen in Fig. 12.1.

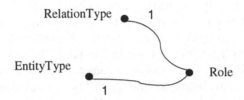

Fig. 12.1. The core syntax model of the PD modeling language

If we have a style format, for example for multiplicities, which has its own data structure, then we can use model composition to add it to the syntax model. See Fig. 12.2 for such an example from [104]. submodel and the model union with the syntax model. Such extensions are therefore simply library entries; the library can be extended.

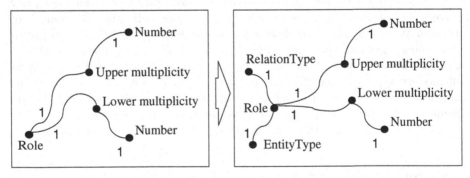

Fig. 12.2. Multiplicity syntax model and union with PD syntax model

Comparison of Syntax Model and Meta Model Approach

The syntax model approach makes no sharp distinction between models of languages and other data models. The metamodeling approach of many visual modeling languages can be subsumed under the syntax model approach.

The metamodeling approach in the narrower sense considers a single problem instance of formal language theory, namely the self-application, hence the prefix *meta*. The syntax model approach is from the outset not self-centered. Syntax models are not primarily intended for other modeling languages. They are intended for all formal languages. Since formal languages are in general many different things, not just modeling languages, the model of a language in general should not be called a metamodel, hence our name syntax model.

But even for the case of self-application the syntax modeling approach allows a more advanced solution. The integrated modeling approach does not need the strict leveling of the metamodeling approach. Due to this strict leveling the metamodeling approach does not capture the relation between types and instances. A precise capture of the type instance relationship approach requires a standpoint, on which both types and instances are in the same data model, and their relationship can be explained. This is a possible further research direction within the syntax modeling approach.

The metamodeling approach is often motivated by likening the metamodel to the model of a CASE tool; some metamodeling proposals came from groups of GUI-based CASE tool developers. In this view the metamodel represents objects in the tool. A particular flexible approach uses this concept as a basis for generic visual tool generators [133] and can even offer advanced features like changing the metamodel on the fly.

A further research direction is to look for a precise understanding in a global community. In our view, all members of the community want to talk about the same objects if they are talking about certain library functions, for example. In the syntax modeling approach the most natural semantics are to assume that one certain artifact resides in one place, in itself a unit system. This idea does not exclude clever replication infrastructures of any kind, since we understand a unit system as a virtual machine, not as a physical server of a site.

The integrated source code paradigm will be the basis for a general theory of tools, including the domain of graphical editor tools as well as structured editors.

12.4 A Closer Look at Languages

An artifact has been characterized as an entity instance in the data model. Our data model is in principle updatable; therefore artifacts can be updated as well. Now the discussions in traditional language theory can be seen as being restricted to constant objects as artifacts, in our terminology messages. Similar to that, messages will play an important role in the integrated source code paradigm as well. For example, the running program will usually be seen as a message – it cannot be changed. Traditional languages can be embedded into the data model. The part of the data model representing non-terminals for this language is formed solely by composition. Identifiers usually form a single entity type. This also implies that even certain low-level checks are not expressed in the syntax, e.g., that a type identifier is not used as a variable identifier. In the abstract syntax of DAL we have used a notation with which we were able to implicitly define several entity types representing identifiers. Our abstract syntax notation then implicitly specified the aforementioned rules, i.e., that a relation type identifier can be used only at appropriate points.

12.4.1 Different Practices, Different Solutions

In the history of programming languages, the concept of declaration is recognized as having led to considerable progress in efficiency. This is chiefly due to the fact that through making declarations mandatory, a common error has been eliminated, namely the erroneous introduction of a new variable due to a typo. In the abstract syntax of DAL, we have demonstrated that one can even support this context-sensitive concept conveniently and highly intuitively within the language syntax itself.

The new source code paradigm brings new editing paradigms. The reference to a variable does not happen through typing in a dumb tool like the editor. It rather happens by choosing an existing instance by an appropriate tool, e.g., a graphical tool. The need for a declaration within the language itself is no longer plausible. The intended safeguard is provided by the editing tool of the language. Therefore languages for structured artifacts often have no declaration concept. The fact that these languages are edited by tools which are more sensitive to their semantics than a text editor compensates for this. The different editing practices therefore lead to different language design solutions.

12.4.2 Names as Comment

The use of tokenization is standard in computer languages, but in typical usage the tokens are not opaque identities, as we find in our data model, and therefore in the syntax model. It is in the problem domain of name conflicts, where the tokens show their nature as being plain text. In standard languages, the same token can be used by chance by different developers in different modules. If these modules have to be used together, a so-called name conflict can arise. The concepts for the solution of name conflicts are deeply intertwined with the language design as a whole.

This is not so in our approach. We consider the textual names as simple comments to the identities. The plain text view of a piece of code is on a completely separate layer of abstraction. The editing of code is primarily the editing of a data structure expressed in the primary data model. A textual piece of code is not code as such, but may be viewed as a putative notation of code. A textual notation has to be imported into the paradigm, by searching for identities of the given names. A name conflict arises at this import step, which is separated from all other semantic aspects.

This has implications for the use of libraries, for example. An identity from a library can be used effectively only by referring to the same identity. The developer can of course search for the library function by a textual name. However, establishing the reference can only happen through a tool which already lives within the information paradigm itself, and which can therefore use the identities within the data model.

12.4.3 Comment as Annotation

In the integrated source code paradigm comment is seen as an annotation of the code. Since the code is a typed data object, comment is discernible from the code by being of a different type. In our source code paradigm we want to treat changes to comment and changes to code differently with respect to versioning. A change in the comment of the code, even if it is comment directly addressing coding issues, is not seen as a change in the program. This is an improvement on the current situation with versioning tools based on the plain ASCII format or on any file format containing code as well as comment.

The structured metaphor makes it also intriguing to think about more structured approaches to comment. A first step is that comment is really pinned to the regarding object, e.g., parameter descriptions are linked to the respective parameter. This also eases somewhat the task of keeping comment up to date, because the editing tool can inform the programmer if comment is outdated since it has lost its referring code; indeed the tool has to do so, because the type definition of the comment requires the comment to be removed, if its referring object is removed.

12.5 The Integrated Source Code Paradigm

An artifact is a composite entity, representing all its parts. The composite entity is updatable. Messages representing a possible state of this composite entity are called versions.

The basic unit of source code management is the single artifact; a source code repository is rather a management concept, which can be postponed for the moment. An artifact is a unit system, which must have a transparent history, and a transparent log. But an artifact has an extended concept of the transparent history, which serves as the translation of the version tree concept from well-known versioning tools. Not only is each previous state accessible, but also for each previous state of a composite object a new successor state can be created. Each such current state is a version; the leaves in the tree are the current versions. The task of a source code repository would then be to bundle such versions.

12.5.1 Source Code Processing

The syntax model naturally considers source code as part of the data model itself. Accordingly, the source code manipulation tools should be expressed in the language itself. We want to use the notion of *source code* for structured artifacts which are created by the user, in contrast to structured artifacts in general, which may of course be the result of a generation process.

The natural concept of possible source code manipulations, which this viewpoint offers, is to see a single step manipulation of an artifact as performing an arbitrary DAL operation on this artifact. The versions are identical with the states in the history of the tool. What versioning tools call a delta is here the DAL update between two states in the history. This concept is a centralized view of source code editing. There is no such concept as a local copy of an artifact. The editors are not tools working on a local state, but terminal sessions working on the repository itself.

We assume the usual editing of the artifacts as being typically performed by a form-oriented interface. Since a form-oriented interface allows only for a statically fixed set of DAL side effects and client page specifications with parameters, this means that such an editor defines a fixed set of DAL operations, which are assumed as the basic editing concepts. The natural editor of an artifact type is the so-called generic editing tool, as explained later.

12.5.2 Identity and Structure of Source Code

Since the syntax model is a proper model, it inherits properties of the data model. There is the possibility to have isomorphic models, with different identities, just like with every composite data type. A system of representatives of isomorphic models can be found through induction over the structure of models.

Isomorphic models can naturally appear in software development. Consider an entity type representing an address as an example, developed by two programmers based on a detailed description. Their editing can yield isomorphic models, but they are not identical since they both use fresh entity instances. There is nothing problematic about this phenomenon, but it is worth mentioning. It is also important to note that if one uses existing artifacts, e.g., if the programmers choose the same address type from a domain model, then the types are identical.

Of course it would be possible to use the representative of the isomorphism class for a type. But one should keep in mind that the use of the concept structural identity is in any case possible. That is, even if the types are non-identical, the programmer can of course use tools to check the isomorphism of the types. In our understanding there is no possibility of defining an ultimate concept of isomorphism anyway.

12.5.3 Worldwide Libraries

The fact that our machine model is in principle a model of a global network has an immediate application for our integrated source code paradigm: it should be seen as a model of a global infrastructure for source code, a worldwide web of libraries. The identity creation mechanism does yield worldwide fresh identities for the pieces of code we create, which allows us to address them uniquely in a global net of libraries.

12.5.4 Source Code Decomposition

We call the modularization of source code in different, separately editable units *source code decomposition*. Source code decomposition as such is a motivated and important type of modularization. There are many other modularization objectives, which include semantic aspects. In many languages source code decomposition is intertwined with other modularization mechanisms, like name spaces. In our language, source code modularization is strictly separated from other modularization mechanisms. The source code modularization concept takes place solely on the syntax model level.

Submodel and Conservative Decomposition

A *submodel* is a substate of the model. We define the *conservative decomposition* of a model to be the decomposition into submodels, which together give the whole model. The decomposition is not required to be disjoint; on the contrary, entity types are typically contained in several submodels.

This method of decomposition has the property that by changing the structure of the decomposition, the resulting model does not change. It is not only equivalent, it is also identical. This is a difference to other decomposition mechanisms, as can be found in many languages, which not only lead to a decomposition of the code, but also to a different structure of the code, even if the code may be equivalent. Take as an example the functional decomposition in many languages, like C, Pascal, but also Java. By forming a separate procedure or method from a block in a piece of code, we introduce not only a decomposition of the code, but also a change in the semantic relation of both pieces. For example, in Java it is not possible to place a body of a loop, which changes local variables of primitive type, easily into a different method. Furthermore the important concept of a file as a code unit is firmly linked to the class concept. A class cannot be spread over different files.

The inverse of decomposition is the composition. The conservative composition of two models is the union of these models. The set of entity instances is the union of the sets of entity instances of the submodels. Each entity instance, which is part of both models, gets all the links from both models. The composition of models is similar to the concept of graph union. The main difference is that models have a more complex structure due to the concept of roles and the identities of relation types.

A generalization of our source code decomposition approach is to utilize the history of the source code creation. Source code is created by a sequence of syntax model editing steps. This log of the update of the syntax model contains in itself the information of the syntax model. The log of updates will be important in the context of roundtrip engineering, which we will discuss in due course.

12.5.5 Replacement

A typical operation in conventional source code notions is the replacement of a token by a subdocument, i.e., the structured variant of the editor's search and replace. In our data model paradigm there is an interesting focus shift, since it becomes obvious that the same identity cannot appear in different places, and there can be only different links to that identity. The replacement works quite similarly: all links of this entity instance are redirected to some other entity instance.

12.5.6 Formal Patterns

A formal pattern is an annotation of a piece of code with a syntax model condition, which holds for that piece of code. Alternatively, it can be defined as the unrolled invocation of an abstraction principle, but with possible subsequent edits. This means that, given a generator, then the pattern is the generator input and the pattern instance is the generator output, which is integrated into the project and further edited. A formal pattern is assumed to be used in a guarded environment, i.e., when editing a source code with a formal pattern it is helpful to have an editor, which watches over the validity of the pattern annotation.

Formal patterns are useful whenever one wants to use an abstraction for the sake of consistency of the code, but one does want to see the resulting code directly, nor the invocation of the abstraction itself. Patterns are therefore characterized by the fact that the lower level is not hidden by use of the high-level principle.

Formal patterns are related to styles, but formal patterns emphasize the generative aspect of the abstraction over the aspect of enforcing structural regularity.

Formal patterns are the best way to integrate generative technologies which need subsequent editing, and are therefore subject to roundtrip engineering phenomena, into the source code paradigm.

An example of a formal pattern is the record manipulation dialogue pattern. This pattern is applicable in enterprise applications, e.g., for core data. There are many data records, which may be inserted, updated, and deleted. The record manipulation dialogue pattern is a generative pattern which yields a formchart for a given data type definition, and which contains the appropriate subdialogue together with all typical dialogue constraints. Such a dialogue pattern can of course be subsequently edited. Using the approach of a formal pattern enables the developer to subsequently change, for example, the data record definition, without losing all edits of the pattern. If, say, the developer has deleted one input facility from the change dialogue, since the corresponding field cannot be changed after it has been inserted, and if later the data record is extended by a completely unrelated field, then the new field is just inserted into the different forms and proper processing of the user input is added, but the other code, including the deleted input facility, is not changed.

12.6 A Flexible Generic Textual Format for Data

We propose a generic textual format GTF for data representation, which allows the discussion of general questions about textual representation. The format enables different representations of the same content prior to knowledge of the types.

A GTF file is a serialization of the state of a DAL model. A GTF file lists all the links of the state, because they comprise the whole state. The entity instances are represented by identifiers. The primitive types have the literals as their identifiers. Since the entity instances are originally supposed to be opaque, they could be random identifiers. For user-written GTF files the user may choose symbolic identifiers. In the integrated source code paradigm we have a general notion of annotating opaque entity instances with names. The relation type of a link is encoded like an additional role of the relation type.

12.6.1 Normal Form

A document according to the textual format is in normal form, if all links of the state are written on separate lines. Each link is a sequence of key/value pairs. they are normal form is the list of all links, each tuple description is complete, and in the same order.

```
// relation types with role names:
Address(person, name, street)
BusinessContact(customer, supplier)

// dump of a state
type=Address person=alice name="Alice" street="queen street"
type=Address person=bill name="William" street="capitol hill"
type=Address person=bert name="Bert" street="queen street"
type=BusinessContact customer=bill person=bert
type=BusinessContact customer=bert person=alice
```

The normal form is not unique, because the order of the tuples is not unique. The order of the roles is not unique either. The textual format allows to reshuffle the information, including the type definition. The following example GTF files will encode the same state.

12.6.2 Grouping

Links with common key-value pairs can be grouped. The common key-value pairs are provided only once, they hold for all indented subsequent lines. In this case the first, non-indented line does not encode a link.

```
type=Address street="queen street"
  person=alice name="Alice"
  person=bill name="William"
person=bert
  type=BusinessContact customer=bill
  type=Address name="Bert" street="fleet street"
type=BusinessContact customer=bert person=alice
```

This principle is recursive:

```
type=Address                                         //encodes no link
  person=bert name="Bert" street="fleet street"      //encodes  a link
  street="queen street"                              //encodes no link
    person=alice name="Alice"                        //encodes  a link
    person=bill name="William"                       //encodes  a link
person=bert type=BusinessContact customer=bill       //encodes  a link
type=BusinessContact customer=bert person=alice      //encodes  a link
```

12.6.3 Syntactic Sugar

The principles of the format are independent from the concrete syntax chosen here. The concrete syntactic elements used in the format here are: line break, indentation for block structure, symbol "=", comment, white space.

The format could allow for defining other representations for key-value pairs or groups thereof. There could be an option to define that "A: B 0..1" is mapped on "id=A attrtype=B lower=0 upper=1". This would allow to define syntactic sugar, just as other languages allow to declare an operator infix notation for binary functions.

The information content of the textual file contains obviously a total order on all links, even across relation types. This could be used to encode ordered lists in an extension of the format.

12.6.4 Application for the Textual Format of Formcharts

In the following we show examples of how formcharts can be described in the textual format. Furthermore it shows how this description of the formchart can be amalgamated with the data model description. The following listing contains different groupings of the same formchart, which is a cutout from the bookshop example shown in Fig. 12.3. These different notations are a direct consequence of the generic properties of the textual format.

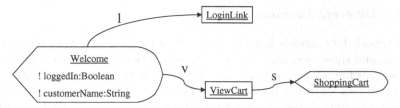

Fig. 12.3. A cutout message storyboard of the bookshop example with custom transition names

```
PageServer(id:pageserverID, source:ClientPage, target:ServerAction)
ServerPage(id:serverPageID, source:ServerAction, target:ClientPage)
Attribute(id:attributeID, source:Message, attributType:Type)

// a normal form
type=Pageserver source=Welcome  id=l target=LoginLink
type=Pageserver source=Welcome  id=v server=ViewCart
type=ServerPage source=ViewCart id=s target=ShoppingCart
type=Attribute  source=Welcome  id=loggedIn attributType=Boolean
type=Attribute  source=Welcome  id=customerName attributType=String

// grouping attributes, but not transitions
type=Pageserver source=Welcome  id=l target=LoginLink
type=Pageserver source=Welcome  id=v server=ViewCart
type=ServerPage source=ViewCart id=s target=ShoppingCart
type=Attribute  source=Wolcome
  id=loggedIn attributType=Boolean
  id=customerName attributType=String

// grouping attributes and transitions separately
type=Pageserver source=Welcome
  id=l target=LoginLink
  id=v server=ViewCart
type=ServerPage source=ViewCart
  id=s target=ShoppingCart
type=Attribute  source=Welcome
  id=loggedIn attributType=Boolean
  id=customerName attributType=String

// grouping attributes and transitions together
source=Welcome
  type=Pageserver id=l target=LoginLink
  type=Pageserver id=v server=ViewCart
  type=Attribute  id=loggedIn attributType=Boolean
  type=Attribute  id=customerName attributType=String
source=ViewCart
  type=ServerPage id=s target=ShoppingCart
```

12.6.5 Different Information Content

Conceptual data models have no linear structure. Serialization requires decisions, and these decisions can be seen as additional information content in the textual file. One additional information content in the given Format are the identifiers for entity instances. We mentioned that this is a general phenomenon of commenting annotation in the integrated source code paradigm.

12.7 Generative Programming

There are two main aspects to our discussion of source code: on the one hand its character as a structured document, and on the other hand its character as a manually edited document. The aspect of structured documents can be discussed independently of the notion of source code as a manually edited document. Structured documents can be especially created as the output of generators.

There are a number of standard processing patterns on structured documents, which are interesting for automated as well as manual processing. This mirrors the fact that source code paradigms like high-level programming languages are not only interesting as formats for manual editing, but also used as output format for generators. The general aspects of manipulating structured documents form therefore one aspect of our discussion. Generative programming is a central concept in software development [72, 98, 99]. A compiler or generator is just a function from the document type to a target document type. The operations available for document manipulations together form our data manipulation language.

12.7.1 Roundtrip Development

We want to distinguish between the required use of generators and the use of generators as a mere organizational pattern for development. As an organizational pattern we understand the case where the generator is used because certain tools, e.g., the compiler, need the generated code in order to perform adequate type checks etc. From a theoretical standpoint the generation process could be deferred until after the development process, in these cases. There are moreover many ad-hoc generators around where the programmer has to edit the code unnecessarily, like in the case of many CASE tools. This creates the need for roundtrip-engineering. In this case the generator use is again an organizational pattern, and roundtrip engineering is avoidable by placing generated code and customizations in separate code units. In object-oriented languages method overriding is used for this purpose. It has to be said though that such separation can be achieved without object orientation as well.

Required generator use on the other hand is the case where the programmer wants to edit the generator output for good reasons. We call this white-box customization. The idea of a generator whose output is subsequently edited creates a number of challenges for source code development and maintenance. If the programmer has to perform white-box customization, he or she urgently needs tool assistance to cope with the case of later change in the generator input, which requires repetition of the generation step and afterwards re-editing. The required tool functionality is a versatile roundtrip engineering.

A typical case of required generator use will be discussed in Sect. 12.7.2. The generator is used there to create a set of initial sources for deliberate editing. In these cases the generator typically produces a high-level format, not a low-level format. Roundtrip engineering is not just a task for tool developers; it requires first and foremost a reflection on the intended semantics. Our approach has the following features.

- We first of all de-emphasize the naming scheme. The user links customizations to opaque identities, not to generated compound names. These identities change exactly in the same circumstances as the generated names would do. The identities of the generated code are annotated with a list of as few elements of the generator input as possible, so that the identities have to change exactly if this list is changing. We call this list the *generation symbol table*.
- In our approach all elements of the generated code can be offered for overriding, depending on the preferences of the generator provider.
- This overriding is purely syntactical; its working can therefore be understood purely syntactically as well. Note that both approaches to customization, white-box editing as well as method overriding, make it hard to assure system properties of the resulting system.

The infrastructure for roundtrip engineering works as follows. Looking at a typical project, the repository can contain generated code by arbitrary generators, perhaps edited afterwards. For each of these generated artifacts, the command which generates them is stored as well. This command can use any elements of the repository as parameters. It is a deterministic DAL command, i.e., immediate subsequent execution is assumed to give an equivalent result. The repository then allows one to keep track of subsequent editing to the generated code. This information is used for roundtrip engineering. A typical activity of roundtrip engineering is the re-execution of a generation step. This is followed by redoing the changes after the generation, if possible. For that purpose the repository transmits all the following data to the generator: the old generator input, the new generator input, the generation symbol table, the log of the edits on the generated code.

The crucial task of the generator is to reuse entity type instances in the newly generated document. This allows for the subsequent simple reapplication of the edit to the generated document. For this reuse of entity type instances the generator technically refers to the generation symbol table; however, in fact this does not have to be done by the generator programmer, but can be automatically achieved.

All edits which do not find an appropriate target in the newly generated document must be reported to the user and the user has to decide on the further processing. The generator can of course still try to help, e.g., by performing pattern matching on the new versus the old code in order to propose better roundtrip offers.

The roundtrip engineering considerations emphasize the aspect that source code is manually edited. The valuable assets created by the programmer's work are therefore the actual manual edits. The first approximation notion is therefore to view the source code as a log of the actual user input to the tools. Here again it helps to view all tools as integrated; hence we assume that the user operates on a single tool, which offers the integrated functionality of all tools necessary for editing. This tool model is therefore the abstract concept behind common integrated development environments (IDEs). Other important concepts will be the concept of a document repository and a release repository.

There is a strict separation between the concepts of source code structuring and the actual semantics of the code. We can define source code manipulation independently of the semantics of the source code format. We have seen that there are a number of concepts which can be discussed solely on the syntactic level, including composition and decomposition, as we experienced in the concept of conservative composition. A source code unit is an instance of a composite data type of a syntax model. A repository is realized by a composite entity type, which we call a repository type. Its contents subsystem is the syntax model of this repository. The log warehouse of the repository has similarities to the data stored by a version archiving tool. The history data model offers the function of retrieving earlier versions.

12.7.2 Generic Translators

A natural case of required generator use is found in the area of form-oriented analysis. We can use a generic translator that takes a data model as an input and creates the form-oriented description of a very generic access system for a database with this data model. This generated access tool contains for each entity type a list of all contained entity instances, and for each instance the linked instances along the different associations. Furthermore it allows update and delete operations. This generic system can be seen as a generic translation of the data model concept into the world of interactive form-oriented systems. The result of the generic translation process is, however, a very schematic tool not yet customized. It is solely a reflection of the basic data structure. But it may be a good starting point for developing the form-based system by customization of this prototype. This way of proceeding is exactly what the concept of roundtrip engineering is for. The developer not only will use the generator output as a convenient starting point, but may also be interested in having the possibility to later change the data model, and having an immediate reasonable update of the form-based description built on this data model. One could think about using annotations on the data model in order to avoid roundtrip engineering. But such solutions will always be expression of personal taste. Those developers which want to straightforwardly customize the system simply want to have a roundtrip engineering tool that meets their desires.

The generic editing tool has one natural application, and that is as the editor in the sense of our integrated source code paradigm. If we think about a tool for editing artifacts in a given format, then the generic editor is the natural choice.

12.7.3 Integrated Development Environments

Many of the aspects mentioned here can be understood as a theoretical foundation of functionality, which can often be found in modern integrated development environments (IDEs). Such systems may offer support for refactoring: a method name can be exchanged at once in the whole project. The versioning tool may be aware that this does not change the semantics and therefore not change the version. These features relate to the concept of names as comment. Most IDEs have syntax-sensitive editors. These editors can follow various paradigms concerning enforcement of indentation, color coding of syntax, supporting naming conventions, etc. IDEs can also support the generative steps in software development, e.g., automatically translate, perform unit checks, etc., and inform the project members of the status of the project.

These features of IDEs can be understood as instances of our pattern concept. A pattern can be a structure or regularity of low-level code, which can be explained as realizing a high-level concept. In this way IDEs realize aspects of our high-level paradigm, but they do not hide the low-level paradigm. As one can see by appreciating the plethora of existing IDEs, this comes at the point where each single aspect of the high-level principle has to be implemented step by step at considerable cost. Furthermore this approach can be said to hinder the understanding of the fundamental principles by the single developer.

The crucial point, however, in which the integrated source code approach has the potential to provide a leap forward compared with the conceptual status of IDEs, is with respect to the concept of the power user. The integrated source code paradigm supports a modular functional approach to source code manipulation features. It motivates a more bare metal type of interface, but also provides a higher conceptual clarity than current IDEs.

13

State History Diagrams

In this chapter we introduce a general notion of finite state modeling that has a tight integration with other modeling views, especially with class diagrams. A state transition diagram in this new notion is called a *state history diagram* [91], SHD for short. SHDs can be used in many circumstances in analysis as well as design. They are especially favorable in cases where we model a system by a finite state machine in order to capture a specific aspect, while the system as a whole is modeled by a class diagram as well. Such models are very widespread, and the formchart is only one example, although indeed a very good example. Other examples include the state of processes in operating systems or the life cycle of components in application servers. We give the operational semantics for general SHDs – not only for bipartite SHDs as they are needed for example for formcharts – in order to clarify the general character of the introduced semantics. The approach chosen here achieves a sound basis for all the special constructs introduced in form-oriented analysis in a rather short and lightweight way. This is achieved through maximal reuse, mainly because we were able to fully reuse the semantics of class diagrams for our new artifacts.

13.1 State History Diagrams and Class Diagrams

Our operational semantics for SHDs are based solely on the semantics of class diagrams. The main idea behind SHDs is the following consideration:

- Class diagrams define the set of possible object nets, i.e., states over the class diagram.
- Finite state machines define the set of possible traces for this state machine.
- Hence finite state machines can be defined as class diagrams, which allow only directed paths as object nets.

SHDs are a semantic unification of class diagrams and state transition diagrams; in fact they are a restriction of class diagrams. We show how SHDs can be defined in the context of UML. As we will see, our semantics are based only on the fundamental semantic concept of core class diagrams, which serve as the semantic foundation in the modeling universe in which UML is located.

If we model a complex system as a finite state machine, this finite state machine is typically only a part of the model. The behavior may depend further on a classical data model. But in many cases the system behavior may especially depend on the history of state transitions. SHDs give a convenient general modeling tool for such systems. As a consequence SHDs allow the specification of temporal constraints on finite state automata without any need for further temporal formalisms, solely through the combination of the already-defined concepts. Submit/response style interfaces will be a special application case. Formcharts, the key diagrams of form-oriented analysis, will then be a simple application of SHDs, though we will support it with our own semantic framework. We then also give precise semantics to the dialogue constraints introduced in DCL.

If a system is modeled with an SHD, the history or trace of the finite state machine is a part of the actual system state. In other words, for each state visit an instance of some class is kept in the actual system state, so that these instances together form a log of the state transition process so far. On this object net we can define constraints concerning the history of state transitions. Hence we can define certain temporal constraints without having to introduce a temporal extension into the constraint language.

In SHDs the log of the state visits is kept as a linked list of object instances. The links represent the transitions between state visits. SHDs are based on the idea of choosing the class diagram for this log in such a way that it is isomorphic to the state transition diagram.

This is possible since STDs and core class diagrams can be modeled by a similar metamodel. The basic metaclasses are nodes and connectors. In STDs the nodes are states and the connectors are directed transitions. In core class diagrams the nodes are classes and the connectors are binary associations.

An SHD is a special class diagram which can be read as an STD at the same time. The consequence of this approach is that a single diagram describes the state machine on the one hand and on the other hand serves at the same time as a class diagram for the aforementioned history of state transitions. Such a class diagram must, however, adhere to rigorous restrictions that will be given in due course.

We adopt the following rules for speaking about SHDs. The diagram can be addressed as an SHD or as an STD or as a class diagram, emphasizing the respective aspect. The nodes are called state classes, the connectors are called transitions and they are associations; their instances are called state changes. A run of the state machine represented by the STD is called a process. The visit of a state during a process over the STD is identified with an instance of the state class and is called a visit. Hence a process is the object net over the

SHD. This object net is a path from the start visit of the process to the current visit. This path is seen as being directed from the start visit. Each prefix of the path is a part of the whole current path. This matches the semantics of the aggregation. Hence all transitions are aggregations. The aggregation diamond points to the later state. In the SHD, however, the transitions are not drawn with diamonds but with single arrows. The associated state classes are called source and target. We will use the SHD for the modeling of formcharts. If a system is used by several clients, each client lives in its own object space. Therefore the singleton property is local to the client's object space. If one were to model all clients accessing a system in a single object space, this could be done by using several SHDs in a single object space. In that case one has to use a slightly modified framework in which the `StartState` is not a singleton, but there is one `StartState` instance for each run of the finite automaton.

13.1.1 Modeling SHDs as Class Diagrams

We have defined SHDs as a restriction of a class diagram, not as a new diagram type. We now give a semantic treatment of this approach in the context of UML. We obtained the definition of SHD's as restricted class diagrams in the following way: SHDs are class diagrams in which all elements are derived from a special semantic modeling framework, the shdframework. Note that we use model-level inheritance here. In the UML context a specification alternative would be a package with stereotypes in which the SHD is defined by meta-model instantiation, instead of model inheritance. But first we adhere strictly to the economy principle, and argue that modeling is more lightweight than metamodeling, therefore we use modeling wherever possible. Secondly our approach allows for a quite elegant formulation of the central SHD semantics, namely that the object nets are paths. In Sect. 13.2 we will discuss the benefits of our modeling approach.

However, we want to use the stereotype notation for pure notational convenience. For that purpose we introduce an auxiliary stereotype package in which for each public element of our framework a stereotype of identical name is introduced which has the metalevel constraint that its instances must inherit the framework class of the same name.

The shdframework is depicted in Fig. 13.1 together with the formchart framework, which extends the shdframework.

In the shdframework we define a hierarchy for classes as well as for associations as shown in Fig. 13.1. Indeed we make intensive use of the concept of association inheritance, in other words the generalization of associations. There have been long debates about the semantics of generalization of associations. We therefore prefer to define the semantics we use here. If an association has n associations, which inherit it directly, then two objects can be connected over only one of the inherited associations. The basic class is `State` and it has an aggregation to itself called `transition`. The ends of `transition` have roles `source` and `target`.

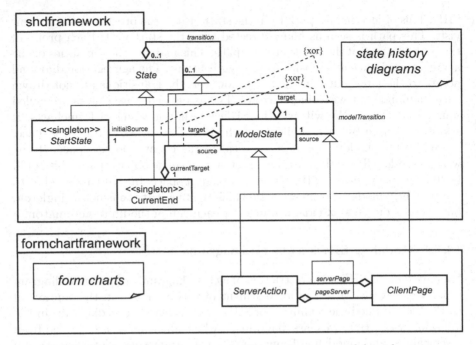

Fig. 13.1. Frameworks for state history diagrams and formcharts

Before we explain how the framework introduces the desired semantics to SHDs, we explain how it should be used in creating SHDs. As mentioned earlier, all elements of an SHD must be derived from the following public elements in the shdframework. All state classes in the SHD must be derived from **ModelState** and all transitions must be derived from **modelTransition**. The marker for the start of the SHD is derived from **StartState**, and its transition to the first state is derived from the unnamed transition to **ModelState**. Only these four elements of SHDs are public. All elements except the class CurrentEnd are abstract, only the classes derived by the Modeler can be instantiated. The singleton stereotype of **StartState** requires that the whole class hierarchy derived from **StartState** has only one instance.

In a concrete SHD of course the generalization dependencies of SHD elements to the framework are not depicted. Instead we make use of the auxiliary stereotypes mentioned earlier. Therefore we are entitled to change the graphical appearance of stereotyped classes in the SHD as we will do especially in formcharts.

The SHD approach is based on our powerful decomposition mechanism, model union. This decomposition mechanism is simply non-disjoint graph decomposition, i.e., graph decomposition with possibly a shared subgraph. Accordingly, the composition mechanism is graph union. A state-based aspect is not modeled by a new diagram type, but exclusively by singling out a submodel of the whole model.

We are showing here that if a system exhibits state based behavior then we can pin this down to model elements. Here we concentrate on special cases, where these model element are part of the plain data model. This is especially useful for the analysis phase, where the model can be adopted.

13.1.2 Constraints on the Object Net

We now explain how the shdframework in Fig. 13.1 formalizes our constraints on the process as the object net over an SHD. We show that the shdframework enforces that the object net is a path.

For this purpose it is necessary that every visit but the start visit must have exactly one predecessor, and every visit but the last visit must have exactly one successor. The formalization of this demand poses two separate problems: on the one hand the formalization of the constraint that each inner node of the path must have exactly one predecessor and successor, and on the other hand the exemption of the start and the end visit in exactly the correct manner. The important problem of guaranteeing that the object net is cycle-free is already achieved by the use of aggregations since aggregations are defined to be cycle-free on the object net level.

We first address the problem of exempting the terminal nodes.

There are two flavors of formalization. First, one could exempt the start visit from the general rule. The second way is to use a technique similar to the sentinel technique in algorithms: an artificial predecessor to the start node is introduced. This artificial visit is of a StartState class, which cannot be revisited. We choose this second method, since it has the advantage that it delegates the semantic details to auxiliary classes. Both classes StartState and ModelState are derived from State. In the same way, the current visit always has an artificial successor from the class CurrentEnd. All states created by the modeler in the SHD shall be derived from ModelState. Each time a new state A is visited, a new instance of A must be created. This new visit gets the old current state as a predecessor and the current end as a successor.

We now discuss how the multiplicities expressed in the class diagram in Fig. 13.1 give the desired semantics and address the second problem, namely the formalization of the constraint that each inner node of the path must have exactly one predecessor and successor.

We sum up these deliberations in the following

Theorem 13.1. *The object net over an SHD is a directed path.*

Proof. If two classes A and B are connected with an association r, then in OCL for an object $a : A$ the group of associated objects $a.r$ is an OCL collection, i.e., a multiset or bag. The multiplicity on the association end specifies the number of elements of the collection, i.e., multiple occurrences counted, not ignored. Objects associated by a derived association $q < r$ are always elements of the collection concerning r, hence $a.q \subset a.r$. This relation is the key for the following multiplicity discussion; if an association end of an abstract association has a multiplicity 1, then exactly one derived association must have exactly one link.

As we have said about SHDs, each transition in the SHD must be derived from `ModelTransition` in the diagram, and each model state must be derived from `ModelState`. This implies that if a model state has several outgoing transitions, they are all derived from `modelTransition`. Hence for an instance of this state only one of these transitions can be instantiated at the same time due to the multiplicities for `modelTransition`. In this way the shdframework introduces an implicit *xor* constraint on all outgoing transitions, and vice versa on all ingoing transitions of a model state. Hence each instance of a model state derived from `modelState` must have exactly one predecessor and one successor. The *xor* constraints that are explicitly modeled in the **shdframework** take care that an instance of a model state can have one of the terminal nodes as a predecessor or successor. We will discuss this for the `StartState`. The Xor constraint responsible for the treatment of the start node is the Xor constraint that connects the `modelTransition` with the transition from `StartState` to `ModelState`. This Xor constraint allows that an instance of a model state can have either another model state instance or a `StartState` instance as a predecessor. In the same way an instance of a model state can have either another model state instance or a `CurrentEnd` instance as a successor. The instances of `StartState` and `CurrentEnd` have only one transition with multiplicity 1, so the instances of these states must have exactly one link attached. Since both classes are singletons, the object net over a formchart contains exactly one object with a single outgoing link, exactly one object with a single ingoing link, and otherwise only objects with exactly one ingoing and one outgoing link. Together with the fact that all associations are aggregations and therefore the object net must not contain cycles, it follows that the object net must be a single directed path.   □

13.1.3 Formcharts as SHDs

Formcharts are bipartite STDs, which we will model now as SHDs. For this purpose we introduce the formchartframework, which introduces specializations of the `ModelState` and `ModelTransition` elements of the shdframework, as shown in Fig. 13.1. Formchart model elements must be derived from the formchartframework elements, except the rather technical start elements, which are still derived directly from the shdframework. Elements of formcharts are therefore also derived from elements of the shdframework, though indirectly. Hence formcharts are SHDs.

The formchart framework enforces by itself that formcharts are bipartite and introduces the known names for formchart elements.

We introduce two subclasses to State: ServerAction and ClientPage. All states in the formchart have to be derived from these classes. We derive aggregations pageServer and serverPage between them from the transition aggregation in order to enforce that formcharts are bipartite: in the formchart all transitions must be derived from either pageServer or serverPage. The usage of the framework for modeling frameworks is shown in Fig. 13.2. Only the derivations of the states are shown, the derivations of the transitions being omitted.

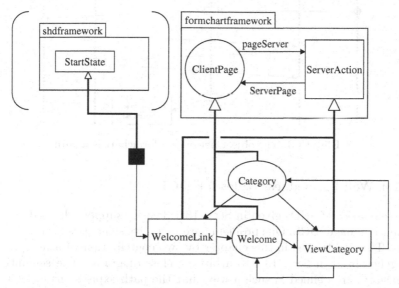

Fig. 13.2. A formchart is derived from the semantic framework

We assume again that each formchart framework element is accompanied by a stereotype of same the name. Each stereotype introduces its own graphical representation. The << ClientPage >> stereotype is depicted by an ellipse, the << ServerAction >> is depicted by a square. In the formchart, ellipses and squares contain only their names.
The << serverPage >> and << pagePerver >> associations are depicted as arrows, even though they are aggregations.
Fig. 13.3 shows a formchart and an example object net over this formchart, depicted actually below the formchart. The start state is omitted. The object net is a path alternating between client states and server actions. If a ModelState in the formchart has no outgoing transition, this state is a terminal state for the dialogue; the dialogue is completed once the state is entered.

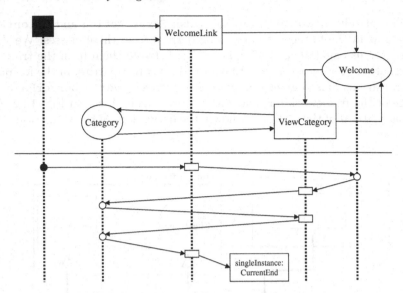

Fig. 13.3. The object net over a formchart is a path

13.1.4 Well-Formedness Rules for DCL

The semantics of SHDs given in Sect. 13.1.3 easily support the dialogue constraint language, DCL. One problem here is to give semantics for path expressions. This is achieved in this chapter by two contributions. Path expressions are generalized in Sect. 13.4 to arbitrary class diagrams. The semantics for formcharts are defined in such a way that the path expressions in DCL map exactly with our general definition of path expressions. Formcharts have new constraint stereotypes for the dialogue constraint language DCL.

The important well-formedness rules concerning the bipartite structure of form charts are already specified by the class diagram in Fig. 13.1. Now we define the well-formedness rules of the different constraint stereotypes introduced in DCL. The placement of the DCL constraints is depicted in Fig. 5.6. In this section we give the formal rules where the new DCL constraints are allowed. These rules are well-formedness rules for formcharts. They are OCL meta-model constraints assigned to the newly introduced stereotypes. Two kinds of DCL constraints are placed on classes, namely client input constraints and server input constraints. The other kinds of constraints are placed at the ends of transitions.

Formally, we define stereotypes for constraints, similar to the stereotypes << invariant >> , << precondition >> , and << postcondition >> for OCL. The new stereotypes apply to constraints at transition ends and are called dialogue constraints. They are derived from the << dialogueconstraint >> stereotype. They are all contained in the formchartframework so that they can be used in a formchart. They conclude the allowed elements within the formchart.

Two of the dialogue constraints, namely client output and server output constraints, share important semantic properties, as we will see in Sect. 13.3. This leads to the intuitive approach to make them specializations of a single constraint type, which we will call << stateoutputconstraint >> . This constraint type can now be understood as a natural constraint already on the SHD level. So the two types of output constraint in the formchart can be understood as the natural dichotomy of this single SHD constraint due to the bipartite structure of the formchart.

The dialogue constraint stereotypes have metamodel constraints as presented in the following. They primarily argue over the constrained element, which can be accessed as `constrainedElement` in the metamodel.

<u>enablingcondition</u>
`constrainedElement→instanceOf(AssociationEnd) and`
`constrainedElement.association→instanceOf(pageServer) and`
`constrainedElement.aggregation=none`

<u>clientoutputconstraint</u>
`constrainedElement→instanceOf(AssociationEnd) and`
`constrainedElement.association→instanceOf(pageServer) and`
`constrainedElement.aggregation=aggregate`

<u>serveroutputconstraint</u>
`constrainedElement→instanceOf(AssociationEnd) and`
`constrainedElement.association→instanceOf(serverPage) and`
`constrainedElement.aggregation=aggregate`

<u>flowcondition</u>
`constrainedElement→instanceOf(AssociationEnd) and`
`constrainedElement.association→instanceOf(serverPage) and`
`constrainedElement.aggregation=none`

<u>serverinputconstraint</u>
`constrainedElement.stereotype=ServerAction`

<u>clientinputconstraint</u>
`constrainedElement.stereotype=ClientPage`

In the metamodel constraints for << serverinputconstraint >> and for << clientinputconstraint >> we use the fact that we have for each framework class a corresponding stereotype which must be assigned to each subclass of the framework class.

Informal metamodel constraints are as follows. Only one constraint of the same stereotype is allowed for the same context. The numbers of flow conditions must be unique. They must not be strictly ascending in order to facilitate model union. For each ServerAction there may be only one flow condition that is not numbered.

13.2 Discussion of Formchart Semantics

We have modeled formcharts by frameworks,i.e., the shdframework and the formchartframework. The semantics presented are directly motivated by our application domain; however, they are also novel operational semantics for STDs in general, independent of the motivation presented. We outline and discuss modeling alternatives in the following.

13.2.1 SHDs and Formcharts by Strict Metamodeling

As we mentioned earlier, a modeling alternative would be a pure metamodel for formcharts. The most general method of introducing new diagrams in UML is given by the metamodeling technique. We therefore could define the formchart elements by strict metamodeling [18], i.e., purely as a framework of stereotypes for metamodel elements of class diagrams. The intention of this approach would be still to define formcharts (or more generally SHDs) as a variant of class diagrams in such a way that it is guaranteed that the object net is a path. The constraints expressed in our framework modeling approach would have to be expressed within the stereotype description. A related topic is the use of the composition notation. One could think of expressing certain multiplicities in the framework implicitly by using composition instead of aggregation. However, composition would be able to express only one direction of the multiplicity at best; furthermore there are different opinions about the exact meaning of composition. Therefore it seems more convenient to stick to aggregation, and to use explicit multiplicities, as was done in the framework.

The diagram in Fig. 13.3 resembles a message sequence chart. However, the diagram is completely different. Above the horizontal line are classes, not instances. Below the line are instances, not method invocations.

13.2.2 Modeling Formcharts with State Machines

UML has its own diagram type for state automata called state machines. State machines are based on David Harel's statecharts [140]. However, state machines have no operational semantics defined within UML, indeed no formal operational semantics are part of the specification. Instead, operational semantics are given by reference to a state machine that is described verbally.

The semantics of statecharts based on pseudo-code are given in [141]. Our definition of SHDs has operational semantics based solely on core class diagrams, the semantic core of UML.

One could model formcharts with UML state machines. For this approach one has to drop the SHD semantics and hence loses support for temporal path expressions. Nevertheless we present the alternatives in the following for reasons of completeness. UML state machines model the behavior of objects by modeling the life cycle of a single object as a finite automaton. There are again two alternatives; we can model the formchart as a bipartite state machine or transform the server actions. The latter alternative means that each page server transition will be transformed to as many statecharts transitions as the targeted server action has outgoing transitions. In that case the flow conditions would become guard conditions directly on the page; the server actions do not appear. In the example of a login page, the page would have two outgoing transitions with event submit, one of them with the guard condition "password valid" the other with guard condition "password invalid," as shown in Fig. 13.4. The guard conditions have to be made exclusive in order to prevent non-deterministic behavior. A variant would be to omit the self-transition with the guard condition "invalid password." However, there is a subtle semantic difference between both variants. That is, in the first variant, the history of state visits could have repeated adjacent visits of the login page state, while in the later alternative there would be only one instance of this state instead.

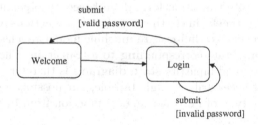

Fig. 13.4. A login subdialogue as UML state machine

The second major alternative would be to model the formchart as a bipartite UML state machine. We need no compound states for formcharts, but we would have to enforce bipartite structure. Server actions would be required to have completion transitions that are triggered automatically upon completion as is known from activities in activity diagrams. The flow conditions in formcharts can be mapped to guard conditions of the server action. However, the flow conditions in our formchart semantics are exclusive since they are mapped to elsif branches of an OCL condition. For the state machine modeling one has to make the guard conditions exclusive, otherwise the semantics of state machines would prescribe non-deterministic behavior.

Except for flow conditions and enabling conditions, DCL constraints cannot be mapped to guard conditions. This is due to the fact that the other conditions like server output and client output constraints are in principle "design by contract" annotations. These DCL conditions would have to be mapped to pre- or postconditions of actions assigned with the transitions in the state machine.

The fact that formcharts use only flat STDs in contrast to hierarchical statecharts does not restrict the expressibility of formcharts due to the fact that formcharts are coupled with an information model. Formcharts can be easily combined with statechart notation if the statechart notation is interpreted as the visualization of parts of the session objects of the information model.

A proposal for representing states by classes can also be found in the state design pattern [119], which describes how an object can delegate its state change to a state object. The object appears to change its state within a finite set of states. The set of states is finite, since each state is represented by a class. The pattern does not prescribe how to model a finite automaton over the state instance set, but discusses procedural implementations. First it proposes implementing the transitions in the so-called Context class using the pattern. An alternative proposal is a table lookup. Both are non-equivalent to the SHD model using associations to model state transitions.

13.2.3 Petri Nets

Petri nets are a state transition formalism based on bipartite graphs. Formcharts resemble Petri nets due to the fact that server actions resemble Petri net transitions. Petri nets as a finite state machine model are classically conceived as being never in a state corresponding to a transition. The main difference between Petri nets and bipartite state diagrams is therefore that the state of a Petri net is not necessarily a single bubble, but possibly a compound state, depending on the type of Petri net, e.g., a function from bubbles to numbers for place/transition nets.

It is possible to give formcharts Petri net semantics. We have outlined how to define the semantics of formcharts based on non-bipartite state machines. Petri net semantics can be given in a similar way by defining only client pages as places and introducing a Petri net transition for every path of length 2 to another client page. Such Petri net semantics, however, involves only trivial transitions, i.e., transitions with one ingoing and one outgoing edge.

13.3 Semantics of Dialogue Constraints

Dialogue constraints have been introduced as stereotypes for constraints. In this section we give the semantics of dialogue constraints by giving for each dialogue constraint a translation into parts of standard OCL constraints. As we will see, all DCL constraints are related to OCL method constraints in their semantics. Accordingly, it is a reasonable choice to map them onto parts of OCL preconditions.

For that purpose we have to make a construction that makes explicit and utilizes the aforementioned unification of structural and behavioral features of formcharts. We have argued that SHDs and therefore formcharts achieve a unification of structural and behavioral semantics, since the relevant temporal evolution of SHDs is already represented in the evolution of its object net, and not just in the evolution of method calls. Now, in order to integrate this view with standard behavioral modeling, especially with OCL method constraints, we have to construct behavioral semantics which are a perfect mirror of the structural features of SHDs. Hence behavioral semantics of SHDs have the task to introduce methods which are called in a defined mandatory way in connection with state changes. These methods serve as contexts for standard OCL constraints, i.e., preconditions and postconditions. The DCL constraints are then mapped onto parts of these constraints.

As in the case of the formchart framework, we first give a behavioral model of SHDs and then give a more restrictive model for formcharts. The behavioral model has the purpose to prescribe which method calls have to be performed in the course of state changes. Partly these method calls can be enforced by the specification tools of our UML notation. Partly, however, we again reach the limits of UML semantics, this time for the behavioral models. As was observed in [73], message sequence charts are unsuited for giving behavioral semantics because they lack the expressibility to specify mandatory behavior. Message sequence charts just specify example interaction sequences. Harel and Damm [73] proposed live sequence charts with richer semantics, which also allows for specification of conditions. We do not need this expressibility for our purposes since in the semantics of formcharts mandatory behavior will be unconditional, as we will see. Therefore we simply specify mandatory behavior as pseudo-code, where necessary.

We define in the abstract class ModelState three methods, enterState(), makeASuperParam(), and changeState(), which perform the handshake between subsequent state visits. The central method is the enterState() method for each state, which has to be called on each newly inserted visit. For that purpose the enterState() method is declared abstract in the ModelState class. Each modeler-defined derived state must overwrite the enterState method. The new visit has to be seen as being the conceptual parameter of its own enterState() method. ModelState replaces the parameter list, therefore we call the ModelState instance a superparameter. Each state has a makeASuperParam() method, which must be called when the state is left, and which constructs the superparameter. The superparameter is passed to the enterState() method in σ-calculus style [1]. This means that the enterState() method is called on the superparameter without method parameters. State changes are performed by a single method changeState() in the old state. The changeState() method of one state calls its own makeASuperParam() and the enter-

State() of the next state. makeASuperParam() and enterState() must not be called from any other method. changeState() is defined final in ModelState. In Java-like pseudo-code:

```
abstract class ModelState extends State {
    // ....
    abstract ModelState makeASuperParam();
    abstract void enterState();
    final void changeState(){
        ModelState aSuperParam = makeASuperParam();
        aSuperParam.enterState();
    }
}
```

The control logic that invokes changeState() of the current visit is not prescribed. However, the only way to change the state is by calling changeState() of the current visit.

13.3.1 State Output Constraints

When we introduced the dialogue constraints, we characterized two of them as the specializations of StateOutputConstraint, the single new constraint type already available on the SHD level. The technical reason for SHDs having a new constraint context is that this new context is conceptually placed on the edge between two states, and it is therefore called transition context. In this newly introduced transition context there is no self keyword, but the role names of the transition ends can be used, especially the role names source and target from the general transition. The role names refer to the ModelState and hence to the corresponding message. The central added value of the state output constraint is the fact that source as well as target are properly typed, i.e., they have the ModelState as type at the respective end.

From the final specification of changeState() as given above it is known that the precondition of enterState() is immediately executed after the postcondition of makeASuperParam(), hence the system state is the same in both constraint contexts. The state output constraint is intended to be executed at that point in time, which can be seen as a single instant; therefore in principle one could use one of the mentioned contexts instead. Semantically therefore we map the state output constraint either onto the postcondition of makeASuperParam() or onto the precondition of enterState(). However, in both contexts there is less typing information available than in the state output constraint. The state output constraint makes use of the fact that in SHDs for each enterState() method the possible predecessors are known from the diagram, and for each changeState() method the possible successors are known. This is captured by the proper typing of source and target.

The more specific dialogue constraints defined for formcharts pay tribute to the more elaborate model of formcharts. In the case of formcharts, the two

classes of states have more specialized semantics than in the case of general
SHDs as we will explain in the following.

It is important to realize that state output constraints must not be mistaken for guard conditions known from state machines. Guard conditions in
state machines specify behavior. State output constraints are on the other
hand "design by contract" constraints. They constrain the possible implementations.

13.3.2 ClientPage Visits

ClientPage visits are the superparameters computed by the preceding Server-
Action makeASuperParam() and offered to enterState(). The ClientPage
methods, however, have to be seen as provided by a browser. enterState()
and makeASuperParam() of a ClientPage are therefore not individually modeled, but conceived as being interpreted by a generic browser concept. This
concept is called the abstract browser. The browser therefore is a parametric
polymorphic concept. The named ClientPage methods are not implemented,
but interpreted by using type reflection on the ClientPage class.

The ClientPage class contains the information that has to be shown to the
user together with interaction possibilities, links, and forms. Since formcharts
are used in the analysis phase, the ClientPage superparameter is assumed to
be a pure content object. The ClientPage superparameter is a hierarchical
constant data type constructed with aggregations. As explained earlier, in
form-oriented analysis we consider an abstract browser as given. The analyst's
view of the browser is a black box taking the content object and delivering a
state change to a ServerAction later. The presentation of the content to the
user and the construction of the method calls to the allowed server actions
according to the SHD is the task of the abstract browser. The analyst assumes
that the page offers a form for each outgoing transition of the ClientPage.
However, in a current ClientPage visit certain forms may be disabled. For this
purpose the ClientPage is assumed to have for each outgoing transition A a
flag formAenabled which specifies whether the transition is enabled. They are
specified by the enabling conditions.

13.3.3 Generation of ServerAction Visits

ServerAction visits are the actual superparameters that are given in a state
change to a ServerAction. The objects are created whenever the user triggers a
state change in the dialogue. The ServerAction superparameter is constructed
by the browser by using the ClientPage visit as a page description. Since
formcharts are, in contrast to concrete technologies like HTML, a strong typed
concept, the type description of the serverAction does not have to be contained
in the ClientPage visit, but the default parameters and the enabled flags have
to be provided. The abstract browser constructs the new ServerAction visit
from the user input.

The information model is updated by a side effect of the server action, for which form-oriented analysis explicitly makes no strict specification requirements. A typical specification of the side effect would be to specify a single method call in the side effect. Business operations can be decomposed; the top layer is formed by the side effects of server actions. Server actions are executed atomically and are therefore multi-user safe operations on the information model.

13.3.4 Enabling Conditions

The outgoing transitions in the class diagram for each ClientPage depict the statically allowed page changes. Often a certain form should be offered only if certain conditions hold, e.g., a bid in an auction is possible only if the auction is still running. Since the page shown to the user is not updated unless the user triggers a page change, the decision whether to show a form or not has to be taken in the changeState() leading to the current ClientPage visit. The enabling condition is mapped to a part of a precondition of enterState().

```
enterState()
pre: formAEnabled = enablingConditionA
pre: formBEnabled = enablingConditionB
```

Alternatively each enabling condition can be seen as a query that produces the Boolean value that is assigned to formXenabled. Typically, the same constraint has to be re-evaluated after the user interaction. In the example above, the auction may end while the user has the form on the page. Then the same OCL expression is also part of another constraint stereotype, for especially << serverinputconstraint >> or << flowcondition >> .

13.3.5 Server Input Constraint

These constraints appear only in incomplete models or models labeled as TBD, to be defined [158]. A server input constraint expresses that the ServerAction is assumed to work correctly only if the server input constraint holds. In a late refinement step the server input constraint has to be replaced by transitions from the ServerAction to error handlers. The context of the server input constraint is the ServerAction visit. Server input constraints are not preconditions in a "design by contract" view, since server input constraint violations are not exceptions but known special cases.

13.3.6 Flow Conditions

Flow conditions are constraints on the outgoing transitions of a ServerAction. The context of flow conditions is the ServerAction visit. The semantics of flow conditions can be given by mapping all flow conditions of a state onto parts of a complex postcondition on this.makeASuperParam(). This postcondition has an **elsif** structure. In the **if** or **elsif** conditions the flow conditions appear in the sequence of their numbering. The flow condition must be evaluated on the system state before executing the state change; hence the flow condition has to be transformed by adding the modal operator pre to all state accesses.

In the **then** block after a flow condition, it is assured that a visit of the targeted ClientPage is the new Current State. In the final **then** block the same check is performed for the target of the serverPage transition without a flow condition.

13.3.7 Client Output Constraints and Server Output Constraints

Client output constraints and server output constraints are specializations of state output constraints and live in the new transition context.

13.3.8 Path Expressions in DCL

As an introduction to the general concept of path expressions in OCL we explain path expressions in DCL. Path expressions allow the expression of a condition about the path that was taken up to then by the dialogue within the state diagram. In formcharts a test on whether the dialogue has chosen a fixed single path can be tested with the new along OCL feature. The path is written backwards in time. The along feature simply tests whether the chosen object exists. More generally constraints are important in which it is tested whether the path has certain properties as long as it remaines in a subdialogue. Hence the path has to be restricted to a subdialogue. The concept of formchart features is viable in this approach. Formchart features must not be mistaken for OCL features. The word feature is derived in the context of formcharts from the requirements engineering community.

Path expressions that are restricted to paths allowed in a feature are written in DCL by the feature name in square brackets. Formally this concept is a shorthand notation. DCL path expressions are mapped to general path expressions as introduced in Sect. 13.4. For this purpose, formchart features are not just diagrams, but come along with a class definition. For each feature diagram a **ModelState** with the name of the diagram is created with a transition to itself, again with the feature name. All model states in the feature as well as the transitions shown in the feature are implicitly derived from these two elements. This is made explicit in Fig. 13.5.

13.3.9 Discussion of DCL Semantics

We have given the semantics for DCL constraints by mapping them to OCL pre- and postconditions. For that purpose we have introduced behavior into

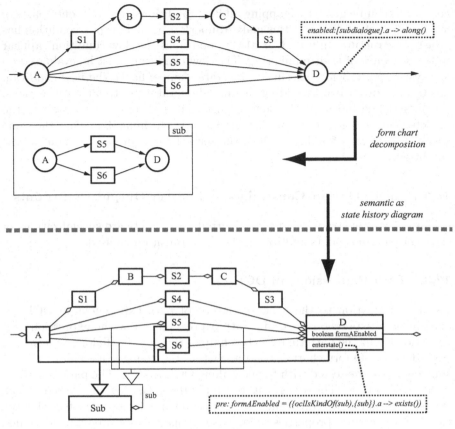

Fig. 13.5. Semantics of path expressions in DCL

our semantics for SHDs. In this section we want to discuss briefly an alternative model. As it turns out, it is possible to model DCL constraints as OCL constraints of the stereotype invariant. As the authors of OCL state explicitly in [314], OCL is ambiguous with respect to the question, at which point in time an invariant must hold. In that respect it differs from Eiffel [219], where invariants are specified to hold at each instant at which the instance is observable to clients. We can specify for our model that all OCL class invariants must hold immediately after each state transition of our formchart. At this instant we assume the superparameter of the new state to be fully constructed. Astonishingly, we can now map all DCL constraints to invariants. Generally, pre- and postconditions cannot be mapped to invariants. Since we have seen that DCL constraints map easily to pre- and postconditions, it is at least remarkable that such a mapping of DCL constraints to invariants is possible. Indeed, these alternative semantics of DCL will be possible only because of the unified character of our STD semantics. The key argument is that we can give an OCL expression which can be used as part of an invariant, and as such specify that this OCL invariant is executed only for the current visit and therefore only once for each visit. This condition is simply a check whether the current visit is the currently last in the path. Due to the sentinel technique used in modeling SHDs, this can be recognized by checking whether the succeeding state is the currentEnd:

`self.target->isTypeOf(CurrentEnd)`

The key technique in modeling a DCL constraint A as invariant is now the conjunction of this expression with A. By doing so we find that A is evaluated only for the current visit.

The technique shown above may have the advantage that no behavioral model is needed for formcharts, but has also disadvantages, namely in context with flow conditions. The result of flow conditions has to be stored in the state.

13.4 Path Expressions

We now define path expressions for collecting objects along the transitive closure of link paths, called gathering in the following. The notation is needed to give semantics to the "along" notation of the DCL used for example in writing enabling conditions during form-oriented analysis. However, path expressions have a justification in their own right. We start with an unrestricted wildcard notation for expressing path navigations. Consider the following OCL expression:

A
`*.C`

For every arbitrary fixed object of the context type A the expression denotes the bag of objects of target type C that are reachable from the context type object along a path of links, i.e., not just directly connected objects, but all reachable objects are gathered. Consider the example given in Fig. 13.6. It shows the bag resulting from the application of the above expression to a concrete object net. An object that is reachable along several link paths occurs more than once in the bag, one time for each path. Only cycle-free link paths, in the object net are considered, i.e., link paths, in which each object is visited only once. This ensures finiteness of the result bag.

Theorem 13.2. *A path expression specifies a finite bag.*

Proof. By definition of the path expression there is a one-to-one correspondence between the object occurrences in the result bag and the cycle-free paths. There can be only as many cycle-free paths in the object net as there are permutations of the objects. Hence the number of cycle-free paths and therefore the number of bag elements is finite.   □

With respect to a possible generalization hierarchy of the classes, only such link paths are considered for which the links are instances of connected, but strictly interchanging, associations in the class diagram. Therefore the object aC3:C in the current example does not belong to the result set of the above expression, because, following the link path, from the viewpoint of the start object the connected object aB':B' is of type B and has no link to the object aC3:C. The above expression has the same meaning as the following OCL expression:

<u>A</u>
self.v.y→union(self.w.y)→union(self.x)

Recall from the latter expression that in OCL a multi-step navigation is a shorthand notation for the repeated application of collect and therefore yields a bag.

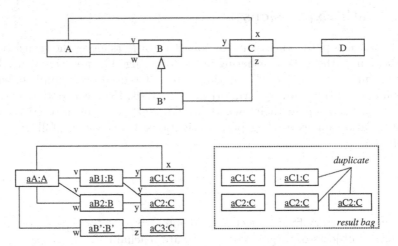

Fig. 13.6. An example class and object diagram, together with the result bag of the path expression *.C, applied to the only instance of Class A

The wildcard notation may be used straightforwardly for writing constraints on cyclic class diagrams based on aggregations, too. The semantics remain the same, except that a path is only considered, if all aggregation links point in the same direction. Consider the example in Fig. 13.7. The following constraint yields the set of leaves for an object tree which is accessed through its root node:

<u>Root</u>
*.Leaf→asSet

This expression has only non-trivial counterparts in UML. A notation like path expressions is clearly needed. Cyclic class diagrams with aggregations are the backbone of proven object-oriented patterns, both from problem domains and solution domains , e.g., the structural kernels of both the composite design pattern and the organization hierarchies analysis patterns [117] are trees.

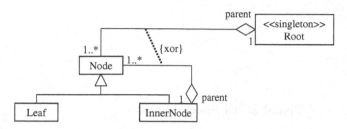

Fig. 13.7. UML tree definition

We proceed with the general notation for path expressions, which is summarized in the following expression:

```
ContextType
{oclConstraint,{package.associationName,..}}.GatheringType
```

The path expression consists of a structured wildcard and the type of the objects that are to be gathered. The structured wildcard is a constraint on the link paths that may be followed to gather objects. The wildcard consist of an OCL constraint and an association constraint which is a set of association specifications. In a valid link path, every object must fulfill the given OCL constraint. There are subtle typing aspects of this mechanism. The OCL constraint of a path expression is not tight to a single context; it must be evaluated with respect to objects of possibly different types. This is not a problem if all classes of the underlying class association path have a common supertype and the OCL constraint is written in terms of this type. Otherwise the expression must be made general enough by first questioning the type of the object.

Furthermore, in a valid link path every link must adhere to the association constraint. This constraint is a set of association specifications. A link in a valid link path must be an instance of an association which is a generalization of one of the associations specified in the association constraint. The modeler specifies an association by giving its qualified name consisting of a package name and the association name. If the model is not structured by packages, only an association name suffices. Association names are unique in packages. If the association specification is an empty set, the link path is not constrained with respect to the links.

The structured wildcard is a powerful narrowing mechanism, e.g., to exclude object net cycles from constraints involving path expressions. It is exploited later to give semantics to path expressions of dialogue constraint language used in formcharts.

At least consider the first path expression in unrestricted wildcard notation on page 267. It is a shorthand notation for the following verbose path expression.

<u>A</u>
{true,∅}.C

Semantics of Visual State Specialization

In Fig. 6.8 we have shown how an enabling condition based on path expressions can be shown graphically by multiple specializations of a state in the formchart, which have to be distinguished by apostrophes. This distinguishes this kind of multiple specializations from the concept of multiple occurrences. Now we have to give precise semantics to this method in the following way: if a state occurs more than once in a formchart diagram, these occurrences represent distinct anonymous subclasses of the state, called substates. If the same system is specified with a formchart with only one representative of the state, then whenever this state is visited an instance of the according substate is instantiated. The parent state is effectively abstract since it cannot be instantiated through the formchart operational semantics. Therefore the state named S5 has to get path-dependent enabling conditions because for each of its substates it can proceed only through one of the outgoing edges.

14

Semantics of the Data Model

The PD modeling language and DAL are based on the well developed relational theory, encompassing relational algebra and tuple relational calculus. This theory provides semantics for relational operations like they are used in SQL and DAL. The mathematical interpretation of the state of a PD model was already discussed in Chapter 7. In this chapter therefore we will focus on the temporal aspects of our system modeling approach. Furthermore we discuss some alternatives to the basic PD model semantics and some related aspects.

14.1 Semantics of the Temporal Model

The temporal model is important to give semantics to temporal constraints. The temporal model has been sketched in the first part as a log file of the system, in which all updates are stored. In this section we give the semantics of the temporal model. This definition will be no extension of the data model, i.e., we do not have to augment or change the static model. Instead, the definition of the temporal model will be an application of the modeling method introduced so far. The idea is that, basically, temporal expressions are reduced to static state expressions. However, in this procedure we will have to assume one type of temporal constraint to be fundamentally given, and this is the permanence constraint. We will give a discussion and a comparison with other approaches to temporal modeling afterwards.

14.1.1 The History as Log Warehouse

In order to give semantics to temporal properties we make a certain assumption about the constitution of the systems which use our data model. For our theoretical considerations it is helpful to assume that all systems keep a so-called log of their update operations. This is, by the way, indeed the case for a very important type of real machines, for which our model is intended, namely for databases. We assume that this log is stored according to our data modeling approach. The log is of course not part of what we usually call the system state, so the logged system and its log are only subsystems in the combined whole system, which we call the *history aware system*. A log contains for each update operation the undo and redo information. In the log we perform only inserts, no updates or deletes. Together with the fact that we store the log in our data model, the log is actually what is usually called a data warehouse, so we call it the *log warehouse*.

The log stores implicitly the information of all previous states. The model of all states parameterized by a state identifier is called the *history data model*. For a site s the history data model is gained from the *data model of presence* by introducing the new entity type `stateid`, and increasing the arity of every relation type by connecting it with `stateid`. Given a stateid, then the *present state graph* for this stateid can be obtained by selecting all links connected with this stateid. The history data model is a view of the log, using aggregation functions.

14.1.2 Discussion of Temporal Formalisms

Temporal constraints are necessary to create a connection between different states in the first place. It creates a structure in the state space, which is connected with the constraints on the data model. Without temporal constraints, all states stay unconnected, and represent arbitrary contents fulfilling the static constraints.

The history warehouse semantics are in our view the most intuitive formalism for studying formal properties of temporal systems, if they are effectively finitely bounded in time. Other approaches, like temporal logic, can be expressed in the history warehouse approach. They differ only in technicalities. We will see that in other definitions there will be structurally equivalent steps, so that one can conceive the different approaches as basically one idea in different notations. Temporal databases [289, 280] represent again a different concept.

14.1.3 Executable Temporal Specification

Through the use of the history warehouse, we can identify an executable subset of all possible temporal specifications. The history warehouse is an executable model, although this does not imply that it is very efficient. Theoretically it can be said that fixed relational queries of an appropriate SQL-like langauge are polynomial in size of the state, hence this holds for the history warehouse as well. However, in practical terms it may often be quite prohibitive. It has to be kept in mind that SQL queries are often too complex as well, as soon as they need too many joins. But having said that, we should not forget that for small data sets as used in examples, such as a few dozens of tuples per table, the history warehouse is fairly often executable. We therefore can easily identify executable temporal constraints as executable programs in the history warehouse. This is an extremely valuable concept, since it allows us to combine temporal modeling and testing, for example. Moreover, parts of the history warehouse have in many applications a natural interpretation as being some typical business logic, like bookkeeping.

14.1.4 Temporal Aspects of the Message Based Network Model

Our network model is non-deterministic concerning the runtime of individual message transmissions, the user input and some of the site functionalities. Assume we want to argue about the temporal development of a whole network.

Clocks may run differently in different unit systems. This can become apparent for the timestamps of messages; a message can be sent later in the sender's local time than it was received in the recipient's local time. Globally, this can be sorted out if the local clocks run at least correctly in that they are never reset to an earlier date. The local timed Web consists of clocked subsystems with *site clocks*. A network message has an identity, a sender site, a delivery time in the sender site time, a recipient site, and an arrival time in the recipient site time. A message flow is directed from the sender to the recipient. For all directed circles of message flows, there is at least one site in the circle, where the arrival time of the incoming message is earlier than the delivery time of the outgoing message.

A *global time order* is an absolute order of all locally issued timestamps. The timestamps of two different sites may not be ordered, but for each single clocked subsystem the timestamps are correctly ordered. A global time order can be assigned ex post.

Each site has state identities which have a timestamp. Each state refers to one executed transaction for one incoming message. This notion incorporates the virtually serial view on transaction processing. The transaction execution time and the waiting time of the message in the waiting bag can be subsumed under the message transmission time. The State identities with greater timestamp are later states.

Each possible evolution of this network up to a certain point in time is a *net evolution trace for fixed sites*, NETFS. This is an assignment of state sets to the state identities fulfilling the semantics of the messaging paradigm. For each NETFS, there is a bag of messages currently under way.

Each NETFS fixes this non-determinism. Arguing over different NETFS at the same time is a *contrafactual theory*. The NETFS form a prefix tree.

Our network model is non-deterministic concerning the message runtimes, the user input and some of the site functionalities. Each NETFS fixes this non-determinism. Arguing over different incompatible NETFS is a *contrafactual theory*. The NETFS form a prefix tree.

14.2 Alternative Fundamental Models

14.2.1 Abstract Syntax Models

Our data modeling language is already very lean due to the use of constraint libraries as the main tool of introducing modeling elements. However, the reader interested in language design may ask whether the language is minimal. There is no such thing as an objectively minimal language, since the definition depends on the definition of the measure with which we compare different data modeling languages. Hence the question whether a language is minimal may be interesting, but in some sense there is no single answer to it.

The search for minimality is perhaps best characterized as an instance of the economy principle (principle of parsimony) known as Ockham's razor. But we think the main insights in discussing parsimony are the gained equivalences, i.e., proven possible reductions, not so much the actual reduction. Or to make it even more precise, in performing simplifications of a theory, starting from a complicated one and proceeding to simpler equivalent theories, there comes a tradeoff point, where any further reduction comes at a cost. Indeed it is our opinion that the usage of a minimal theory is often decisively less abstract than the use of a less minimal, but appropriate, theory. That is, the usage of the minimal theory can lead easily to models which basically repeat in every model the semantic basics of the theory. As we will see, there is besides the notion of minimality a notion of appropriateness. This notion of appropriateness is in our opinion the notion of problem orientation. A reduction of a theory towards minimality beyond the point of maximal problem adequacy is a loss of abstraction.

In fact the one central concept which has to be mentioned in this concept is the very notion of termini. As we have mentioned earlier, collections of term definitions are like libraries. This concept of libraries is the best key for understanding the limitations of minimality discussions. If a minimal theory is used, libraries emerge. But then at the surface of these libraries, the language is as complicated as any other. This discussion could surely be elaborated even further, but we leave it at this point.

Quintessentially, our syntax model can be called an abstract syntax model.

Universal Models

The DAL model which we have introduced is only one possible model, but it has two properties, namely it is problem oriented and relational universal. Relational universal refers to the fact that it belongs to a class of models which are equivalent to the relational model in a certain sense. Problem oriented refers to the fact that the model incorporates in its structure important elements of the intended application domain, namely interacting distributed transactional-relational persistent systems.

A relational universal model must be able to encode the relational model. Note that models may look like generalizations, but may be simply equivalent. This resembles a fundamental definition of potentially infinite sets as being sets which are isomorphic to a proper subset. For every sufficiently powerful modeling approach you can find a more general second approach, which clearly contains the first approach as a part and is therefore a proper extension. However, vice versa, under an appropriate notion of equivalence, you can always interpret the latter approach as a proper part of the first approach as well.

For example, the binary DAL modeling approach, which has been defined to be the DAL modeling approach with only binary relations, is clearly a proper subset of the general DAL modeling approach with arbitrary arities. However, you can as well encode a higher arity DAL modeling approach in the binary DAL modeling approach, by introducing every relation in a higher arity model into a new entity type in the resulting binary model. Every role in the higher arity model becomes a new binary relation with a multiplicity 1..1 at the former role's entity type. The image of all higher arity DAL models is a proper subset of the set of all binary DAL models, because this mapping generates only binary relations, which have at least one multiplicity 1..1. The mapping is, however, injective, since, as you may check for yourself, every model and even the already binary models are mapped to a new model. The mapping accordingly contains no information loss. Every model of the new kind can be uniquely transformed back into a higher arity model. A certain irritation may arise due to the fact that one will of course use the full binary modeling approach, not just the subset, which is characterized as the image of the mapping. Then one has to be aware that the mapping characterizes some models as redundant, i.e., every model which is an image of another binary model. The latter model is smaller, but contains the same information. The last aspect of this example we want to turn our attention to is that the higher arity modeling approach is of course itself subject to possible extensions. One possible extension is the introduction of higher-order relations, as is done in the HERM model [290]. Again this extended model can be modeled in the higher arity model. Basically one has to say that the use of such a concept is nothing more than a matter of taste. In most data modeling approaches this concept is deliberately forbidden, because to every higher-order model one can trivially find an equivalent non-higher-order model.

Problem-Oriented Models

The data model as well as the functionality model incorporate knowledge about the application domain. The model is built along the structure of important target paradigms, chiefly SQL, i.e., both the data definition part called DDL as well as the data manipulation part DML. The model aims mainly at abstracting from notational peculiarities and offering a unified view of the paradigms.

The main thing which is not formally incorporated into the paradigm is the underlying cost model. The relational structure, which our model shares with SQL, can be said to be primarily motivated by some cost measure, not by comprehensibility. Perhaps the most important cost measure in this context is relative time, i.e., the execution time expressed relative to the speed of the underlying platform.

The model language fosters expressions which lead to efficient execution on the typical target platforms, chiefly modern relational databases. The decision in favor of this paradigm is of course alleviated by the fact that it leads to comprehensible models, and has turned out to be intuitive.

Our modeling language has been chosen on the one hand to be directly translatable to SQL, and on the other hand to have an advantageous and simple semantic basis. One goal of this model is to allow building a more complex model on top of this model exclusively by the use of the inbuilt modularization mechanisms. Furthermore the model does not aim at being minimal in its primary presentation.

One novel idea is that the offered language kernel is indistinguishable from a library invocation. Hence the code using the offered language kernel is not tied to the fact that the offered language kernel is the actual language core. In principle the language kernel can be substituted by another kernel, on which the offered language kernel is implemented. This is of course another aspect of the concept of abstract models.

14.2.2 A Reductionist Syntax Model

At this point we want to discuss a concrete alternative to the mentioned model, which goes a step further towards minimality. In order to show one of the possible reductions of the PD data model, we introduce the so-called reductionist model. The rationale behind this model is that associations have no type, and there is no special concept of roles. The concept of roles in the PD model allows for relation types, which connect more than once to the same entity type. More generally, it is helpful for entity types, which are connected to one other entity type across more than one relation type.

The reductionist model uses only entity types and a single binary relation between entities. The bundle of concepts comprising roles, relation types, directions, etc., is realized by using *sibling entity types*. These are entity types that are in a one-to-one relation to each other. There are again two natural alternatives, either a peer-to-peer cluster of sibling types, or a central type surrounded by sibling types.

The PD semantics can be implemented as a library on top of the reductionist semantics. A simple translation is to identify roles with sibling types. Since the single relation in the reductionist model is binary, it is natural to treat binary relations as special, so it is natural to restrict the discussion to binary PD models. A binary relation in the PD model is mapped to two sibling types of the respective entity types, and the current set of links of the relation is expressed by the set of links between these two sibling types. Relations of higher arity have to be simulated basically by the relationship concept, which was introduced as a constraint in the Chap. 7, i.e., they have to be expressed as independent entity types. In the reductionist model it becomes fairly obvious that there is a certain redundancy in having identities for relation types as well as for roles. Relation types can be replaced by using one of the sibling types.

From the view of the reductionist model, the PD model becomes the flavor of a mere pattern, e.g., the pattern that a sibling type of one cluster is used only in relation to one sibling type of another cluster. The reductionist model therefore makes it immediately plausible to explore other patterns. One very interesting pattern for example makes use of the fact that a sibling type can participate in more than one relation type. We call it commutativity modeling, since it puts more emphasis on commutativity diagrams. Then a sibling type would be used to represent a commutativity role.

The reductionist model has basically the same structure for all data models, making the different data models really rather constraints on a basic model than structural descriptions. The reductionist semantics have an entity repository U and a general relation type G and constraints on them. Types are no inbuilt language concept, neither for entities nor for relation types. Types are realized by using one constant entity instance for each type. The entities of that type are represented by all entities linked to that entity instance. It is called entity identifier in the following.

Thus multiple relation types between two entities can be simulated by using different sibling entity identifiers. In this way the single relation type is sufficient. In the reductionist model the states are exactly mathematical directed graphs.

A query to the reductionist data model contains in the FROM clause only a list of names, no types. The FROM clause in DAL has been identified to be a dependent product, whereby the attribute dependent refers to the enforcement of typing. Accordingly, in the reductionist access language, the from clause is simply the set or records, I^U. The enforcement of typing is translated into new join expressions in the where clause. For every variable v and its entity identifier e we get a basic clause WHERE (v G e).

One can argue that there is one aspect about associative models which gives a particular motivation for considering the reductionist model as the basic semantics of associative models. This is the fact that in the semantics of the relational access operations there is a concept of navigation from the type to its instances. Take the query *SELECT title FROM book*. The query is accessing all instances of the type book. This is a language feature (an aspect of its semantics) that is in this form absent in many other languages. Particularly, it is not a classic concept of object orientation. This may be the reason behind the fact that object-oriented modeling languages, like OCL for UML, do not have the same expressive power as SQL, since certain SQL operations violate the paradigm in some interpretation. The reductionist model now captures in a natural way a fundamental property of associative models, like the relational model and the IR model. The link between an instance and its entity identifier expresses this navigability, and captures the most fundamental aspects of tables in relational databases: the accessibility of the whole collection of current entity instances.

The concept of the reductionist model has interesting relations to the area of semi-structured data models, which has received increased attention.

14.2.3 A Web of Paradigms

The concept of exchanging the language kernel which we earlier outlined leads to a shift in the notion of what a theory should be. The very operational insight that one can exchange the language kernel is an expression of a more general vision, namely the vision to establish with a theoretical approach not only a single paradigm but a *web of paradigms*. The choice of the basic building blocks of our model is more a pragmatic one than a fundamental one. There is no such thing as a fundamental model.

As an example, this holds true for the net-based metaphor. We could have based the model on a kind of single server paradigm. All data could be assumed to be in the same data space. We could give semantics to our net-based model within this centralized model.

The use of the net-based model can be seen as an instance of a general software engineering principle, which is in some sense the opposite to the principle of data abstraction. It is the principle to base a certain functionality on a library, which is as well as possible in its semantic guarantees. This makes the software artifact as flexible as possible: it can be based on every library, which offers stronger properties.

An instance of this property is the rule to use the weakest transactional isolation level which is possible for specifying a given business rule. This specification of course always allows use of stronger isolation levels, where it comes at no cost.

14.2.4 Alternative Minimal Paradigms

It is very informative to think about a number of other paradigms, which one can easily devise, and which are very plausible as a fundamental model, depending on the personal objective. One desire, for instacne, could be to have no longer a distinction between entity types and relation types. A model which would fulfill this, and which would combine this with the flavor of the presented reductionist model, would be a model which actually uses the so-called S-expressions known from LISP as the basic data model. We therefore call it the LISP model. The model has a single type, which is a type of pair records. Each pair has two entries, traditionally called CAR and CDR in LISP, and an identity of course. These pairs are used to represent the links of the data model. Because the pairs have identities, they can be used as entity instances as well. This model immediately allows for the so-called higher-order relations we have mentioned earlier; since the links have identity as well in this model, one can insert links which refer to a link. A possible argument for this model, moreover, is the fact that the complexity of the state is proportional to the number of entities, i.e., every element of a state over this model can be identified by a single identity, while in the reductionist model the links can be identified only by two identities. We prefer the reductionist model chiefly because it follows from the outset some patterns which have been judged to be good practices, e.g., separation between relations and entities.

Both models, the reductionist and the LISP model, introduce a distinction between both the partners in the link. This ordering is purely structural. One may ask whether one can go without ordering. Indeed, this leads to two possible models. The first model is the graph model, which uses plain mathematical undirected graphs as states. In this model one has to find appropriate workarounds for self-associations. However, a similar construction such as the translation of roles in the case of the reductionist model will do. The obvious translation of the undirected approach to the LISP model is a model which uses unordered pairs with an identity.

14.3 Discussion

We close our considerations with a reflection on four topics which point at characteristics of our application domain. We start with the concept of a black-box model and discuss how this fits into our message based modeling paradigm.

14.3.1 Black-Box Model of Enterprise Applications

Black-box modeling is a classical specification approach. A single enterprise application installation can be modeled as a *black box*. This black box is an automaton, which has an internal state. The exact nature and structure of the state is not specified, only its *behavior*, i.e., its action and reaction. Every *implementation*, i.e., realization of its internal state, which produces a behavior as specified, fulfills the specification. A specification can, however, be a proposed implementation, but typically on an abstract machine. We call that an *executable specification*. Every implementation which behaves like the proposed implementation fulfills the specification.

The black-box concept gives another intuitive argument why it is desired to understand messages as being passive objects essentially different from systems. That is, the goal of the behavioristic approach is to understand the system through its communicative behavior, which requires that the messages as data do not pose the same problem as the systems. The goal here therefore is to perform a reduction: the system is reduced to an understanding of the messages. Such a reduction is not achieved by models, where the exchanged messages are objects of the same type themselves, i.e., certain object-oriented models.

There are different possible models for the behavior of a black box. We use a message-based model, with optional extensions. In this message-based model, time is only the concept of before/after, i.e., it is only an order, not a quantity. We specify our systems as *computational automata*. A *computational automaton* is specified by giving its *state transition function*. We specify systems by the state transition function:

```
system: message × state → state × listof(message)
```

In specifying the state transition function we have also to specify the *state type*, which is a part of both the argument type as well as the return type of the state transition function. In the operation of the automaton the state transition function is repeatedly invoked and each consecutive invocation of the state transition function receives the state from the return value of the previous invocation and provides the new current state for the next invocation of the state transition function.

The structure of the state transition function and its interpretation determine the kind of automaton under consideration. Especially, the remaining parts of the argument type specify the input, and the remaining parts of the return type specify the output. In our system model, the system receives a single message, and reacts with a list of return messages. The model extends naturally to a model of a net of systems. Each system has an address. A message has a sender address, a recipient address, and a message body. The net infrastructure moves messages from the sender to the recipient. For each system in the net, which we will call *node*, the state transition function is performed on each incoming message. The model includes a tacit assumption of queues in front of each node, which, however, appear only in the form of the simplifying assumption that each server is always idle at the moment it receives a new message. A node is not obliged to send a return message to the node which has sent it a message.

Clients in the system can be conceived as nodes, which allow the user to see received messages and to create and send new messages. We will use two well-defined concepts of clients in the future. The first will be a conceptual net browser, which allows us to see and store all received messages and to communicate with all nodes. The second client will be a conceptual session browser, which supports a single, possibly endless session with a single node, which is assumed to consist of alternating messages from the browser client to the server, and then the server to the browser, and so forth.

14.3.2 Data Separability

Data separability means that data are separable from the functions and can be accessed from multiple applications. The same contract data can be accessed from the call center as well as from the accounting office. The notion of integrity constraints can be defined with respect to this concept as such as functionality, which is in this paradigm rather an aspect of the structure of data than functionality in the behavioral meaning of the word.

We call a system *data based* if it supports the concept of the *complete report*. The intuition is that the state of the current database is open to inspection in its entirety. The complete report is in its simplest form the printout of all tables, which requires the translation of opaque foreign keys in random numbers.

In business modeling data separability is a concept, which occurs naturally. The concept of the message system model offers an explanation, why this still goes together with the concept of black-box modeling. The data separability is a consequence of the fact that the system can be understood thhrough its message communication with the outside world.

14.3.3 Transactions in Business Logic and Database Technology

A key concept in modeling enterprise applications is the concept of the business transaction. A business transaction is an operation of a system, which forms a single whole. Examples of transactions are the purchase of a flight at the end of a selection process, or the transfer of money between two accounts. A key property of a transaction is that even in a concurrent system, the transaction appears to have exclusive access to the data during its operation, i.e., during the operation of the transaction no other operation can change the same data. We call this a virtual serial view on the data that is available within a transaction. For modeling purposes, it is sufficient

Transactional databases use elaborated and sophisticated methods to ensure that the transaction can achieve this view, while still allowing the concurrent processing of many transactions. This service of transactional databases comes at a cost: an ongoing transaction on the system may be aborted from the database itself, if the database sees no possibility to achieve the virtual serial view.

14.3.4 Enterprise Application Installations

In this last reflection we want to come back to the concept of nonfunctional requirements with a special focus on the issues addressed by embedding specifications. Enterprise applications share important characteristics with other data-centric applications. In contrast to office applications, for example, the installation of an enterprise system for professional use is a heavyweight process, which involves a commitment by the performing organization. In contrast, if you install a word processor and you write a letter, say, even an important one like a contract, which is then sent and becomes effective, you nevertheless can obviously remove the word processor, and often you can even remove the text file, if the printed contract is stored. Enterprise applications are totally different. Setting up an enterprise application is not just more demanding concerning hardware resources. In order to get the application operational, you not only have to provide a considerable amount of core data, which are different from the business rules and are stored as data, but which nevertheless have rather configurationally character and hence are different from the steadily streaming operational data. You also have to make a commitment that this enterprise application is your operational database, which has a status equally important as your accounting documents and hence has a high-reliability demand. The concrete deployed instance of an enterprise application is a singular, long-lived, and mission-critical concept. Such deployed instances can be hard to move, in any sense of the word, from version to version, from server to server, or even physically. The idea of extracting the data, playing them on another place and having them run again is naive and not achievable in practice. Important vendors pay a lot of attention to migrating and update concerns. We call a deployed instance an *installation*. Many terms and concepts also relate in subtle ways to this fact, e.g., the distinction between the backend servers and the clients in an enterprise application. That is, the clients are again rather of a volatile and lightweight nature as the aforementioned office application, hence the client–server asymmetry is not just created by technological demands. The notion of cluster computers refers to the strategy of making server hardware units as lightweight as clients. You have a complete layer, which is created by a varying number of identical cluster hardware units. Only the layer as a whole is a heavyweight concept, and cannot be simply dropped. The single hardware units in contrast can be exchanged or augmented on demand.

15

Semantics of Web Signatures

This chapter formalizes the semantics of the reverse engineering tool JSPick introduced in Sect. 10.2 and the semantics of the typed server pages technology NSP introduced in Chap. 11.

First, the JSPick semantics are given as a pseudo-evaluation. Then the notions of client page description safety and client page type safety are made precise by the NSP coding guidelines in Sect. 15.2. The NSP coding guidelines target the developer: correct NSP code is very natural and the NSP coding guidelines are easy to learn. Finally, these coding guidelines are formalized in Sect. 15.3 by a Per Martin-Löf-style type system.

15.1 Formal Semantics of Web Signature Recovery

This section formalizes the semantics of the core functionality of the reverse engineering tool JSPick, i.e., the recovery of a high-level description of form parameters. The semantics are formalized as a pseudo-evaluation. A pseudo-evaluation runs a program with non-standard values instead of concrete values for the purpose of static program analysis. The pseudo-evaluation technique was introduced with type checking in the GIER ALGOL compiler [228, 227], where a program is executed on types instead of values. Another early usage of the pseudo-evaluation technique is object code optimization [176] in ALGOL compilers. Pseudo-evaluation has been taken up with other, more sophisticated notions of program analysis [231] like data flow analysis [203] or abstract interpretation [67], each with other emphases.

In JSPick pseudo-evaluation is preceded by parsing a program with respect to an non-standard abstract syntax, called pseudo-syntax in the sequel, that consists only of constructs that are relevant with respect to the desired program analysis. The pseudo-evaluation is formalized as a semantics function, i.e., in denotational style. The original paper on pseudo-evaluation [228] gives an operational-style specification with respect to stack transformations.

15.1.1 The Pseudo-Syntax Specification

First the JSPick pseudo-syntax is given by an extended context-free grammar. In the grammar used the production rules of an extended context-free grammar may have regular expressions as right hand sides. Non-terminals are underlined. The syntactic category that corresponds to a given non-terminal is depicted in bold face. The JSPick pseudo-syntax consists of controls as basic building blocks plus sequencing, if structure, if–else structure, switch structures, and loop. JSPick does not distinguish between completed and uncompleted switch structures in the sense of NSP for the following reason: in NSP it is a coding convention that all branches of a switch structure must be ended by a break statement. But in JSPick this cannot be demanded, because JSPick is designed as a tool for existing code. Fortunately it does not pose a problem: a useful form type inference can be defined with respect to another switch structure distinction. JSPick distinguishes between unique and arbitrary switch structures. In a unique switch structure all branches end with a break statement and the last branch is a default branch. All other switch structures are arbitrary switch structures.

$$\underline{pseudo} ::= (\underline{element})+$$

$$
\begin{aligned}
\underline{element} ::= \quad &\underline{control} \\
&|\ \text{if}\ \underline{pseudo} \\
&|\ \text{ifElse}\ \underline{pseudo}\ \underline{pseudo} \\
&|\ \text{switch}^{\text{arbitrary}}\ (\underline{pseudo})+ \\
&|\ \text{switch}^{\text{unique}}\ (\underline{pseudo})+ \\
&|\ \text{loop}\ \underline{pseudo}
\end{aligned}
$$

The usual types of HTML/XHTML controls are supported. Every control node carries information about the name of the targeted formal parameter. The set of names is not specified.

$$\underline{control} ::= \underline{controltype}\ \underline{name}$$

$$
\begin{aligned}
\underline{controltype} ::= \quad &\text{text}\ |\ \text{textarea}\ |\ \text{password} \\
&|\ \text{hidden}\ |\ \text{checkbox}\ |\ \text{radiobutton} \\
&|\ \text{singleselect}\ |\ \text{multipleselect}
\end{aligned}
$$

$$\underline{name} ::= n \in \boldsymbol{name}$$

The types that are assigned to targeted formal parameters as part of a form type are given by a little context-free grammar, too. A type can be either a basic type or a basic type together with an array annotation. The basic types differ from the control types of the pseudo-syntax. There is no distinction between single select menus and multiple select menus. The various pseudo-controls are introduced.

$$\underline{\text{parametertype}} ::= \underline{\text{basictype}} \mid \underline{\text{basictype}} \; []$$

$$\underline{\text{basictype}} ::= \quad \text{TEXT} \mid \text{TEXTAREA} \mid \text{PASSWORD}$$
$$\mid \text{HIDDEN} \mid \text{CHECKBOX} \mid \text{RADIOBUTTON}$$
$$\mid \text{SELECT}$$
$$\mid \text{VARIOUS}$$

15.1.2 The Semantics Function of Pseudo-Evaluation

The semantics of JSPick form type inference are specified as a semantics function (15.1) that maps a pseudo-syntax tree to a form type. A form type is a finite partial function that assigns types to parameter names. Initially the semantics function is applied to the entire content of a form.

$$[\![\_]\!] : \boldsymbol{pseudo} \to \boldsymbol{name} \nrightarrow \boldsymbol{parametertype} \qquad (15.1)$$

In order to define the semantics function it is helpful to have an auxiliary function (15.2) at hand that yields the contained basic type for every parameter type.

$$\Downarrow \_ \; : \boldsymbol{parametertype} \to \boldsymbol{basictype}$$

$$\Downarrow t = \begin{cases} t & , \; t \in \boldsymbol{basictype} \\ t' & , \; t = t'[\,] \end{cases} \qquad (15.2)$$

The form type of a single control is defined only for the formal parameter that is targeted by the control. If the control is a multiple select menu the parameter is assigned the select basic type and an array annotation. If it is a single select menu the parameter is assigned the select basic type only. In all other cases simply the control type is assigned to the parameter, without array annotation.

$$[\![controltype \; name]\!] =$$
$$\lambda n. \begin{cases} \bot & , \; n \neq name \\ \text{TEXT} & , \; controltype = \text{text} \\ \text{TEXTAREA} & , \; controltype = \text{textarea} \\ \text{PASSWORD} & , \; controltype = \text{password} \\ \text{HIDDEN} & , \; controltype = \text{hidden} \\ \text{CHECKBOX} & , \; controltype = \text{checkbox} \\ \text{RADIOBUTTON} & , \; controltype = \text{radiobutton} \\ \text{SELECT} & , \; controltype = \text{select} \\ \text{SELECT}[\,] & , \; controltype = \text{multipleselect} \end{cases} \qquad (15.3)$$

The if construct is semantically equivalent to an arbitrary switch structure and the if–else construct is semantically equivalent to a unique switch structure in the way defined in Eqs. (15.4).

$$[\![\texttt{if } p]\!] = [\![\texttt{switch}^{\texttt{arbitrary}} p]\!]$$
$$[\![\texttt{ifElse } p_1 \, p_2]\!] = [\![\texttt{switch}^{\texttt{unique}} p_1 \, p_2]\!] \tag{15.4}$$

Equation (15.5) defines how a form type is assigned to a unique switch structure. Note that free occurrences of the meta type variable t are implicitly existentially quantified in the equations of this section. For a unique switch structure it is ensured that exactly one branch is executed. This fact can be exploited to possibly infer a single parameter type for a targeted formal parameter. Assume an arbitrary fixed name. If none of the branches yields a control that targets that name, the switch structure does not, too. If all branches always target that name with exactly one control the complete switch does so, too. If at least one branch targets the name but it is not sure that it produces exactly one control, the switch targets the name with a control array. Equally, if at least one branch targets the name and at least one branch does not target the name, the switch targets the name with a control array. If all branches target the name with the same kind of control, the switch targets the name with this uniquely known control, otherwise it targets the name with the special various control.

$$[\![\texttt{switch}^{\texttt{unique}} \quad p_1 \ldots p_n]\!] =$$
$$\lambda n . \begin{cases} \bot & , \underset{1 \leq i \leq n}{\forall} ([\![p_i]\!] n) \uparrow \\ t & , \underset{1 \leq i \leq n}{\forall} ([\![p_i]\!] n) = t \in \textbf{\textit{basictype}} \\ \texttt{VARIOUS} & , \underset{1 \leq i \leq n}{\forall} ([\![p_i]\!] n) \in \textbf{\textit{basictype}} \\ t[\,] & , \underset{1 \leq i \leq n}{\forall} (([\![p_i]\!] n) \uparrow \lor \Downarrow ([\![p_i]\!] n) = t \in \textbf{\textit{basictype}}) \\ \texttt{VARIOUS}[\,] & , else \end{cases} \tag{15.5}$$

For an arbitrary switch structure it is not certain that exactly one of the branches is executed. Therefore the switch structure either does not target a given name or targets that name with a control array. Apart from this, arbitrary switches are equal to unique switches with regard to the form type. Therefore Eq. (15.6) immediately arises from Eq. (15.5) by dropping the second and third line.

$$[\![\texttt{switch}^{\texttt{arbitrary}} \quad p_1 \ldots p_n]\!] =$$
$$\lambda n . \begin{cases} \bot & , \underset{1 \leq i \leq n}{\forall} ([\![p_i]\!] n) \uparrow \\ t[\,] & , \underset{1 \leq i \leq n}{\forall} (([\![p_i]\!] n) \uparrow \lor \Downarrow ([\![p_i]\!] n) = t \in \textbf{\textit{basictype}}) \\ \texttt{VARIOUS}[\,] & , else \end{cases} \tag{15.6}$$

A loop targets every formal parameter that is targeted by its body with a control array.

$$\llbracket \texttt{loop } p \rrbracket = \lambda n \,.\, \begin{cases} \perp & ,(\llbracket p \rrbracket n)\uparrow \\ (\Downarrow(\llbracket p \rrbracket n))[\,] & ,else \end{cases} \tag{15.7}$$

The form type of sequences of document parts is defined in Eq.(15.8).

$$\llbracket p_1 \ldots p_n \rrbracket = \\ \lambda n \,.\, \begin{cases} \perp & , \underset{1 \le i \le n}{\forall} (\llbracket p_i \rrbracket n)\uparrow \\ \llbracket p_i \rrbracket n & , \underset{1 \le i \le n}{\exists !} (\llbracket p_i \rrbracket n)\downarrow \\ \texttt{radiobutton} & , \underset{1 \le i \le n}{\forall} ((\llbracket p_i \rrbracket n)\uparrow \;\vee\; \Downarrow(\llbracket p_i \rrbracket n) = \texttt{radiobutton}) \\ & \wedge \underset{1 \le i \le n}{\exists} ((\llbracket p_i \rrbracket n) = \texttt{radiobutton}) \\ t[\,] & , \underset{1 \le i \le n}{\forall} ((\llbracket p_i \rrbracket n)\uparrow \;\vee\; \Downarrow(\llbracket p_i \rrbracket n) = t \in \textbf{\textit{basictype}}) \\ \texttt{VARIOUS}[\,] & , else \end{cases}$$

$$\tag{15.8}$$

Assume a sequence of document parts and that at least one of the parts targets a given name. If there is only one part that targets the name and furthermore the part targets the name with a single control then it is safe that the sequence targets the name with this single control. If all parts that target the name provide the same kind of control other than radio buttons, then the sequence targets the name with an array of the given control. Radio buttons are special, because together they provide a control. If a name is assigned a radio button and an array annotation this means only that it is not certain whether a radio button control is generated; it cannot mean that possibly more than one control is generated. Therefore if all document parts that target a given name provide radio buttons and at least one part is safe to provide a single radio button control, the sequence targets the name with a single radio button control. JSPick treats the generation of a one single radio button as a correct alternative, too. This treatment of radio buttons once more points up that JSPick is a tool for existing code: lots of web designers deliberately use a single radio button this way as a kind of check box, though this is not in accordance with recommended good practice, as in [220]. As a last rule, if several parts target a given name with different kinds of control, the sequence targets the name with an array of various controls.

15.2 Coding Guidelines for Typed Server Pages

There are two kinds of coding guidelines. The parameter guidelines which deal with client page type safety, and the structure guidelines which deal with client page description safety. The guidelines are declarative characterizations of valid NSP code, and are informal descriptions of demands placed on NSP code. The resulting notion of correctness can be checked statically and guarantees client page type and description safety. The NSP parameter guidelines allow the adaptation of typed programming discipline to the context of server pages development.

In the discussion of coding guidelines passive NSP code is considered as generated code. Such passive NSP code is a variant of XHTML code. It is ensured that generated NSP tags will cause the generation of valid XHTML eventually. The mapping of NSP tags to valid XHTML is given canonically.

15.2.1 Basic Parameter Guidelines

We now give the NSP parameter guidelines for formal parameters of basic type. NSP distinguishes between basic types, array types, and form message types. The notion of form message type is introduced in Sect. 15.2.3: a user-defined type may be explicitly defined as a form message type; then NSP offers tag support for gathering composed data of form message type. In NSP/Java the basic types encompass the Java primitive types and every object type, i.e., every user-defined type or arbitrary Java API type.

Formal Parameters of Primitive Type

For a formal int parameter either one type correct input control, hidden control, single select menu, or at least two type correct radio buttons must be provided.

A form encompassing a type correct input control cannot be submitted if the data entered by the user are not a number. Similarly a formal int parameter implicitly requires an entry by the user. The necessary concept of active direct input controls was explained in Sect. 11.1.3. A hidden control may target a formal int parameter, as long as its contained expression has int as type; such an expression cannot evaluate to a null object, because int is a primitive Java type. For the same reason a single select menu may target a formal int parameter. Alternatively a set of radio buttons may target the parameter. It must contain at least two radio buttons. An int radio button set or single select menu always produces a unique value, because of the concept of NSP active single select controls introduced in Sect. 11.1.5.

A formal int parameter may be constrained to be targeted by an interactive widget. The param tag has a widget attribute which may be set to required for this purpose. If a widget is required, the targeting control must not be a hidden parameter. Besides this exception the parameter guideline is the same. Requiring an interactive widget is a powerful concept that allows for the precise specification of a dialogue method as an editable method call offered to the user by means of a web signature.

The int type is the only NSP/Java instance of the general notion of an NSP direct input supported primitive type. Other language amalgamations may support more primitive types by a direct input widget in a way that follows the parameter guidelines just introduced.

The dual notion of an NSP direct input supported primitive type is that of an NSP ordinary primitive type. The float type is an example of such a type. For a formal float parameter exactly one type correct hidden control, a single select menu, or at least two type correct radio buttons must be provided.

Formal Boolean Parameters

The Boolean type needs specific parameter guidelines. It is supported by an instance of the check box mechanism as explained in Sect. 11.1.6. The Boolean type is an NSP specific primitive type.

For a formal Boolean parameter either exactly one check box or one type correct input hidden control must be provided. If the widget attribute is set to required, the formal parameter must be targeted by exactly one check box. It is not allowed to use other controls like direct input or a select menu for targeting a Boolean formal parameter. We feel that, with respect to user interaction, the Boolean type is inextricably connected to the notion of check box and this is expressed by the current parameter guideline.

Formal Object Type Parameters

Every non-primitive Java type is termed object type. For a formal parameter of object type at most one type correct hidden control, a single select menu, or at least two type correct radio buttons must be provided. Very importantly, it is not allowed to provide any control for a formal parameter of object type. If no control is provided, the system will automatically fill in a null object on submission.

For a formal parameter of object type the widget attribute may be set to required, too. Then exactly one type correct single select menu or at least two type correct radio buttons must be provided. It is not longer allowed just to omit any kind of control: the purpose of the required widget attribute is to ensure that an interaction capability is offered to the user. In general there is no direct input capability for an object type and possible interaction capabilities are single select menus or a set of radio buttons. However, as opposed to formal parameters of primitive type, requiring a widget does not guarantee valuable data on submission, because nothing prevents a data item provided by, for example, a select menu from being a null object. This leads to another kind of NSP object type.

Direct input supported object types are distinguished from ordinary object types. Examples of direct input supported object types in NSP/Java are the Integer type and the JDBC API type Date [316]. For a formal parameter of such type the above parameter guidelines are applicable, except for the possibility to additionally target a parameter by the type correct input control. Beyond this, the formal parameter tag has an entry attribute for such types. This entry attribute may be set to required. Then for a formal parameter exactly one type correct input control must be provided. Furthermore the system statically ensures that every targeting input control dynamically ensures data entry. As discussed above, only this can prevent a null object from being submitted.

Formal String Parameters

The Java type String is another example of an object type that is supported by an active direct input control. Actually it has three such controls: the usual input field, a password field, and the text area control. The parameter guidelines are the same as the ones for types like Integer or Date, except for the additional input controls that are handled in the same way as the input field. The only subtle difference concerning the input controls has already been described in Sect. 11.1.3: no null object will be transmitted at any time.

Furthermore, it can be specified that a formal String parameter must be targeted by the specific password control or by the specific text area control. The widget attribute is used for this purpose. If it is set to password exactly one password field must be provided, and analogously for the text area widget.

15.2.2 Parameter Guidelines for Arrays

A web signature may encompass formal array parameters. A formal array parameter may be targeted by an arbitrary mix of controls, as long as all controls are type correct and valid with respect to the contained items' type. The valid controls for a formal array parameter encompass the controls that are valid for a completely unconstrained formal parameter of the respective contained items' type. An unconstrained formal parameter is a parameter for which no widget is required or specified and no entry is explicitly required. Furthermore, type correct value check boxes and select menus are valid controls for array parameters. The number of controls is not constrained for all kinds of controls, except for radio buttons. If a radio button targets a formal array parameter there must be at least a second radio button targeting the same parameter.

For example, a formal int array parameter may be targeted by an arbitrary mix and number of type correct input controls, hidden controls, single select menus, value check boxes, select menus, and perhaps a set of at least two radio buttons.

A formal parameter of array type is optional. If no control targets the parameter the system will automatically pass a null to the dialogue method on submit. It is not possible to give requirements for a formal array parameter. The emphasis of the NSP array mechanism is on support for gathering array data in forms. If a constrained dynamic data structure is desired, complex message types and their respective facilities described in Sect. 15.2.3 may be used.

NSP offers sophisticated support for gathering array data in forms. Listing 15.1 shows a form that targets a dialogue method that excepts an Integer array x and an int array y. Nine input fields are generated for the parameter x. Input widgets for Integer values are optional by default. If the user does not enter a value into a field this field is just ignored. All fields that have received valid user data together provide the submitted actual array parameter. If the user does not enter any data a null object will be provided by the system for the parameter x on submission. Another nine input fields are generated for the parameter y. Input widgets for int values are required by default. The user must enter valid data in all the fields, otherwise the form cannot be submitted. The submitted array is guaranteed to have a length of nine.

Listing 15.1 NSP: gathering data for an array parameter

```
01  <form callee="N"><java>
02    for {int i=0; i<9; i++){</java>
03      <input type="int" param="x"></input><java>
04    }
05    for {int i=0; i<9; i++){</java>
06      <input type="Integer" param="y"></input><java>
07    }</java>
08    <submit></submit>
09  </form>
```

As a second opportunity it is possible to explicitly specify the index of an array item. For this purpose the input field tag may contain an index element. The content of such an index element must be a Java int expression. If explicit definition of array element indexes is chosen, the specification should be unique. Furthermore the specification should be complete. Array items that have a redundant index or do not have an explicit index are attached arbitrarily to the array.

Listing 15.2 is oriented towards the example from Listing 15.1. A loop generates nine input fields for the parameter x. This time fields not filled out by the user cannot simply be ignored. Instead of this null objects are inserted at the specified positions. Another input field is generated behind the loop. It has index 10. There is no input field with index 9 targeting the parameter x. If the form is submitted, again a null object will be inserted as the ninth element. Another ten input fields are generated for the parameter y. These fields must be filled out. Again there is no input field with index 9 targeting the parameter y. If the form is submitted, this will result in a dynamic type error, because the system must fail to insert an appropriate value for this missing element of primitive type.

Listing 15.2 NSP: gathering data for an indexed array parameter

```
01 <form callee="N"><java>
02   for {int i=0; i<9; i++){</java>
03    <input type="Integer" param="x">
04        <index> i </index>
05    </input><java>
06 }</java>
07    <input type="Integer" param="x">
08        <index> 10 </index>
09 </input><java>
10   for {int i=0; i<9; i++){</java>
11    <input type="int" param="y">
12        <index> i </index>
13    </input><java>
14 }</java>
15    <input type="int" param="x">
16        <index> 10 </index>
17 </input>
18    <submit></submit>
19 </form>
```

15.2.3 Parameter Guidelines for Form Messages

In NSP objects of user-defined types can be used as hidden parameters, select menu items, and radio button or check box values. But NSP offers tag support for gathering data of user-defined type in forms, the so-called NSP form message mechanism. Input or selection capabilities for the single attributes of an object or of a complex object net may be offered to the user. A special object element that resembles the with construct in MODULA-2 [318] enables the construction of data records. Similarly the group element of the XForms [106] technology enables the construction of semi-structured data entered by the user.

In order to be supported in the way described above a user-defined type must be explicitly marked as a form message type. In a concrete language amalgamation marking a user-defined type as a form message type may be defined by a naming convention or as implementing a marker interface. In general a form message is a record of attributes. The attributes are the fields that are supported by the form message mechanism. The user-defined type underlying a form message type may have auxiliary fields. Therefore, for every programming language amalgamation a naming convention must be defined for form message types that distinguishes attributes from auxiliary fields. In NSP/Java the naming convention of the Java Beans [137] component model is chosen. A form message type is a Java Bean. A form message type attribute is a Java Bean property.

In this chapter we visualize form message types as class diagrams. These diagrams are drawn within a defined perspective, which is a kind of specification perspective in the sense of [116, 64]. The perspective abstracts away from possible concrete naming conventions. Only form message type attributes occur in the diagram, i.e., auxiliary fields are not visualized. Attributes that have form message type are visualized as associations; all other form message type attributes are visualized as object attributes. The associations are navigated and carry the attribute's name as role name. No methods occur in the diagrams. For instance, with respect to the NSP/Java naming convention, a class denotes a Java Bean, object attributes and associations denote Java Bean properties. In the diagrams all associations are compositions in order to emphasize that all object nets gathered by the user are trees. That is, we follow [237] where aggregations may form cycles, but constrain the respective link relationship to be transitive and antisymmetric. Compositions are aggregations with an additional constraint: an object must not be a direct part of several composites. This means that, although it can be part of several composites because of the transitivity of the composition relationship, it must be identified with one unique composite object. All this amounts to saying that object net instances of class diagrams with aggregations are only directed acyclic graphs; and object net instances of class diagrams with compositions are only trees.

A first introductory example is given by the form message type Person in Fig. 15.1 and the form in Listing 15.3. The example is already sufficient in order to state the NSP parameter guidelines for form message types. The form targets a web signature that consists of a formal parameter customer of type Person. Within the form data for an object net consisting of a Person object and an Address object may be entered; on submit the respective object net is constructed. More concretely, on submit a Person object and an Address object are created. Furthermore, a pointer to the Address object is created which automatically becomes the address attribute of the Person object. A formal parameter of form message type must be targeted by at most one object element. Like the control tags, the opening object tag has a param attribute for this purpose. The object element contains controls and possibly further object elements for the attributes of the targeted parameter. Note that the NSP parameter guidelines apply recursively, i.e., from a form's viewpoint a form message type can be understood as a nested formal parameter type.

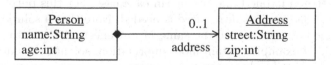

Fig. 15.1. Example form message type

Listing 15.3 NSP: gathering form message type data

```
01 <form callee="target">
02   <object param="customer">
03     <input type="String" param="name"></input>
04     <input type="int"    param="age"></input>
05     <object param="adress">
06       <input type="String" param="street"></input>
07       <input type="int"    param="zip"></input>
08     </object>
09   </object>
10 </form>
11
12 // web signature of target
13 <param name="customer" type="Person"></param>
```

The form in Listing 15.4 targets a web signature that consists of a formal array parameter customers, and the array items' type is again the type Person given in Fig. 15.1. A formal array parameter of form message type may be targeted by an arbitrary number of object elements (Listing 15.4, line 3, line 10), as long as the NSP parameter guidelines are fulfilled recursively for each object element. The single object nets may be explicitly indexed. An object element may contain an index element for this purpose (Listing 15.4, line 4, line 11).

An object element may be given a uniquely identifying name with the optional id attribute (Listing 15.4, line 3, line 10). Then controls and object elements for gathering data for form message type attributes can occur anywhere. They have to reference the object element they belong to by its identifying name. Input controls (Listing 15.4, e.g., line 19) and object tags (Listing 15.4, line 7) have an optional in attribute for this purpose. Identifying and referencing object elements provides a convenient way for allowing arbitrary form layout. With object element nesting only, some desired occurrences of controls that contradict the rigid structure of layout elements could not be realized. Note that the XForms technology even introduces decoupling of controls from forms [106] for similar reasons. The respective attributes are the id attribute and the ref attribute. Listing 15.4 yields an example, where data for two object nets are gathered. Data for the attributes of each object net are gathered in one table column in each case. For this purpose, the referencing mechanism just introduced is needed. Note that a solution based on nested tables cannot achieve the same layout effect. If the data cells of the given minimal example contain more information, so that the data cells of a row have different heights, correct alignment is no longer ensured.

A formal parameter of form message type is optional. It is possible not to provide an object element for it. On submit the system will pass a null object to the receiving dialogue method. Again it becomes important that

Listing 15.4 NSP: gathering distributed form message type data

```
01 <form callee="target">
02 <table>
03   <tr><td><object param="customers" id="first">
04            <index>1</index>
05             <input type="String" param="name"></input>
06            </object>
07            <object param="adress" id="firstPart" in="first">
08            </object>
09       </td>
10       <td><object param="customers" id="second">
11            <index>2</index>
12             <input type="String" param="name"></input>
13            </object>
14       </td>
15   </tr>
16   <tr><td><input type="int" param="age" in="first"></input></td>
17       <td><input type="int" param="age" in="second"></input></td>
18   </tr>
19   <tr><td><input type="String" param="street" in="firstPart">
20            </input>
21       </td>
22       <td></td>
23   </tr>
24   <tr><td><input type="int" param="zip" in="firstPart"></input>
25       </td>
26       <td></td>
27   </tr>
28 </table>
29 </form>
30
31 // web signature of target
32 <param name="customers" type="Person[]"></param>
```

the notion of form message type attribute is subsumed under the notion of formal parameter. For example, the first object element in line 3 of Listing 15.4 possesses an object element for the Address attribute in line 7, but the second object element in line 10 does not possess an object element for this attribute. Very importantly, though a formal parameter of form message type is optional, this is not carried over to its contained attributes. An object element may not be provided, but if it is, the NSP parameter guidelines apply to the contained attributes; for example, an int attribute would be required.

For formal parameters data entry may be specified as required with the data attribute (Listing 15.6, line 2). For a parameter of form message type this enforces that exactly one object element is provided for it.

The fact that formal parameters of form message type are optional enables the support of cyclic user-defined data in forms. The form in Listing 15.5 targets a web signature that consists of a formal parameter of type PersonList. The type PersonList, which is a dynamic data structure, is given in Fig. 15.2. In the example form input capabilities for three list elements are given. On submit an object net of three list elements is created. For the next pointer of the third element a null object is filled in. Dynamic creation of input capabilities for dynamic data structures in a statically type-safe manner is possible by recursive definitions of dialogue submethods, which are introduced in Sect. 11.2.2.

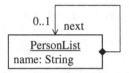

Fig. 15.2. Example cyclic form message type

Listing 15.5 NSP: gathering data for dynamic data structures

```
01 <form callee="target">
02   <object param="customers">
03     <input type="String" param="name"></input>
04     <object param="next">
05       <input type="String" param="name"></input>
06       <object param="next">
07         <input type="String" param="name"></input>
08         <object param="next">
09           <input type="String" param="name"></input>
10         </object>
11       </object>
12     </object>
13   </object>
14 </form>

// web signature of target
<param name="customers" type="PersonList"></param>
```

NSP defines a fine granular mechanism for putting constraints on the attributes of user-defined data. For this purpose a parameter element that defines a formal parameter of form message type may contain constraints elements. Each of the constraints elements must uniquely refer to a form message type that is involved as a part in the definition of the formal parameter type.

A constraints element contains a param element for every attribute of the form message type it refers to. The param element can be used to pose on the attributes one or several of the constraints that have been introduced in Sect. 15.2.1:

- data=required
- widget=required
- widget=password
- widget=textarea

The mechanism is not recursive. The param elements of a constraint specification must not contain further constraints elements.

Listing 15.6 gives examples of constraints on user-defined data attributes. Consider the form message type given in Fig. 15.3. Again it is PersonList – as in Fig. 15.2 – but this time the type's attribute has a form message type. The attribute's type is Person, which has already served as an example (Fig. 15.1), but this time the multiplicity of the address association has changed from 0..1 to 1, which means that the address attribute is required this time. In Listing 15.6 a formal parameter of type PersonList is defined. The constraint specification in line 3 to line 6 means that the person attribute is required. That is, whenever an object element for gathering data for a list element for the actual parameter is generated, it must contain an object element for its person attribute. There is no additional constraint posed on the next attribute. It must be optional, because it forms a cycle in the class diagram. Further constraint specifications ensure, for example, that for every Person object, the user has to enter a name, a street, and a zip code. Note that it would not be sufficient to constrain the street attribute and zip attribute of the type Address to be required in order to achieve this (Listing 15.6, line 13, line 14). The address attribute of the type Person must be required for this purpose, too (Listing 15.6, line 10). Without requiring the address attribute, the whole address is optional. Requiring only street and zip code just enforces that these are required in the case when an object element for the address is actually generated.

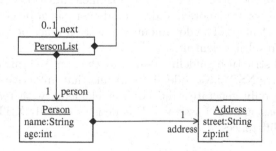

Fig. 15.3. Example complex form message type

Listing 15.6 NSP: constraints on form message type attributes

```
01 // web signature of target
02 <param name="customers" type="PersonList" data="required">
03   <constraints type="PersonList">
04     <param name="person" data="required"></param>
05     <param name="next"></param>
06   </constraints>
07   <constraints type="Person">
08     <param name="name" data="required"></param>
09     <param name="age"></param>
10     <param name="address" data="required"></param>
11   </constraints>
12   <constraints type="Address">
13     <param name="street" data="required"></param>
14     <param name="zip" data="required"></param>
15   </constraints>
16 </param>
```

15.2.4 Document Structure Guidelines

The NSP coding guidelines for ensuring client page type safety have been described in Sects. 15.2.1 to 15.2.3; we now complete the discussion by describing the remaining coding guidelines concerning client page description safety.

The first basic structure guideline demands that an NSP always only generates well-formed XML. The NSP document must be a well-formed XML document and the Java block structure must be compatible with the XML block structure. The latter means that for every XML tag the corresponding dual tag must occur in the same block; however, as a necessary exception to this the Java tags are ignored. Java tags must be considered merely as switches between the programming language and the markup language with respect to the document structure. In technical terms Java opening and closing tags are go-betweens of different lexical states. This can be reformulated more concisely in the following way. The document must be well-formed XML. Then the Java tags are ignored, and instead every Java block is considered a new document element. The document in question must be well-formed with respect to the resulting element set.

The second structure guideline demands that an NSP always only generates valid passive NSP/Java code. This means that an active NSP document fragment must only generate valid content elements with respect to its directly encompassing tags. Passive NSP code is essentially XHTML except for the following differences:

- some element properties are supported by content elements instead of attributes;
- some elements, e.g., the form element and the control elements, are modified;
- some new elements are introduced, e.g., the param element and the call element;
- some content elements are not required, though their counterparts are required in XHTML.

The first three differences pose no problems. The modifications introduced are resolved when the final page, i.e., the XHTML page that is sent to the browser, is generated. The fourth difference is discussed in the sequel. The coding guideline must be discussed with respect to the finally called page.

In XHMTL [304] some elements require that a certain kind of content element appears at least once. In NSP these demands are dropped for pragmatic reasons, not for technical reasons. For example, in XHTML a list must contain at least one item. A table must contain at least one row. A table row must contain at least one table data cell. A select list must contain at least either one option or one group of option. However, most of these constraints are artificial, because browsers can, and current browsers do, cope with violations of these constraints in a naturally sensible way. For example, lists without items, tables without rows, and table rows without data cells are just not displayed. Moreover, some of these constraints are ineffectual. For example, although an item is required for a list, it is not required that a list must not be empty.

15.3 Formal Definition of the NSP Type System

In this section the semantics of the typed server pages technology NSP are made more precise. A Per Martin-Löf [206, 207, 233] style type system is given to specify type correctness for a crucial subset of NSP. The NSP coding guidelines in Sect. 15.2 give an informal explanation of NSP type correctness. They are easy to learn and will help in everyday programming tasks, but may give rise to ambiguity. A precise description of the static semantics of NSP languages is desired. The formal Core NSP type system provides a succinct precise definition at the right level of communication. A formal type system definition makes it easier to adapt results from the vast amount of literature on type systems to the NSP approach, especially concerning type inference and type checking algorithms.

We formalize the type system of Core NSP, which is the amalgamation of NSP concepts with a minimal imperative programming, which encompasses assignments, command sequences, a conditional control structure, and an unbounded loop. The tag set of Core NSP consists of the most important elements for writing forms as well as some nestable text layout tags. The programming language types of Core NSP comprise records, arrays, and recursive types for modeling all the complexity found in the type system of a modern high-level programming language. The web signatures of Core NSP embrace server page type parameters; that is, higher-order server pages are modeled. Tags for server-side calls to server pages belong to the language; that is, functional server page decomposition is modeled.

15.3.1 Core NSP Grammar

An abstract syntax of Core NSP programs is specified by a context-free grammar. In the grammar non-terminals are underlined and terminals are not emphasized. This is in contrast to BNF standards like [167] or [70]; however, it fosters readability significantly. Every non-terminal corresponds to a syntactic category. In the grammar a syntactic category is depicted in bold face. A Core NSP program is a whole closed system of several server pages. A page is a parameterized core document and may be a complete web server page or an include server page.

$$
\begin{aligned}
\underline{\text{system}} &::= \underline{\text{page}} \mid \underline{\text{system}}\ \underline{\text{system}} \\
\underline{\text{page}} &::= \text{<nsp name=`'}\underline{\text{id}}\text{">}\ \underline{\text{websig-core}}\ \text{</nsp>} \\
\underline{\text{websig-core}} &::= \underline{\text{param}}\ \underline{\text{websig-core}} \mid \underline{\text{webcall}} \mid \underline{\text{include}} \\
\underline{\text{param}} &::= \text{<param name=`'}\underline{\text{id}}\text{" type=`'}\underline{\text{parameter-type}}\text{"/>} \\
\underline{\text{webcall}} &::= \text{<html>}\ \underline{\text{head}}\ \underline{\text{body}}\ \text{</html>} \\
\underline{\text{head}} &::= \text{<head><title>}\ \underline{\text{strings}}\ \text{</title></head>} \\
\underline{\text{strings}} &::= \varepsilon \mid \underline{\text{string}}\ \underline{\text{strings}} \\
\underline{\text{body}} &::= \text{<body>}\ \underline{\text{dynamic}}\ \text{</body>} \\
\underline{\text{include}} &::= \text{<include>}\ \underline{\text{dynamic}}\ \text{</include>}
\end{aligned}
$$

There are some basic syntactic categories. The category id is a set of labels. The category string consists of character strings. A character string does not contain white spaces. We work with abstract syntax and therefore do not have to deal with white-space handling problems like the one described in [31]. The category parameter-type consists of the possible formal parameter types, i.e., programming language types plus page types. The category supported-type contains each type for which a direct manipulation input capability exists. The respective Core NSP types are specified in Sect. 15.3.3.

$$
\begin{aligned}
\underline{\text{string}} &::= s \in \textbf{String} \\
\underline{\text{id}} &::= l \in \textbf{Label} \\
\underline{\text{parameter-type}} &::= t \in \mathbb{T} \cup \mathbb{P} \\
\underline{\text{supported-type}} &::= t \in \mathbb{B}_{supported}
\end{aligned}
$$

Parameterized server pages are based on a dynamic markup language, which combines static client page description parts with active code parts. The static parts encompass lists, tables, server-side calls, and forms with direct input capabilities, namely check boxes, select lists, and hidden parameters, together with the object element for record construction.

Core NSP comprises list and table structures for document layout. All the XML elements of the dynamic markup language are direct subcategories of the category dynamic, which means that the grammar does not constrain arbitrary nesting of these elements. Instead of that the manner of use of a document fragment is maintained by the type system. We delve further on this in Sect. 15.3.2.

The rest of the static language parts address server-side page calls, client-side page calls, and user interaction. A call may contain actual parameters only. The call element may contain no element, too. As a matter of taste the special character ε_{act} for empty contents is used in the Core NSP grammar to avoid redundant production and typing rules for the call element.

Core NSP comprises expression tags for direct writing to the output and code tags in order to express the integration of active code parts with layout. The possibility to integrate layout code into active parts is needed. It is given by reversing the code tags. In this way all Core NSP programs can be easily related to a convenient concrete syntax.

Core NSP is not a working programming language. It possesses only a set of very interesting features to model all the complexity of NSP technologies. Built-in operations, i.e., a sufficiently powerful expression language, must be added. But this would just result in a more complex type system without providing more insight into static NSP semantics. Instead Core NSP aims to specify the typed interplay of server pages, the interplay of static and active server page parts, and the non-trivial interplay of the several complex types, i.e., user-defined types and arrays, which arise during dynamically generating user interface descriptions.

The imperative sublanguage of Core NSP comprises statements, command sequences, an if–then–else construct, and a while loop. The only statement is assignment. Expressions are just variable values or deconstructions of complex variable values, i.e., arrays or user-defined typed objects.

```
dynamic ::=  dynamic dynamic
         | ε | string
         | ul | li
         | table | tr | td
         | call
         | form | object | hidden | submit
         | input | checkbox
         | select | option
         | expression
         | code
```

```
        ul ::= <ul> dynamic </ul>
        li ::= <li> dynamic </li>
     table ::= <table> dynamic </table>
        tr ::= <tr> dynamic </tr>
        td ::= <td> dynamic </td>

         call ::= <call callee=''id"> actualparams </call>
  actualparams ::= ε_act | actualparam actualparams
  actualparam ::= <actualparam param=''id"> expr </actualparam>
         form ::= <form callee=''id"> dynamic </form>
       object ::= <object param=''id"> dynamic </object>
       hidden ::= <hidden param=''id"> expr </hidden>
       submit ::= <submit/>
        input ::= <input type=''supported-type" param=''id"/>
     checkbox ::= <checkbox param=''id"/>
       select ::= <select param=''id"> dynamic </select>
       option ::= <option>
                     <value> expr </value>
                     <label> expr </label>
                 </option>

   expression ::= <expression> expr </expression>
         code ::= <code> com </code>
          com ::= </code> dynamic <code>

          com ::=   stat
                  | com ; com
                  | if expr then com else com
                  | while expr do com

         stat ::= id := expr
         expr ::= id | expr.id | expr[expr]
```

15.3.2 Core NSP Type System Strength

The grammar given in Sect. 15.3.1 does not prevent arbitrary nestings of the several Core NSP dynamic tag elements. Instead necessary constraints on nesting are guaranteed by the type system. Therefore the type of a server page fragment comprises information about the manner of use of itself as part of an encompassing document.

As a result some context-free properties are dealt with in static semantics. There are pragmatic reasons for this. Consider an obvious example first. In HTML forms must not contain other forms. Furthermore some elements like the ones for input capabilities may only occur inside a form. If one wants to take such constraints into account in a context-free grammar, one must create a non-terminal for document fragments inside forms and duplicate and appropriately modify all the relevant production rules found so far. If there exist several such constraints the resulting grammar would quickly become unmaintainable. For that reason the Standard Generalized Markup Language supports the notions of exclusion and inclusion exception. The declaration of the HTML form element in the HTML 2.0 SGML DTD [63] is the following:

```
<!ELEMENT FORM - - %body.content -(FORM) +(INPUT|SELECT|TEXTAREA)>
```

The expression -(FORM) uses exclusion exception notation and the expression +(INPUT|SELECT|TEXTAREA) uses inclusion exception notation exactly for establishing the constraints mentioned. Indeed the SGML exception notation does not add to the expressive power of SGML [319], because an SGML expression that includes exceptions can be translated into an extended context free grammar [184]. An extended context-free grammar is a context-free grammar with production rules that may have regular expressions as right hand sides. The transformation algorithm given in [184] produces $2^{2^{|N|}}$ nonterminals in the worst case. This shows: if one does not have the exception notation at hand then one needs another way to manage complexity. The Core NSP way is to integrate necessary information into types; the resulting mechanism formalizes the way the Amsterdam SGML parser [313] handles exceptions. The Amsterdam SGML parser deals with exceptions by keeping track of excluded elements in a stack.

Furthermore, in NSP the syntax of the static parts is orthogonal to the syntax of the active parts, nevertheless both syntactic structures must regard each other. For example, HTML or XHTML lists must not contain elements other than list items. The corresponding SGML DTD [163] and XHTML DTD [305] specifications are

```
<!ELEMENT (OL|UL) - - (LI)+> resp. <!ELEMENT ul (li)+>
```

In Core NSP the document fragment in Listing 15.7 is considered correct.

Listing 15.7 Core NSP: combining static and dynamic document parts

```
01 <ul>
02    <code> x:=3; </code>
03    <li>First list item</li>
04    <code>
05      if condition then </code>
07        <li>Second list item</li> <code>
08      else </code>
09        <li>Second list item</li> <code>
11    </code>
12 </ul>
```

Line 2 must be ignored with respect to the correct list structure. Furthermore it must be recognized that the code in lines 4 to 11 correctly provides a list item. Again excluding the wrong documents by abstract syntax amounts to duplicating production rules for the static parts that may be contained in dynamic parts.

A Core NSP type checker has to verify uniquely the naming of server pages in a complete system, which is a context-dependent property. It has to check whether include pages provide correct elements. The way Core NSP treats dynamic fragment types fits seamlessly to these tasks.

15.3.3 Core NSP Types

We now simultaneously introduce the types of Core NSP and the subtype relation between types.

- Core NSP types. There are types for modeling programming language types, and special types for server pages and server page fragments in order to formalize the NSP coding guidelines. The Core NSP types are given by a family of recursively defined type sets. Every type represents an infinite labeled regular tree.
- Core NSP subtyping. The subtype relation formalizes the relationship of actual client page parameters and formal server page parameters by strictly applying the Barbara Liskov principle. A type A is a subtype of another type B if every actual parameter of type A may be used in server page contexts requiring elements of type B. The subtype relation is defined as the greatest fix point of a generating function. The generating function is presented by a set of convenient judgment rules for deriving judgments of the form $\vdash\ S < T$.

Note that the original Liskov substitution principle [197] is the following: if for each object o_1 of type S there is an object o_2 of type T such that for all programs P defined in terms of T, the behavior of P is unchanged when o_1 is substituted for o_2, then S is a subtype of T.

Notational Issues

First we summarize some notation that is used in the sequel. A part of the notation stems from the Z mathematical toolkit notation [283, 320, 147]. The notational elements needed and their meaning are given by the following table:

◁   Domain restriction (Z notation). A tuple (x, y) is a member of $S \lhd R$ if and only if (x, y) is member of R and x is member of S.

◁   Domain anti-restriction (Z notation). A tuple (x, y) is a member of $S \lhd R$ if and only if (x, y) is member of R and x is not member of S.

(*dom R*) Domain of a relation or function (Z notation).

⇻   Finite partial function.

$t \downarrow$ Defined (relations). $R(x, y) \downarrow$ is true iff $(x, y) \in R$.
$d \downarrow$ Defined (functions). $F(x) \downarrow$ is true iff $x \in (dom\ F)$.
$t \uparrow$ Undefined (relations). $R(x, y) \uparrow$ is true iff $(x, y) \notin R$.
$d \uparrow$ Undefined (functions). $F(x) \uparrow$ is true iff $x \notin (dom\ F)$.

Programming Language Types

In order to model the complexity of current high-level programming language type systems, the Core NSP types comprise basic types $\mathbb{B}_{primitive}$ and $\mathbb{B}_{supported}$, array types $\mathbb{A}$, record types $\mathbb{R}$, and recursive types $\mathbb{Y}$. $\mathbb{B}_{primitive}$ models types for which no null object is provided automatically on submit. $\mathbb{B}_{supported}$ models types for which a direct manipulation input capability exists. Note that $\mathbb{B}_{primitive}$ and $\mathbb{B}_{supported}$ overlap because of the int type. The set of all basic types $\mathbb{B}$ consists of the union of $\mathbb{B}_{primitive}$ and $\mathbb{B}_{supported}$. Record types and recursive types play the role of user-defined form message types. The recursive types allow for modeling cyclic user-defined data types. Core NSP works solely with structural type equivalence [40], i.e., there is no concept of introducing named user-defined types, which would not contribute to the understanding of NSP concepts. Enumeration types $\mathbb{E}$, i.e., subtype polymorphism in the narrow sense of [40], could be introduced in order to specify the behavior of radio button tag structures. The types introduced so far and the type variables $\mathbb{V}$ together form the set of programming language types $\mathbb{T}$.

$$\mathbb{T} = \mathbb{B} \cup \mathbb{V} \cup \mathbb{A} \cup \mathbb{R} \cup \mathbb{Y}$$

$$\mathbb{B} \quad = \quad \mathbb{B}_{primitive} \cup \mathbb{B}_{supported}$$

$$\mathbb{B}_{primitive} = \quad \{\texttt{int}, \texttt{float}, \texttt{boolean}\}$$

$$\mathbb{B}_{supported} = \quad \{\texttt{int}, \texttt{Integer}, \texttt{String}\}$$

$$\mathbb{V} \quad = \quad \{X, Y, Z, \ldots\}$$
$$\cup \{\texttt{Person}, \texttt{Customer}, \texttt{Article}, \ldots\}$$

Type variables may be bound by the recursive type constructor μ. Overall free type variables, i.e., type variables free in an entire Core NSP system and complete Core NSP program, represent opaque object reference types. It is a usual economy not to introduce ground types in the presence of type variables [39]. Similarly in Core NSP example programs free term variables are used to model basic constant data values.

For every programming language type, there is an array type. According to subtyping rule (15.9) every type is a subtype of its immediate array type. In commonly typed programming languages it is not possible to use a value as an array of the value's type. But the Core NSP subtype relation formalizes the relationship between actual client page and formal server page parameters. It is used in the NSP typing rules targeted to constrain data submission. A single value may be used as an array if it is submitted to a server page.

In due course we informally distinguish between establishing subtyping rules and preserving subtyping rules. The establishing subtyping rules introduce initial NSP-specific subtypings. The preserving subtyping rules are just the common judgments that deal with defining the effects of the various type constructors on the subtype relation. Judgment rule (15.10) is the preserving subtyping rule for array types.

$$\mathbb{A} = \{\, \text{array of } T \mid T \in \mathbb{T} \setminus \mathbb{A} \,\}$$

$$\frac{}{\vdash T < \text{array of } T} \tag{15.9}$$

$$\frac{\vdash S < T}{\vdash \text{array of } S < \text{array of } T} \tag{15.10}$$

A record is a finite collection of uniquely labeled data items, its fields. A record type is a finite collection of uniquely labeled types. In [250] record types are deliberately introduced as purely syntactical and therefore ordered entities. Then permutation rules are introduced that allow record types to be equal except for their ordering. In other texts, such as [2] or [268], record types are considered unordered from the beginning. We take the latter approach: a record type is a partial function from a finite set of labels to the set of programming language types. Rule (15.12) is just the necessary preserving subtyping rule for records.

$$\mathbb{R} = \textbf{Label} \rightarrowtail \mathbb{T}$$

$$\frac{T_j \notin \mathbb{B}_{primitive} \quad j \in 1 \ldots n}{\vdash \{l_i \mapsto T_i\}^{i \in 1 \ldots j-1, j+1 \ldots n} < \{l_i \mapsto T_i\}^{i \in 1 \ldots n}} \tag{15.11}$$

$$\frac{\vdash S_1 < T_1 \ldots \vdash S_n < T_n}{\vdash \{l_i \mapsto S_i\}^{i \in 1 \ldots n} < \{l_i \mapsto T_i\}^{i \in 1 \ldots n}} \qquad (15.12)$$

The establishing subtyping rule (15.11) states that a shorter record type is a subtype of a longer record type, provided the types are equal with respect to labeled type variables. At first sight this contradicts the well-known rules for subtyping records [39] or objects [1]. But there is no contradiction, because these rules describe hierarchies of feature support and we just specify another phenomenon: rule (15.11) models an actual record parameter being automatically filled with null objects for the fields of non-primitive types that are not provided by the actual parameter, but expected by the formal parameter.

The Core NSP type system encompasses recursive types for modeling the complexity of cyclic user-defined data types.

$$\mathbb{Y} = \{ \mu X . R \mid X \in \mathbf{V}, R \in \mathbb{R} \}$$

$$\frac{\vdash S[^{\mu X.S}/_X] < T}{\vdash \mu X.S < T} \qquad (15.13)$$

$$\frac{\vdash S < T[^{\mu X.T}/_X]}{\vdash S < \mu X.T} \qquad (15.14)$$

Recursive types may be handled in an iso-recursive or an equi-recursive way. The terms iso-recursive and equi-recursive stem from [69]. In an iso-recursive type system, a recursive type is considered isomorphic to its one-step unfolding and a family of unfold and fold operations on the term level is provided in order to represent the type isomorphisms. A prominent example of this purely syntactical approach is [2]. In an equi-recursive type system like the one given in [19], two recursive types are considered equal if they have the same infinite unfolding. We have chosen to follow the equi-recursive approach along the lines of [123] for two reasons. First, it keeps the Core NSP language natural; no explicit folding and unfolding are needed. More importantly, though the theory of an equi-recursive treatment is challenging, it is well understood and some crucial results concerning proof techniques and type checking of recursive typing and recursive subtyping like [41, 9, 270, 177] are elaborated in an equi-recursive setting. Actually, compared to iso-recursive typing, equi-recursive typing is a Curry-style [19], i.e., implicit, typing discipline, and therefore its theory is more challenging, or in more practical terms, constructing a type checker is more challenging.

The subtype relation adequately formalizes all the advanced NSP notions like form message types and higher-order server pages as may be checked against the examples given in Sect. 15.2.

In the Core NSP type system types represent finite trees or possibly infinite regular trees. A regular tree is a possibly infinite tree that has a finite set of distinct subtrees only [66]. More precisely these type trees are unordered, labeled, and finitely branching – note that we treat records as unordered tuples from the outset. Type equivalence is not explicitly defined, it is given implicitly by the subtype relation: the subtype relation is not a partial order but a preorder and two types are equal if they are mutual subtypes. The subtype relation is defined as the greatest fixed point of a monotone generating function on the universe of type trees [123]. The Core NSP subtyping rules provide an intuitive description of this generating function. The subtyping rules for left folding (15.13) and right folding (15.14) provide the desired recursive subtyping. Rules for reflexivity and transitivity are given by (15.15) and (15.16).

$$\overline{\vdash T < T} \tag{15.15}$$

$$\frac{\vdash R < S \qquad \vdash S < T}{\vdash R < T} \tag{15.16}$$

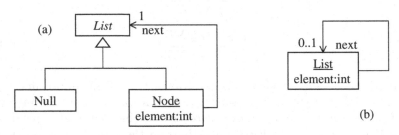

Fig. 15.4. List definitions

A Digression on Core NSP Recursive Record Subtyping

Normally sum or variant types are used in order to provide some finite data to be inhabited in recursive types. There is no sum or variant type in Core NSP. Instead the establishing record subtyping rule (15.11) makes it possible that finite data may be submitted to a formal parameter of recursive type. For example, the finite data gathered in Listing 15.8 have the recursive type given by subtype derivation (15.17).

$$e \equiv_{\text{DEF}} element$$
$$n \equiv_{\text{DEF}} next$$

$$\begin{aligned}
&\vdash \{e \mapsto int, n \mapsto \{e \mapsto int, n \mapsto \{e \mapsto int\}\}\} \\
&< \{e \mapsto int, n \mapsto \{e \mapsto int, n \mapsto \{e \mapsto int, n \mapsto \mu X.\{e \mapsto int, n \mapsto X\}\}\}\} \\
&= \mu X.\{e \mapsto int, n \mapsto X\}
\end{aligned} \tag{15.17}$$

Listing 15.8 Core NSP: gathering data of recursive type

```
01 <object param="list">
02   <input param="element" type="int"/>
03   <object param="next">
04     <input param="element" type="int"/>
05     <object param="next">
06       <input param="next" type="int"/>
07     </object>
08   </object>
09 </object>
```

Interestingly the record subtyping rule (15.11) is more generally appropriate for a direct formalization of cyclic data type definitions found in the usual object-oriented languages. Consider the definition of possibly infinite lists in the Haskell [178] code fragment (15.18). The null data constructor for the left summand is needed in order to explicitly enable finite lists.

$$\texttt{data List = NULL | NODE \{element :: Int, next :: List\}} \qquad (15.18)$$

The direct counterpart of this data type definition in an object-oriented language is depicted as a class diagram in Fig. 15.4(a) – the diagram is drawn within an implementation perspective in the sense of [116, 64]. A more appropriate way of modeling lists in an object-oriented programming language is given in Fig. 15.4(b). Basically the 1 multiplicity of the navigated association in 15.4(a) is replaced by an $0..1$ multiplicity in 15.4(b). It is possible to define lists this way, because in an object-oriented language every object field of complex type that is not constructed is implicitly provided as a null object. This mechanism is exactly the one formalized by subtyping rule (15.11). To see this, note that the lists defined in (15.18) and 15.4(a) both have type $\texttt{List}_{expl}$ given in (15.19) and 15.4(b) has type $\texttt{List}_{impl}$ given in (15.20) provided that subtyping rule (15.11) is present. The variant notation in the sequel is taken from [134].

$$\texttt{List}_{expl} \equiv_{DEF} \mu List.[\texttt{NULL} : \{\}, \texttt{NODE} : \{element \mapsto \texttt{int}, next \mapsto List\}]$$
$$(15.19)$$

$$\texttt{List}_{impl} \equiv_{DEF} \mu List.\{element \mapsto \texttt{int}, next \mapsto List\} \qquad (15.20)$$

Server Page Types

In order to formalize the NSP coding guidelines the type system of Core NSP comprises server page types $\mathbb{P}$, web signatures $\mathbb{W}$, a single complete web page type $\square \in \mathbb{C}$, dynamic fragment types $\mathbb{D}$, layout types $\mathbb{L}$, tag element types $\mathbb{E}$, form occurrence types $\mathbb{F}$, and system types $\mathbb{S}$.

A server page type is a functional type that has a web signature as argument type. An include server page has a dynamic document fragment type as result type, and a web server page the unique complete web page type.

$$\mathbb{P} = \{ \, w \to r \mid w \in \mathbb{W}, \, r \in \mathbb{C} \cup \mathbb{D} \, \}$$

$$\mathbb{W} = \textbf{Label} \rightarrowtail (\mathbb{T} \cup \mathbb{P})$$

$$\mathbb{C} = \{\square\}$$

A web signature is a record. This time a labeled component of a record type is either a programming language type or a server page type; that is, the type system supports higher-order server pages. Notably a clean separation between the programming language types and the additional NSP-specific types is kept. Server page types may be formal parameter types, but these formal parameters can be used only by specific NSP tags. Server pages deliberately become no first class citizens, because in this way the Core NSP models conservative amalgamation of NSP concepts with a high-level programming language.

The preserving subtyping rule (15.12) for records equally applies to web signatures. The establishing subtyping rule (15.11) must be slightly modified resulting in rule (15.21), because formal parameters of server page type must always be provided, too.

Subtyping rule (15.22) is standard and states that server page types are contravariant in the argument type and covariant in the result type.

$$\frac{T_j \notin \mathbb{B}_{primitive} \cup \mathbb{P} \quad j \in 1 \ldots n}{\vdash \{l_i \mapsto T_i\}^{i \in 1 \ldots j-1, j+1 \ldots n} < \{l_i \mapsto T_i\}^{i \in 1 \ldots n}} \tag{15.21}$$

$$\frac{\vdash w' < w \qquad \vdash R < R'}{\vdash w \to R < w' \to R'} \tag{15.22}$$

A part of a core document has a document fragment type. Such a type consists of a layout type and a web signature. The web signature is the type of the data, which is eventually provided by the document fragment as part of an actual form parameter. If a web signature plays the part of a document fragment type it is also called a form type. The layout type constrains the usability of the document fragment as part of an encompassing document. It consists of an element type and a form occurrence type.

$$\mathbb{D} = \mathbb{L} \times \mathbb{W}$$

$$\mathbb{L} = \mathbb{E} \times \mathbb{F}$$

$$\frac{\vdash S_1 < T_1 \quad \vdash S_2 < T_2}{\vdash (S_1, S_2) < (T_1, T_2)} \tag{15.23}$$

Subtyping rule (15.23) is standard for products and applies both to document fragment and layout types. An element type partly describes where a document fragment may be used. Document fragments that are sure to produce no output have the neutral document type ∘. Examples for such neutral document parts are hidden parameters and pure Java code. Document fragments that may produce visible data like string data or controls have the output type •. Document fragments that may produce list elements, table data, table rows, or select list options have type **LI**, **TD**, **TR**, and **OP** respectively. They may be used in contexts where the respective element is demanded. Neutral code can be used everywhere. This is expressed by rule (15.24).

$$\mathbb{E} = \{\, \circ, \bullet, \mathbf{TR}, \mathbf{TD}, \mathbf{LI}, \mathbf{OP} \}$$

$$\frac{T \in \mathbb{E}}{\vdash \circ < T} \tag{15.24}$$

The form occurrence type further constrains the usability of document fragments. Fragments that must be used inside a form, because they generate client page parts containing controls, have the inside form type ⇓. Fragments that must be used outside a form, because they generate client page fragments that already contain forms, have the outside form type ⇑. Fragments that may be used inside or outside forms have the neutral form type ⇕. Rule (15.25) specifies that such fragments can play the role of both fragments of outside form and fragments of inside form type.

$$\mathbb{F} = \{\, \Downarrow, \Uparrow, \Updownarrow \}$$

$$\frac{T \in \mathbb{F}}{\vdash \Updownarrow < T} \tag{15.25}$$

$$\mathbb{S} = \{\, \Diamond, \surd \}$$

An NSP system is a collection of NSPs. NSP systems that are type correct receive the well type ◇. The complete type √ is used for complete systems. A complete system is a well-typed system where all used server page names are defined, i.e., are assigned to a server page of the system, and no server page names are used as variables.

15.3.4 Type Operators

In the NSP typing rules in Sect. 15.3.6 a central type operation, termed form type composition $\odot$ in the sequel, is used that describes the composition of form content fragments with respect to the provided actual superparameter type. First an auxiliary operator $*$ is defined, which provides the dual effect of the array item type extractor $\Downarrow$ in Chap. 15.1. If applied to an array the operator leaves the type unchanged, otherwise it yields the respective array type.

$$T* \equiv_{\text{DEF}} \begin{cases} \text{array of } T & , T \notin \mathbb{A} \\ T & , else \end{cases}$$

The form type composition $\odot$ is the cornerstone of the NSP type system. Form content provides direct input capabilities, data selection capabilities, and hidden parameters. On submit an actual superparameter is transmitted. The type of this superparameter can be determined statically in NSP, and is called the form type of the form content, see Sect. 15.3.3. Equally document fragments, which dynamically may generate form content, have a form type. Form type composition is applied to form parameter types and describes the effect of sequencing document parts. Consequently form type composition is used to specify typing with respect to programming language sequencing, loops, and document composition.

$$w_1 \odot w_2 \equiv_{\text{DEF}} \begin{cases} \bot \ , \textbf{if } \exists (l_1 \mapsto T_1) \in w_1 \bullet \exists (l_2 \mapsto T_2) \in w_2 \bullet \ l_1 = l_2 \wedge P_1 \in \mathbb{P} \wedge P_2 \in \mathbb{P} \\ \bot \ , \textbf{if } \exists (l_1 \mapsto T_1) \in w_1 \bullet \exists (l_2 \mapsto T_2) \in w_2 \bullet \ l_1 = l_2 \wedge T_1 \sqcup T_2 \ undef. \\ \\ (\textbf{dom } w_2) \triangleleft w_1 \ \cup \ (\textbf{dom } w_1) \triangleleft w_2 \\ \cup \left\{ \left(l \mapsto (T_1 \sqcup T_2)* \right) \ | (l \mapsto T_1) \in w_1 \ \wedge \ (l \mapsto T_2) \in w_2 \right\}, \ \textbf{else} \end{cases}$$

If a document fragment targets a formal parameter of a certain type and another document fragment does not target this formal parameter, then and only then does the document resulting from sequencing the document parts target the given formal parameter with unchanged type. That is, with respect to non-overlapping parts of form types, form type composition is just union. With antidomain restriction notation, see page 304, this is specified succinctly in line 3 of the $\odot$ operator definition.

Two document fragments that target the same formal parameters may be sequenced if the targeted formal parameter types are compatible for each formal parameter. NSP types are compatible if they have a supertype in common. The NSP subtype relation formalizes when an actual parameter may be submitted to a dialogue method: if its type is a subtype of the targeted formal parameter. So if two documents have targeted parameters with compatible types in common only, the joined document may target every dialogue method that fulfills the following: formal parameters that are targeted by both document parts have an array type, because of sequencing a single data transmission cannot be ensured in either case. The array items' type must be a common supertype of the targeting actual parameters. This is formalized in line 4 of the $\odot$ operator definition: for every shared formal parameter a formal array parameter of the least common supertype belongs to the result form type. The least common supertype of two types is given as the least upper bound of the two types, which is unique except for the equality induced by recursive subtyping itself. Consider the following example application of the $\odot$ operator:

$$\{l \mapsto \texttt{int}, n \mapsto \{o \mapsto \texttt{int}, p \mapsto \texttt{String}\}\} \qquad (T_1)$$
$$\odot \{m \mapsto \texttt{int}, n \mapsto \{o \mapsto \texttt{int}, q \mapsto \texttt{String}\}\} \qquad (T_2)$$

$$= \begin{array}{l} \{\, l \mapsto \texttt{int}, \\ \quad m \mapsto \texttt{int}, \\ \quad n \mapsto \texttt{array of}\{o \mapsto \texttt{int}, p \mapsto \texttt{String}, q \mapsto \texttt{String}\} \\ \} \end{array} \qquad (T_3)$$

In the example two form fragments are concatenated, the first one having type T_1, the second one having type T_2. The compound form content will provide int values for the formal parameters l and m. It will provide two actual parameters for the formal parameter n. The record stemming from the first form fragment can be automatically filled with a null object for a formal q parameter of type String, because String is a non-primitive type. Analogously, the record stemming from the second form fragment can be automatically filled with a null object for a formal p parameter. The compound form document therefore can target a dialogue method with web signature T_3.

The error cases in the $\odot$ operator definition are equally important. The $\odot$ operator is a partial function. If two document fragments target the same formal parameter with non-compatible types, they simply cannot be sequenced. The $\odot$ operator is undefined for the respective form types. More interestingly, two document fragments that should be composed must not target a formal server page parameter. This would result in an actual server page parameter array which would contradict the overall principle of conservative language amalgamation introduced in Chap. 11. If desired, page array types must be introduced by tag support.

Form type composition can be characterized algebraically. The web signatures form a monoid ($\mathbb{W}$, $\odot$, $\emptyset$) with the $\odot$ operator as monoid operation and the empty web signature as neutral element. The operation $(\lambda v.v \odot w)_w$ is idempotent for every arbitrary fixed web signature w, which explains why the typing rule (15.37) for loop-structures is adequate.

15.3.5 Environments and Judgments

In the NSP type system two environments are used. The first environment Γ is the usual type environment. The second environment Δ is used for binding names to server pages, i.e., as a definition environment. It follows from their declaration that environments are web signatures. All definitions coined for web signatures immediately apply to the environments. This is exploited for example in the system parts typing rule (15.59).

$$\Gamma : \mathbf{Label} \twoheadrightarrow (\mathbb{T} \cup \mathbb{P}) = \mathbb{W}$$

$$\Delta : \mathbf{Label} \twoheadrightarrow \mathbb{P} \qquad \subset \mathbb{W}$$

The Core NSP identifiers are used for basic programming language expressions, namely variables and constants, and for page identifiers, namely formal page parameters and server pages names belonging to the complete system. In some contexts, e.g., in hidden parameters or in select menu option values, both page identifiers and arbitrary programming language expressions are allowed. Therefore initially page identifiers are treated syntactically as programming language expressions. However, a clear cut between page identifiers and the programming language is maintained, because the modeling of conservative amalgamation is an objective. The cut is provided by the premises of typing rules concerning such elements where only a certain kind of entity is allowed, e.g., in the statement typing rule (15.29) page identifiers are prevented from becoming program parts.

The Core NSP type system relies on several typing judgments:

$$\begin{array}{ll}
\Gamma \vdash e : \mathbb{T} \cup \mathbb{P} & e \in \mathbf{expr} \\
\Gamma \vdash n : \mathbb{D} & n \in \mathbf{com} \cup \mathbf{dynamic} \\
\Gamma \vdash c : \mathbb{P} & c \in \mathbf{websig\text{-}core} \\
\Gamma \vdash a : \mathbb{W} & a \in \mathbf{actualparams} \\
\Gamma, \Delta \vdash s : \mathbb{S} & s \in \mathbf{system}
\end{array}$$

Eventually the judgment that a system has complete type is targeted. In order to achieve this, different kinds of types must be derived for entities of different syntactic categories. Expressions have programming language types or page types consequently along the lines just discussed. Both programming language code and user interface descriptions have document fragment types, because they can be interlaced arbitrarily and therefore belong conceptually to the same kind of document. Parameterized core documents have page types. The actual parameters of a call element together provide an actual superparameter, the type of which is a web signature and is termed a call type. All the kinds of judgments so far work with respect to a given type environment. If documents are considered as parts of a system they must mutually respect defined server page names. Therefore subsystem judgments have to be given additionally with respect to the definition environment.

15.3.6 Typing Rules

The notion of Core NSP type correctness is specified as an algorithmic type system. In the presence of subtyping there are two alternatives for specifying type correctness with a type system. The first one is by means of a declarative type system. In such a type system a subsumption rule is present. Whenever necessary it can be derived that an entity always has each of its supertypes. Instead, in an algorithmic type system reasoning about an entity's supertypes happens in a controlled way by fulfilling typing rule premises. Both approaches have their advantages and drawbacks. The declarative approach usually leads to more succinct typing rules. However, reasoning about type system properties may become complicated in the declarative approach – cut elimination techniques may have to be employed. In the algorithmic approach the single typing rules may quickly become complex; however, an algorithmic type system is easier to handle in proofs.

For Core NSP an algorithmic type system is the correct choice. Extra premises are needed in some of the typing rules, e.g., in the typing rule for form submission. In some rules slightly more complex type patterns have to be used in the premises, e.g., in the typing rules concerning layout structuring document elements. However, in the Core NSP type system this extra complexity fosters understandability.

The typing rules are presented by starting from basic building blocks and moving to more complex building blocks. The typing rule (15.26) allows for extraction of an identifier typing assumption from the typing environment. Rules (15.27) and (15.28) give the types of selected record fields and indexed array elements respectively.

$$\frac{(v \mapsto T) \in \Gamma}{\Gamma \vdash v : T} \tag{15.26}$$

$$\frac{\Gamma \vdash e : \{l_i \mapsto T_i\}^{i \in 1...n} \qquad j \in 1...n}{\Gamma \vdash e.l_j : T_j} \tag{15.27}$$

$$\frac{\Gamma \vdash e : \textbf{array of } T \qquad \Gamma \vdash i : \textbf{int}}{\Gamma \vdash e[i] : T} \tag{15.28}$$

Typing rule (15.29) introduces programming language statements, namely assignments. Only programming language variables and expression may be used, i.e., expressions must not contain page identifiers. The resulting statement will not produce any output. It is possible to write an assignment inside forms and outside forms. If it is used inside a form it will not contribute to the submitted superparameter. Therefore a statement has a document fragment type which is composed of the neutral document type, the neutral form type, and the empty web signature. The empty string, which is explicitly allowed as content in NSP, obtains the same type by rule (15.30).

$$\frac{\Gamma \vdash x : T \qquad \Gamma \vdash e : T \qquad T \in \mathbb{T}}{\Gamma \vdash x := e \ : \ ((\circ, \updownarrow), \emptyset)} \tag{15.29}$$

$$\overline{\Gamma \vdash \varepsilon : ((\circ, \updownarrow), \emptyset)} \tag{15.30}$$

Actually in Core NSP the programming language and user interface description language are interlaced tightly by the abstract syntax. The code tags are just a means to relate the syntax to common concrete server pages syntax. The code tags are used to switch explicitly between programming language and user interface description and back. For the latter the tags may be read in reverse order. However, this switching does not affect the document fragment type and therefore the rules (15.31) and (15.32) do not, too.

$$\frac{\Gamma \vdash c : D}{\Gamma \vdash <\mathtt{code}> c </\mathtt{code}> : D} \tag{15.31}$$

$$\frac{\Gamma \vdash d : D}{\Gamma \vdash </\mathtt{code}> d <\mathtt{code}> : D} \tag{15.32}$$

Equally basic as rule (15.29), rule (15.33) introduces character strings as well-typed user interface descriptions. A string's type consists of the output type, the neutral form type, and the empty web signature. Another way to produce output is by means of expression elements, which support all basic types and get by rule (15.34) the same type as character strings.

$$\frac{d \in \mathbf{string}}{\Gamma \vdash d : ((\bullet, \updownarrow), \emptyset)} \tag{15.33}$$

$$\frac{\Gamma \vdash e : T \quad T \in \mathbb{B}}{\Gamma \vdash <\mathtt{expression}> e </\mathtt{expression}> : ((\bullet, \updownarrow), \emptyset)} \tag{15.34}$$

Composing user descriptions parts and sequencing programming language parts must follow essentially the same typing rule. In both rule (15.35) and rule (15.36) premises ensure that the document fragment types of both document parts are compatible. If the parts have a common layout supertype, they may be used together in server pages contexts of that type. If in addition to that the composition of the parts' form types is defined, the composition becomes the resulting form type. Form composition was explained in Sect. 15.3.4.

$$\frac{d_1, d_2 \in \mathbf{dynamic}}{\Gamma \vdash d_1 : (L_1, w_1) \quad \Gamma \vdash d_2 : (L_2, w_2) \quad L_1 \sqcup L_2 \downarrow \quad w_1 \odot w_2 \downarrow}{\Gamma \vdash d_1 \, d_2 : (L_1 \sqcup L_2, w_1 \odot w_2)} \tag{15.35}$$

$$\frac{\Gamma \vdash c_1 : (L_1, w_1) \qquad \Gamma \vdash c_2 : (L_2, w_2) \qquad L_1 \sqcup L_2 \downarrow \qquad w_1 \odot w_2 \downarrow}{\Gamma \vdash c_1; c_2 \; : \; (L_1 \sqcup L_2, w_1 \odot w_2)} \tag{15.36}$$

The loop is a means of dynamically sequencing. From the type system's point of view it suffices to regard it as a sequence of twice the loop body as expressed by typing rule (15.37). For an if–then–else structure the types of both branches must be compatible in order to yield a well-typed structure. Either one or the other branch is executed, so the least upper bound of the layout types and least upper bound of the form types establish the adequate new document fragment type.

$$\frac{\Gamma \vdash e : \texttt{boolean} \qquad \Gamma \vdash c : (L, w)}{\Gamma \vdash \texttt{while } e \texttt{ do } c \; : \; (L, w \odot w)} \tag{15.37}$$

$$\frac{\Gamma \vdash e : \texttt{boolean} \qquad \Gamma \vdash c_1 : D_1 \qquad \Gamma \vdash c_2 : D_2 \qquad D_1 \sqcup D_2 \downarrow}{\Gamma \vdash \texttt{if } e \texttt{ then } c_1 \texttt{ else } c_2 \; : \; D_1 \sqcup D_2} \tag{15.38}$$

Next the typing rules for controls are considered. The submit button is a visible control and must not occur outside a form; in Core NSP it is an empty element. It obtains the output type, the inside form type, and the empty web signature as document fragment type. Similarly an input control obtains the output type and the inside form type. But an input control introduces a form type. The type of the input control is syntactically fixed to be a widget supported type. The param attribute of the control is mapped to the control's type. This pair becomes the form type in the control's document fragment type. Check boxes are similar. In Core NSP check boxes are only used to gather Boolean data. Hidden parameters are not visible. The value of the hidden parameter may be a programming language expression of arbitrary type or an identifier of page type.

$$\frac{}{\Gamma \vdash \; < \texttt{submit/} > \; : \; ((\bullet, \Downarrow), \emptyset)} \tag{15.39}$$

$$\frac{T \in \mathbb{B}_{supported}}{\Gamma \vdash \; < \texttt{input type} = \text{``}T\text{''} \texttt{ param} = \text{``}l\text{''} / > \; : ((\bullet, \Downarrow), \{(l \mapsto T)\})} \tag{15.40}$$

$$\frac{}{\Gamma \vdash \; < \texttt{checkbox} \quad \texttt{param} = \text{``}l\text{''} / > \; : \; ((\bullet, \Downarrow), \{(l \mapsto boolean)\})} \tag{15.41}$$

$$\frac{\Gamma \vdash e : T}{\Gamma \vdash \; < \texttt{hidden param} = \text{``}l\text{''} > e < /\texttt{hidden} > \; : \; ((\circ, \Downarrow), \{(l \mapsto T)\})} \tag{15.42}$$

The select element may only contain code that generates option elements.

Therefore an option element obtains the option type **OP** by rule (15.44) and the select element typing rule (15.43) requires this option type from its content. An option element does not have its own param element. The interesting type information concerning the option value is wrapped as an array type that is assigned to an arbitrary label. The type information is used by rule (15.43) to construct the correct form type. In this way no new kind of judgment has to be introduced for select menu options.

$$
\frac{\Gamma \vdash d : ((\mathbf{OP}, \updownarrow), \{(l \mapsto \text{array of } T)\})}{\Gamma \vdash \begin{array}{l} < \texttt{select} \quad \texttt{param} = \text{``}l\text{''} > \\ \quad d \\ < /\texttt{select} > \end{array} : ((\bullet, \Downarrow), \{(l \mapsto \text{array of } T)\})} \tag{15.43}
$$

$$
\frac{\Gamma \vdash v : T \qquad \Gamma \vdash e : int \qquad l \in \mathbf{Label}}{\Gamma \vdash \begin{array}{l} < \texttt{option} > \\ \quad < \texttt{value} > v < /\texttt{value} > \\ \quad < \texttt{label} > e < /\texttt{label} > \\ < /\texttt{option} > \end{array} : ((\mathbf{OP}, \updownarrow), \{(l \mapsto \text{array of } T)\})} \tag{15.44}
$$

The object element is a record construction facility. The enclosed document fragment's layout type lasts after application of typing rule (15.45). The fragment's form type is assigned to the object element's param attribute. In this way the superparameter provided by the enclosed document becomes a named object attribute.

$$
\frac{\Gamma \vdash d : (L, w)}{\Gamma \vdash < \texttt{object param} = \text{``}l\text{''} > d < /\texttt{object} > : (L, \{(l \mapsto w)\})} \tag{15.45}
$$

The form typing rule (15.46) requires that a form may target only a server page that yields a complete web page if it is called. Furthermore the form type of the form content must be a subtype of the targeted web signature, because the Core NSP subtype relation specifies when a form parameter may be submitted to a dialogue method of given signature. Furthermore the form contents must be allowed to occur inside a form. Then the rule (15.46) specifies that the form is a visible element that must not be contained inside another form.

$$
\frac{\Gamma \vdash l : w \to \square \qquad \Gamma \vdash d : ((e, \Downarrow), v) \qquad \vdash v < w}{\Gamma \vdash < \texttt{form} \quad \texttt{callee} = \text{``}l\text{''} > d < /\texttt{form} > : ((e, \Uparrow), \emptyset)} \tag{15.46}
$$

Now the layout structuring elements, i.e., lists and tables, are investigated. The corresponding typing rules (15.47) to (15.51) do not affect the form types and form occurrence types of contained elements. Only document parts that have no specific layout type, i.e., are either neutral or merely visible, are allowed to become list items by rule (15.47). Only documents with list layout type may become part of a list. A well-typed list is a visible element. The rules (15.49) to (15.51) work analogously for tables.

$$\frac{\Gamma \vdash d : ((\bullet \vee \circ, F), w)}{<\texttt{li}> d <\texttt{/li}> \ : \ ((\mathbf{LI}, F), w)} \tag{15.47}$$

$$\frac{\Gamma \vdash d : ((\mathbf{LI} \vee \circ, F), w)}{<\texttt{ul}> d <\texttt{/ul}> \ : \ ((\bullet, F), w)} \tag{15.48}$$

$$\frac{\Gamma \vdash d : ((\bullet \vee \circ, F), w)}{<\texttt{td}> d <\texttt{/td}> \ : \ ((\mathbf{TD}, F), w)} \tag{15.49}$$

$$\frac{\Gamma \vdash d : ((\mathbf{TD} \vee \circ, F), w)}{<\texttt{tr}> d <\texttt{/tr}> \ : \ ((\mathbf{TR}, F), w)} \tag{15.50}$$

$$\frac{\Gamma \vdash d : ((\mathbf{TR} \vee \circ, F), w)}{<\texttt{table}> d <\texttt{/table}> \ : \ ((\bullet, F), w)} \tag{15.51}$$

As the last core document element the server-side call is treated. A call element may only contain actual parameter elements. This is ensured syntactically. The special character $\varepsilon_{\mathsf{act}}$ acts as an empty parameter list if necessary. It has the empty web signature as call type. Typing rule (15.54) makes it possible for several actual parameter elements to uniquely provide the parameters for a server-side call. Rule (15.52) specifies that a server call can target an include server page only. The call element inherits the targeted include server page's document fragment type, because this page will replace the call element if it is called.

$$\frac{\Gamma \vdash l : w \to D \qquad \Gamma \vdash as : v \qquad \vdash v < w}{\Gamma \vdash <\texttt{call} \quad \texttt{callee} = \text{``}l\text{''} > as <\texttt{/call}> \ : \ D} \tag{15.52}$$

$$\frac{}{\Gamma \vdash \varepsilon_{\mathsf{act}} : \emptyset} \tag{15.53}$$

$$\frac{\Gamma \vdash as : w \qquad \Gamma \vdash e : T \qquad l \notin (dom \ w)}{\Gamma \vdash \begin{array}{l} <\texttt{actualparam} \quad \texttt{param} = \text{``}l\text{''} > \\ \quad e \\ <\texttt{/actualparam}> as \ : \ w \cup \{(l \mapsto T)\} \end{array}} \tag{15.54}$$

With the typing rules (15.55) and (15.58) the arbitrary document fragment may become an include server page, with the document fragment's type becoming the server page's result type. A document fragment may become a complete web page by typing rules (15.56) and (15.58) if it has no specific layout type, i.e., is neutral or merely visible, and furthermore is not intended to be used inside forms. The resulting server page obtains the complete type as result type. Both include server page cores and web server page cores start with no formal parameters initially. With rule (15.57) parameters can be added to server page cores. The rule's premises ensure that a new formal parameter must have another name than all the other parameters and that the formal parameter is used in the core document type correctly. A binding of a type to a new formal parameter's name is erased from the type environment.

$$\frac{\Gamma \vdash d : D \qquad d \in \mathbf{dynamic}}{\Gamma \vdash\ <\texttt{include}> d <\texttt{/include}> :\ \emptyset \to D} \tag{15.55}$$

$$\frac{\Gamma \vdash d : ((\bullet \vee \circ, \updownarrow \vee \Uparrow), \emptyset) \qquad t \in \mathbf{strings} \qquad d \in \mathbf{dynamic}}{\Gamma \vdash \begin{array}{l} <\texttt{html}> \\ <\texttt{head}><\texttt{title}> t <\texttt{/head}><\texttt{/title}> \\ <\texttt{body}> d <\texttt{/body}> \\ <\texttt{/html}> :\ \emptyset \to \Box \end{array}} \tag{15.56}$$

$$\frac{\Gamma \vdash l : T \qquad \Gamma \vdash c : w \to D \qquad l \notin (dom\ w)}{\Gamma \backslash (l \mapsto T) \vdash \begin{array}{l} <\texttt{param}\ \ \texttt{name} = \text{``}l\text{''}\ \ \texttt{type} = \text{``}T\text{''}/> \\ c : (w \cup \{(l \mapsto T)\}) \to D \end{array}} \tag{15.57}$$

$$\frac{\Gamma \vdash l : P \qquad \Gamma \vdash c : P \qquad c \in \mathbf{websig\text{-}core}}{\Gamma \backslash (l \mapsto P), \{(l \mapsto P)\} \vdash\ <\texttt{nsp}\ \ \texttt{name} = \text{``}l\text{''}> c <\texttt{/nsp}> :\ \Diamond} \tag{15.58}$$

A server page core can become a well-typed server page by rule (15.58). The new server page name and the type bound to it are taken from the type environment and become the definition environment. An NSP system is a collection of NSPs. A single well-typed server page is already a system. Rule (15.59) specifies system compatibility. Rule (15.60) specifies system completeness. Two systems are compatible if they have no overlapping server page definitions. Furthermore the server pages that are defined in one system and used in the other must be able to process the data they receive from the other system, therefore the types of the server pages defined in the one system must be subtypes of the ones bound to their names in the other system's type environment.

$$\frac{\begin{array}{c} s_1, s_2 \in \mathbf{system} \qquad (dom\ \Delta_1) \cap (dom\ \Delta_2) = \emptyset \\ ((dom\ \Gamma_2) \lhd \Delta_1) < ((dom\ \Delta_1) \lhd \Gamma_2) \\ ((dom\ \Gamma_1) \lhd \Delta_2) < ((dom\ \Delta_2) \lhd \Gamma_1) \\ \Gamma_1, \Delta_1 \vdash s_1 : \Diamond \qquad \Gamma_2, \Delta_2 \vdash s_2 : \Diamond \end{array}}{((dom\ \Delta_2)\lhd\Gamma_1) \cup ((dom\ \Delta_1)\lhd\Gamma_2),\ \Delta_1 \cup \Delta_2 \vdash s_1\ s_2\ :\ \Diamond} \tag{15.59}$$

$$\frac{\begin{array}{c} \Gamma \in \mathbb{R} \\ (dom\ \Delta) \cap bound(s) = \emptyset \\ \Gamma, \Delta \vdash s : \Diamond \end{array}}{\Gamma, \Delta \vdash s : \sqrt{}} \tag{15.60}$$

Typing rule (15.60) specifies when a well-typed system is complete. First, all of the used server pages must be defined; that is, the type environment is a pure record type. Secondly, server page definitions may not occur as bound variables somewhere in the system.

Theorem 15.1. *Core NSP type checking is decidable.*

Proof. Core NSP is explicitly typed. The Core NSP type system is algorithmic. Recursive subtyping is decidable. The least upper bound can be considered as a union operation during type checking – as a result a form content is considered to have a finite collection of types, which are each checked against a targeted server page if rule (15.46) is applied. □

Part IV

Conclusion

A Comparison of Modeling Methods

This chapter discusses representative system modeling approaches and techniques. Some of the methods discussed have gained widespread attention in the past, others represent recent efforts in the areas indicated. The aim of the chapter is to comprehend the opinions stated in this book. Alternative articulations of the new standpoints are provided by comparing them with the standpoints of other approaches.

Information systems hold data, and provide functionality to the user. Therefore we first discuss user interface modeling and data modeling in their own right. A review of model-oriented specification languages is provided. We proceed with the two major comprehensive approaches, structured analysis and object-oriented analysis. Finally the current discussion on model-driven architecture is taken into account.

16.1 User Interface Modeling

The form-based interface is the poor cousin of HCI of the human–computer interaction (HCI) community. This did not reduce the practical importance and ubiquity of this kind of interface. The HCI community has naturally believed that over time the crude looking form-based interfaces will be replaced by advanced GUI-based interfaces. However, it seems by now that many new interface metaphors have not been able to provide real added value to the cases where form-based interfaces are used. The typical usage of a textual input field, e.g., the collection of a new username, apparently cannot be improved in most cases. Hence the form-based interface seems destined to remain with us in the future.

User interface modeling has become a recognized area of research with the advent of GUIs. A major milestone in the research on user interface modeling is the Seeheim model [249, 131], which defines a reference architecture for user interface management systems (UIMS), see Fig. 16.1. This reference model has served as the starting point for intense research that is still underway [281].

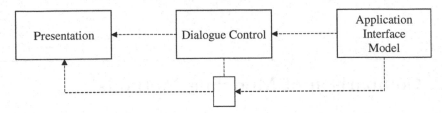

Fig. 16.1. The Seeheim model of user interfaces

State diagrams have been used for a long time in user interface specification [246], partly with the objective of user interface generation [281]. The elaborate approaches [309, 310, 173] target user interface specification only at a fine-grained level, in our terminology concerning page interaction. Another early approach [146] targeted the modeling of push-based, form-based systems like the already discussed single-user desktop databases.

DENIM and SILK [191, 229] are informal interactive tools that support the early stages of user interface design. They enable the execution of electronic sketches of user interface prototypes. PICTIVE [223, 224, 225] (Plastic Interface for Collaborative Technology Initiatives through Video Exploration) is a design method for the participatory creation of software interfaces for interactive systems.

The form-oriented user interface model applies the concept of black-box abstraction to direct manipulation interfaces. The pages presented to the user are edited by partially using direct manipulation. One can roughly say that input of primitive data is keyboard oriented, while manipulating opaque references is mouse-based. Moreover navigation is rather mouse based, but in any case there are certainly many exceptions to these trends. The form-oriented viewpoint abstracts from the details of page change. We want to call this the *transparency* of input devices; the usage of these input devices is considered to be intuitive, and therefore the particular technologies can be seen as being invisible. The user has the impression of entering the input directly.

16.2 Web Site Modeling

16.2.1 Hypertext Modeling

The conceptual modeling of hypertext is a separate domain, which has been intensively studied since the beginning of interest in hypertext [232]. A reference model for hypertext based on formal specification with Z is [136]. A complete methodology for hypermedia design called RMM is presented in [172]. The aim to reduce the necessary navigation primitives is addressed in WebML [45], which we discuss in the next section. The conceptual modeling of navigation was also addressed in the ViewNet approach [325]. These named approaches are modeling content in logical collections of information elements. As such these approaches are related to modeling of information architectures [262] as represented by content management systems. In the early contribution of Zhaneg and Pong [324] statecharts are employed to give semantics to frame-based, scrolling-based hypertexts. The approach HMBS (Hypermedia Based on Statecharts) discusses patterns for modeling advanced concepts such as hierarchical views, access control, versioning and navigational contexts [240].

All the named hypertext modeling approaches do not use bipartite transition descriptions. The system response in these approaches is unconditional. These approaches therefore also have no direct connection to constraint writing.

16.2.2 Modeling Web Sites

WebML [45] is a visual language for the conceptual modeling of complex web sites, in which all concepts are defined visually as well as in XML. WebML offers icons for page elements for composing web sites, e.g., catalogue pages and single item views. The model of the web sites involves a number of orthogonal divisions, called structural model, composition model, navigation model, presentation model, and personalization model. The structural model is in principle a semantic data model described in XML. The composition model is a description of page content based on the data model. The navigation model describes hyperlinks between the pages, with a distinction between so-called contextual links, which are induced by the structure of the data model, and non-contextual links, which are freely defined. The WebML approach can therefore be seen as an advanced and customizable successor of model-driven interface generators [281]: the basic idea of such systems is to generate all contextual links from the model. Advanced systems like WebML offer on the other hand the possibility to choose between the contextual links as well as to use freely definable links. Links in WebML are directed edges, which lead typically from pages to pages and therefore form a non-bipartite navigation model. WebML also offers a mechanism for accessing so-called generic external operations by model elements called operation units [46]. Operation units have conditional output similar to server actions in form-oriented analysis, but perform asynchronous computations. They are activated by a designated link and can afterwards perform operations of arbitrary length. They can then leave content in other WebML-modeled units.

A solution for managing web applications that addresses both semantic and managerial issues is [118].

16.3 Data Modeling

16.3.1 Properties of Relational Modeling Languages

As we have said, many data modeling languages like ER diagrams, UML, etc., as well as our DAL, have important commonalities, and the central commonality is that they have so-called relational semantics. The key element of these relational semantics is the way the connections between different data types are established. In fact one can say that even UML, which is usually conceived as a primarily object-oriented language, not least because of the way it is presented by its creators, is in contrast rather a primarily relational language, with object-oriented extensions. In fact a closer investigation shows that the object-oriented and the relational features are rather loosely connected.

The characterizing concept of relational semantics is the way in which collections associated with a single object are modeled. The best way to illustrate the key difference between relational semantics and third generation languages, i.e., C, Java, but also Algol etc., is by looking at an example that represents the general concepts. A paradigmatic example is a purchase order with a list of posts. If you model an order in a third generation language, you typically have a record data type representing the header of the order, e.g., containing the customer ID, the date of the order, etc. Furthermore the order record contains a field that is a collection of order lines, which is typically a polymorphic collection type from a library, or the inbuilt array type of the language. Hence the order header refers to the order lines. On the other hand, in the relational paradigm that you find in relational databases as well as in typical constraint languages for class diagrams, the order lines contain a reference to the order header, but not vice versa, i.e., the order header does not contain a reference to the order lines. If you want to obtain the list of order lines of the order, you make a request to the system with the following meaning: "show me all order lines which refer to this header." In this way the complete order is obtained by a query executed afresh each time it is used, but in the conventional sense the order is not stored as a composite data object. The clue to relational databases is that behind the scenes, the data record types you define are embedded in an automated indexing framework which is totally transparent to the user, but which enables the database software to offer a powerful query language, which can answer the above request efficiently [272].

Generally speaking, in third generation languages used for describing efficient data structures and algorithms, a collection is modeled explicitly in the state as a linked data structure, i.e., a linked list containing references to all members. In a relational model each member of the collection holds a reference to an object representing the collection, the so-called foreign key. The collection associated with the object is created only on demand as the result of an operation, namely a query, which searches for all objects of a given type, which have the right reference.

16.3.2 Domain Models

Based on the discussion of real-world modeling in Sect. 9.4, this section reconsiders the notion of domain model. A *domain model* is a library of data models, which are to be used in a business domain. The domain model deals with models that are needed for the exchange between organizations or persons or models that an organization may use internally, since it is impossible to define a strict border.

Note that from our viewpoint this is the whole definition of ontologies. Specifically, we again do not suggest that an ontology describes objects in the real world. In our view, the clearest conception of domain-specific enterprise systems is simply that their model contains the ontology as a submodel. This is a precise point about ontologies. The assumption that the ontology models objects in the real world may be a nice intuition, but it is a matter of taste and not precise.

Ontologies are the basic intuition between semantic data modeling techniques, which are declared as being real-world modeling. However, the real-world modeling conception once more turns out to contain an explanation that is arguably more confusing than clarifying. There is a possible elaboration of the real-world modeling concept, which talks of types in the world. This approach depicts a relation between the structure of the data model and the structure of the world, not between the state of the data model and the actual state of the world. However, the error here is arguably the indicative in the statement that the data model depicts facts in the real world. An acceptable version would be an affirmative one: we want to create the data model so that it represents our view of the real world.

The use of a domain model in different systems creates interoperability. There is no restriction on the types of constraints that may be used in a domain model. Due to the integration of functionality in the data model, the domain model may therefore contain business rules. A model of an enterprise system typically contains parts besides the domain model.

Domain model entity types are abstract entity types. Consider the date type as an example. A date can be read in different formats. All attributes expressing the respective formats are connected with the date object. They are furthermore connected by constraints, which state the mutual format conversion. Domain models typically will be used only in parts. Consider an address record as an example. A system may want to use a part of the address record. One of the practical problems here is related to the question of multiplicities. The domain model should contain one address entity type, which offers an extensive list of attributes about the user.

16.4 Model-Oriented Specification Languages

Formal system specification languages can be divided into algebraic specification languages and model-oriented specification languages [148]. Algebraic approaches [326, 126] are completely axiom-based: axioms are the sole means to specify abstract data types. Model-oriented approaches are rather two-staged. First the state of an abstract state machine, the model, is explicitly specified by means of type constructors, then operations are specified with respect to the model. In order to explain this difference, a typical example is often used: the stack. In a model-oriented specification language [171, 25] the stack can be modeled simply by a sequence of items, while with an algebraic specification language, the stack specification looks like the following:

$$pop(push(s,i))=s$$

In the following section we use the well-known specification language Z [283] as an example for the model-oriented approach. Reports on the usage of the specification language Z for the refactoring of the IBM CICS Application Programming Interface are provided by [60, 145].

16.4.1 The Z Specification Language

The aim of Z is perhaps best pointed out in the phrase *specification using mathematics* [147]. In Z systems are specified as functions. For stateful systems Z uses an automaton model for the specification of system states. The model, called the state machine model in [320], describes the system as an automaton with a state from a potentially infinite state space and a state transition function. The system description therefore consists of a specification of the space of possible states and the operations on the state. Z allows specification of update operations that lead to state changes, Δ operations for short, and pure queries, called $\varXi$ operations.

There are certain connections between Z and our approach as well as notable differences. First of all Z as well as our approach use an automaton model for the system description, but it is important to understand that the counterpart to the state in a Z specification is not the state of the dialogue model, but the current object net over the data model in form-oriented analysis. It is the formchart, where form-oriented analysis goes beyond the Z specification paradigm. In Z all operations are at first hand conceived as being applicable at any time. In form-oriented analysis on the other hand operations are applicable only if they are options of the current client page. Hence form-oriented analysis offers a specification point for the availability of operations. One main additional specification concept in form-oriented analysis is therefore the support of conditional accessibility of operations based on a finite state machine. But beyond the finite automaton as such, form-oriented analysis offers support for specifying constraints in the form of dialogue constraints. Form-oriented analysis also offers support for conditional system response. Such conditional response is a first-class concept in form-oriented analysis since in the formchart server actions can branch to different client pages. In Z such conditional system response must be coded into the single response type. Hence the return type in Z must be an EITHER–OR type, built from the different response types.

16.4.2 Direct Access to the Abstract Interface

Form-oriented analysis has in common with the model-oriented specification approach the abstract machine system viewpoint. However, with respect to the form-oriented user interface model we assume that the virtual machine is not placed in an abstract environment, but that it has a direct interface to the user. We call this concept the *embedded virtual machine*.

The form-oriented user interface model and the terminal concept connected with this model have a pivotal role because they are supposed to provide direct access for the user to the model. In that sense we call the form-oriented interface a human–model interface – in contrast to the term human–computer interface. The concept of the human-model interface is in some sense also the counter-paradigm of the real-world modeling approach. In the real-world modeling approach the relation between model and world is established by an elusive connection, which is different from both. In our approach the intuition behind the model is not a certain ontology, but a hypothetical situation, namely the imagination of the completed model. The semantics of the model are basically captured in the preamble:

"Suppose you sit in front of a new system. Then it will have the following properties..."

The human–model interface concept makes sure that we have this kind of unambiguity about how the model has to be understood. In that form we can access the model, with the form-oriented interface as the connection. This concept has to be seen in the wider framework of the embedded virtual machine paradigm.

The embedded virtual machine adds a crucial specification element to an abstract machine model or a data type definition. Those concepts are understood as living in an abstract environment, e.g., as a purely mathematical definition. The actual usage of such a model is by no means defined, as we will explain below. The embedded virtual machine is a mathematical definition plus a clearly separated embedding specification. The embedding specification is naturally related to other non-functional specifications, and should therefore be dealt with in the context of these non-functional demands.

16.5 Structured Analysis

Structured analysis [264, 85, 86, 263, 265] is a consistent approach for modeling enterprise applications that has been proven by years of experience in companies. Structured analysis methods are based on the elaboration of hierarchical DFDs. Well-known structured analysis methods are the SADT (Structured Analysis and Design Technique) method [86, 201] and the standardized IDEF0 (Integration Definition of Function Modeling) method [226]. We will discuss structured analysis along the lines of the concrete method of modern structured analysis [323], because it is a widespread method, too, and uses convenient methods for the data modeling part. Structured analysis is in extensive use in the industry even today, and is used for both business modeling and system modeling. The approach is well-suited for form-based tasks, as can be seen by early the contributions [297], and it works especially well for the analysis of combined manual and automatic processes.

16.5.1 Modern Structured Analysis

Early tutorials on structured analysis are [121, 122, 79]. Modern structured analysis offers integration of a semantic data model and a data dictionary with an asynchronous DFD. The asynchronous DFD has proven to be useful in systems analysis. With respect to interfaces the asynchronous semantics of such diagrams are known to lack important state-based semantics concerning the timing of user interaction. The new interaction models of our method provide exactly the missing state-based semantics, yet they are indeed much more compatible with modern structured analysis than other state diagram types.

Modern structured analysis defines several analysis-level artifacts, namely leveled DFDs, data dictionaries, entity–relationship diagrams, pseudo-code – called structured English – decision tables, and decision trees. They together form the structured specification called the target document. The method is deliberately ambiguous with respect to the semantics of the several notational elements of the DFDs and therefore relies heavily on the intuition of the modeler. Conditions for the mutual correctness of the diagrams are defined as so-called balancing rules. The balancing rules cover type correctness rules as well as name space rules.

16.5.2 Data Flow Diagrams

A DFD describes the data flow in the system between processes and other instances. A DFD is a directed graph. Edges and nodes are labeled. There are three kinds of nodes:

- *Processes.* Processes are data processing units. They are depicted by bubbles.
- *Stores.* Stores make up the system state. They are depicted by two parallel horizontal lines.
- *Terminators.* Terminators serve as data sources and data sinks. They are depicted by squares.

The edges are called flows. DFDs are typed, the type system being given by the data dictionary concept. The labels on the edges and on stores represent entries in the data dictionary. Terminators represent incoming or outgoing data flows. Figure 16.2 shows a possible DFD for the login and registration capabilities of a system like our example bookstore.

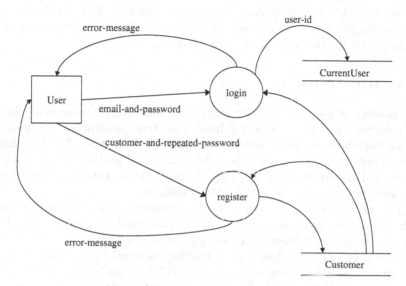

Fig. 16.2. Data flow diagram of a system login and registration feature

DFDs can be decomposed, see also Fig. 6.3. Only processes are subject to decomposition. A single process can be replaced by a complete DFD called the subdiagram. The dependency between edges connected to the process and the terminators in the subdiagram is explained in a balancing rule: the data flows connected to a process must be constructed from the data flows connected to the terminators of the subdiagram for that process. DFDs can be conceived as a concurrency model. The edges of the DFD represent pipes for messages with a fixed type specified in the data dictionary. If a process has two ingoing data flows, the diagram does not specify e.g., whether the process needs messages each time from both ingoing flows or only one message from an arbitrary ingoing flow [120]. This ambiguity is designed to focus deliberation on the aspects of pure typed flow of data. The decomposition of DFDs is functional decomposition. Since the processes are decomposed by subdiagrams, this resembles the specification of subprograms in programming languages. However, the sub-DFDs cannot be reused in different places of the specification. The hierarchical decomposition is hence only targeted at the partitioning of the specification.

DFDs may seem superficially similar to formcharts, but are completely different. While a formchart is bipartite, a DFD is not. In a DFD the different types of nodes may be combined freely. Moreover, the semantics of a DFD are different from the formchart semantics. Especially the DFD is no state diagram; on the contrary it exhibits parallelism and non-determinism as explained above. There are no strict temporal relations between ingoing and outgoing messages in a DFD. In a formchart obviously a state must be entered before it can be left exactly once on exactly one outgoing edge. Furthermore the decomposition mechanisms are completely different. While in DFDs a process can be decomposed into a complete data flow itself, in formcharts such a decomposition is neither intended nor possible.

16.5.3 Data Dictionary

The concept of a data dictionary plays a key role in structured analysis. The data dictionary is a list of hierarchical data type definitions. Formally this means that data dictionary entries are algebraic data types. Data dictionary types represent messages sent along flows or stored in data stores. Data dictionary entries are immutable values. A change to an entry in a store has to be understood as an exchange of whole messages.

The data dictionary structured analysis resembles the user message model of form-oriented analysis, but there is an important difference through the concept of opaque references. In modern structured analysis there is actually a concept of keys, based on a naming convention, for integrating the data dictionary with the semantic data model: keys are named like the entity types with an additional symbol. In form-oriented analysis, the key concept is transformed into a fully elaborated semantic concept in the form of the opaque reference mechanism.

16.5.4 Object-Oriented Extensions of Structured Analysis

Given the success of structured analysis, some work has been done in constructing object-oriented extensions of structured analysis. The Object–Process Methodology OPM [88, 89] deliberately avoids the partition of different modeling artifacts in different diagrams and uses a joint representation of processes and object-oriented information. It sets itself in contrast to object-oriented modeling techniques as discussed in the next section. In the FOOM methodology [275, 276] an object-oriented extension of structured analysis is given in such a form that two initial diagram types are used, a class diagram and a so-called OO-DFD. The authors of FOOM claim to gain superior results in comparison with OPM [277]. These methods aim at employing the advantageous elements from structured analysis as well as from object orientation in a single method.

16.6 Object-Oriented Analysis and Design

16.6.1 Object-Oriented Analysis

There are a remarkable number of different object-oriented analysis (OOA) methods, e.g., [279, 54, 205, 284, 59]. OOA is based on the intuition that the object-oriented metaphor, which was at this time already firmly introduced in the programming languages world, can serve as a viable metaphor for analysis as well.

Object-oriented analysis takes a different approach to system modeling than structured analysis. Structured analysis proceeds by describing the key functional processes in the problem domain and structuring them in the DFD. The data model originally takes the form of a data dictionary that annotates the DFD.

In object-oriented analysis according to Coad and Yourdon [54] the analysis starts by identifying the concepts of the problem domain, which are conceived as classes of objects. Objects are seen as encapsulations of data in the form of attributes. In a second step the interconnections of classes are elicited in the form of associations and generalization hierarchies. Behavioral aspects are identified in the next stage in the form of services offered by objects.

The results of object-oriented analysis vary strongly. Kamath et al report significant advantages [179]. It has been observed in [200] that OOA is best applied to a new project and does not work well with re-engineering of legacy applications.

UML provides a modern, object-oriented modeling approach, which is primarily used for design or especially for implementation purposes. In the analysis phase the primary role of UML is currently its use as a replacement for ER diagrams, hence class diagrams are used in their reduction to data models. UML as a universal modeling language is now well established: in February 2003 IBM announced the completion of its $2.1 billion acquisition of Rational Software Corporation. A focus of the current discussion is on specialized modeling languages built on the universal language UML [278, 18]. Such profiles are now in the early stages of development.

16.6.2 The Origins of Object Orientation

Object orientation is in the first instance a programming language paradigm. It was introduced by the language Simula [288, 185]. Simula started as a discrete event simulation language – at the early stages its designers Dahl and Nygaard also called it Monte Carlo Compiler [236]. Later the language Smalltalk [156] developed at Xerox PARC took up the object-oriented metaphor. In these days the Xerox PARC laboratory pushed the direct manipulation interface [287], the mouse input device [112], and the window-based interface [182]. A widespread viewpoint considers object-oriented programming chiefly as a data abstraction technique [196].

Object orientation is indeed successful on the design and implementation level. Object-oriented design (OOD) is especially relevant with respect to the justification of OOA, since one of the main goals in a pervasive object-oriented development process is to create synergies through the tight paradigmatic integration of the different development steps [48]. Several principles that describe the advantages of OOD have been identified [55, 56, 192]. One important principle is the Hollywood Principle *don't call us, we'll call you*, which refers to the object-oriented style of customizing behavior by overwriting methods. Another key principle is the *don't ask what kind* principle, which refers to the way in which subtype polymorphism is used by client objects. Both principles support separation of concerns. Note that disciplined approaches to customizing behavior – hooks or callbacks – are possible without object orientation.

The object-oriented paradigm is a mélange of the following notions:

- real-world simulation;
- vivid desktop metaphors;
- data abstraction;
- low coupling and high cohesion design.

The theory of object orientation, i.e., the semantics of object-oriented programming languages, has turned out to be rather complicated [1, 2].

16.6.3 The Use-Case-Driven Approach

In the use-case-driven approach to OOA [174] use cases are employed in order to describe the functionality of the user interface. However, it is now commonly agreed that interaction diagrams of the use cases describe the system by examples, but do not yield a specification, i.e., a description of all possible system usages [74], which is often desired. The interaction models of our method in contrast provide a true specification of the system.

OOA through a use-case-driven approach was popularized by Jacobson [174]. This approach begins by identifying use cases of the problem domain, together with actors which use them, in a coarse-grained diagram. A use case diagram for the example bookstore is shown in Fig. 16.3. Use cases are described by scripts that have the task of storyboarding scenarios of user interaction [28]. The scripts are textual, sequential descriptions of user interactions. Based on the use cases analysis classes are identified, especially boundary objects, with which the actors are conceived to communicate. The scripts can now be transformed to interaction diagrams showing the actors enacting on the boundary classes [175, 188].

The use-case-driven approach may yield a description specification of an analysis-level system interface description which is not a specification in the strict sense. The system usage is described only through singular cases, which are depicted in a sequential manner, e.g., as a message sequence chart. Message sequence charts are expressively weak [73]. Furthermore the system usage

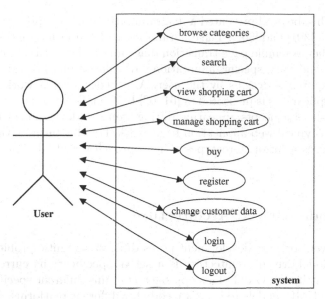

Fig. 16.3. Jacobson-style use case diagram of the example bookstore. The content of the use case diagram is similar to the bullet list on page 23

is depicted in a non-hierarchical manner. The interaction with form-based systems is modeled as a fine-grained sequential activity [174]. Use-case-driven modeling even for small examples becomes unwieldy.

The use-case-driven approach to object-oriented software engineering has become a widely acclaimed analysis technique. From the beginning [267, 174] to state-of-the-art versions [175] of this approach the recommended human computer interface specification techniques have been oriented towards the modeling of object-oriented GUIs and event-based user interfaces in contrast to form-based interfaces. As a consequence the use-case-driven modeling approach does not have the two-staged structure of interaction as is introduced for form-oriented analysis.

Use cases are defined as typical usages of the system. In a form-oriented user interface model, the basic flow and the alternative flows of a use case correspond to paths in the diagram. The complete diagram can be considered as the compact notation of the set of all use cases. In form-oriented analysis every use case is a feature.

16.6.4 User Interface Modeling Approaches with UML

Within the UML community the discussion about dealing with the user interface is still underway [71]. UML*i* [282] is a proposed visual language for presenting user interfaces. The new artifacts are basically visualizations of page components. The method is tightly coupled with the use-case-driven approach. Schwabe et al presented a diagrammatic tool for representing web interaction in [301] and [302]. The diagrams are called user interaction diagrams (UIDs). They resemble page transition diagrams without server actions. Very restrictive and very specific annotations are placed on the transitions concerning required selections by the user. A stereotype framework specifically for web applications is presented in [61, 62] by Conallen. This approach allows the design-level concepts appearing during web site development to be modeled with a typical web application framework. For this purpose the Conallen approach uses a set of stereotypes. The approach targets design rather than analysis.

16.7 Model-Driven Architecture

Model-driven software development poses difficult semantic problems [132].

The Model-driven architecture is a set of specifications currently under development by the OMG. This approach contains different specifications on how to use UML models to generate code for different platforms. The model-driven architecture does not specify which extent of model elements has to be translated into the target platform. Tools which generate code skeletons from these associations and attributes only can be subsumed under the model-driven architecture, as well as tools which automatically translate certain OCL annotations into code.

A goal for this approach is to use UML as a platform-independent notation and to generate code for different platforms. One disadvantage, however, is that this kind of platform independence is a subjective one. Indeed, if one takes a closer look at the proposals, i.e., the platforms from which this approach wants to abstract, one finds technologies like Java, which of course claim to be platform independent themselves. This shows that platform independence is a subjective viewpoint of one technology – in the views of other technologies, though, this platform-independent technology then appears as a platform in itself. Interestingly, this is not even a contradiction, it just shows that there is one more platform, which is independent of other platforms. The problem is only that many such platforms or technologies think that they themselves are more than a platform, even to say above other platforms, at least concerning the level of abstraction. However, developers of other platforms understandably do not agree with this judgment – platform independence lies finally in the eye of the beholder.

One basic problem here is that each of the newly emerging platform-independent approaches is based on a simple translation approach. The argument is that, from the code provided in the new format, some code can be generated in the other formats. The downside of this is, however, that they provide no innovative argument why this new format is more than simply another format adding to the complexity of our system landscape. In fact, a look at today's technology landscape shows quickly that the latter is simply the case. Hence platform independence is a fairly weak argument for any new technology; it is rather a sales trick to get new customers. For establishing a new technology there must be firmer arguments.

Another typical subtlety, which makes it easy to detract from some new technology, is the comparison between a new technology's vision and an old technology's reality. For the critical reader, it is important to realize that such a comparison is basically unfair. The great vision of the new technology, which did not have to experience all the problems of the reality, always does sound easy and consistent and able to overcome all the problems of the current system landscape. And, in fact, since the technology is not yet established, no one actually know for sure whether it will encounter a problem, and what this problem would be. So there is no possibility to compare the new technology's reality with the old technology's reality. But there is of course another possibility of a learned – and indeed fair – comparison: by comparing the new technologies' vision with the old technologies' vision – with the initial ideas, as they were put forward when these technologies were introduced. And then one would indeed see that these technologies, e.g., fourth generation languages, already had most of the visionary goals a long time ago. In other words, the pretender's new clothes are often old hat – if not, some really novel idea comes in.

There is a tendency within discussions on UML to move away from the visual aspects of UML towards the metamodeling aspects. It may, however, not be clear if this is really a fruitful development. This is because the de-emphasizing of visual modeling which we have recommended as well is something different from using a visual language non-visually, or even demotivating visual modeling. A language designed for visual modeling is usually full of support for visual modeling and is therefore not streamlined enough for non-visual modeling. The visualization of models has advantages which must not be diminished. Visualization is certainly an intuitive way of presentation and in the case of UML it is obvious that it provides for many developers a considerable fun factor, perhaps even supporting team spirit. It also provides a more friendly appearance for many technical documents, and adds some kind of authority to them. So diminishing these visualization aspects would certainly reduce one of the values of the visual modeling approaches, perhaps even the most important contribution of UML, even if this visual approach is not an original contribution of UML, but of ER modeling.

The essence of de-emphasizing visual modeling is rather to keep the modeling approach simple in itself, instead of tailoring it to a visual modeling method. In that regard, this de-emphasizing does not fit UML. The metamodel of UML is indeed best considered as the data model of a visual tool, since it contains many concessions to the need for visual representation. Indeed, the complexity of the metamodel is one of the reasons why UML has become fairly obviously a platform of its own. One example in this regard is the representation of the aspect whether an association is an aggregation or composition or none of them. This is modeled with an attribute of enumeration type in the association ends. Without going into the details of how this works, it is important to point out that this approach already is not able to capture multiple partial orders, for example, as is possible in the PD modeling language we have introduced. UML instead supports only one partial order at a time. Moreover, the particular metamodel of UML does provide considerably fewer semantics than the PD approach with its much simpler structure of having only constraints. In the PD modeling approach, for instance, every constraint can be combined with every other constraint just by applying both. In UML, however, in the case of aggregation/composition there is no way of telling from the metamodel that the composition implies an aggregation. This leads to considerable semantic problems, especially if composition and aggregation appear together in a diagram. These problems are obviously not inherent problems of the described phenomena, but problems generated by the particularities of the metamodel.

Another motivation for the model-driven architecture is the conception that a UML model is more abstract than the target platforms, e.g., code. Although one can argue that even abstraction is in the end sometimes a matter of taste and therefore it is immediately legitimate to see UML as more abstract, we want to investigate in which regard we can find substantial grounds for doing so. In looking for hard reasons we want to exclude insufficient ones beforehand. A format should not be called abstract alone

- because of being a generator input instead of a generator output. Hence the fact that the generators in mind use UML as input and generate C# as output does not prove that UML is more abstract.
- because it is visual in contrast to being ASCII-based.
- because it has another source code partitioning policy. That is, the fact that in UML a model does have multiple classes in one file, while Java has only one public class per file, does not mean that UML is more abstract.
- because it has another syntactical organization of the code. Hence the fact that an association in the UML model is obviously accessible from all participating classes does not create a higher abstraction than in programming languages. Note that this opinion also implies that the basic element of aspect-oriented programming is not per se an increase in abstraction, even if it may be seen by some as a nice feature – there is no contradiction.
- because it contains only a syntactically defined subset of another format, such as containing basically only a choice of the non-terminals slightly transformed in another notation. That is, just because one part of UML models, and perhaps the most popular part contains only signatures but no code, does not mean it is more abstract.

The remaining candidates for why UML could be called more abstract are the relational semantics incorporated from ER, the "design by contract" specification strategy with OCL, incorporated from Eiffel, or the dynamic binding of object orientation. The sad thing is that these three elements are mutually not sufficiently integrated. The relation-based semantics are not integrated with object orientation, because the state participation is undefined and the relational semantics do not fit the encapsulation principle. OCL does not care much about the object-oriented structure; instead it navigates along the core ER diagram. However, OCL is not as powerful as the relational calculus, at least not without workarounds using the metalevel.

Given a "design by contract" specification in a class, what is the implication of this specification for the subclasses? Our answer is based on the Barbara-Liskov principle. The subclasses must fulfill stronger constraints. For the application of this rule it is important not to use preconditions as such since preconditions are not constraints; the notation with pre- and postconditions has to be translated into a single temporal constraint which combines both parts and which has the form if(precondition)then postcondition. The rule stated above that the constraints have to be stronger in subclasses has to be applied to this constraint as a whole.

A rarely mentioned fact should be taken into account, namely that on the specification level this demand is achievable purely syntactically. This works by adding the constraint of the superclass by logical conjunction to the constraint of the subclass. This again opens up another possibility: the demand can be dropped and built into the semantics, stating that the conditions of the superclasses remain. Under this rule, as one can see, dynamic binding looks much different on the specification level than in the target platforms. While in the target platforms the method of the superclass can be completely replaced, the specifications can only be extended.

However, we have pinpointed one element in the feature set of UML, which is more abstract in some sense than a programming language, and this is simply the fact that UML allows for declarative specifications. However, this kind of abstraction has been around for a long time, and it has simply not prevailed as a useful tool for typical industry programming projects. The crucial problem is, and always has been, that it is so abstract that it is not executable. There is no automatic tool to translate all the specifications into code, as we mentioned earlier. As a consequence, e.g., regarding inheritance, this means that the constraint conservation rule cannot be checked in programming paradigms.

UML has added no new solutions for the problems, which have for decades impeded any effort to use this specification technology in everyday project work.

The advantage of our approach with regard to the model-driven architecture is that our approach has a defined notion of high-level programming which can be translated to target platforms. The emphasis here is not on providing yet another version of platform independence, but on abstracting from technical details by the use of the high-level programming paradigm. One instance of this is that our approach offers an integrated transactional virtual machine model, tailoring it to fit enterprise systems modeling.

Summary

We want to summarize the concepts of form orientation. Form-oriented analysis is a holistic approach to software development of a certain ubiquitous kind of system, which is characterized by our definition of submit/response style interaction. Form-oriented analysis pursues a neutral concentration on the everyday tasks of the working software developer. It integrates software development best practices with a couple of entirely new concepts on the level of an abstract software system viewpoint. Then concepts are derived on all levels of technology. Form-oriented analysis introduces new artifacts, namely page diagrams, form storyboards, and formcharts, which differ in formality and expressiveness.

This book presented two kinds of contributions. The first kind concerns the modeling process of submit/response style applications. The most important contributions of this kind are summarized in Sect. 17.1. The second kind of contributions concerns advances of a general nature. These advances go beyond the immediate application within form-oriented analysis, but the application of these concepts in form-oriented analysis is more than sufficient justification of them. We summarize contributions of this kind in Sect. 17.2.

17.1 Contributions to Modeling Form-Based Systems

Form-oriented analysis brings the following benefits for the analysis of submit/response style systems:

Domain-Specific Modeling. Our modeling contributions start from a defined application domain. The modeling methods are developed towards this concrete area. We do not start out with the claim of presenting a universal method, able to model all systems from embedded systems to computing grids. Of course we can expect to find other application areas for our approaches. But they will show up through time. This approach is therefore a more patient one.

Black-Box Modeling at the User Interface. We follow a particularly fundamental and mature approach to system modeling, namely the black-box modeling approach. The interface of our black box is the user interface, hence the only computer interface that can be touched by the user. In order to make the black-box modeling work we have to define the human–computer interaction paradigm we want to use, namely submit/response style systems.

Submit/Response Style Systems. The human–computer interaction is modeled as a strictly alternating message exchange between user and system. The system messages have the character of reports; they do not change once they have been sent to the user. After submission of a form the next page is shown automatically. In the submit/response style user interface model the user action of providing a message to the system is intricately combined with the previous system message in that the form is embedded into the report and the presented information can be directly and symbolically reused by the user. Submit/response style systems are successful, due to their advantageous software system architecture, which fosters scalability and maintainability.

Two-Staged Interaction Paradigm. Submit/response style systems are the natural solution for a wide range of business and administrative applications. Working with submit/response style systems has cognitive advantages because of an inherently easy form metaphor. The next message the user wants to send to the system appears as a form, which can be edited by the user and then submitted. Therefore submit/response style systems follow a two-staged interaction paradigm. The work is divided by single explicit system interaction points into protected bunches of work concerning editing single forms. Form-oriented analysis relies on defined user interface modeling as an integral part of requirements specification and analysis. It exploits the two-staged interaction paradigm to define bipartite state transition diagrams for modeling user interfaces, namely form storyboards and formcharts.

Transparency of Page Interaction. In modeling the submit/response style interface we have an elegant abstraction from the detailed workings of the input devices. There is no need to model the fine-grained interaction of the user with the page in order to fill out forms and to navigate between input forms. This user interaction is *transparent*, i.e., the user and the modeler have the impression that the user works directly on the form.

Direct Manipulation of Opaque References. The form metaphor goes beyond the paper form metaphor, especially concerning the dealing with references to entities in the system. The user can manipulate the references abstractly, without seeing their internal representations, i.e., as numerical keys or whatever. This knowledge not only can be used to create new widgets for conventional browsers, it can also be used to create a novel integrated client concept altogether.

Page Diagrams. How could you start working on a project developing a web-based application? You could start by painting the system welcome page on a blackboard. Then you could continue to paint more and more pages and to connect them with arrows representing links or possible form submissions.

This would be a rational way to actuate modeling of a submit/response style software system. Page diagrams offer a conceptual basis. Though natural, the outlined process may quickly become bulky. But with a good concept of model decomposition the process can be intuitively split into manageable parts. Well-understood page diagram modeling will help. Page diagrams are coarse-grained state transition diagrams.

Form Storyboards. Form storyboards are designed with respect to informal communication between domain experts and system analysts. The special way that signatures of server actions are visualized as forms make form storyboards capable of serving as mock-up prototypes. Form storyboards can be transformed into formcharts without structural friction.

Fully Typed Modeling. Using the fundamental concept of static typing rigorously in the modeling approach pays off. The static types give an easy interpretation of the finiteness of the state model. We can use the type system itself as the definition language for pages as well as for forms. The type system therefore replaces a markup language and immediately yields maximal separation of content from presentation. The pure type description of the pages and forms creates a user interface model, which is bare metal and high-level at the same time. The consistent use of the type system also allows for an unprecedented amount of reuse. For example, the same record definition may be used in the page description, the form definition, the database model, as well as in all mediating business operations.

Formcharts. Formcharts depict the bipartite state machine of a dialogue model. They are used for rigorous software system specification. They are annotated with precise dialogue specifications and are integrated with a layered data model.

Model Union. The defined model composition of form-oriented diagrams is based on pure graph union. As a result, model pieces resulting from a decomposition are again self-contained models. However, they are themselves no model elements. The concept of model union we describe is simple yet versatile. It keeps the management of the models orthogonal to the models.

Feature-Driven Approach. Consider the following simple system requirement: the user wants to reach an overview page from everywhere. In a use-case-based approach it is not obvious how to model this feature. A use-case-driven requirement elicitation can easily fail in finding this feature. The form-oriented diagrams introduce a notation for system state collections, which enables modeling general features. Model decomposition ensures the maintainability of features.

Layered Data Modeling. Form-oriented analysis explicitly admits nontransparency for phenomena that are well understood and which can and must be considered during early phases of software engineering. In form-oriented analysis the data model is layered. It consists of an information model for persistent data and a user message model for data that are exchanged during human–system interaction. Data types of the information model have defined semantics with respect to the message model: every information model type implicitly introduces an opaque reference type.

Dialogue Specification. Dialogue specifications annotate the formchart. They are written with respect to both the layered data model and the dialogue history. For every formchart element several kinds of specifications are predefined and given semantics. Several kinds of specifications can be identified that constitute no specification overhead because they can be recovered directly during system implementation.

Taking Transactions Seriously. Transactions are of crucial importance for enterprise applications. The achievement of the sophisticated transactional core technologies, the database and the transaction monitor, is the establishment of a virtual machine, in which every transaction client has a virtual serial view of the transactional core system. These transactional clients are supposed to finish transactions quickly and automatically. The transactional paradigm has such serious implications that it dominates the system architecture. Many universal modeling techniques fail to address transactionality with adequate high priority. Our modeling method gives the transactional paradigm a central and leading role. In a strict ranking of priorities it is decided that nice metaphors like object orientation are not of great use if there is no clear compatibility with transactionality.

Dialogue Patterns. Form-oriented analysis is not about modeling bottle receivers, traffic lights, coffee machines, elevators, etc. The world of form orientation is the mundane world of forms, i.e., purchase orders, receipts, invoices, etc. What are the workflow patterns dealing with these entities with respect to human–computer interactions? Form orientation enables the formulation of such dialogue patterns: from the outset examples from real-world enterprise applications are provided.

Forward and Reverse Engineering of Presentation Layers. The language Angie is a specification language for web-based presentation layers that is oriented towards the NSP type system. The language Angie can be seen as a textual format of formcharts. It is exploited by the tools JSPick and Angie. The JSPick tool is a design recovery tool for Java Server Pages based web presentation layers. JSPick generates high-level system descriptions in an Angie dialect. The Angie tool generates a complete Java Server Pages based prototypical dialogue from a high-level system description.

Strongly Typed Server Pages. The NSP technology is a server pages technology that is fully integrated with the concepts of form-oriented analysis. A notion of correctness is defined that can be statically checked and ensures a type-safe interplay of generated forms and targeted server pages as well as the generation of valid documents with respect to a defined user interface description language. A formal definition of the static semantics of the NSP technology has been given as a Per Martin-Löf style type system.

17.2 Contributions to Modeling in General

Artifact Orientation. We do not prescribe a process. Instead we pursue artifact orientation from the outset. Well-understood artifacts are a key in software development in their own right. The implicit objective of some state-of-the-art software processes is to decouple artifacts from processes, however, resulting in sometimes complex, e.g., spiral or two-dimensional structures. Despite defined tailoring, some of these processes tend towards clumsy prescriptiveness and micro management. There are a great many project driving forces. They are different in every project. We doubt that it is possible to have a general purpose software development process, unless it is ultra-lightweight. Artifact orientation is about posing a permanent question: how to proceed in order to contribute most effectively to the growth and quality of a defined project-dependent artifact set.

High-Level Programming. A constraint-based specification is in general not executable. It can be incomplete, unique, or unsatisfiable. Moreover, it can be redundant. The satisfiability is in general not a mechanically decidable question. This not only limits automatic generation of systems, it may also be unwanted from a modeling point of view, since both the generator and the modeler may find it hard to understand some models. High-level programming refers to the concept of having a programming paradigm on the same level as the constraint specification paradigm, which allows a guaranteed unique and executable specification to be given. This is in many cases the more natural definition, e.g., for a simple insert operation the specification with pre- and postconditions can be cumbersome in comparison to an insert command. Imperative-style programming is not necessarily less abstract than declarative.

Business Logic Modeling. Our modeling method gives an implicit definition of what business logic is supposed to be. The models in our method are business logic. These models contain only information on the abstraction level of business programming. Our models can be viewed as being executable on a virtual business machine. This virtual business machine is in fact a worldwide net of businesses interacting with each other and with their clients. Our modeling method presents a logical view on applications, just as SQL provides a logical view on data. Business modeling forms a defined abstraction layer. We propose to use business modeling as a fixed part of an artifact-oriented software development approach. It is the core of the functional specification of a system.

Business Logic Programming. The combination of the concepts of business modeling and high-level programming is business logic programming. It can be seen as the continuation of the concept of fourth generation languages for enterprise applications. It is a conceptual abstraction from and consequent extension of 4GLs towards non-proprietary solutions, whereas 4GLs have become typically product-specific solutions.

The Business Web. The basic programming paradigm and therefore the virtual machine of our high-level programming approach is the transactional business network, the business web. This is a virtual distributed execution platform that spans organizations. We have identified message-based communication as the feasible paradigm which allows the realization of the virtual machine on current platforms. The abstract machine model consists of a set of automata, which represent enterprise systems, and which communicate by messages. This network and automaton model allow a transactional coupling of systems so that each message to an automaton is processed in a local transaction on this automaton.

Non-Universal Programming. By avoiding WHILE type loops or freestyle recursion a high-level programming paradigm can even be made total, i.e., programs always terminate. This non-Turing-universality can be found, for example, in SQL. Even if the restrictions found there may be too restrictive, it must be said that typical classes of business logic do not need computational universality. A high-level programming paradigm can help in making it necessary to explicitly enable higher complexity classes.

Transactional Programming. The high-level programming paradigm of choice for transactional applications is imperative in its style, but due to the possibility of user aborts this paradigm goes beyond other imperative paradigms in crucial aspects. The same has to be said with respect to the update commands themselves, which have concurrent semantics not found in many other imperative programming paradigms.

State History Diagrams. State history diagrams unify statecharts and class diagrams. The visit of a state implicitly causes the instantiation of an object, so that the history of a state machine run is given by a history object path. This log warehouse is used in form-oriented analysis to give precise though still lightweight semantics to the temporal aspects of the dialogue constraint language.

History Log Warehouse. Many typical tasks in enterprise applications can be seen as accessing logged data, i.e., write-only data. The history log warehouse is an operational approach to temporal modeling, which identifies executable temporal queries. It serves as a basis for a fundamental understanding of business logic patterns. It allows a more regular business logic design.

Integrated Source Code Model. The models and programs are seen as data and are therefore instances of ordinary data types. The modeling methods including the form-oriented interface can be used to define source code manipulation on a high level. The integrated source code model can abstract from many problems like name collisions.

Bipartite Modeling of Finite Aspects. The bipartite modeling we have introduced for formcharts is valuable for all finite state modeling problems, where the finite state model is only an aspect of the system and is accompanied by a more complex system model. As a complex state we see every system, which is described by a data model and actual algorithms acting on the data model. The specification of such finite state behavior by a bipartite state machine enforces the separation of concerns. The finite state machine alternates between receptive states, which listen for the next event, and reactive states, which react to an event and are left automatically in order to return to a receptive state. These bipartite finite state models have the natural property that a single event type leads to a single transition from a receptive to a reactive state. The bipartite structure actually models a fact of the system, namely that the system does change the state with the reception of the event. The bipartite model pays tribute to the fact that in the addressed type of complex systems the reaction is indeed a computation and therefore extended in time, even if it is terminated automatically. Bipartite modeling is the cornerstone of the user interface model of form-oriented analysis.

References

1. M. Abadi, L. Cardelli. A Theory of Primitive Objects – Untyped and First-Order Systems. In: Proceedings of the International Conference on Theoretical Aspects of Computer Software, LNCS 789. Springer, 1994, pp.296–320.
2. M. Abadi, L. Cardelli. A Theory Of Objects. Springer, 1996.
3. A. Abran, J.W. Moore, P. Bourue, R. Dupuis (Eds.). SWEBOK – Guide to the Software Engineering Body of Knowledge, Trial Version 1.00. IEEE Press, May 2001.
4. D.H. Akehurst, B. Bordbar. On Querying UML Data Models with OCL. In: The Unified Modeling Language, Modeling Languages, Concepts, and Tools, 4th International Conference, LNCS 2185. Springer, 2001.
5. B. Alabiso. Transformation of Data Flow Analysis Models to Object Oriented Design. In: Proceedings of the Conference on Object-Oriented Programming Systems, Languages and Applications 1988 (OOPSLA 1988). ACM Press, 1988.
6. C. Alexander. A Pattern Language – Towns, Buildings, Construction. Oxford University Press, 1977.
7. C. Alexander. Patterns in Architecture. Keynote Speech, OOSPLA '96 – Object-Oriented Programming, Systems, Languages, and Applications. Conference Video, 1996.
8. G. Alonso, F. Casati, H. Kuno, V. Machiraju.Web Services – Concepts, Architectures and Applications. Springer, 2004.
9. R.M. Amadio, L. Cardelli. Subtyping Recursive Types. ACM Transactions on Languages and Systems, vol. 15, no. 4., pp.575–631, September 1993.
10. K.W. Angell. Python Server Pages (PSP), Part I. Dr. Dobbs Journal, January 2000.
11. G. Antoniol, G. Canfora, G. Casazza, A.D. Lucia. Web site reengineering using RMM. In: Proceedings of the International Workshop on Web Site Evolution, pp.9–16, March 2000.
12. Aristotle. Metaphysics.
13. Aristotle. Poetic.
14. Aristotle. Rhetoric.
15. D. Atkins et al. Integrated Web and Telephone Service Creation. Bell Labs Technical Journal, vol. 2, no.1, 1997.
16. D. Atkins et al. Experience with a Domain Specific Language for Form-based Services. Software Production Research Department, Bell Laboratories, Lucent Technologies, 1997.

17. D. Atkins et al. Mawl: a domain-specific language for form-based services. In: IEEE Transactions on Software Engineering, vol. 25, no. 3, pp.334–346, 1999.
18. C. Atkinson, T. Kühne. Strict Profiles: Why and How. Proceedings of UML'2000, LNCS 1939. Springer, 2000.
19. H.P. Barendregt. Lambda Calculi with Types. In: S. Abramsky, D.V. Gabbay, T.S.E. Maibaum (Eds.), Handbook of Logic in Computer Science, vol. 2, pp.118–331. Clarendon Press, 1992.
20. K. Beck. Extreme Programming Explained – Embrace Change. Addison-Wesley, 2000.
21. H.D. Benington. Production of Large Computer Programs. In: Proceedings of the ONR Symposium on Advanced Programming Methods for Digital Computers, June 1956.
22. T. Berners-Lee, D. Connolly. Hypertext Markup Language – 2.0, RFC 1866. Network Working Group. November 1995.
23. P.A. Bernstein, E. Newcomer. Principles of Transaction Processing – For the Systems Professional. Morgan Kaufmann, 1997.
24. P.V. Biron, A. Malhotra. XML Schema Part 2: Datatypes. W3C Recommendation, May 2001.
25. D. Bjørner, C.B. Jones (Ed.). The Vienna Development Method: The Meta-Language. LNCS 61. Springer, 1978.
26. B.W. Boehm. A spiral model of software development and enhancement. IEEE Computer, vol. 21, no. 5, pp.61–72, 1988.
27. B.W. Boehm et al. Software Cost Estimation with Cocomo II. Prentice Hall, 2000.
28. G. Booch. Object-Oriented Analysis and Design, Benjamin/Cummings, 1994.
29. J.R. Borck. WebSphere Studio Application Developer 4.0. JavaWorld, March 2003.
30. D. Box et al. Simple Object Access Protocol (SOAP) 1.1 – W3C Note, May 2000.
31. T. Bray, J. Paoli, C.M. Sperberg-McQueen, Eve Maler. Extensible Markup Language (XML) 1.0 (Second Edition). World Wide Web Consortium, 2000.
32. F.P. Brooks. The Mythical Man-month – Essays on Software Engineering. Addison-Wesley, 1975.
33. Frederick P. Brooks. No Silver Bullet – Essence and Accidents of Software Engineering. IEEE Computer, vol.20, no.4, April 1987.
34. D. Budgen, S. Burgees. A Simple Tool for Temporal Indexing of Hypertext Documents. In: IEEE Computer, vol. 31, pp.52–53, December 1998.
35. M.H. Butler. Current Technologies for Device Independence – HP Labs Technical Report HPL-2001-83. Hewlett-Packard Company, April 2001.
36. D. Cabeza, M. Hermenegildo. WWW Programming using Computational Logic Systems (and the PILLOW/CIAO Library). In: Proceedings of the Workshop on Logic Programming and the WWW, in conjunction with WWW6, April 1997.
37. D. Cabeza, M. Hermenegildo. The PiLLoW Web Programming Library Reference Manual. The CLIP Group, School of Computer Science, Technical University of Madrid, 2000.
38. D.M. Campbell, B.Czejdo, D.W. Embley. A Relationally Complete Query Language for an Entity-Relationship Model, In: Proceedings of the 4th International Conference on Entity-Relationship Approach, pp.90–97, October 1985.
39. L. Cardelli. Type systems. In: Handbook of Computer Science and Engineering. CRC Press, 1997.

40. L. Cardelli, P. Wegner. On Understanding Types, Data Abstraction, and Polymorphism. In: Computing Surveys, Vol. 17, No. 4, pp. 471–522. ACM, 1985.
41. F. Cardone, M. Coppo. Type Inference with Recursive Types: Syntax and Semantics. Information and Computation, vol. 92, no. 1, pp. 48–80, 1990.
42. R.G.G. Cattell (Ed.). The Object Database Standard: ODMG 2.0. Morgan Kaufmann, 1997.
43. M.V. Cengarle, A. Knapp. A Formal Semantics for OCL 1.4. In: The Unified Modeling Language, Modeling Languages, Concepts, and Tools, 4th International Conference, LNCS 2185. Springer, 2001.
44. Central Computer and Telecommunications Agency. IT Infrastructure Library – Service Support. Renouf, 2000.
45. S. Ceri, P. Fraternali, S. Paraboschi. Web Modeling Language, (WebML): a modeling language for designing Web sites. Proceedings of the 9th. International World Wide Web Conference, Elsevier, 2000, pp.137–157.
46. S. Ceri, P. Fraternali, A. Bongio, A. Maurino. Modeling data entry and operations in WebML, WebDB 2000, Dallas, 2000.
47. A.F. Chalmers. What is This Thing Called Science? University of Queensland Press, 1999.
48. D. de Champeaux, L. Constantine, I. Jacobson, S. Mellor, P. Ward, E. Yourdon. PANEL: Structured Analysis and Object Oriented Analysis. In: Proceedings of ECOOP/OOPSLA'90. ACM Press, 1990.
49. P.P.-S. Chen. The Entity-Relationship Model – Toward a Unified View of Data. ACM Transactions on Database Systems, vol.1, no.1, pp.9–36, March 1976.
50. E.J. Chikofsky, J.H. Cross, II. Reverse engineering and design recovery: A taxonomy. IEEE Software, pp.13–17, January 1990.
51. E. Christensen, F. Curbera, G. Meredith, S. Weerawarana. Web Services Description Language (WSDL) 1.1. Ariba, International Business Machines Corporation, Microsoft. July 2001.
52. J. Clark, S. DeRose. XML Path Language (XPath) Version 1.0 – W3C Recommendation 16. World Wide Web Consortium, November 1999.
53. T. Clark, J. Warmer (Eds.). Object Modeling with the OCL: the Rationale behind the Object Constraint Language. LNCS 2263. Springer, 2002.
54. P. Coad, E. Yourdon. Object-Oriented Analysis. Prentice Hall, 1990.
55. P. Coad. Object Models – Strategies, Patterns, and Applications. Yourdon Press, 1995.
56. P. Coad, D. North, M. Mayfield. Strategies and Patterns Handbook. Object International, Inc. 1997.
57. K.A.L. Coar, D.R.T Robinson .The WWW Common Gateway Interface – Version 1.1, Internet-draft, June 1999.
58. E.F. Codd. The Relational Model for Database Management: Version 2. Addison-Wesley, 1990.
59. D. Coleman, P. Arnold, S. Bodoff, C. Dollin, H. Gilchrist, F. Hayes, P. Jeremes. Object-Oriented Development – The FUSION Method. Prentice Hall, 1994.
60. B.P. Collins, J.E. Nicholls, I.H. Sørensen. Introducing Formal Methods: the CICS experience with Z. Technical Report TR 12.2777, IBM Hursley Park, December 1990.
61. J. Conallen. Modeling Web Application Architectures with UML. Communications of the ACM, vol. 42, no. 10, pp.63–70, 1999.
62. J. Conallen. Building Web Applications with UML. Addison Wesley, 2003.

63. D.W. Connolly. Document Type Definition for the HyperText Markup Language, level 2. World Wide Web Consortium, 1995.
64. S. Cook, J. Daniels. Designing Object Systems: Object-Oriented Modeling with Syntropy. Prentice Hall, 1994.
65. S. Cook, A. Kleppe, R. Mitchell, B. Rumpe, J. Warmer, A. Wills. The Amsterdam Manifesto on OCL. Object Modeling with the OCL – The Rationale behind the Object Constraint Language, pp. 115–149. Springer, 2002.
66. B. Courcelle. Fundamental Properties of Infinite Trees. In: Theoretical Computer Science 25, pp.95–169. North-Holland, 1983.
67. P. Cousot. Program Analysis: The Abstract Interpretation Perspective. SIGPLAN Notices, vol. 32, pp.73–76, 1997.
68. K. Cox, T. Ball, J.C. Ramming. Lunchbot: A tale of two ways to program web services. Technical Report BL0112650-960216-06TM, AT&T Bell Laboratories, 1996.
69. K. Crary, R. Harper, S. Puri. What is a recursive module? In: Proceedings of the ACM Conference on Programming Language Design and Implementation, pp.50–63, May 1999.
70. D. Crocker P. Overell (Eds.). Augmented BNF for Syntax Specifications: ABNF. RFC 2234. Network Working Group, November 1997.
71. J.F. e Cunha, N.J. Nunes. Towards a UML Profile for Interaction Design: The Wisdom Approach. Proceedings of UML'2000, LNCS 1939, Springer 2000.
72. K. Czarnecki, U. Eisenecker. Generative Programming – Methods, Tools, and Applications. Addison-Wesley, 2000.
73. W. Damm, D. Harel. LSCs: Breathing Life Into Message Sequence Charts. Technical Report CS98-09, The Weizmann Institute of Science, Dept. of Applied Mathematics and Computer Science, April 1998.
74. W. Damm, D. Harel. LSCs: Breathing Life Into Message Sequence Charts. Formal Methods in System Design, vol. 19, pp.45–80, 2001.
75. J.D. Davidson, S. Ahmed. Java Servlet Specification, v2.1a. Sun Press, 1999.
76. J.D. Davidson, D. Coward. Java Servlet Specification, v2.2. Sun Press, 1999.
77. M. Davis. Struts, an open-source MVC implementation. IBM developerWorks, February 2001.
78. P. Delisle. Java Server Pages Standard Tag Library – version 1.0. Sun Microsystems, June 2002.
79. T. DeMarco. Structured Analysis and System Specification. Prentice Hall, 1979.
80. B. Demo, A. DiLeva, P. Giolito. An Entity-Relationship Query Language. In: Proceedings of the IFIP WG8.1 Working Conference on Theoretical and Formal Aspects of Information Systems, pp.19–32. North-Holland, 1985.
81. B. Demuth, H. Hussmann, S. Loecher. OCL as a Specification Language for Business Rules in Database Applications. In: The Unified Modeling Language, Modeling Languages, Concepts, and Tools, 4th International Conference, LNCS 2185. Springer, 2001.
82. S. DeRose, E. Maler, D. Orchard. XML Linking Language (XLink) Version 1.0 – W3C Recommendation. World Wide Web Consortium, June 2001.
83. A. van Deursen, P. Klint, J. Visser. Domain-Specific Languages: An Annotated Bibliography. ACM SIGPLAN Notices, vol. 35, no. 6, pp.26–36, June 2000.
84. Deutsches Institut für Normung. Deutsche Industrienorm DIN 66001. Sinnbilder für Datenfluß und Programmablaufpläne. DIN, September 1966.
85. M.E. Dickover. Principles of Coupling and Cohesion for Use in the Practice of SADT. Technical Publication 039. SofTech Inc., 1976.

86. M.E. Dickover, C.L. McGowan, D.T. Ross. Software design using SADT. In: Proceedings of the 1977 Annual Conference. ACM Press, 1977, pp. 125–133.
87. E.W. Dijkstra. Go to statement considered harmful. Communications of the ACM, vol. 11, no. 3, pp.147–148, 1968.
88. D. Dori, M. Goodman. From Object-Process analysis to Object-Process design. Annals of Software Engineering, vol. 2, pp.25–50, 1996.
89. D. Dori. Object-Process Methodology applied to modeling credit card transactions. Journal of Database Management, vol. 12, no. 1, pp.4–14, 2001.
90. D. Draheim, G. Weber. An Introduction to Form Storyboarding. Technical Report B-02-06, Institute of Computer Science, Freie Universität Berlin, March 2002.
91. D. Draheim, G. Weber. An Introduction to State History Diagrams. Technical Report B-02-09, Institute of Computer Science, Freie Universität Berlin, March 2002.
92. D. Draheim, G. Weber. Form Charts and Dialogue Constraints. Technical Report B-02-08, Institute of Computer Science, Freie Universität Berlin, March 2002.
93. D. Draheim, G. Weber. Strongly Typed Server Pages. In: Proceedings of the 5th Workshop on Next Generation Information Technologies and Systems, LNCS 2382. Springer, 2002.
94. D. Draheim, E. Fehr, G. Weber. JSPick – A Server Pages Design Recovery Tool. In: Proceedings of the 7th European Conference on Software Maintenance and Reengineering. IEEE Press, 2003.
95. D. Draheim, G. Weber. Storyboarding Form-Based Interfaces. In: Proceedings of INTERACT 2003 – the 9th IFIP TC13 International Conference on Human-Computer Interaction. IOS Press, 2003.
96. D. Draheim, E. Fehr, G. Weber. Improving the Web Presentation Layer Architecture. In: X. Zhou, Y. Zhang, M.E. Orlowska (Eds.), Web Technologies and Applications, LNCS 2642. Springer, 2003.
97. D. Draheim, G. Weber. Modeling Submit/Response Style Systems with Form Charts and Dialogue Constraints. In: Proceedings of the Workshop on Human Computer Interface for Semantic Web and Web Applications, LNCS 2889. Springer, 2003.
98. D. Draheim, C. Lutteroth, G. Weber. Factory: Statically Type-Safe Integration of Genericity and Reflection. In: Proceedings of the 4th International Conference on Software Engineering, Artificial Intelligence, Networking, and Parallel/Distributed Computing. ACIS, 2003.
99. D. Draheim, C. Lutteroth, G. Weber. An Analytical Comparison of Generative Programming Technologies. Technical Report B-04-02, Institute of Computer Science, Freie Universität Berlin, January 2004.
100. D. Draheim, G. Weber. Specification and Generation of Model 2 Web Interfaces. In: Proceedings of the 6th Asia-Pacific Conference on Computer-Human Interaction. LNCS 3101 Springer, 2004.
101. D. Draheim, G. Weber. Co-Knowledge Acquisition of Software Organizations and Academy. In: Proceedings of the 6th International Workshop on Learning Software Organisations. LNCS 3096. Springer, 2004.
102. D. Draheim, C. Lutteroth, G. Weber. Source Code Independent Reverse Engineering of Dynamic Web Sites. Technical Report B-04-10, Institute of Computer Science, Freie Universität Berlin, June 2004.

103. D. Draheim, C. Lutteroth, G. Weber. Generator Code Opaque Recovery of Form-Oriented Web Site Models. In: Proceedings of the 11th IEEE Working Conference on Reverse Engineering. IEEE Press, 2004.

104. D. Draheim, G. Weber. The Data Access Languages DAL and TDAL. Research Report UoA-SE-2004-2, Department of Computer of Computer Science, University of Auckland, October 2004.

105. M. Dubinko, S. Schnitzenbaumer, M. Wedel, D. Raggett. XForms Requirements – W3C Working Draft. World Wide Web Consortium, April 2001.

106. M. Dubinko, L.L. Klotz, R. Merrick, T.V. Raman. XForms 1.0. – W3C Working Draft. World Wide Web Consortium. August 2002.

107. ECMA – European Computer Manufacturer's Association. Standard ECMA-262 – ECMAScript Language Specification. ECMA Standardizing Information and Communication Systems, 1999.

108. R. Elmasri, G. Wiederhold. GORDAS: A Formal High-Level Query Language for the Entity-Relationship Model. In: Proceedings of the 2nd Conference on the Entity-Relationship Approach to Information Modeling and Analysis. North-Holland, 1981.

109. M.A. Emmelhainz. EDI: A Total Management Guide. Van Nostrand Reinhold, 1993.

110. G. Engels, M. Gogolla, U. Hohenstein, K. Hulsmann, P. Lohr-Richter, G. Saake, H.-D. Ehrich. Conceptual modeling of database applications using an extended ER model. Data & Knowledge Engineering, vol. 9, no. 4, pp.157–204, 1992.

111. G. Engels, U. Hohenstein. SQL/EER – Syntax and Semantics of an Entity-Relationship-Based Query Language. In: Information Systems, vol. 14, no. 3, pp.209–242, 1992.

112. W.K. English, D.C. Engelbart, M.L. Berman. Display Selection Techniques for Text Manipulation. IEEE Transactions on Human Factors in Electronics, vol. 8, pp.5–15, 1967.

113. R.T. Fielding, J. Gettys, J.C. Mogul, H. Frystyk, L. Masinter, P. Leach, T. Berners-Lee. Hypertext Transfer Protocol – HTTP/1.1. RFC 2616. IETF – Network Working Group, The Internet Society, June 1999.

114. D. Flanagan. JavaScript: The Definitive Guide. O'Reilly, 2002.

115. J. Foreman, K. Brune, P. McMillan, R. Rosenstein. Software Technology Review. Software Engineering Institute, Carnegy Mellon University, July 1997.

116. M. Fowler. UML Distilled – Applying the Standard Object Modeling Language. Addison-Wesley, 1997.

117. M. Fowler. Analysis Patterns: Reusable Object Models. Addison-Wesley, 1997.

118. A. Gal, J. Mylopoulos. Towards Web-Based Application Management Systems IEEE Transactions on Knowledge and Data Engineering, vol. 13, no. 4, pp. 683–702, 2001.

119. E. Gamma et al. Design Patterns. Addison-Wesley, 1995.

120. C. Gane. Rapid Systems Development Using Structured Techniques and Relational Technology. Prentice Hall, 1989.

121. C. Gane, T. Sarson. Structured Systems Analysis: Tools & Techniques. Improved System Technologies. New York, 1977.

122. C. Gane, T. Sarson. Structured Systems Analysis: Tools & Techniques. Prentice Hall, 1979.

123. V. Gapayev, M.Y. Levin, B.C. Pierce. Recursive Subtyping Revealed. SIGPLAN Notices, vol. 35, no. 9., pp.221–231. ACM Press, 2000.

124. Gartner Group. Survey Results: The Real Cost of E-Commerce Sites. Gartner Group, 1999.

125. M. Gogolla, M. Richters. On Constraints and Queries in UML. The Unified Modeling Language – Technical Aspects and Applications, Physica-Verlag, 1998, pp.109–121.

126. J.A. Goguen, J.W. Thatcher, E.G. Wagner. An Initial Algebra Approach to the Specification, Correctness and Implementation of Abstract Data Types. IBM Research Report RC 6487, 1976.

127. J. Gosling, B. Joy, G. Steele, G. Bracha: The Java Language Specification. Addison-Wesley, 1996.

128. M. Grand. Patterns in Java – A Catalog of Reusable Design Patterns. Wiley, 1998.

129. P. Graunke, S. Krishnamurthi, S. van der Hoeven, M. Felleisen. Programming the web with high-level programming languages. In European Symposium on Programming, 2001.

130. J. Gray, A. Reuter. Transcation Processing: Concepts and Techniques. Morgan Kaufmann, 1993.

131. M. Green. A Survey of Three Dialogue Models. ACM Transactions on Graphics, vol. 5, no. 3, pp.244–275, 1987.

132. M. Große-Rhode. Semantic Integration of Heterogeneous Software Specifications. Springer, 2004.

133. J. Grundy, N. Zhu, J. Hosking. Pounamu: a meta-tool for multi-view visual language environment construction. In: Proceedings of the IEEE Symposium on Visual Languages and Human-Centric Computing. IEEE Press, 2004.

134. C.A. Gunter. Semantics of Programming Languages – Structures and Techniques. The MIT Press, 1992.

135. H. Haas, D. Orchard. Web Services Architecture Usage Scenarios – W3C Working Draft. World Wide Web Consortium, July 2002.

136. F. Halasz, M. Schwartz. The Dexter hypertext reference model. Communications of the ACM, vol. 37, no. 2, pp.30–39, February 1994.

137. G. Hamilton (Ed.). Java Beans version 1.0.1. Sun Microsystems, July 1997.

138. M. Hanus. Server side Web scripting in Curry. In Workshop on (Constraint) Logic Programming and Software Engineering (LPSE2000), London, July 2000.

139. M. Hanus. High-level server side Web scripting in Curry. In: Practical Aspects of Declarative Languages, Proceedings of the 3rd International Workshop, LNCS 1990. Springer, 2001.

140. D. Harel. Statecharts: a Visual Formalism for Complex Systems. Science of Computer Programming, Elsevier Science, 1987, pp.231–274.

141. D. Harel, A. Naamad. The Statemate Semantics of Statecharts. ACM Transactions on Software Engineering and Methodology, vol. 5, no. 4, pp.293–333, 1996.

142. A.E. Hassan, R.C. Holt. Towards a Better Understanding of Web Applications. Proceedings of WSE 2001: International Workshop on Web Site Evolution, November 2001.

143. A.E. Hassan, R.C. Holt. Architecture Recovery of Web Applications. Proceedings of ICSE 2002: International Conference on Software Engineering, May 2002.

144. A.E. Hassan, R.C. Holt. A Visual Architectural Approach to Maintaining Web Applications. Annals of Software Engineering – Volume 16 – Special Volume on Software Visualization, 2003.

145. I.J. Hayes. Applying Formal Specification to Software Development in Industry. IEEE Transactions on Software Engineering, vol. 11, no. 2, pp.169–178, 1985.

146. P.J. Hayes. Executable Interface Definitions Using Form-Based Interface Abstractions. Advances in Human-Computer Interaction, vol. 1, pp.161–189, 1985.

147. I. Hayes. Specification Case Studies. Prentice Hall, 1993.

148. I. Hayes, C.B. Jones, J.E. Nicholls. Understanding the differences between VDM and Z. Newsletter of the British Computing Society, Formal Aspects of Computing Science Special Interest Group and Formal Methods Europe, series I, vol. 1, no. 1, pp.7–30, Autumn 1993.

149. C.A.R. Hoare. An Axiomatic Basis for Computer Programming. Communications of the ACM, vol. 12, no. 10, pp. 576–580, 1969.

150. P. Hudak, P. Wadler (Eds.). Report on the Programming Language Haskell Version 1.1. Computer Science Departments, Glasgow University and Yale University, August 1991.

151. J. Hughes. Generalising Monads to Arrows. Science of Computer Programming, vol. 37, pp.37–111, 2000.

152. R. Hull, R. King. Semantic database modeling: Survey, applications, and research issues. ACM Computing Surveys, vol. 19, no. 3, pp.201–260, 1987.

153. IBM Object-Oriented Technology Center. Developing Object-Oriented Software – An Experience-Based Approach. Prentice Hall, 1997, out of print.

154. IBM Corporation. Flowcharting Techniques. Technical Publication C20-8152-1, IBM Corporation, 1969.

155. IBM Corporation Software Group. Sabre Turns TPF Data into Business Asset with WebSphere MQ. IBM Corporation, 2002.

156. D. Ingalls. The Smalltalk-76 Programming System. In: Proceedings of the 5th Annual ACM Symposium on Principles of Programming Languages. ACM Press, 1987.

157. Institute of Electrical and Electronics Engineers. IEEE Standard 610.12-1990, IEEE Standard Glossary of Software Engineering Terminology, Software Engineering Standards Committee of the IEEE Computer Society, New York, 1990.

158. Institute of Electrical and Electronics Engineers. IEEE Standard 830-1993, Recommended Practice for Software Requirements Specifications, Software Engineering Standards Committee of the IEEE Computer Society, New York, 1993.

159. International Function Point User Group. Function Point Counting Practices, Release 4.1. IFPUG, May 1999.

160. International Telecommunication Union. Recommendation X.500: Information Technology – Open Systems – Interconnection – The Directory: Overview of concepts, models and services. ITU-T, 1999.

161. International Organization for Standardization. International Standard ISO 1028:1973. Information processing – Flowchart symbols. ISO, 1973.

162. International Organization for Standardization. International Standard ISO 5807:1985. Information processing – Documentation symbols and conventions for data, program and system flowcharts, program network charts and system resources charts. ISO, 1985.

163. International Organization for Standardization. International Standard ISO 8879. Information Processing – Text and Office Systems – Standard Generalized Markup Language (SGML). ISO, 1986.

164. International Organization for Standardization. International Standard ISO 9000-3:1991(E). Quality management and quality assurance standards – Part 3:

Guidelines for the application of ISO 9001 to the developement, supply and maintenance of software. ISO, 1991.

165. International Organization for Standardization. International Standard ISO 9241-10. Ergonomic Requirements for Office Work with Visual Display Terminals (VDTs) – Part 10: Dialogue Principles. ISO, 1991.

166. International Organization for Standardization. International Standard ISO 9001:1994(E). Quality systems – Model for quality assurance in design, developement, production, installation and servicing. ISO, 1994.

167. International Organization for Standardization. International Standard ISO/ICE 14977. Syntactic metalanguage – Extended BNF. ISO, 1996.

168. International Organization for Standardization. International Standard ISO/IEC 10744-1992(E). Information technology – Hypermedia/Time-based Structuring Language (HyTime). ISO, 1996.

169. International Organization for Standardization. International Standard ISO/IEC 16262. ECMAScript: A general purpose, cross-platform programming language. ISO, 1998.

170. International Organization for Standardization. International Standard 9075:1999. Information Technology – Database Language SQL. ISO, 1999.

171. International Organization for Standardization. International Standard ISO/IEC 13568. Information Technology, Z Formal Specification Notation, Syntax, Type System and Semantics. ISO 2002.

172. T. Isakowitz, E.A. Stohr, P. Balasubramanian. RMM: A Methodology for Structured Hypermedia Design. Communications of the ACM, vol. 38, no. 8, pp.34–44, 1995.

173. R.J.K. Jacob. Using Formal Specifications in the Design of a Human-Computer Interface. Communications of the ACM, vol. 26, no. 4, pp.259–264, 1983.

174. I. Jacobson. Object-Oriented Software Engineering: A Use Case Driven Approach. Addison-Wesley, 1992.

175. I. Jacobson, G. Booch, J. Rumbaugh. The Unified Software Development Process. Addison-Wesley, 1999.

176. J. Jensen. Generation of machine code in ALGOL compilers. BIT – Nordisk Tidskrift for Informations-Behandling, vol. 5, pp.235–245, 1965.

177. T. Jim, J. Palsberg. Type inference in systems of recursive types with subtyping. Manuscript, 1999.

178. S.P. Jones (Ed.). Report on the programming language Haskell 98. Technical Report YALEU/DCS/RR-1106, Yale University, CS Dept., February 1999.

179. Y.H. Kamath, R.E. Smilan, J.G. Smith. Reaping Benefits with Object-Oriented Technology. AT&T Technical Journal, vol. 72, no. 5, pp.14–24, 1993.

180. K. Kang, S. Cohen, J. Hess, W. Novak, A. Peterson. Feature-Oriented Domain Analysis (FODA) Feasibility Study. Carnegie Mellon Software Engineering Institute, Technical Report CMU/SEI-90-TR-021, 1990.

181. N. Kassem and the Enterprise Team. Designing Enterprise Applications with the Java 2 Platform, Enterprise Edition. Sun Microsystems, 2000.

182. A. Kay. The Reactive Engine. PhD thesis, University of Utah, September 1969.

183. C.F. Kemerer. Reliability of Function Points Measurement – A Field Experiment. Communications of the ACM, vol. 36, no.2, pp.85–97, 1993.

184. P. Kilpeläinen, D. Wood. SGML and Exceptions. Technical Report HKUST-CS96-03, Department of Computer Science, University of Helsinki, 1996.

185. B. Kirkerud. Object-oriented Programming with Simula. Addison-Wesley, 1989.

186. G.E. Krasner, S.T. Pope. A Cookbook for Using the Model-View-Controller User Interface Paradigm in Smalltalk-80. Journal of Object-Oriented Programming, August/September, pp.26–49, 1988.

187. D. Kristol, L. Montulli. HTTP State Management Mechanism. RFC 2109, Network Working Group. February 1997.

188. P. Kruchten. The Rational Unified Process. Addison-Wesley, 1999.

189. D.A. Ladd, J.C. Ramming. Programming the Web: An application-oriented language for hypermedia services. In 4th International World Wide Web Conference, 1995.

190. P.J. Landin. The Next 700 Programming Languages. Communications of the ACM, vol. 9, no. 2, pp. 157–165, March 1966.

191. J.A. Landay, B.A. Myers. Interactive Sketching for the Early Stages of User Interface Design. In: Proceedings of Human Factors in Computing Systems. ACM Press, May 1995, pp. 43–50.

192. C. Larman. Applying UML and Patterns. Prentice Hall, 1998.

193. H.D. Lasswell. The Structure and Function of Communication in Society. In: Bryson, Lyman (Ed.), The Communication of Ideas. Institute for Religious and Social Studies, 1948, pp. 37–51.

194. R. Lerdorf, K. Tatroe. Programming PHP. O'Reilly, 2002.

195. J. Liberty, D. Hurwitz. Programming APS.NET. O'Reilly, 2002.

196. B. Liskov. Keynote Address – Data Abstraction and Hierarchy. Addendum to the Proceedings on Object-oriented Programming Systems, Languages and Applications. ACM Press, 1987.

197. B. Liskov. Data Abstraction and Hierarchy. SIGPLAN Notices, vol. 23, no. 5, pp. 17–34, May 1988.

198. S.W. Loke, A. Davison. Logic Programming with the World-Wide Web. In: Proceedings of the 7th ACM Conference on Hypertext, ACM Press, pp.235–245, 1996.

199. G.A. Di Lucca, A.R. Fasolino, F. Pace, P. Tramontana, U. de Carlini. WARE: A Tool for the Reverse Engineering of Web Applications. In: 6th European Conference on Software Maintenance and Reengineering. IEEE, 2002.

200. R. Malan, D. Coleman, R. Letsinger. Lessons Learned from the Experiences of Leading-Edge Object Technology Projects in Hewlett-Packard. ACM SIGPLAN Notices, vol. 30, no. 10, pp.33–46, 1995.

201. D.A. Marca, C.L. McGowan. SADT: structured analysis and design technique. McGraw-Hill, 1987.

202. V.M. Markowitz. ERROL: an entity-relationship role oriented query language. In: Proceedings of the 3rd Conference on the Entity-Relationship Approach. North-Holland, 1983.

203. T.J. Marlowe, B.G. Ryder. Properties of data flow frameworks – A unified model. Acta Informatica, vol. 28, pp.121–163, 1990.

204. J. Marsh, D. Orchard. XML Inclusions (XInclude) Version 1.0 – W3C Working Draft. World Wide Web Consortium, May 2001.

205. J. Martin, J.J. Odell. Object-Oriented Analysis and Design. Prentice Hall, 1992.

206. P. Martin-Löf. Constructive Mathematics and Computer Programming. In: Logic, Methodology and Philosophy of Science, VI, 1979, pp.153–175. North-Holland, 1982.

207. P. Martin-Löf. Intuistionistic Type-Theory. Bibliopolis, 1984.

208. B. Matzke. ABAP/4 – Programming the SAP R/3 System (Second Edition). Addison-Wesley, 1999.
209. S. Mazzocchi, R. Rocha. Extensible Server Pages. The Apache Software Foundation, 2001.
210. S. McGlashan et al. Voice Extensible Markup Language (VoiceXML) Version 2.0, W3C Working Draft, October 2001.
211. P. McJones (Ed.). The 1995 SQL Reunion: People, Projects and Politics. SRC Technical Note 1997-018, Digital Systems Research Center, August 1997.
212. E. Meijer. Server-side Scripting in Haskell. Journal of Functional Programming, 2000.
213. E. Meijer, D. Leijen, J. Hook. Client-Side Web Scripting with HaskellScript. In: Practical Aspects of Declarative Languages (PADL), LNCS 1551, pp.96–210. Springer, 1999.
214. E. Meijer, Mark Shields. XMλ – A Functional Language for Constructing and Manipulating XML Documents. 2000.
215. E. Meijer, D. van Velzen. Haskell Server Pages – Functional Programming and the Battle for the Middle Tier. Electronic Notes in Theoretical Computer Science 41, no. 1, Elsevier Science, 2001.
216. A.O. Mendelzon, Z.-Q. Zhang. A Graphical Query Language for Entity-Relationship Databases. In: Proceedings of the 3rd Conference on the Entity-Relationship Approach, pp.441–448. North-Holland, 1983.
217. B. Meyer. Applying "design by contract." IEEE Computer, vol. 25, no. 10, pp.40–51, October 1992.
218. B. Meyer. Design by Contract. In: Dino Mandroli, Bertrand Meyer (Eds.), Advances in Object-Oriented Software Engineering. Prentice Hall, 1992.
219. B. Meyer. Eiffel, the Language. Prentice Hall, 1992.
220. Microsoft Developer Network. Official Guidelines for User Interface Developers and Designers. Microsoft Corporation, 2002.
221. Microsoft Corporation. Microsoft Agent – Software services to enhance the user interface of applications and Web pages. Data Sheet. Microsoft Corporation, 1999.
222. R. Mordani, J.D. Davidson, S. Boag. Java API for XML Processing Specification, v1.1. Sun Microsystems, 2001.
223. M.J. Muller. PICTIVE – an exploration in participatory design. In: Proceedings of the SIGCHI Conference on Human Factors in Computing Systems. ACM Press, 1991, pp. 225–231.
224. M.J. Muller. Retrospective on a year of participatory design using the PICTIVE technique. In: Procceddings of the SIGCHI Conference on Human Factors in Computing Systems. ACM Press, 1992, pp.455–462.
225. M.J. Muller, D.M. Wildman, E.A. White. Equal opportunity PD using PICTIVE. Communications of the ACM, vol. 36, no. 4, pp.64–66, 1993.
226. National Institute of Standards and Technology. Integrated Definition for Functional Modeling (IDEF0), Draft Federal Information Processing Standards Publication 183. U.S. Department of Commerce, December 1993.
227. P. Naur. The Design of the GIER ALGOL Compiler. BIT. Nordisk Tidskrift for Informations-Behandling, vol. 3, pp.124–140 and 145-166, 1963.
228. P. Naur. Checking of operand types in ALGOL compilers. BIT. Nordisk Tidskrift for Informations-Behandling, vol. 5, pp.151–163, 1965.

229. M.W. Newman, J. Lin, J.I. Hong, J.A. Landay. DENIM: An Informal Web Site Design Tool Inspired by Observations of Practice. Human-Computer Interaction, vol. 18, no. 3, pp. 259–324, 2003.

230. T. Nguyen, V. Srinivasan. Accessing Relational Databases from the World Wide Web. Proceedings of the 1996 ACM SIGMOD, 1996.

231. F. Nielson, H. Nielson, C. Hankin. Principles of Program Analysis. Springer, 1999.

232. J. Nielsen. The Art of Navigating through Hypertext. Communications of the ACM, vol. 33, no. 3, pp.296–310, 1990.

233. B. Nordström, K. Peterson, J.M. Smith. Programming in Martin-Löfs Type Theory. The International Series of Monographs on Computer Science. Clarendon Press, 1990.

234. K. Nørmark. Programming World Wide Web Pages in Scheme. Sigplan Notices, vol. 34, no. 12, pp.37–46, December 1999.

235. K. Nørmark. Programmatic WWW authoring using Scheme and LAML. The 11th International World Wide Web Conference 2002, March 2002.

236. K. Nygaard, O.-J. Dahl. The Development of the SIMULA Languages. The 1st ACM SIGPLAN Conference on History of Programming Languages, pp.245–272. ACM Press, 1978.

237. Object Management Group. OMG Unified Modeling Language Specification, version 1.5, March 2003.

238. Object Management Group. UML 2.0 OCL Specification, OMG Adopted Specification ptc/03-10-14, October 2003.

239. Office of Government Commerce Staff. Ict Infrastructure Management. Bernan, 2002.

240. M.C.F. Oliveira, M.A.S.T. Turine, P.C. Masiero. A Statechart-based Model for Hypermedia Applications. ACM Transactions on Information Systems, vol. 19, no. 1, pp.28–52, ACM Press, 2001.

241. J.K. Ousterhout. Tcl and the Tk Toolkit. Addison-Wesley, 1994.

242. J.K. Ousterhout. Scripting: Higher-Level Programming for the 21st Century. Computer, vol. 31, no. 3, pp.23–30, 1998.

243. M.C. Paulk. How ISO 9001 Compares with the CMM. IEEE Software, vol. 11, no. 1, pp. 74–83, January 1995.

244. M.C. Paulk, B. Curtis, M.B. Chrissis, C.V. Weber. Capability Maturity Model, Version 1.1. IEEE Software, vol. 10, no. 4, pp.18–27, 1993.

245. M.C. Paulk, C. Weber, S. Garcia, M.B. Chrissis, M. Bush. Key Practices of the Capability Maturity Model Version 1.1. Carnegie Mellon Software Engineering Institute, Technical Report CMU/SEI-93-TR-025, February 1993.

246. D.L. Parnas. On the use of transition diagrams in the design of a user interface for an interactive computer system. Proceedings of the 24th National Conference. ACM Press, 1969, pp. 379–385.

247. D.L. Parnas. A Technique for Software Module Specification with Examples. Communications of the ACM, vol. 15, no. 5, pp.330–336, 1972.

248. E. Pelegri-Llopart, L. Cable. Java Server Pages Specification, v.1.1. Sun Press, 1999.

249. G.E. Pfaff. User Interface Management Systems. Springer, 1985.

250. B.C. Pierce. Types and Programming Languages. MIT Press, 2002.

251. G. Poonen. CLEAR: A Conceptual Language for Entities and Relationships. In: W. Chu, P.P. Chen (Eds.), Centralized and Distributed Systems, pp.194–215. IEEE Computer Society, 1980.

252. M.E. Porter. Strategy and the Internet. Harvard Business Review, March, pp.63–78, 2001.
253. S. Powers. Developing ASP Components. O'Reilly, 1999.
254. A.N. Prior. Past, Present and Future. Oxford Clarendon Press, 1967.
255. C. Queinnec. The Influence of Browsers on Evaluators or, Continuations to Program Web Servers. International Conference on Functional Programming, ACM, Montreal, Canada, November 2000.
256. E. Quinn. Application Server Market Share – A Different Angel. Hurwitz Balanced View Bulletin. Hurwitz Group Inc., December 2001.
257. D. Raggett, Arnaud Le Hors, Ian Jacobs. HTML 4.01 Specification – W3C Recommendation. World Wide Web Consortium, December 1999.
258. J.C. Ramming. PML: A Language Interface to Distributed Voice-Response Units. ICCL Workshop: Internet Programming Languages. LNCS 1686, pp.97–112. Springer, 1999.
259. E. Raymond (Ed.). The Jargon file, version 4.3.1, June 2001.
260. M. Richters, M. Gogolla. On Formalizing the UML Object Constraint Language OCL. Proceedings of the 17th International Conference on Conceptual Modeling (ER98), LNCS 1507. Springer, 1998.
261. W. Roesner. DESPATH: An ER Manipulation Language. In: Proceedings of the 4th International Conference on the Entity-Relationship Approach, pp.72–81. IEEE Computer Society, 1985.
262. L. Rosenfeld, P. Morville. Information Architecture for the World Wide Web. O'Reilly, 1998.
263. D.T. Ross. Structured Analysis (SA): A Language for Communicating Ideas. IEEE Transactions on Software Engineering, vol. 3, no. 1, pp. 16–34, January 1977.
264. D.T. Ross, J.W. Brackett. An approach to structured analysis. Computer Decisions, vol. 8, no. 9, pp. 40–44, Sept. 1976.
265. D.T. Ross, K.E. Schoman. Structured Analysis for Requirements Definition. IEEE Transactions on Software Engineering, vol.3, no. 1, pp. 6–15, January 1977.
266. W.W. Royce. Managing the Development of Large Software Systems. Proceedings of the IEEE WESCON Conference, August 1970, pp.1–9. IEEE, 1970.
267. J. Rumbaugh, M. Balaha, W. Premerlani, F. Eddy, W. Lorenson. Object-Oriented modeling and design. Prentice Hall, 1991.
268. D. Sangiorgi, D. Walker. The π-calculus – A Theory of Mobile Processes. Cambridge University Press, 2001.
269. A.-W. Scheer. ARIS – Business Process Modeling. Springer, 1999.
270. T. Sekiguchi, A. Yonezawa. A complete type inference system for subtyped recursive types. In: Proceedings of Theoretical Aspects of Computer Software, LNCS 789, pp.667–686. Springer, 1994.
271. Private communication with B. Selic and J. Warmer, October 2000.
272. D. Shasha, P. Bonnet. Database Tuning: Principles, Experiments, and Troubleshooting Techniques. Morgan Kaufmann, 2002.
273. M. Shields, E. Meijer. Type-indexed Rows. In: Proceedings of the 28th Annual ACM SIGPLANSIGACT Symposium on Principles of Programming Languages (POPL'01), ACM Press, pp.261–275, 2001.
274. A. Shoshani. CABLE: A Chain-Based Language for the Entity-Relationship Model. In: Proceedings of the 1st International Conference on the Entity-Relationship Approach. North-Holland, 1980.

275. P. Shoval. ADISSA: architectural design of information systems based on Structured Analysis. Information System, vol. 13, no. 2, pp.193–210, 1988.

276. P. Shoval, I. Frumermann. OO and EER conceptual schemas: a comparison of user comprehension. Journal of Database Management, vol. 5, no. 4, pp.28–38, 1994.

277. P. Shoval, J. Kabeli. FOOM: Functional- and Object-Oriented Analysis and Design of Information Systems – an Integrated Methodology. Journal of Database Management, vol. 12, no. 1, pp.15–25, 2001.

278. D. D'Souza, A. Sane, A. Birchenough. First Class Extensibility for UML – Packaging of Profiles, Stereotypes, Patterns. Proceedings of the UML'99, Fort Collins, LNCS 1723. Springer, 2000.

279. S. Shlaer, S.J. Mellor. Object-Oriented Systems Analysis: Modeling the World in Data. Pearson Education, Yourdon Press Computing Series, March 1988.

280. R.T. Snodgrass (Ed.). The TSQL2 Temporal Query Language. Kluwer Academic Publishers, 1995.

281. P.P. da Silva. User Interface Declarative Models and Development Environments: A Survey. Proceedings of 7th International Workshop on Design, Specification and Verification of Interactive Systems, Limerick, Ireland, LNCS 1946. Springer, June 2000, pp.207–226.

282. P.P. da Silva, N.W. Paton. UMLi: The Unified Modeling Language for Interactive Applications. Proceedings of the UML'2000, York, LNCS 1939. Springer, 2000.

283. J.M. Spivey. The Z Notation. Prentice Hall, 1992.

284. P. Sully. Modelling the World with Objects. Prentice Hall, 1993.

285. Sun Microsystems. Java Remote Method Invocation Specification, revision 1.50. Sun Microsystems, October 1998.

286. Sun Microsystems. Java Object Serialization Specification, revision 1.43. Sun Microsystems, November 1998.

287. I.E. Sutherland. Sketchpad – A Man-Machine Graphical Communication System. In: Proceedings of AFIPS Spring Joint Computer Conference, pp.328–346, 1963.

288. Svensk Standard. Databehandling – Programsprak – SIMULA, SS 636114, 1987.

289. A. Tansel (Ed.). Temporal Databases: Theory, Design, and Implementation. Benjamin/Cummings, 1993.

290. B. Thalheim. Entity-Relationship Modeling. Foundations of Database Technology. Springer, 2000.

291. S. Thatte (Ed.). Specification: Business Process Execution Language for Web Services Version 1.1, May 2003.

292. P. Thiemann. Modeling HTML in Haskell. Practical Applications of Declarative Programming, PADL'00, LNCS 1753. Springer, January 2000.

293. P. Thiemann. A typed representation for HTML and XML documents in Haskell. February 2001.

294. P. Thiemann. Wash/CGI: Server-side Web Scripting with Sessions and Typed, Compositional Forms. Practical Aspects of Declarative Languages (PADL'02). January 2002.

295. H.S. Thompson, D. Beech, M. Maloney, N. Mendelsohn. XML Schema Part 1: Structures. W3C Recommendation, May 2001.

296. TPC Benchmark W (Web Commerce). Transaction Processing Performance Council, 2000.

297. D. Tsichritzis. Form Management. Communications of the ACM, vol. 25, no. 7, pp.453–478, 1982.
298. S. Tucker Taft, R.A. Duff (Eds.). Ada 95 Reference Manual: Language and Standard Libraries. International Standard ISO/IEC 8652:1995(E), LNCS 1246. Springer, 1995.
299. C.R. Turner, A.L. Wolf, A. Fuggetta, L. Lavazza. Feature Engineering. In: Proceedings of the 9th International Workshop on Software Specification and Design, pp. 162–164. IEEE, 1998.
300. P. Ursprung, C.A. Zehnder. HIQUEL: An Interactive Query Language to Define and Use Hierarchies. In: Proceedings of the 3rd Conference on the Entity-Relationship Approach. North-Holland, 1983.
301. P. Vilain, D. Schwabe, C.S. de Souza. Modeling Interactions and Navigation in Web Applications. Proceedings of 7th International Workshop on Design, Specification and Verification of Interactive Systems, Salt Lake City, Utah, LNCS 1921. Springer, 2000, pp.115–127.
302. P. Vilain, D. Schwabe, C.S. de Souza. A Diagrammatic Tool for Representing User Interaction in UML. Proceedings of the UML'2000, York, LNCS 1939. Springer, 2000.
303. J. Vlissides. The Hollywood Principle. C++ Report, vol. 8, February 1996.
304. W3C HTML working group. XHTML 1.0 The Extensible HyperText Markup, W3C, 2000. Language.
305. W3C HTML working group. Extensible HTML version 1.0 Strict DTD, W3C, 2000.
306. M. Wahl, A. Coulbeck, T. Howes, S. Kille. Lightweight Directory Access Protocoll, version 3: Attribute Syntax Definitions, RFC 2252. Network Working Group, December 1997.
307. M. Wahl, T. Howes, S. Kille. Lightweight Directory Access Protocoll, version 3, RFC 2251. Network Working Group, December 1997.
308. L. Wall, T. Christiansen, J. Orwant. Programming Perl. O'Reilly, 2000.
309. A.I. Wasserman. A Specification Method for Interactive Information Systems. Proceedings SRS – Specification of Reliable Software, IEEE Catalog No. 79 CHI1401-9C, IEEE, 1979, pp.68–79.
310. A.I. Wasserman. Extending State Transition Diagrams for the Specification of Human-Computer Interaction. IEEE Transaction on Software Engineering, vol. 11, no. 8, 1985, pp.699–713.
311. G.H. Watson. Strategic benchmarking – How to rate your company's performance against the world's best. Wiley, 1993.
312. M. Wallace, C. Runciman. Haskell and XML: Generic combinators or type-based translation? In: Proceedings of the ICFP'99, ACM SIGPLAN Notices, vol. 34, no. 9, pp.148–159, September 1999.
313. J. Warmer, S. van Egmond. The implementation of the Amsterdam SGML parser. Electronic Publishing, vol. 2, no. 2, pp.65–90, July 1989.
314. J. Warmer, A.G. Kleppe. The Object Constraint Language. Addison-Wesley, 1999.
315. E. Whelan, F. McGrath. A Study of the Total Life Cycle Costs of an E-Commerce Investment. Evaluation and Program Planning, vol. 125, pp.191–196, 2002.
316. S. White et al. JDBC API Tutorial and Reference. Addison-Wesley, 1999.

366   References

317. R. Winter. Formal Validation of Schema Clustering for Large Information Systems. Americas Conference on Information Systems, Pittsburgh, PA, August 25-27, 1995.
318. N. Wirth. Programming in MODULA-2, 3rd Edition. Springer, 1985.
319. D. Wood. Standard generalized markup language: Mathematical and philosophical issues. In: J. van Leeuwen (Ed.), Computer Science Today. Recent Trends and Developments, LNCS 1000, pp.344–365. Springer, 1995.
320. J.B. Wordsworth. Software Developement with Z – A Practical Approach to Formal Methods in Software Engineering. Addison-Wesley, 1992.
321. XSL. The Extensible Stylesheet Language Family. Addison-Wesley, 2000.
322. XSL Transformations (XSLT) – W3C Recommendation. World Wide Web Consortium, November 1999.
323. E. Yourdon. Modern Structured Analysis. Yourdon Press, Prentice Hall, 1989.
324. Y. Zheng, M.-C. Pong. Using Statecharts to Model Hypertext. In: Proceedings of the ACM Conference on Hypertext. ACM Press, 1992, pp. 242–250.
325. J. Ziegler. ViewNet – Conceptual Design and Modeling of Navigation. Proceedings of INTERACT'97.
326. S.N. Zilles. Algebraic Specification of Data Types. Project Mac Progress Report 11, Massachusetts Institute of Technology, 1974.

Index

4GL *see* fourth generation language

Extensible Server Pages
    XSP   206

ABAP-4   5
abstract data object   9
abstraction   166
abstraction level   74
ACID   123
action set chart   **74**
Algol   328
application server   12
applied science   166
architecture description languages   150
architecture diagram   194
arity   **111**
ASP   194
atomicity   123
automatic generation   193

backward ring terminal   **129**
binary PD model   **111**
bipartite typed state machine   49
black-box abstraction   9, 138, 163, 173,
    279, 326, 344
block structure   194
bookshop   23
bookstore example   *see* webshop
    example
business culture   165
business web   348

C   328

CGI   *see* Common Gateway Interface
change history   194
checkpoint   **125**
CICS   11
class diagram   23
click-dummy   40
client page   **49**
    description safety   201, 204
    type safety   201, 204
client page instance   **49**
clone   **133**
clone parts   **133**
COCOMO   *see* Constructive Cost
    Model
Cocoon   206
combined multiplicity   **126**
commercial off-the-shelf   11, 150
Common Gateway Interface   204
commutativity diagram   **130**
complex web site   327
composite entity type   **131**
composition model   327
computer game   172
concatenation   **130**
conceptual model   *see* conceptual
    modeling
conceptual modeling   194, 327
conservative decomposition   **239**
consistency   123
constraint   **113**, 125
    composition constraint   **131**
    contexts   **125**
    expression   **125**

if constraint   **129**
immutable composition   **136**
nand constraint   **128**
permanence   **136**
remote subscriber constraint   **140**
subset constraint   **128**
xor constraint   **129**
Constructive Cost Model   167
content/layout separation   203
contents subsystem   **131**
CONTEXT   **119**
contrafactual theory   **273**
Core NSP   299
    grammar   300

DAL   328
    updates   **113**
debugging information   196
deletion of a link   **113**
DENIM   326
dependent product   115
descriptive approach   74, 165
descriptiveness   *see* descriptive
    approach
design by contract   260, 263, 264
design recovery   193
desktop agent   172
desktop databases   13, 41, 326
desktop metaphor   13, 172
detouring relation type   **114**
dialogue model   **50**, 55
dialogue specification   **66**
dialogue specification language   **66**
dialogue steps   11
direct manipulation   326
direction   **113**, 114
documentation   193
documentation tool   193
domain expert view   43
drag and drop   13, 172, 214
durability   123
dynamic semantics   **113**

e-commerce   9
editable method call   41
electronic data interchange   9
embedding specifications   **183**
empowerment   7, 165, 172
engineering   170

enterprise application   9
enterprise resource planning   9
enterprise system   9
entity instance   **112**
entity relationship approach   328
entity type   **111**
ER   *see* entity relationship approach
evaluation order   **69**
executable specification   74
Extensible Markup Language   209, 327
Extensible Server Pages   206
external references set   **114**
external relation types   **114**

feature   **102**
fine-grained interaction   41
flat decomposition mechanism   **100**
flight reservation   9
FOR loop   **122**
form storyboard   **41**
form type   193, 194
formal parameter   194
formchart   **55**
    arrow   55
    ellipse   55
    readability   56
    rectangle   55
formchart decomposition   **99**
formchart elements   56
formlike view   **13**
forward ring terminal   **129**
forward role   **113**
fourth generation language   347
FPA   *see* Function Point Analysis
fresh entity instance   **112**
full information system model   **51**
Function Point Analysis   167
functional dependency   130, 179
functional dependent order   **130**

global time order   **273**
glue   150
GROUPBY   120
guideline   196

HCI   325
high-level description   283
higher-order server pages   214
HTML   203
HTTPRequest   193

HTTPResponse 193
human–computer interaction 9
human–computer interface 9
hypermedia design 326
hypertext 326

IDEs 247
immediate status 14
informality 23
information architecture 327
information model 60, **62**
information system model **49**
initial selection base **115**
input capability 194
input device 326
INSERT 119
insertion of a link **113**
insight models 167
integrated development environments
    247
interface metaphors 325
inverse order **129**
isolation 123
isomorphism **133**
isoterminal **113**
IT expert view 43

J2EE 11
Java 203, 288, 292, 328
Java Bean 292
Java Beans 203
Java Server Pages 203
Java Servlets 203
javadoc 193
join entity type **132**
joins 115
JSP *see* Java Server Pages
JSP actions 203
JSPick 193
  control
    multiple select menu 194
    pseudo-control 195
    radio button 194
    various-control 195

keyboard 326
know-how 167
knowledge transfer 168

labeled product 115

layered data model 49
learning 167
learning organizations 167
leveling 100
linear programming 167
link **112**
linked **112**
local modality **53**
log warehouse 271, 272, 348
lower multiplicity **126**
lower multiplicity number **126**

mail client 9
major multiplicities **126**
many **126**
Markov chains 167
markup language 194
master relation type **131**
mathematical models 166
maximal **131**
message
  network message 273
message storyboard **46**, 242
messages 41
metadata 173
mock up 40, 345
Model 2 architecture 214
model graph **111**
model union **97**
model-driven architecture 325
model-oriented specification 325
modeler 56
modeling alternatives 74
monotonic modeling **98**
Monte Carlo simulation 167, 335
multi-tier system 11
multi-user abstracted model **108**
multi-user declared model **108**
multi-user exception 108
multi-user safe model **108**
multidependent entity types **132**
multiplicity 113, **126**

navigation 326
navigation model 327
navigation primitive 326
navigational structure 194
net evolution trace for fixed sites **273**

NETFS   *see* net evolution trace for
    fixed sites
non-modality   172
notification   **140**

object-oriented analysis   325
office suites   41
online transaction processing   9
opaque identity   60
opaque reference   **60**
opaque reference facade   **60**
ORDER BY   120
outgoing relation type   **114**
ownership   172

packaging   100
page change   10
page diagram   **36**
page edits   10
page image   **43**
page interaction   326
page signature   193
pages with active content   **53**
partial order   **129**
partial order diagram   **129**
PD model   **109**
Per Martin-Löf   299
persistent data   23
personalization model   327
PHP   194
PICTIVE   326
plug components   150
poor cousin of HCI   325
port   150
power user   163, 172, 233
prescriptiveness   *see* descriptive
    approach
presentation layer   41, 193
presentation model   327
primary working model   **108**
primitive type   **114**
primitive update   **113**
problem domain   165, 166, 182, 269,
    335, 336
project scope   165
projection   115
pseudo-evaluation   193, 283
pure form-based paradigm   **51**
push-based   326

queuing theory   167

real word   173, 174, 329
refinement   107
refresh   13
relation type   **111**
relation type path   **113**
relational calculus   115
relationship   **127**
relationship uniqueness   **127**
reload vs. refresh   13
remote publisher   **140**
REPORT   **120**
reports   41
repository   **112**
requirement   **102**
response page principle   **14**
result set   116
reverse engineering   193, 196, 283
reverse role   **113**
ring terminal   **129**
RMM   326
roles   **111**
ROLLBACK   **122**
running example   VI, 23

SABRE   9
SAP   5
    consolidation system   12
    development system   12
    production system   12
    transportation system   12
SAP R/3   12
screen   23
screen diagram   **40**
screen transaction   11
search criteria   23
Seeheim model   325
SELECT   119
semantic data model   327
semantical framework   74
server action   16, **49**
server input declared model   **108**
server input safe model   **108**
service interface   9
session   9, 204
sessionless interface   9
shared model   **63**
SHD   *see* state history diagram

shelf components   150
shopping cart   10
signature model   **107**
SILK   326
Simula   335
simulation models   167
single-staged interaction   41
social interaction   167
software management   165
software process   165
Software Technology Review   168
solution domain   166, 171, 269
source code   238
source code analysis   194
source code decomposition   239
source name   *see* transition source
   name
specification language   193
specifying models   167
spreadsheet applications   41
SQL queries   115
state   **112**
state design pattern   260
state diagram   326
state history diagram   53, 67, 249, **249**,
   348
state instances   **104**
state set   **104**, 191
state specialization   104, 270
static constraints   **125**
static pages   194
static semantics   **112**
statistical models   167
strong typing   41
structural invariant   **125**
structural invariant context   **125**
structural joins   **115**
structural model   327
structured analysis   325
structured artifact   **233**
structured editor   53, 231, 235
style guide   74
submission form metaphor   **13**
submit   55
submodel   **114**, 239
subsystem   **114**
   clocked   273
superparameter   59, **59**
SWEBOK   168

syntax model   233, **234**
   syntax model of the PD modeling
      language   234
system interface   41, 193
system modeling   9, 325

TACID   *see* transparent ACID
tag libraries   203
target name   *see* transition target
   name
targeted formal parameter   194
team server   229, 230
temporal constraints   **135**
textual input   325
TPC-W   23
transactional invariant   **125**
transactional invariant context   **125**
transactions   **113**
transition source name   **57**
transition target name   **57**
transparent ACID   **123**, 125, 139
trivial upper multiplicity   **126**
two-staged interaction   11

UIMS   *see* user interface management
   system
UML   *see* Unified Modeling Language
Unified Modeling Language   7, 73, 250,
   328, 335
unique attribute   **127**
upper multiplicity   **126**
upper multiplicity number   **126**
user identity   **124**
user interface generation   326
user interface management system   325
user message model   **59**
user message system model   **51**
user perspective   9
user session   49

ViewNet   326
virtual world   172
visual language   327
visual state specialization   **104**, 270

WARE   194
weak entity type   **131**
web presentation layer   193, 214
WebML   326, 327

webshop
    new customer   23
webshop example
    Angie specification   191
    browsing categories   23, 26, 84
    buying   23, 29, 38, 89
    changing customer data   23, 29, 92
    login   23, 24, 76
    logout   23, 24, 76
    registration   23, 24, 76
    search   23, 30, 84
    shopping cart   23, 29, 87

WHILE loop   **122**
white-box abstraction   173
widget annotation   **45**
widget constraints   **95**
word-of-mouth communication   168
work product   172

XHTML   206
XML   *see* Extensible Markup
        Language

Z notation   304, 326